D0099858

JUL 29 '95

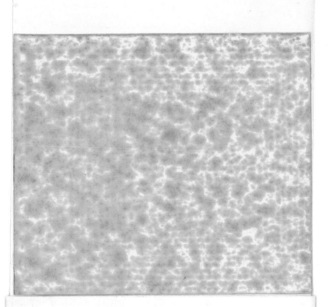

HIGHLINE COLLEGE LIBRARY
P.O. BOX 98000
DES MOINES, WA   98198-9800

CHINA
KOREA
AND
JAPAN

CHINA KOREA AND JAPAN

The Rise of Civilization in East Asia

GINA L. BARNES

With 217 illustrations

THAMES AND HUDSON

For David

© 1993 Thames and Hudson Ltd, London

First published in the United States of America in 1993 by
Thames and Hudson Inc., 500 Fifth Avenue,
New York, New York 10110

Library of Congress Catalog Card Number 93-60205

Printed and bound in Slovenia by Mladinska Knjiga

Contents

Preface

The East Asian countries of China, Japan and the Koreas[1] are of ever-increasing importance in today's world. Modern differences in political and economic systems, customs, languages and national characters sometimes obscure the fact that these three countries boast a common heritage of great historical depth. Several current books serve as syntheses of, or specialist texts for, the archaeology and early history of one or another of these three areas (see Further Reading: Preface and Chapter 1). The present book, however, is the first regional synthesis of East Asian archaeology and early history, tying together the major early developments within the entire region.

This book outlines the social and political developments within the modern countries of China, Korea and Japan up to and including the 8th century AD. This is a natural cut-off point in the history of the region because it marks the maturation of governmental systems in all three areas based on a shared religion (Buddhism), state philosophy (Confucianism), and bureaucratic structure (founded on 'administrative law'). Prior to this date, the areas of modern Korea and Japan had a developmental trajectory rather different from China. I will be focusing on the evidence for initial differentiation and the trends for eventual integration of these areas. In one sense, it would be misleading to refer to the region as 'East Asia' until this integration was achieved – thus the rise of civilization in these three countries is actually the story of the formation of East Asia.

Background

Much of the current commonality among East Asian countries is due to the extraordinary influence of the early-developing Chinese civilization on its eastern neighbours, particularly the diffusion of Buddhism and Confucianism into the early states. This is not to say, however, that the later societies growing out of these states were carbon copies of China and lacked their own unique natures. One of the reasons for Japan's ascendancy in the modern world is her unusual development of a complex merchant economy and middle-class culture during the pre-modern Edo period (1603–1868). In fact, Japan's historical relations with the outside world can be mapped in pendulum-like swings from active solicitation and absorption of foreign culture to periods of isolationist incubation leading to the development of a rich and infinitely refined native culture. Such isolationism also took hold periodically on the

Korean Peninsula, with the pre-modern Choson period (1392–1910) being popularly called the 'Hermit Kingdom'. Only in recent times (in the Meiji period from 1868 to World War I and during the post-World War II period) has Japan looked to the West during her phases of foreign receptivity. Before this, China was a natural magnet for Japan, Korea and all other peoples of eastern Eurasia.

The crucial period of active importation and adoption of Chinese ways occurred in the 6th and 7th centuries. The contemporaneous governments of the Korean Peninsula (Shilla)[2] and the Japanese Islands (Yamato) both looked at that time to the Sui and Tang Dynasties on the China Mainland for administrative patterns after which they could model their new states. Among the items borrowed were the gridded city plan of the Tang capital, the regional administrative system, and codes of law. One should not, however, make the mistake of thinking that this extraordinary period of receptivity characterized all previous interaction between peoples of the China Mainland, the Korean Peninsula and the Japanese Islands. The fallacies in doing so are several, as iterated below.

One fallacy is to think that such countries as 'China', 'Korea' and 'Japan' existed in those earlier periods. They did not. The East Asian landscape was much more politically and culturally varied, and if the above terms are used in this book, they refer only to geographical areas rather than to political entities unless otherwise specified. A second fallacy is to think that the flow of cultural influence was all unidirectional from the China Mainland eastwards to the Peninsula and Islands. It was not. Constant interaction linked smaller areas of East Asia, and within those spheres, contact and exchange was multi-directional. Moreover, there was considerable influence throughout the ages from the Eurasian steppe region and from Southeast Asia. Finally, it is wrong to think that all areas were constantly in touch so that development occurred in concert. It did not. Just as in historical times, there were periods of intense interaction and periods of relative isolation between these geographical areas. By treating the cultural histories of the modern East Asian countries together, it is possible to gain a sense of the mosaic of early peoples, cultures and polities which cross-cut what are now modern national boundaries. Although each East Asian nation today claims portions of the mosaic for its individual history, the ancient entities belong to no one and no thing other than their own time and place. Nationalistic views of local development are hereby eschewed.

For any particular topic, there are vast differences in the quality and quantity of archaeological data available in the different East Asian countries. Such inherent biases in the evidence are exploited to full advantage in this book, and no attempt is made to give 'equal coverage' to the individual archaeologies of the three nations. On the other hand, attempts are made to elicit comparable data from the three countries on developmental topics of interest. In doing so, some rich or well-known details may be excluded in order to provide a regional context for understanding the role of that case within a broader framework.

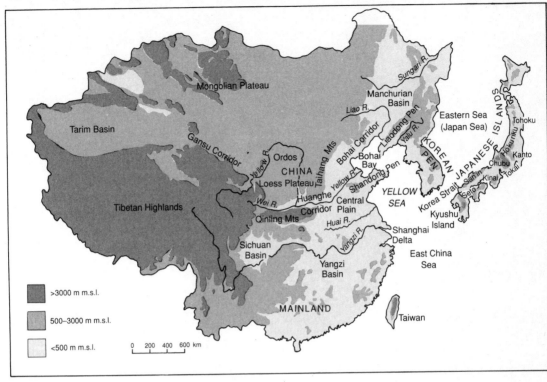

1 The geography of East Asia centring on the Yellow Sea.

Objectives

This book thus serves as a regionally integrated introduction to the archaeologies and early histories of the modern nations of China, Korea and Japan for readers approaching the subject for the first time. Both East Asian enthusiasts who are unacquainted with archaeological methods and archaeology enthusiasts who know little about East Asia are catered for. Since no assumptions are made about readers' knowledge of East Asian languages, an attempt has been made to cite English-language literature wherever possible so that topics of interest can be pursued independently. An effort has also been made to keep East Asian place and personal names to a minimum for easy assimilation.

The aim of this book is to describe and account for the major socio-cultural developments in East Asia through the millennia to AD 800. Data are integrated across the region within successive time-frames to make it possible to achieve this overview. However, a prior grasp of each East Asian country's sequence is necessary to understand the overview, since this book employs local chronologies and cultures as its building blocks. Before embarking on the major task, therefore, an 'Orientation' is provided by discussing the changing nature of archaeological enquiry into prehistoric, protohistoric and historic periods

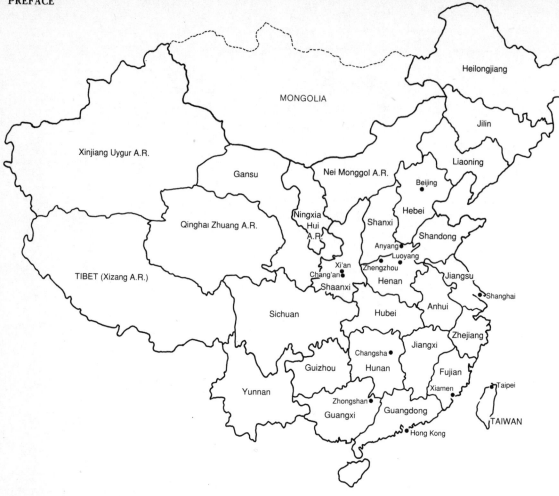

2 Chinese provinces and cities. Autonomous regions (A.R.), with Taiwan, Hong Kong, Mongolia and major cities (dots).

and tracing the individual sequences of Chinese, Japanese and Korean culture histories. In the former discussion, many of the anthropological concepts employed in the book are introduced and defined for those not familiar with the discipline.

Grounding

fig. 1

The central geographical point of reference for this text is the 'Yellow Sea Basin', which begins at the Shanghai Delta and runs up the east coast of the China Mainland to the mouths of the Yellow River in the northwest (whose transported loess soils make the Yellow Sea yellow) and the Liao River in the northeast (draining the lower Manchurian Basin), then down the west coast of the Korean Peninsula to Kyushu Island. Internally, the pinching in of the Shandong and Liaodong peninsulae divides the Bohai Bay region in the north from the Yellow Sea itself. The latter is open-ended on the south, grading into the East China Sea which laps at the western edge of the Ryukyu Islands and

3 Modern Korean provinces and cities. Some provinces occur in north-south pairs (N, S); the demilitarized zone (DMZ) is marked by a double dotted line, and major cities by dots.

Tumen R.

N. Hamgyong

Yalu R.

S. Hamgyong

N. P'yongan

S. P'yongan

P'yongyang

Taedong R.

Hwanghae

DMZ

Kyonggi · Ch'unch'on

Seoul

Kangwon

Han R.

N. Ch'ungch'ong

S. Ch'ungchong Ch'ongju N. Kyongsang

Kongju

Puyo

Kum R.

Naktong R.

Taegu

Chonju

N. Cholla

Kyongju

S. Kyongsang Kimhae

S. Cholla Chinju Ch'angwon Pusan

Kwangju

Mok'po

Chejudo Island

Cheju

Hokkaido Island

1

2

6

3

7

4

Honshu Island

5

8

9

13

14

12

Oki Islands

10

16 15

Kyoto

11

17 Tokyo

20

19 18

Tsushima Islands

37

36

29

24

21

23 22 Tokyo Bay

38

35

30

28

25

Nara

39

34

26

Osaka 27

Inland Sea

40

33

32

31

Shikoku Island

44

45

41

46

42

43

Kyushu Island

Ryukyu Islands

47

Okinawa Island

1 Hokkaido	13 Tochigi	25 Mie	37 Shimane
2 Aomori	14 Gunma	26 Nara	38 Hiroshima
3 Iwate	15 Chiba	27 Wakayama	39 Yamaguchi
4 Miyagi	16 Saitama	28 Osaka	40 Fukuoka
5 Fukushima	17 Tokyo	29 Kyoto	41 Oita
6 Akita	18 Kanagawa	30 Hyogo	42 Miyazaki
7 Yamagata	19 Yamanashi	31 Tokushima	43 Kagoshima
8 Niigata	20 Nagano	32 Kochi	44 Saga
9 Toyama	21 Gifu	33 Ehime	45 Ngasaki
10 Ishikawa	22 Shizuoka	34 Kagawa	46 Kumamoto
11 Fukui	23 Aichi	35 Okayama	47 Okinawa
12 Ibaragi	24 Shiga	36 Tottori	

4 Modern Japanese prefectures and major cities (dots).

nominally ends at Taiwan. To the east of the Korean Peninsula lies the Eastern Sea, more commonly known as the Japan Sea.

Several terms have been devised here to refer to parts of East Asia without using modern nation-state designations. 'Pen/Insular' and 'Pen/Insulae' refer to the combined areas of the Korean Peninsula and the Japanese Islands, whereas the term 'Peninsular' is used specifically to refer to the Korean Peninsula. On that Peninsula, names of the five major rivers (the Yalu, Taedong, Han, Kum and Nakdong) are used as geographical locators. Within the Japanese archipelago, areas on the four main islands are often referred to by sub-regions: Tohoku, Kanto, Chubu, Tokai, Hokuriku, Kinai, and San'in. In addition, the Inland Sea area of western Japan is here referred to as the Seto region. Finally, new terms have been coined to refer to the land areas underlying the Yellow Sea and Inland Sea when they were exposed as broad plains during the glacial phases of the Pleistocene period: the Yellow Plain and Seto Plain, respectively. The entire northeastern landmass that was exposed during the maximum period of lowered sea level is referred to as East Asialand.

The 'China Mainland' refers to the body of the present-day Peoples' Republic containing the Central Plain, the Yangzi Basin in central China, the Sichuan Basin in the southwest, and the mountainous southeastern coastal region. The main rivers of north and south China respectively will be referred to by their Western names: the Yellow River (called the Huanghe in northern Chinese) and the Yangzi River (called the Changjiang in northern Chinese). The Huanghe Corridor is that section of the Yellow River between its bend to the north and its emergence on to the Central Plain. The northwestern portion of the great hook of the Yellow River encompasses the arid region known as the Ordos. The Huai River and Qinling mountain range have marked the division between the north and south Mainland at various times in the past.

Beyond the China Mainland lie the Manchurian Basin to the northeast, the Mongolian Plateau to the north, and the Tarim Basin to the northwest. The Bohai Corridor connects the Central Plain to the lower Manchurian Basin, drained by the Liao River; the upper Manchurian Basin is drained to the north by the Sungari River. The Gansu Corridor connects the Wei River valley, a tributary of the Yellow River, to the Tarim Basin. Today, this entire northern region is characterized by increasing aridity from the Pacific coast towards Inner Asia, with Manchurian forests grading into Mongolian steppe and steppe desert towards the true sand desert and oases of the Tarim Basin. In the past, however, the central and western arid areas were once colonized by greater tracts of forest and grasslands, leading to human patterns of settlement somewhat different from those seen today. The Tibetan Highlands are not dealt with at all in the present work.

Discussions of sites in East Asian countries usually refer to their locations in the modern prefectures and provinces of the individual countries. Maps of these administrative divisions are provided, though references to such divisions are kept to a minimum in the body of the text.

figs 2–4

Limitations

The problems in writing this book have been threefold. First, it proved a challenge to tie together the data from China with those from Korea and Japan. As mentioned above, the view that East Asia forms a coherent region is one of hindsight. In dealing with the material from the bottom up, so to speak, intra-regional differentiation is considerable. Since what is commonly recognized as 'civilization' developed so much earlier on the China Mainland than in the Pen/Insular region, and because the latter derived a great many of its institutions and much of its material culture from the former, it has been difficult to avoid dealing first with the Mainland sequence and then with the Pen/Insular sequence, though an effort has been made to avoid Sino-centrism. A similar problem is the built-in contradiction generated by treating East Asia as a self-contained region while avoiding national boundaries within the region. And, of course, East Asia cannot be understood fully without reference to phenomena outside its modern boundaries.

Second, the abundance of information available for East Asian archaeology is far in excess of that presented in this book. Anyone who is already familiar with the region's archaeology will invariably find the exposition here compressed to a fault. Rather than concentrate on details, which are provided in other publications, the aim has been to exemplify general trends and principles and to pinpoint controversies. With ongoing discoveries and resolution of controversies, details will soon be outdated. It is hoped that the framework given here will provide the means to integrate such changing perspectives and new information, so that while aspects of the content might soon be obsolete, the approach will continue to be useful.

Third, despite the surfeit of materials in certain categories such as pottery and bronze, data relating to some problems which are theoretically important in understanding the major transitions – for example, domestication of plants and animals – are scarce in East Asia. Furthermore, what data do exist are often lopsided, with more information available from one region than from another. For example, despite the differences in country size, the number of Palaeolithic sites in Japan is in the thousands, but only in the hundreds in China and in scores in Korea. Palaeolithic skeletal material comes almost exclusively from China, and the sites in Japan are almost exclusively Late Palaeolithic. These imbalances have been used to advantage in structuring the chapters, but a balanced treatment of all East Asian areas must be relegated to the future.

Style

Romanization
Romanization of foreign words employs the Pinyin system for Chinese, the McCune-Reischauer system for Korean, and the modified Hepburn system for Japanese. It was not, however, possible to include diacratic marks over Korean and Japanese vowels.

There is tremendous variation in Korean spellings in the Western-language literature. These derive from competing romanization systems based respectively on the structure of syllables in isolation or the pronunciation changes between adjacent syllables as they affect each other. For example, Songguk-ri (rendered structurally) becomes Songgungni (as pronounced). McCune-Reischauer romanization is a pronunciation-based system and is adopted here, but even within it there are variations.[3] Pinyin uses some letters whose pronunciation is not obvious to the uninitiated. These letters are as follows (Pinyin in capitals, Wade-Giles versions in parentheses):

C (ts') followed by a vowel is pronounced like English ts in 'bitsy'; Pinyin ch, however, is like English ch.
Q (ch') is like English ch but subtly different in sound from Pinyin ch.
SHI (shih) is like American-English 'sure', with a retroflex r sound.
SI (ssu), ZI (tzu), CI (tz'u): the vowel in these syllables is similar to American-English 'could'.
X (hs) is like English sh, but subtly different in sound from Pinyin sh.

In the text, if Asian personal names are given in full, the surname appears in small capitals.

Dates

Dating the past is almost a field unto itself in archaeology and can be quite complicated. For the general purposes of this book, it was decided to keep references to dates as non-technical as possible. Two different schemes are employed for referring to dates. The first is the standard BC/AD distinction for time before and after the beginning of the Christian era, even though the history of Christianity is irrelevant to the region under study. The second is the phrase 'years ago', which has been used in place of the scientific convention of BP, meaning years 'before present'. This latter phrase was developed in conjunction with radiocarbon dating, where 'present' refers to a specific year – 1950. Most dates have been rounded off for easy consumption. For the uninitiated, it is often difficult to use both BC and BP or years ago simultaneously, resulting as they do in c. 2000 years difference in dates. For example, 1000 BC was 3000 years ago. This is particularly crucial for the date of the end of the 'Ice Age', which was 10,000 years ago or 8000 BC.

References

Suggested books and articles for 'Further Reading' are provided for each chapter at the end of the book; the general references were chosen for their capacity to elaborate on the cultures and periods presented in the chapter, while the specific references were chosen for their unique contributions. Special reviews of East Asian archaeology bibliographies also exist, to which the reader is guided in the Further Reading section. Controversies, detailed arguments and data on specific topics mentioned in the text can, of course, be followed up through the works cited in the Notes to the Text. Picture credits and citations for boxes, tables, figures and plates are listed separately in Sources of Illustrations. All the works referred to in the Notes to the Text, Sources of Illustrations, and Further Reading section are listed in the Bibliography.

Five maps interspersed throughout the text (*figs 16, 43, 59, 100* and *110*) show the locations of sites mentioned in text and captions.

Acknowledgments

I would first and foremost like to thank my publishers for the long leash they allowed me for writing this book. Their encouragement, patience and editorial suggestions have been crucial to its production and are all much appreciated. Crane Begg applied his superb drawing skills to many of the illustrations at short notice, greatly enhancing the visual presentation. Previous drafts of the text were read and commented on by several colleagues, including Sarah Allan, Paul Bahn, Andrea Barnes, Gary Crawford, Nicola Di Cosmo, Clive Gamble, Sue Hughes, Mark Lewis, Michael Loewe, Jessica Rawson, and Don Wagner. I am grateful for their rescue from several pitfalls, though sometimes I have overridden their good advice, and the interpretations presented here are my responsibility alone. David Hughes has borne the brunt of a decade's lamentations during the gestation of this book. To him I owe my sanity and my profound thanks for his limitless support. His thoroughgoing critique of the text has without doubt made it a more readable book.

CHAPTER 1

Orientation

Human society in East Asia extends back at least a million years, and each of the modern East Asian countries has its own scheme of how to divide this time-span into archaeological periods and developmental stages. Because most of the research into these millennia is undertaken within national boundaries, these schemes must be respected; however, they do result in the confusing situation that any particular archaeological 'period' is not regional but only national in scope! Moreover, such Western names as Palaeolithic (meaning 'old stone age') and Neolithic ('new stone age') are routinely applied to certain East Asian periods when they might not be exactly comparable to their Western namesakes. This is particularly the case with 'Neolithic', and it will be used here only to refer to developments on the China Mainland and not to the Jomon or Chulmun cultures as sometimes seen.

fig. 5

Archaeological data have been given primacy in this book, but the onset of written history generates documentary sources that often overshadow excavated information. Methods of research and interpretation thus change with the availability of written records, and the discipline of archaeology has three clearly different approaches depending on the prominence of documentary evidence. These are prehistoric, protohistoric and historic archaeology, all of whose natures will be discussed in the first half of this chapter. This same section also introduces several basic archaeological concepts and specialist terms used in the rest of the book. The second half of this chapter provides an overview of the sequence of periods in the modern East Asian nations. The periods are categorized in terms of the 'different archaeologies', so that the general concerns raised here can be applied to the individual sequences in the following chapters.

Different 'archaeologies'

Prehistoric archaeology

Archaeological research on societies extant before the advent of written history constitutes 'prehistoric archaeology'. This includes research on the evolution of our modern human species (*Homo sapiens sapiens*) and ancestral species (such as *Homo erectus*). The first prehistoric period is the Palaeolithic, which is divided differently in the various East Asian countries according to the nature of the local data. The Early or Lower Palaeolithic is characterized at both its beginning and end by changes in the human population (Chapter 3), while the

Upper or Late Palaeolithic period in East Asia witnessed the development of refined stone tool technologies (Chapter 4).

The entire Palaeolithic period falls within the Pleistocene geological era, popularly known as the Ice Age. Recent research has revealed that there were potentially seventeen major glaciations during the Pleistocene – not just the four classically defined glacial periods (termed Günz, Mindel, Riss and Würm in Europe but named Boyang, Lushan, Dagu and Dali in China).[1] No large ice-sheets formed in East Asia despite these multiple cold periods: glaciers were confined to isolated high peaks, and the major changes consisted of alternating dry and humid phases triggering different successions of flora and fauna. Nevertheless, the formation of glaciers and ice-sheets elsewhere in the world did affect sea levels in East Asia, which rose and fell as much as 120 m, alternately exposing and drowning sections of coastal land which were of potential use to human groups. After the last maximum cold period 18,000 years ago, the climate began to warm and the Ice Age is arbitrarily agreed to have ended 10,000 years ago.

The geological time period since the end of the Pleistocene is known as the Holocene, our own era. The early millennia of the Holocene are often referred to as the 'postglacial' period. A significant feature of the time between 8000 BC and AD 1 was the warming of the climate to levels higher than today's average and its subsequent cooling off, with a concomitant rise in sea levels to higher than present heights (the marine transgression) and then their slight regression. The parts of East Asialand that had been exposed during the glacial maximum were submerged again between *c*. 4000 and 2000 BC, bringing the sea right up to the edges of the major Pen/Insular mountain chains.[2] It is no coincidence that archaeological sites show an increased exploitation of sea resources from 8000 BC onwards.

Human groups around the world began domesticating local plants and animals in the early Holocene, initiating the Neolithic periods of prehistoric archaeology. In East Asia, the term 'Neolithic' is ambiguously employed: for China, it refers to agricultural society (Chapter 6), while in Korea and Japan it is sometimes used in its more literal sense of 'new stone' – that is, the era defined by the introduction of polished stone tools. The Pen/Insular societies (Chulmun and Jomon) of the postglacial period are in fact characterized by their polished stone tools and ceramics but not by agriculture (Chapter 5). The subsistence systems in those societies – that is, their methods of food procurement – focused on the hunting of animals and sea mammals, the collection of plant foods and shellfish, and fishing. The tending of some plants might have been practised, but this horticultural activity contrasts with major investments in cropping and animal husbandry characterizing fully agricultural societies. The establishment of an agricultural economy seems to have been a prerequisite for mature political development around the world.

Within Western prehistoric archaeology, there are two conflicting ways of describing stages of social development. The European tradition concentrates on the type of material employed in successive stages: stone, bronze and iron.[3]

From these we have the terms Palaeolithic (for chipped stone tool use), Neolithic (for polished stone tool use), Bronze Age and Iron Age. By contrast, the American tradition of social evolutionary thought concentrates on the form of social organization rather than the material technology. Thus, we have the idealized succession of band, (tribe), chiefdom and state (with 'tribe' as a disputed optional stage), according to the degree of political centralization and status differentiation.[4] In applying either or both of these Western schemes to the East Asian sequences, confusions and inconsistencies arise because each term carries with it a heavy load of preconceived images and meanings. To make matters even more complicated, Marxist scholars in China and Japan use an early form of Western evolutionary theory, based on the ideas of Lewis Henry Morgan,[5] which does not coincide with its more modern American version.

For example, it is within the later Chinese Neolithic period (Chapter 7), as defined by Chinese archaeologists, that we see the emergence of both centralized and hierarchical societies that would be termed 'chiefdoms' in the American evolutionary system. According to their own Marxist mode of interpretation, Chinese archaeologists describe the Neolithic as encompassing the transition from 'matriarchal' to 'patriarchal' society and focus exclusively on the clan as the basic form of social organization. As another instance, the Chinese Bronze Age (Chapter 8) is considered to be the age of 'slave society' by Chinese Marxists, but is identified as the period of state formation by American evolutionists. The state itself played no role in the European tripartite, material-based developmental scheme from which the Neolithic period's name is derived. Finally, the appearance of 'class society' or pronounced social stratification – which serves as the foremost threshold for state formation in American social evolutionary theory – is currently being sought by Japanese Marxist archaeologists in the Jomon period, while American researchers are content to search for evidence of chiefdom development among the Jomon. For the American evolutionists (including myself), social stratification in the Japanese Islands is not thought to have occurred until much later – at the end of the 3rd century AD. The European criteria of bronze and iron are of no more help in understanding social development in East Asia than in the Americas, where highly stratified societies managed to operate without these working metals at all. Nevertheless, the terms 'Bronze Age' and 'Iron Age' are retained here to refer to sections of the East Asian sequence because these metals were indeed important to the social mechanics of the periods in question – the Shang and Zhou periods, ending with the appearance of iron towards the close of Middle Zhou (Chapters 8, 9, 10). It should be recognized, however, that the natures of the societies referred to as Bronze or Iron Age are often quite different from those of their European counterparts.

Protohistoric archaeology

Box 1   The advent of writing marks a tremendous watershed in the operation of ancient societies as well as in archaeology's role in elucidating them. To be able to draw on the records of the people themselves not only gives us an inside perspective on how they thought, but also provides us with innumerable details not recoverable through the excavation of decayed and incomplete material remains. Neither material nor documentary evidence is without bias or a direct 'reflection' of reality: the former often does not survive well or at all and may even serve to mask rather than represent realities, and the latter was often manipulated during its writing for specific purposes. Used together, however, they complement each other in their kinds and quantities of information; and of course, archaeological evidence gives a much longer-term view than does written evidence.

The amount of information accessible from inscriptions or written documents is less in the decades or centuries during which a writing system is being developed and perfected than when writing is fully developed and in common use for recording history. This transitional period between the prehistoric and the historic is called the 'protohistoric', but it is usually rather subjectively defined, depending on how individual researchers view the informative potential of the sequence.

Another meaning of 'protohistoric' applies to societies having no writing system themselves but which have been documented in print by their neighbours. Such cases involve problems in interpretation because the written materials usually reflect the needs and perspectives of the neighbours, not the people being documented. Writing was invented on the China Mainland, and only much later was the script borrowed by surrounding peoples. As a result, there is a long period for which there are only Chinese documents to augment the material records of those societies – documents which are undoubtedly a biased and less than fully informed source of evidence.

The term 'protohistoric' is thus used in this book to refer to periods in which societies are known through fragmentary or indirect textual references. These include the Shang and Zhou periods for the China Mainland (Chapters 8, 9), for which inscriptions on bronze and bone and texts on bamboo and wooden slips are known. The Iron Age, Proto-Three Kingdoms and Three Kingdoms periods on the Korean Peninsula, and the Yayoi and Kofun periods in the Japanese archipelago, are also protohistoric in nature (Chapters 11, 13, 14).

Historic archaeology
The archaeology of fully historic periods presents special methodological problems in integrating the divers kinds of information offered by material remains and written records. There are three main ways of dealing with these problems. The first is the traditional 'handmaiden' or what is called here the 'Illustrator' approach,[6] in which archaeological data play a subservient and passive role to history: they are used to substantiate and illustrate what is already assumed to be known from the written records. This approach encourages a 'see it for yourself' attitude to archaeology and is heavily employed in museums. The second is the 'Elaborator' approach, which uses archaeological data to investigate what is *not* known from the historical records.

BOX 1
Documentary Sources

Marks and signs incised on Neolithic pottery of the China Mainland constitute the earliest stage of writing in East Asia (a). Their meanings are as yet unknown, but similar symbols cast on to Shang-period bronzes are deciphered as emblems of different elite clans or occupational groups (b). The first full sentences – the beginning of East Asian history – occur on the so-called 'oracle bones' in the Shang period: bovid shoulder blades (scapulae) and freshwater turtle under-shells (plastrons) (c) used in divination procedures. These were inscribed with a variety of information, such as the diviner's name or the oracular content. Some inscriptions also occur on bronzes of the period (d), and these become more common in the Zhou period as oracle bones declined in use. Inscribed stones are known from the Middle Zhou onwards (e), and in the Late Zhou and Han periods inked inscriptions on bamboo or wood slips form the major body of excavated writing (f).

All of the above stand in contrast to what are termed the transmitted documents, handed down through the ages in manuscript form. These have specific interpretational problems deriving from different editions, copying errors, and the like. Moreover, they were usually written for a specific ideological purpose to the exclusion of other data. The major historical documents shedding light on the 1st millennium BC are the Early Zhou *Yijing* (Book of Changes), *Shangshu* (Book of Documents), and *Shijing* (Book of Poetry); and the Middle and Late Zhou *Chunqiu* (Spring and Autumn Annals), *Guoyu* (State Discourses), *Yili* (Book of Etiquette), The Confucian Analects, *Zuozhuan* (Zuo Chronicle), The Elegies of Chu, and the writings of various philosophers. These were all written in the context of competing states during an era generally known in the West as the time of Confucius (Box 2).

The compilation of court histories began in the Han period. Two of the first were the *Shiji* (Records of the Grand Historiographer),

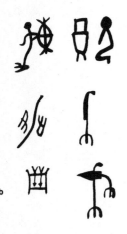

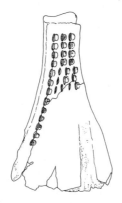

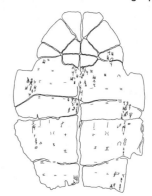

which contains a history of the Zhou period, and the *Hanshu* (History of the Former Han Dynasty). Among the works of the early 1st millennium AD, the *Houhanshu* (History of Later Han) and the *Weizhi* (Wei Chronicles) are of great significance to East Asian archaeology as a whole, for although Han-period society on the China Mainland was fully historical, its neighbours remained without systems of writing until approximately the 4th century AD. Intentional ethnographic reconnaissance by embassies of the Han court, however, garnered much information about these societies which was recorded in the dynastic histories. The Chinese written perspective on other East Asian cultures and peoples is then complementary to the archaeological record of indigenous development and change.

Some time between the 4th and 6th centuries AD, possibly in conjunction with the spread of Buddhism and Buddhist sutra texts, the emerging state societies of Pen/Insular East Asia adopted the Chinese script in their court dealings. Nevertheless, few early documents have survived, and the earliest extant records from Japan are the 8th-century court chronicles, the *Kojiki* and *Nihon Shoki*. The earliest written records surviving in Korea are much younger: the *Samguk Sagi* and *Samguk Yusa* date respectively from the 12th and 13th centuries, though they were compiled from earlier documents no longer extant.

It is worth noting here that the adoption of the Chinese writing system by societies speaking early forms of the Korean and Japanese languages was most inappropriate. The latter belong to a completely different language family from Chinese – the Altaic – and are related to Mongolian and Turkic in a large arc across northern Eurasia. These languages all have inflected verbal and adjectival forms, in contrast to the uninflected Chinese languages. The representation of inflected forms using the Chinese script became a great challenge to all Asian societies which adopted it. The Pen/Insular societies eventually developed supplementary scripts more phonetic in nature – the *han'gul* alphabet for Korean and the *kana* syllabaries for Japanese, which are used in conjunction with (or sometimes independently of) Chinese characters.

e

f

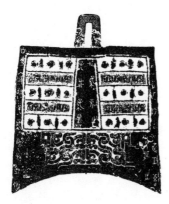

d

In this sense archaeology serves to complement history, providing the missing data of 'what history doesn't tell you'. The third approach is that of the 'Challenger', which is disputative and substitutive: archaeological data are used to correct impressions misleadingly garnered from the written evidence. In practical terms, one can integrate archaeology and history using the 'Illustrator' and 'Elaborator' approaches to produce a holistic synthesis, or one can keep the two forms of data separate using the 'Elaborator' and 'Challenger' approaches, either to see what each tells us in turn or to test one against the other. Elements of all three approaches are used in the protohistoric and especially the early historic chapters (Chapters 12, 15).

East Asian chronologies

The Chinese sequence

fig. 5
Box 2
The material cultures of the early historic societies of China were systematically studied as long ago as the 13th century by Neo-Confucian scholars in one of the world's oldest traditions. It was, nevertheless, a foreign researcher who introduced the modern discipline of prehistoric archaeology to China early in the 20th century. Johan Gunnar Andersson, a Swedish geologist affiliated with the Geological Survey of China, is usually credited with the first discoveries (in the 1920s) of Neolithic painted pottery sites and Palaeolithic human and
fig. 16 artifactual remains at the site of Zhoukoudian.[7]

The skeletal materials excavated in 1921 from Zhoukoudian, the first Palaeolithic site to be discovered in China, include specimens of modern humans (*Homo sapiens sapiens*) and our ancestral species (*Homo erectus*). The earliest dates for *Homo erectus* and the beginning of the Chinese Palaeolithic are in the order of between 1 million and 1.3 million years ago, though the exact dating is disputed (Chapter 3). *Homo* evolved on the African continent about 2 million years ago at the beginning of the Pleistocene. *Homo erectus* thence migrated out to colonize southern Europe and Asia, and the transition to modern humans is presumed to have taken place worldwide between about 100,000 and 45,000 years ago. Academic circles are currently wracked by great debates on the nature of this transition, and the skeletal evidence from China is crucial to the outcome.

The subsequent Palaeolithic record for the China Mainland is 'bottom heavy' in that there are more finds and data for earlier in the sequence than later. There is currently a considerable gap for the period between 14,000 and 7000 BC, during which very little is known of lifeways transitional from the mobile hunting and gathering societies of the Palaeolithic (nominally ending at 8000 BC) to the emergence of agriculture.

The beginning of the Chinese Neolithic period is being pushed back regularly as new excavations reveal ever earlier evidence for agriculture. Currently, agricultural sites are known from the 7th millennium BC, but ceramics have been dated even earlier (Chapter 4). The Chinese Neolithic is relatively long and rather diverse, lasting until 2000 BC and encompassing the transformation from agricultural society to class society. This prehistoric period featured innumerable regional cultures with their own characteristic artifacts,[8] which this book cannot even begin to describe. Instead, the two chapters devoted to this period examine respectively the development of agricultural society in the Early Neolithic (Chapter 6) and the increasing status differentiation which gave rise to a political elite in the Late Neolithic (Chapter 7). The designation 'Middle Neolithic' is adopted here to refer to agricultural societies of the late 4th and 3rd millennia BC, though this term is not generally found in the Chinese archaeological literature.

Following the Late Neolithic is the protohistoric Shang period of early state formation (*c.* 2000–1027 BC). 'Shang', a term derived from textual sources, is commonly used in four distinct and sometimes contradictory ways as the name of 1) the archaeological period, 2) a protohistoric ethnic group, 3) a particular style of bronzes, and 4) an early state. In the most simplistic descriptions of the Shang period, the Shang people are portrayed as ruling the Shang state, which is marked archaeologically by the distribution of Shang-style bronzes. As an archaeological period, however, it encompassed several other regional bronze traditions as well. Here, the Shang period is defined as beginning with bronze vessel production regardless of possible differences in ethnic, political or cultural affiliations among bronze-users in the 2nd millennium BC (Chapter 8). As such, the Shang period is the first phase of the Chinese Bronze Age, followed by the second phase, the Zhou (Chapter 9).

The protohistoric Zhou period (1027–221 BC) traditionally begins with the overthrow of the Shang king and clan by a rival ethnic group, the Zhou. This is a historically attested event, though the date is much debated; 1027 is chosen for use here. The lengthy Zhou period is traditionally segmented by historians into Western or Royal Zhou (1027–771 BC) and the Eastern Zhou periods of Spring and Autumn (771–475 BC) and Warring States (475–221 BC). For simplicity's sake, these three periods are referred to here as Early (Western), Middle (Spring and Autumn) and Late (Warring States) Zhou. With the advent of the Zhou period, numerous competing states and statelets proliferated across the north China Mainland and beyond. A significant feature of the 1st millennium BC was the emergence of mounted nomads on the northern Zhou frontiers (Chapter 10).

During the Late Zhou, seven states emerged as major rivals: Qi, Qin, Yan, Qiao, Wei, Han, and Chu. The period ended with the Qin's conquest of the others in 221 BC and the proclamation of a united Qin Dynasty (221–206 BC). The fully historic Han Dynasty (206 BC–AD 220) soon succeeded it, continuing the centralization and bureaucratization begun by Qin. The territorial and economic expansion achieved under the Han has earned it the reputation of being an 'empire'. The Han period as defined here consists of three dynasties: the Western or Former Han dynasty (206 BC–AD 8) and the Eastern or Later Han Dynasty (AD 25–220) surround the brief Xin Dynasty (AD 9–23). Also for simplification, I will refer to these as the Early, Middle and Late Han periods.

The fall of Han resulted in the partitioning of the China Mainland into three

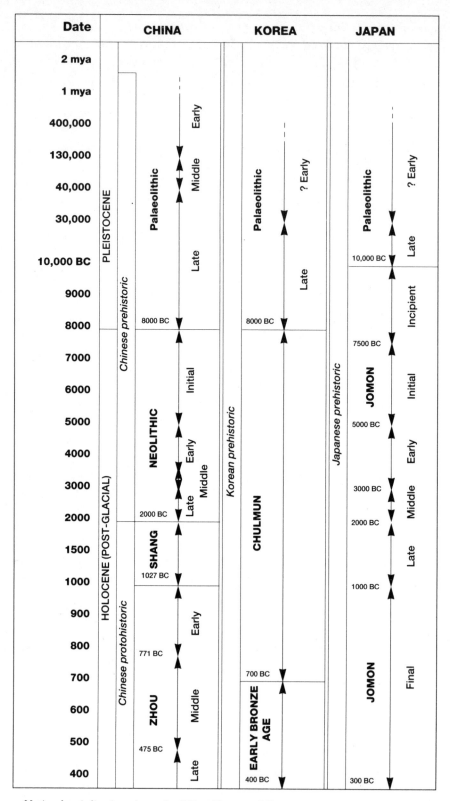

5 National periodization schemes for China, Korea, and Japan.

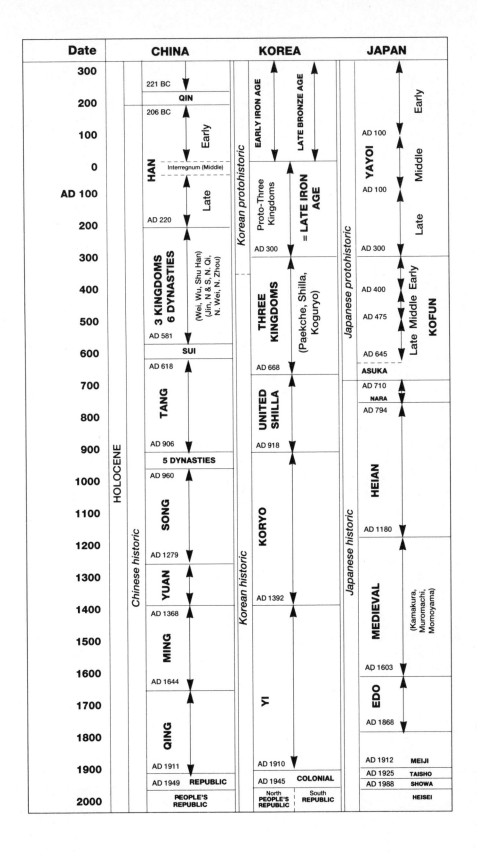

main states – Wei (220–65), Wu (222–80) and Shu (221–63) – and many minor statelets. The traditional historic period encompassing this time of disunity and strife is the Three Kingdoms Six Dynasties (220–581). Only in the late 6th century was the region reunited under one rule, the Sui Dynasty (581–618), which then led into the florescence of Chinese culture under the Tang Dynasty (618–907).

The Korean sequence

fig. 5   Archaeology in Korea is a relatively new discipline. Introduced by the Japanese during the period of colonial occupation (1910–45), archaeological research did not take off among indigenous scholars until the 1970s. Although Japanese researchers reported possible Palaeolithic finds, the existence of such early material was not substantiated until 1962.[9] Now dates of 400,000 years ago are claimed for certain sites, but these are not yet accepted. Thus as yet there is no firm date for the earliest Palaeolithic remains on the Korean Peninsula (Chapter 3).

In the postglacial period after 8000 BC, the Peninsula was occupied by groups subsisting on fish, shellfish and plant foods such as nuts; they used ceramics and polished stone tools but initially practised no agriculture. The archaeological culture is known by its ceramic name, the Chulmun, and the Chulmun period (*c.* 6000–700 BC) is regarded by some as the Korean Neolithic (Chapter 5), but this appellation will be avoided here. Towards the end of this prehistoric period, millet began to be cultivated, and rice agriculture may have been introduced from the China Mainland via processes very poorly understood at present. The Korean Bronze Age (700 BC–AD 1) was initiated by an influx of bronze weapons of a Manchurian Basin type (Chapter 10). Iron was introduced into the northern Peninsula from the China Mainland around 400 BC, and the last few centuries of prehistory (400–1 BC) are jointly referred to as the Late Bronze Age and the Early Iron Age.

In 108 BC Han Dynasty troops from the China Mainland conquered the northern Peninsula and integrated that region into the Han empire's system of military commanderies (Chapter 13). Such commanderies were newly created Han administrative units that co-existed with older units often referred to as 'principalities'. Archaeologically, the protohistoric commandery period on the Peninsula (AD 1–300) is referred to as the Late Iron Age, or as the Proto-Three Kingdoms period, because it is viewed as the formative period for the emergence of the three Korean kingdoms of Koguryo, Paekche and Shilla in the subsequent Three Kingdoms period (300–668). Since the period name Proto-Three Kingdoms is somewhat teleological, I shall refer to the period as the Late Iron Age.

The Three Kingdoms period is marked archaeologically by monumental mounded tomb burials for the rulers (Chapter 14); it must not be confused with the Three Kingdoms Six Dynasties period of the China Mainland. Developing after the collapse of the commandery system in AD 313, the Peninsular Three Kingdoms are viewed as the first Korean states. By 668, Shilla had conquered its rivals and united the Korean Peninsula under one rule. Unified Shilla (668–935) adopted several administrative units and techniques from Tang Dynasty China; though fully historic in its own age, no documents other than wooden tablets survive from this period (Chapter 15).

The Japanese sequence

The Jomon period was the first prehistoric period to be discovered and *fig. 5* documented in Japan, through the excavation of a shellmound in 1877 by an American zoologist, E.S. Morse, who was teaching at Tokyo University. Firm evidence of Palaeolithic occupation, however, was not obtained until 1949. As in China and Korea, dating of the beginning of the Palaeolithic period is still highly controversial (Chapter 3). Japan has provided the most abundant and best-quality materials from the Late Palaeolithic period by which to trace the development of modern human culture in the region (Chapter 4).

At present, Japan lays claim to the world's earliest-known ceramic vessels at *c.* 10,000 BC. These are used to mark the beginning of the Jomon period, a long period of lifeways based mainly on hunting, gathering and fishing that existed in the Islands between 10,000 and 300 BC (Chapter 5). The manufacture and use of pottery by Jomon groups was facilitated by a sedentary rather than mobile lifestyle, which was in turn made possible by the postglacial richness of resources in the Japanese Islands. The Jomon period nominally ended with the introduction of rice agriculture from the continent (Chapter 11).

The ensuing Yayoi period of early agricultural society (300 BC–AD 300) is named after the site in Tokyo where pottery of this period was first excavated. The development of this kind of pottery was formerly believed to have accompanied the adoption of rice agriculture; now, however, the introduction of rice and the emergence of typical Yayoi ceramics are known to have been independent events. Currently, there is a schism among Japanese archaeologists concerning whether to define the Yayoi period on the basis of the presence of rice agriculture or on the presence of Yayoi ceramics. This book employs the traditional ceramic date for the beginning of the Yayoi period (300 BC) so that rice agriculture is acknowledged for some Final Jomon groups. The transition from prehistory to protohistory occurred in the Middle Yayoi period when the Insular societies came into contact with the Han Dynasty (Chapter 13) and were documented in Han court chronicles.

The Late Yayoi period witnessed gradual political centralization and the development of status hierarchies. Such processes culminated in the emergence of class society by AD 300, from which time large mounded tombs (*kofun*) were built for the elite. The protohistoric Kofun period (AD 300–710), defined by this burial tradition, also saw the formation of the first Japanese state and the emergence of court society (Chapter 14). Writing and Buddhism were adopted from the continent in the 5th and 6th centuries, and urbanism took off with temple and palace construction. The succeeding, fully historic Nara period (AD 710–94) began with the move to a new capital city, and the full bureaucratization of the state was accomplished before the period ended (Chapter 15).

CHAPTER 2

Archaeology Emergent

The discipline of archaeology as practised today in East Asia is essentially an import from the West. Yet each country into which it was introduced had its own traditions of antiquarianism which bequeathed a whole set of local outlooks and problems to the developing discipline. Moreover, the co-option of the majority of archaeological activity by the modern states has given the discipline a function in the growth of nationalism in the region. I shall set the stage here for this phenomenon by tracing the early structure of archaeological enquiry and its modern organization.

Antiquarianism

The present East Asian governments follow a long tradition of claiming continuity with the first centralized regimes of the distant past: the Shang of 3200 years ago for China; Yamato of 1500 years ago for Japan; and the Three Kingdoms of at least 1500 years ago for the Koreas. Between then and now, the perceived continuities were maintained not only through written history but also through a concern with the transmission of elite material culture.

Box 2   The first instance of antiquarianism, in Song-Dynasty China (AD 960–1279), focused on the revival of ancient court culture.[1] Interest in the past was excited by the rediscovery of Confucianism in reaction to the other-worldly concerns of Buddhism. Scholarship came to focus more on secular subjects, and sophisticated historiographical methods were developed. Confucianism encouraged empiricism in the cataloguing of bronzes and jades dating from the Shang to Han Dynasties lodged in imperial and private collections. Surprisingly modernistic techniques of observation and representation were deployed in measuring the artifacts, drawing their profiles, describing their decoration, and copying any inscriptions. Reproductions of many objects were then made for use in court ceremonies, giving the rituals an authenticity based on historical precedent.

Contemporaneously with Song in 12th-century Japan, concern grew for the preservation of 'court etiquette' as ancient court society gave way to a militaristic feudal order. Not only were the intangible aspects of bureaucratic ranks and positions studied but also the material aspects of palace architecture, banqueting utensils, dress, weaponry, etc.[2] This concern subsequently encompassed actual palace and tomb sites of previous emperors; and in 1692 the first recorded excavations in Japan took place as a regional *daimyo* dug two tombs to investigate a stone inscription.[3] A similar excavation was undertaken in 1748 in southeastern Korea by the father of a local governor; he 'excavated six ancient tombs to see if they were the lost tombs of his ancestors from the Koryo Dynasty'.[4]

Beginning in the 19th century, the revival of Neo-Confucian scholarship encouraged objective observation and 'investigation into things', resulting in popular scholarly pursuit that focused on objects. In Japan, major exhibitions of curious rocks and artifacts were held, and the many catalogues and treatises written about such collections demonstrate that these scholars not only followed the principles of systematic study but also employed techniques of description and classification,[5] echoing the pioneering antiquarianism of Song. These subsequently became the foundation for Japanese archaeological research.

It was characteristic of antiquarian thought in these countries that material objects from the past were assigned to peoples or ages which were named in historical documents. In other words, concepts of the past were entirely confined to written history – a limitation that also plagued early European antiquarianism.[6] No populations or time periods apart from those described in the documents could possibly be imagined, especially since the documents often incorporated the mythological creation of the universe and humankind and so provided a ready-made history back to the beginning of time. The great contribution of modern archaeology was not the introduction of methods of observation, description and excavation, which as noted above were all variously present in the antiquarianism of the region. It was the introduction of the possibility of a past – the very 'idea of prehistory' – that resided external to written history and was accessible through excavation.[7]

Archaeology from the West

Inherent in antiquarianism was the knowledge that ancient objects could be found in or on the ground. Also, the general locations of former palaces or capitals were known and even visited for information.[8] But the concept of a 'site' (especially ones that were non-imperial in nature) that could be investigated systematically through excavation to reveal something of the lifeways of past peoples was only introduced with archaeology.

The beginning of the discipline in Japan is usually attributed to the American zoologist Edward S. Morse, who arrived in Japan in 1877 a mere twelve years after the publication of the seminal book by Sir John Lubbock, *Pre-historic Times*,[9] that broke the historical grip on thoughts about the past in England. In China, credit for the introduction of archaeology in the 1920s goes to the Swedish geologist J.G. Andersson. Both of these individuals, though not archaeologists themselves, demonstrated through systematic excavation the potential for prehistoric research about a past which was not included in the written documents. The Insular Jomon and Mainland Palaeolithic and Neolithic cultures were all defined during these initial archaeological activities.

BOX 2
Confucius and his Impact

The man we know today as Confucius (K'ung fu-tzu or Kongzi, 551–479 BC) was born into a family of the lower aristocracy in the Middle Zhou state of Lu. He grew up to become a minor court official who, at the age of 60, left his native state to serve as an independent political advisor to a series of other Zhou states. His self-defined mission in life was to effect a return to the 'golden age' of moral politics represented by the founder of the Zhou Dynasty. His mobile career was both stimulated and enabled by monumental changes in social organization at the transition from the Middle to the Late Zhou, when the power and authority of the traditional feudal aristocracy was being challenged by the growing ministerial class (Chapter 9).

Confucius taught moderation and harmony in all things in an era of incredible violence and change. His conception of good government was based on an analogy with the family and was at once authoritarian and hierarchical: children honour parents (filial piety), wives obey husbands, husbands serve lords, and lords serve the ancestors. Yet, he was an egalitarianist who believed that human nature was fundamentally good and that the practice of 'loyalty, reciprocity, dutifulness, filial and fraternal affection, courtesy, friendship and good faith' among individuals would lead to the natural emergence of moral leaders. The loss of morality in a ruler came to be seen, through Confucianist eyes, as

It is sometimes argued that the introduction of archaeology has been an instrument of Western imperialism. The case of the Korean Peninsula shows that it could also be an instrument of 'Eastern imperialism', since archaeology was begun in Korea by Japanese colonial archaeologists between 1910 and 1945. The government used many of the projects and interpretations of Peninsular archaeology to justify the subordination of Korea to Japan during its period of annexation, but the actual quality of the archaeology conducted in this period was so high that the resulting publications are still necessary reference material today.[10]

It is interesting to note that in all three of the above cases, local students were not explicitly trained to carry on archaeological activities in these countries. The discipline became fully established only later with the renewed initiative of resident scholars themselves. Ironically, however, the eras of establishment again coincided with heavy Western influence as students and scholars began to travel abroad. HAMADA Kosaku, an art historian, studied with Flinders Petrie in the loss of the 'Mandate of Heaven' to rule, and such a leader could justifiably be overthrown.

Confucius also accepted students without regard to social class, thus setting a precedent for an emphasis on merit that underlay the bureaucratic examination system. He was a cult figure within the state school system of the Han Dynasty (206 BC–AD 220), and the Confucian Classics became the object of proper study for all aspiring bureaucrats. From the 5th to the 11th century AD his teachings were somewhat overshadowed by concern with Buddhism, but they underlay the powerful and prestigious administrative system of the Tang Dynasty (618–907) which was widely copied by other East Asian states (Chapter 15). Confucianism was revived during the Song Dynasty (960–1279) in a Neo-Confucian movement which brought a 'new historical consciousness' to politics.

Neo-Confucianism had two major impacts on the study of the past. In the 11th century, it stimulated a revival of ancient court rituals using many of the artifacts of the early dynasties as known from accidental discoveries and extant imperial collections. Confucius himself believed that one could restore the ancient (Early Zhou) social order through the practice of the proper rites and rituals, and now the Song Court attempted a return to the golden age using his means! In the 18th century, Qing Dynasty Neo-Confucianists propounded that the essence of things could never be grasped through meditation but only by 'wide learning, careful investigation, exact thinking, clear reasoning, and sincere conduct'. These attitudes, activated by Neo-Confucianists in Japan, gave rise to indigenous scientific study of the wonders of nature and of ancient artifacts.

England and introduced Petrie's techniques of *stratigraphic* excavation to Japan in 1917.[11] HARADA Yoshito, who travelled through Europe and America in 1921–3, also brought back knowledge of new techniques.[12] In 1923 LI Chi, the 'father of modern Chinese archaeology',[13] finished his studies at Harvard University, and was followed by LIANG Ssu-yung, who participated in excavations run by Alfred V. Kidder;[14] XIA Nai studied at the Institute of Archaeology in London between 1935 and 1939, and eventually he went on to serve as director of the Institute of Archaeology in Beijing until his death in 1986. And in the 1950s KIM Won-yong, the doyen of Korean archaeology, studied art history at New York University, becoming the first in a long line of Korean archaeologists to enrol in American Ph.D. programmes. Needless to say, the institutions within which these individuals developed their countries' archaeological disciplines were also Western forms of organization: museums, universities, scholarly societies, and journals.   *fig. 6*

Before moving on to discuss the local characteristics of archaeology in the

	★ Japan	▲ Korea	● China
1092			● 'An Illustrated Study of Ancient Things' (*Kaogutu*) published by the N. Song scholar Lu Dalin
1871	★ Imperial Household (later National) Museum established		
1876	★ First cultural properties protection law passed		
1877	★ Omori shellmound excavation by Edward S. Morse, naming of Jomon pottery		
1884	★ Excavation of Mukogaoka shellmound, discovery of Yayoi pottery		
	★ Anthropological Association of Tokyo (for prehistorians) formed by Tsuboi Shogoro		
1889			● Grum-Grzimailo brothers (Russia) investigate Chinese Turkistan
1892			● Grenard and de Rhine (France) to Chinese Turkistan
1893	★ Anthropological Institute founded at Tokyo University		
1895–6			● Torii Ryuzo (Japan) investigates Liaodong Peninsula and Taiwan
1896			● Sven Hedin (Sweden) to Chinese Turkestan (Xinjiang Province)
	★ Launching of Archaeological Society of Japan and its publication, *Kokogaku Zasshi*		
1897	★ Law for the Preservation of Ancient Temples and Shrines		
1900	★ First site listing compiled by Tokyo University		
1905			● Torii Ryuzo researches Manchuria
1907	★ First archaeology course taught at Kyoto University by Hamada Kosaku		
1908		▲ Royal Household Museum of Choson Kingdom established	
1910		▲ Korean Peninsula annexed by Japan, committee for archaeological investigation established	
1913	★ Department of Archaeology formed at Kyoto University		
1915		▲ Museum of Colonial Government established, later becomes the National Museum	
1917–19	★ First stratigraphic excavations at Ko and Satohama sites		
1919	★ Law for the Preservation of Historic Sites, Scenic Spots, and National Monuments		
1920			● J.G. Andersson 'discovers' the Chinese Palaeolithic at Zhoukoudian and the Painted Pottery Neolithic at Yangshao-cun
1922	★ First book on archaeological methods: *Tsuron Kokogaku*		
1925	★ Law requiring compilation of site lists (published 1925–9)		
1926			● Publication of *Critical Reviews of Ancient History*, advocating archaeological study of the past

6 Institutional histories for East Asian archaeology

★ Japan ▲ Korea ● China	
1927–34	● Folke Bergman leads Sino-Swedish expedition to Xinjiang
1928	● Founding of Institute of History and Philology, Academia Sinica ● Discovery of Black Pottery Neolithic at Longshan, Shandong Province
1928–37	● Excavation of Anyang by Institute of History and Philology
1927	★ Tokyo Archaeological Society founded by MORIMOTO Rokuji
1929	★ Law for the Preservation of Ancient Temples and Shrines changed to Law for the Preservation of National Treasures ● Excavation of first complete skull of *Sinanthropus pekinensis* by PEI Wenzhong at Zhoukoudian
1930	▲ Formation of the colonial Society for Study of Korean Antiquities
1931	● Stratigraphic excavations at Hougang establish cultural sequence
1936	★ *Minerva* debate establishing 'idea of prehistory'
1944	● Dunhuang Institute for Cultural Relics established
1946	▲ Founding of the National Museum of Korea after liberation from Japanese colonial rule ▲ The first excavation by Korean archaeologists, Houchong Tomb, Kyongju
1948	★ Founding of Japanese Archaeological Society
1949	★ Discovery of Japanese Palaeolithic by AIZAWA Tadahiro ● Chinese Academy of Sciences (CAS) established
1950	▲ Beginning of Korean War, suspension of archaeological work for the decade ● Initiation of *Wenwu Cankao Zihao* publication, changing to *Wenwu* in 1959
1952	★ Law for the Protection of Cultural Properties (combined 1919 and 1929 laws) ★ Nara National Cultural Properties Research Institute (Nabunken) established for the excavation of the Heijo Palace ● Institute of Archaeology founded under CAS ● Archaeology major established at Beijing University
1953	★ Founding of the Society of Archaeological Studies and beginning publication of *Kokogaku Kenkyu*, originally called *Watakushi-tachi no Kokogaku* ● Cenozoic Research Laboratory reorganized into Institute of Vertebrate Palaeontology and Palaeoanthropology (IVPP), and beginning publication of *Vertebrata Palasiatica* ● Initiation of *Kaogu Xuebao* publication
1954	★ Law amended to provide for 'buried cultural properties'
1959	● Initiation of *Kaogu* publication

	★ Japan	▲ Korea	● China

1960–2	★ First site registration activities by prefectural Boards of Education at central government's request; registration maps (published 1965–8)	
1961		▲ Department of Archaeology established at Seoul National University, publication of *Kogo Misul* begins ▲ Bureau of Cultural Properties established
1962		▲ Discovery of Korean Palaeolithic by G. Bowen ▲ Cultural Properties Protection Law promulgated
1965	★ *Nihon no Kokogaku* series published, landmark in cultural history studies	
1966–76		● Excavations suspended during Cultural Revolution
1968	★ Agency for Cultural Affairs established	
1969		▲ Korean Atomic Energy Research Institute (KAERI) and radiocarbon lab established
1972		● Zhoukoudian Museum and other schools and institutes reopened after Cultural Revolution; journal publications recommenced
1973	★ Asuka and Fujiwara Palace Site Research Department and Asuka Historical Museum established at Nabunken	
1974	★ Centre for Archaeological Operations (CAO) established at Nabunken	
1975		▲ Institute of Cultural Properties established in Seoul ● Article 12 in Chinese Constitution requires proletariat control over scientific research
1976		▲ Consolidation of the Korean Archaeological Society and publication of *Hanguk Kogo-Hakbo*
1977		● Chinese Academy of Social Sciences (CASS) founded
1981		● Anthropology Department formed at Zhongshan University
1982	★ Founding of the Japanese Society for Scientific Studies on Cultural Property and co-option of *Kokogaku to Shizen Kagaku* as the Society's journal	
1983		● Cultural Properties Law co-opting buried materials as national property
1984		● Opening of Anthropology Department at Xiamen University
1985		▲ First Ph.D. programme in archaeology initiated at Seoul National University
1991		● Regulation for foreign participation in archaeological work promulgated
1992	★ Membership in the Japanese Archaeologists' Association opened up internationally	

East Asian countries, it should be mentioned that subsequent to the post-war communist take-overs in North Korea and China, a specific Western interpretational framework – that of Marxist historical materialism – was imported.[15] According to this theoretical framework, societies around the world move through specific developmental stages: matriarchal clan society, patriarchial clan society, slave society, feudalism, capitalism, then finally communism.[16] Archaeological remains in these countries are generally assigned to these immutable stages but only as loose alternatives for period names, without heavy theorizing or excessive interpretation. Thus it has been said that efforts at least in China to apply historical materialism to archaeological data have resulted only in 'indifferent success'.[17]

Modern organization

In East Asia today, archaeological excavation is mainly a government concern. The active institutions are government research institutes and museums, and the majority of the data being generated through excavation are subject to the time, budget and space restrictions of rescue archaeology. This means that locations of digs are generally determined not by specific research problems but where construction projects are planned. The degree of university involvement in rescue archaeology varies from country to country. In China and Korea, university teams can be called out to large projects when needed, such as the recent dam-site excavations in South Korea. In Japan, however, universities boycotted rescue excavations in the early 1970s because increasing governmen-   plate 2
tal demands for their participation left insufficient time to fulfil their teaching and academic commitments. This boycott led to the complete separation of rescue and academic excavation activity, with the government developing a huge bureaucracy of public archaeologists.[18] In all East Asian countries, academic excavations are poorly funded and small in scale, although there has recently been a significant effort in Japan to increase government support for research archaeology.

The structure of government archaeology is similar in all East Asian countries, since Japan's early organizational framework served as a model during her colonial period in the first half of this century. The seminal unit in Japan was the Commission for the Protection of Cultural Properties, which operated under the Ministry of Education at the national level with branches in the prefectural governments in Japan. This hierarchy was duplicated in China and Korea, and it is through this government administrative structure that current cultural properties laws are administered. In addition to these government offices there are state-run research institutes and museums, any of which might field teams of archaeologists to deal with sites threatened by development.

Separate from this hierarchy are the universities, both state and private. Some university museums co-operate in excavation projects; others merely serve as repositories for the excavated materials.

Japan

In 1968, a new Agency for Cultural Affairs was established within the Ministry of Education to take over the functions of the original Commission for the Protection of Cultural Properties. Archaeological resources (termed 'buried cultural properties') came to be administered under the Monuments Division, which liaised with Cultural Affairs Sections within the prefectural governments. This was the beginning of bureaucratic archaeology in Japan whereby each prefecture installed its own archaeological teams to investigate sites threatened by construction and development, as required by law.[19] The recruiting of trained personnel into government service has resulted in a nationwide staff of 4670 public archaeologists in 1992,[20] in addition to 622 archaeologists working at universities. The former were originally employed by the prefectural Boards of Education, either full-time or temporarily for specific projects; now they are increasingly employed by archaeological resource centres which are established by the prefectural governments as adjunct contract units. These centres operate as autonomous foundations, but their standard of work is compatible with the prefectural units because they are all centralized under the Agency for Cultural Affairs. Moreover, continuing training opportunities for all public archaeologists are offered by the Centre for Archaeological Operations (CAO), created in 1974.

The CAO is affiliated to the Nara National Cultural Properties Research Institute (Nabunken), which was established in 1952 for the investigation of the 8th-century Heijo Palace site. The CAO is a self-contained research, advisory, and training unit catering for the needs of government archaeology throughout the nation. Its permanent staff travel to sites being excavated to give advice, and they run training courses several times a year for select groups of prefectural archaeologists.

The Law for the Protection of Cultural Properties (1952, 1954) in Japan is very non-Western in that it makes no distinction between public and private land. This is in great contrast, for example, to the corresponding laws in the United States, which apply only to state-owned land. In Japan, all buried objects are decreed to be the property of their original owners (however many centuries in the past!); and if they or their descendants cannot be located, the state takes custody of them. Before the mid-1970s, the important materials were retained and sent to the Tokyo National Museum for curation; since then, however, almost every prefecture has built a new prefectural museum, and most excavated materials are curated locally. If conservation is necessary and local facilities are not available, artifacts may be sent to the Gangoji Conservation Unit in Nara, which services most government and some academic excavations. In addition to their public museums, many prefectures have built site museums on the model of the Heijo Palace site museum established by Nabunken. Some of these stand in areas containing clusters of ancient monuments (mounded tombs, early provincial centres and temple sites, etc.) which have been designated as historic parks.

These government facilities for archaeology complement those within the university system, where both public and private universities often maintain museums which hold materials from previous discoveries and current academic excavations. Fifteen national and eleven private universities currently run graduate degree programmes in archaeology, while another fifty-three universites offer courses in archaeology.[21]

China

In 1983 China passed a law specifying that all buried materials are national property. It resembles the Japanese law in making no distinction between public and private land. Any buried objects found in the course of construction are to be reported to the Ministry of Culture's Bureau of Antiquities and Museums, and any planned excavations must be licensed by this bureau. Excavations are conducted by a variety of institutions: university archaeological departments (of which more than a dozen offer degrees in archaeology),[22] provincial or local museums, and government institutes.

Three government institutes located in Beijing are directly involved in ongoing archaeological excavation and research. The oldest is the Institute of Vertebrate Palaeontology and Palaeoanthropology (IVPP), which succeeded the pre-war Cenozoic Research Laboratory (CRL). In 1953, the CRL was reorganized into the IVPP and then later affiliated to the Chinese Academy of Sciences (CAS), established in 1949, as one of its seventy-seven attached institutes. Pleistocene studies and the Palaeolithic are the main concerns of the IVPP, which has a branch office at the site of Zhoukoudian. The two other institutes concerned with archaeology – the Institute of Archaeology and the Institute of (Chinese) History – are now administered under the Chinese Academy of Social Sciences (CASS) which was founded in 1977. The Institute of Archaeology has permanent field stations in the cities of Anyang, Xi'an and Luoyang, where ongoing excavations of important protohistorical and early historical sites are conducted. The Institute also maintains about ten teams of archaeologists in Beijing which it can deploy to any area in the country where excavations are necessary. The Institute of History does not participate in excavation but acts as a locus for the analysis of excavated inscriptional material. In addition, there exists the Dunhuang Institute for Cultural Relics, which was established in 1944 and reorganized in 1951 *fig. 110* expressly for the investigation of the Dunhuang Buddhist caves and manuscript material.

Virtually every province and many municipalities have museum facilities to house materials unearthed in their administrative districts, and have their own excavation teams. The Hunan Provincial Museum in Changsha City is unusual in that it was built specifically to house the finds from the Han-period Mawangdui Tomb. Another special museum – in Luoyang City, Henan *fig. 100* Province – is that of a Han-period tomb mound which has been removed from its original location and reconstructed in a park to display its interior paintings. Museums have also been established at many archaeological sites: Banpo, Tahe, Zhoukoudian, Yinxu, Zhangjiapo, and the Shang Palace Museum in *figs 16, 43, 59*

Zhengzhou City. At the national level, there is also the Museum of Chinese Historical Relics and, of course, the Palace Museum in Beijing, which is complemented by the Palace Museum in Taipei, Taiwan.

In addition to museums, designated historical sites constitute an important part of cultural heritage preservation in modern China. Provincial branches of the Bureau of Antiquities and Museums are empowered to designate sites without consultation with the national headquarters. Thus, the provinces have some leeway in deciding for themselves what cultural remains will be preserved as their local heritage.

Interestingly, China has few national archaeological associations. The existing ones usually focus on specific topics or regions and include the recently
plate 15   formed Chinese Rock Art Association and the Society for Circum-Bohai Archaeology. Thus national meetings hosting archaeological discussions of mixed sorts are replaced by international conferences of fixed content. Recent conferences, for example, have dealt with prehistoric culture in South China,
plate 31   bronze drums and bronze cultures in southern China and Southeast Asia, Xia and Shang culture, circum-Bohai archaeology, and 'Dunhuangology'. China is also continuously involved in sending large exhibitions of Chinese archaeological materials abroad; expanded catalogues of these exhibitions, incorporating research and syntheses by major scholars, form a large proportion of the Western-language materials published on Chinese archaeology.

The major national journals for archaeology in China continue to be *Wenwu*, *Kaogu*, and *Kaogu Xuebao*. But the proliferation of local journals under decentralization policies has vastly increased the amount of data and research being published – the problem now being gaining access to these materials outside China.

Korea

The Koreanization of archaeology on the Peninsula has taken place only since 1945. With economic reconstruction occupying the first two decades after the Korean War, archaeological research has really only flourished since the 1970s. The two Korean governments have approached the task in somewhat different ways. South Korean excavations are conducted mainly by the national museums and the universities, whereas in North Korea government institutes play an important role. The Institute of Archaeology and Folklore, under the North Korean Academy of Social Sciences, fields a large archaeological team for excavations.

The National Museum structure inherited from the Japanese colonialists has been expanded in region and scope by the South Korean government. There are currently eight national museums (Seoul, Kyongju, Kwangju,
fig. 3   Ch'ongju, Chonju, Puyo, Kongju, Chinju) with plans for more (Ch'unch'on, Taegu, Kimhae and Cheju). These are located in major cities or ancient cultural centres, supplanting the need for provincial museums, though some
plate 63   municipalities such as Pusan have their own facilities. The tumuli park in Kyongju, with one tomb opened as a site museum, is the oldest of several site

museums; the Murong tomb in Kongju and the Pokch'on-dong and Pangi-dong tomb clusters in Seoul are also preserved as parks where individual tombs can be entered. Amsadong is a Chulmun-period village in Seoul whose pit-house reconstructions are open to the public, and a small site museum displays artifacts of the period.

Most of the national museums field teams of archaeologists, and the finds are eligible for conservation and preservation by the Department of Conservation Science at the Institute of Cultural Properties in Seoul. This Institute is an arm of the Bureau of Cultural Properties under the Ministry of Culture; established in 1975, it now has branches in Kyongju, Mokp'o, Changwon and Puyo, which focus on specific projects.

fig. 3

Several universities in South Korea have active programmes in archaeology, and sixty-one have museums holding large archaeological collections. In contrast to Japan, many Korean archaeologists hold doctoral degrees from the United States and England, but the first Korean Ph.D. programme in archaeology was instituted as recently as 1985 at Seoul National University. One of the main journals, *Hanguk Kogo-Hakbo*, is published by the Korean Archaeological Society (Hanguk Kogohak'oe), with several other more specialized associations producing their own publications as well.

The character of East Asian archaeology

Despite continuing exposure to Western archaeological research, some aspects of East Asian archaeology are still conditioned by traditional concerns: the priority of inscriptional materials in Chinese protohistoric archaeology; the object-orientation of Japanese archaeologists; the search for Korean ethnicity in past cultures; and most interestingly, the common East Asian conception of time deriving from myth and legend. The last is realized in a vocabulary that sees times past as rising off the ground into the heavens, so that the earlier the period, the 'higher' in physical location it is. This gives meaning to the phrase 'the upper limit' of a site's existence as the oldest limit, whereas 'the lower limit' in East Asian terminology means the youngest. These meanings are exactly opposite to the Anglo-American archaeological vocabulary. Such contradictions are simultaneously confusing and enriching. With the input of local ideas into archaeology, the discipline becomes less 'Western' in character.

fig. 7

The recognition of on-the-ground prehistory as opposed to mythological and legendary history took a very long time to emerge in East Asian archaeology. In Japan, although Morse introduced the 'idea of prehistory' with his excavations in the late 19th century, it took over fifty years for Japanese archaeologists to cease equating prehistoric remains with individuals and peoples mentioned in the early chronicles and view them as anonymous cultures. The final incorporation of the idea of prehistory into Japanese archaeology was achieved in 1936 after substantial discussion known as the 'Minerva debate', since it was documented in the Japanese journal entitled *Mineruva* (Minerva).[23] Of course, such cultures are no longer anonymous to

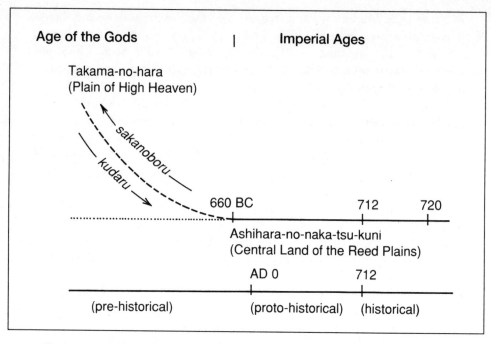

7 *Traditional chronology of early Japanese history, as presented in the Nihon Shoki (compiled in AD 720). The traditional history, extending from fact into legend into myth as it 'ascended' into the past, provided no room for recognition of on-the-ground prehistory (dotted line). The time words in East Asian languages all incorporate the up-down analogy:*

	To go back in time:	To come forward in time:
Japanese	*saka-noboru* 'to climb a hill'	*kudaru* 'to descend'
Chinese	*guoqu* 'to ascend to the past'	*xialai* 'to come down'
Korean	*olla kada* 'to climb up'	*nerida* 'to descend from'

the Japanese, who now commonly speak familiarly of the Jomon and Yayoi peoples as identified exclusively through their material remains.

A second point of variance with the West is in the area of theory. Whereas anthropological archaeology as developed in the United States aims to study the origins and development of humankind, East Asian archaeologists are more locally focused. Tracing the historical roots of their own societies and genetic links between their individual cultures receives top priority, and the re-creation of the lifestyles of former inhabitants in particular periods through the analysis of material culture is the overarching problem which guides all archaeological investigation and synthesis. In this sense, enquiry into past human behaviour as an interesting phenomenon in itself does not enter into the research structure, even though comparative studies with external cultures have been taken up with gusto by Japanese archaeologists in the 1980s. The point of these

Japanese studies is to illuminate the behaviour of past inhabitants of the archipelago, not to integrate the actions of those inhabitants into an understanding of universal human behaviour.

Perhaps the most recent development in archaeological research in East Asia is the increasing shift towards scientific analyses in investigating the details of past activities and material culture. This has manifested itself in China in the chemical analyses of ceramics and metals. Large groups of archaeologists and scientists are now collaborating in investigating ancient technologies, with the results being brought together through large conferences and conference publications of massive scale.[24] The Japanese are also applying scientific techniques to a wide range of materials including wood, bone, botanic remains, etc. The formation of the Japanese Society for Scientific Studies on Cultural Property in 1986 is a measure of the widespread involvement in technological questions, and the society's journal, *Archaeology and Natural Science* (*Kokogaku to Shizen Kagaku*), illustrates the diversity of research topics being undertaken. This development of archaeological science in the country was begun in 1976 with a six-year investment by the Ministry of Education in a programme of multidisciplinary and cross-institutional projects,[25] which resulted in a series of annual conferences and publications.[26] Such studies will probably increase in all East Asian countries in the future, since technological investigations are much more likely to attract funding than theoretical research.

CHAPTER 3

The Earliest Inhabitants
1,000,000–40,000 years ago

The peopling of East Asia

Prior to about one million years ago, East Asia was uninhabited by human beings. Then, according to most palaeoanthropologists, came the migration 'Out of Africa' by the ancestors of modern humans, the early peoples known as *Homo erectus*: '*Homo erectus* . . . travelled widely, and has been nicknamed both Peking Man and Java Man. . . . He had reached Java about a million years ago, and he survived to about 400 thousand years ago in China'.[1] Africa has been considered the locus of early human evolution because of the relative richness of transitional fossils by which to trace the development of the genus *Homo* from the earlier australopithecines, which are absent from other parts of the world. The subsequent broad distribution of *Homo erectus* finds is looked upon as evidence of an actual expansion of the geographical range of the genus *Homo*. This scenario is compatible with the dominant theory of biological evolution, which postulates that species evolution occurs rapidly and only within small reproductively isolated populations.

An opposing view, that *Homo erectus* developed in Asia, is held by some Chinese archaeologists.[2] This view assumes that species evolution can occur on a broad geographic scale among a large interactive population – an assumption which openly challenges the current evolutionary paradigm. The ancestral population, in this case, is thought to have been the ramapithecines – fossil apes which lived between 14 and 8 million years ago across a huge area from eastern Africa to southwestern China.[3] They were first identified in 1931 in northern India, and the majority of finds come from Asia: Lufeng in southern China alone has produced over a thousand teeth and five partial crania.[4]

fig. 16

In the 1960s, it was generally thought that *Ramapithecus* was pre-human in character, but now the majority of palaeontologists consider that the genus was ancestral only to Asian apes such as the giant fossil ape called *Gigantopithecus* and the modern Orang-utan. Unfortunately, there is little evidence of an evolutionary transition from *Ramapithecus* to *Australopithecus*, either in Asia or Africa, and the acknowledged ancestors of *Homo erectus* – the australopithecines – so far occur only in Africa.

This is not to say that australopithecine fossils are not sometimes claimed to exist in Asia. Three molars excavated in 1970 from a southern Chinese cave – plus earlier *Hemanthropus* finds also from the south China Mainland and *Meganthropus* from Java – are identified by local scholars as robust

	palaeomagnetic date (years ago)	fauna	*H. erectus* fossils	stone tool categories
Xihoudu	1,800,000	E. Pleist.	—	core, point, chopper
Yuanmou	1,700,000	E. Pleist.	incisors	scraper
Xiaochangliang	1,000,000	E. Pleist.	—	chopper, scraper
Donggutuo	1,000,000	—	—	point, scraper
Lantian:				
Gongwangling	750–800,000	E. Pleist.	cranium	core, scraper
Chenjiawo	650,000	M. Pleist.	mandible	scraper

8   *Early Pleistocene sites on the China Mainland.*

australopithecines, and articles continue to be published on *Australopithecus* fossils in China. Western scholars, however, disagree with these attributions, classifying these finds instead as *Homo erectus* despite their rather large size. Thus, the lack of universally acknowledged australopithecine fossils from the Mainland renders the Chinese hypothesis of indigenous *Homo erectus* evolution currently unsupportable, interesting though it may be.

Even when the spread of human ancestors 'Out of Africa' is accepted, the date of their appearance in East Asia is hotly debated. Before absolute dating methods were applied to East Asian Palaeolithic materials, the earliest date for *Homo erectus* on the China Mainland was assumed to be about 700,000 years ago at the beginning of the Middle Pleistocene. This date was chosen because no human fossils or stone tools occurred with any Nihewan faunal assemblages of the Early Pleistocene, only with Middle Pleistocene Zhoukoudian fauna.   Box 3 This date has now been challenged by a palaeomagnetic dating programme and the recent discovery of three Palaeolithic sites containing Nihewan faunal assemblages. About 700,000 years ago not only marks the beginning of the Middle Pleistocene but also serves as the boundary – in the world's palaeomagnetic history – between the present epoch of normal polarity and the most recent major reversal of polarity. Lantian, where *Homo erectus* fossils have been recovered from two localities, is now dated before this boundary at 750,000 and 800,000 years ago, while dates of over 1.5 million years ago were obtained for Yuanmou and Xihoudu. However, not all scholars accept these early palaeomagnetic readings, especially from Yuanmou.

The debate over the normal polarity reading at Yuanmou derives from   *fig. 9* differing interpretations of the relative patterning of reversals in the site stratigraphy. The pattern from Yuanmou has been matched with both older (1.61–1.79 million years ago) and younger (0.5–0.73 million years ago) sections of normal polarity within the master sequence. Some claim that the case for the younger dates is reinforced by an analysis of amino acid ratios in animal bones from the Yuanmou stratum, which gave a reading of 0.8 million years ago.[5] Yet

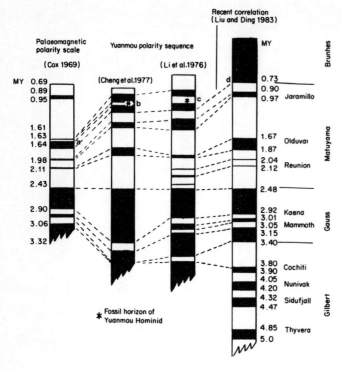

Palaeomagnetic polarity scale
(Cox 1969)

Yuanmou polarity sequence
(Li et al.1976)

Recent correlation
(Liu and Ding 1983)

(Cheng et al.1977)

* Fossil horizon of
  Yuanmou Hominid

9 *Palaeomagnetic dating problems.
Palaeomagnetism is a method of relative
dating based on the fact that magnetic
particles in igneous or sedimentary rocks
align themselves with the earth's magnetic
field as the rocks cool and/or solidify. Their
alignment then preserves the direction and
polarity – which are variable – of the
magnetic field at the time of the rocks'
solidification. Major reversals in the earth's
polarity have been documented in cores
several times for the last 4 million years.*

*The most recent major reversal occurred
between 0.69 and 0.73 million years ago
according to the potassium-argon (K-Ar)
dating of the strata at the reversal boundary.
Thus, 700,000 BP is the approximate
dividing line between the Brunhes Normal
Epoch – continuing to the present – and the
earlier Matuyama Reversed Epoch.
However, these major epochs also entail brief
shifts of polarity within them, and problems
in interpretation most often arise in matching
field data with these minor shifts. The
Yuanmou patterns (b, c) have been matched
to both older dates (around 164 m.y.a) on
the Cox scale (a) and to younger dates
(c. 0.73 m.y.a.) in a recent correlation (d).*

even this claim is not free from controversy, since this date, falling within a
period of reversed polarity, contradicts the younger palaeomagnetic dates of
normal polarity which it is supposed to support.

fig. 10 In view of all these difficulties, a tentative date of one million years ago is
given here as the beginning of the Chinese Palaeolithic. This is bound to change
as the details of the mechanics and timing of the initial peopling of Asia are
clarified in what is one of the more interesting research problems in
understanding Early Palaeolithic East Asia.

Homo erectus at Zhoukoudian

Homo erectus fossils are known from a number of sites on the China Mainland.
Primary among them is Locality 1 at Zhoukoudian. This cave site has yielded
the largest number of *Homo erectus* fossils in the world – so numerous that they
can be used as a group to study individual variation within the species. Among
the forty-odd individuals represented, 40 per cent belong to children under age
14, with only 2.6 per cent attributed to people over 50.[6] Alas, the Zhoukoudian
fossils themselves were lost in shipment during World War II, but plaster casts
made before shipping are still available for research. It is possible that the
originals will be recovered one day, since claims – none substantiated as yet –
continue to filter in of their rediscovery in somebody's loft.[7]

The Zhoukoudian fossils are crucial to current debates on the emergence of
modern humans in the Late Pleistocene, and other data from the site are also in

China	Japan–Korea	Geological era
		Early Pleistocene 1,600,000–700,000 years ago
Early Palaeolithic 1,000,000–200,000 years ago	Early Palaeolithic? ?400,000–30,000 years ago	
Middle Palaeolithic 200,000–50,000 years ago		Middle Pleistocene 700,000–130,000 years ago
		Late Pleistocene 130,000–10,000 years ago
Late Palaeolithic 50,000–10,000 years ago	Late Palaeolithic 30,000–10,000 years ago	

10   Palaeolithic phases in East Asian archaeology.

the forefront of controversies surrounding the nature of *Homo erectus* habitation in Asia. Locality 1 has consistently been portrayed in the archaeological literature as a cave inhabited by *Homo erectus,* who built fires in the interior to keep warm and cook food. This homey scenario – based on tens of thousands of animal bones and stone tools from the thirteen cultural layers spanning several hundred thousand years – has recently been challenged by both Chinese and Western archaeologists.[8] After long debate, these scholars have now agreed on several reinterpretations while disagreeing on other points. No one thinks that the thick ash layers in the cave were produced entirely by these early humans, but Chinese archaeologists point to ash heaps positioned

11   The Zhoukoudian cave sites. Locality 1 shown in cross-section and the later-occupied Upper Cave shown positioned above it. These are only two of scores of localities excavated at Zhoukoudian in the past 50 years. The current cave (G) is surrounded by ancient cultural layers (A/a, B/b, C/c) and loci of Homo erectus *finds (SA-SG). The stratigraphic layers (1-11) contain Quartz horizons (Q1-3).*

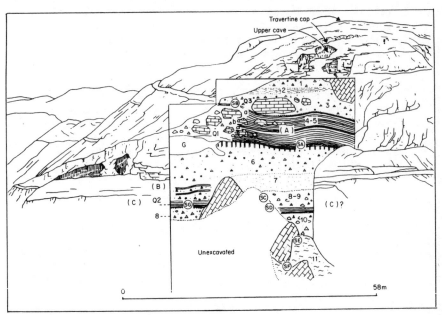

BOX 3
Fossil Faunas

Phases of the Palaeolithic period are sometimes distinguished by a rough classification based on the percentage of extinct species occurring in faunal assemblages recovered from East Asian sites. In Early Palaeolithic assemblages, 40–60 per cent of species are now extinct; in Middle Palaeolithic, 20–30 per cent; and in Late Palaeolithic, only 10 per cent. In addition, the assemblages of different time periods are populated by distinctive animal types or groups of animals, whose presence in a site will give the investigator a clue as to the age of the assemblage and perhaps to the climate at that time. Faunal dating, using these principles, is an extremely crude guide to real age and tends to mask regional and temporal oscillations. Nevertheless, it is a commonly used technique, and references to standard faunal groups as age indicators pepper the Palaeolithic literature.

In East Asia, different animal assemblages represent the northern and southern Mainland as divided by the Qinling mountain range. The southern mammals belong to the Ailuropoda-Stegodon (panda-elephant) fauna, referred to here as the southern fauna. Animals of this group imply a warm climate; for example, the panda and bamboo rat both inhabit southern bamboo groves, and the tapir and orang-utan are common to the humid tropical forests. The occurrence of any of these southern animals above the Qinling boundary indicates that a warm phase of climate prevailed in the north. The southern fauna was overall remarkably stable throughout the Pleistocene in contrast to the northern fauna, whose composition changed several times in accordance with climatic variations. Still, in the south individual genera or species of animals had limited spans of existence. These individuals are used as temporal markers to date southern sites, whereas the dates of northern sites are known from entire complexes of animals.

Throughout the Pleistocene, the northern fauna was a mixture of animals of the temperate forest (bear, deer, squirrel, monkey, etc.) and the grassland (horse, bison, gazelle, etc.), and several rough chronological complexes of animals have been established. The Early Pleistocene or Nihewan fauna seldom occurs in archaeological sites because most early human sites on the China Mainland date to the Middle Pleistocene. The Middle Pleistocene fauna of the north is often referred to as the Sanmen or

Zhoukoudian fauna; it is characteristic of most Early Palaeolithic sites in the north between 700,000 and 200,000 years ago. Succeeding it in the Late Pleistocene is the Loess fauna, which is augmented during the last glacial phase by the Mammoth fauna.

The traditionally recognized diagnostic types for these faunal divisions are given below, but it must be noted that these do not reflect the phase divisions within the groupings that are currently being developed. It is no longer acceptable to assign several sites to the Middle Palaeolithic, for example, and assume they are contemporaneous; after all, this period lasted for half a million years and entailed major changes in climate and in the animals roaming the land.

Nihewan fauna
Myospalax tingi (mole rat)
Elephurus bifurcatus (deer)
Eucladoceros boulei (deer)
Cervus (Rusa) elegans (red deer)

Sanmen/Zhoukoudian fauna
Megaloceros pachyosteus (giant deer)
Homo erectus (early humans)

Loess fauna
Megaloceros ordosianus (giant deer)
Bubalus wansjocki (water buffalo)
Bos primigenius (auroch)

Mammoth fauna
Mammuthus (mammoth)
Alces (elk; moose)

Southern fauna
Pongo (orang-utan)
Gigantopithecus (giant ape)
Ailuropoda (giant panda)
Megatapirus (giant tapir)
Rhinoceros sinensis (rhino)
Stegodon orientalis (stegodont)

within the ash layers and on a limestone slab which they think were hearths. A few burnt bones such as several horse jaw and teeth fragments give clear, visible evidence of roasting; other evidence of heating not visible to the naked eye is expected to be ascertained by scanning electron microscopy. It is certain that at least hyenas lived in the cave, as evidenced by the presence of their coprolites and hundreds of bones gnawed by them. *Homo erectus* may have scavenged their kill, since some of the animal bones bear tool marks in addition to signs of gnawing. Most of the thousands of bones in the cave layers had been introduced by denning animals; only 1 per cent of the recovered bones exhibit clear evidence of human modification. Whether any of these were used as tools rather than being scraped for meat is controversial.

The variety of animals at Locality 1 includes some of the species which Peking Man, Woman and Child exploited for food. Such animals also reflect changes in the climate through time. In the absence of radiometric dating when Zhoukoudian was first excavated, groupings of warm-phase and cold-phase mammals were used to assign the layers to successive climates and periods. Layers 11 to 5 display a gradual progression from the cold-climate Zhoukoudian fauna (e.g. marmot, cave bear, wild cat and hyena) to the warm-climate south China fauna (e.g. straight-tusked elephant, water buffalo, and porcupine) and then back to cold again.[9] These shifts in climate were estimated to have occurred between 500,000 and 200,000 years ago on this biostratigraphic evidence. Recently, several sophisticated dating methods have been applied to the Locality 1 strata.[10] For example, uranium series determinations date Layers 1–3 to 230,000 years ago; Layers 6–7 to 350,000; Layers 8–9 to more than 400,000; and Layer 12 to at least 500,000 years ago, all conforming with the biostratigraphic estimates. Since these new dating methods are quite expensive, many Palaeolithic sites in China are still dated through the relative means of their faunal assemblages and stone tool typologies.

Behind the 'Bamboo Curtain'

The stone tool assemblages of *Homo erectus* on the Mainland were characterized in 1949 by Hallam Movius, Jr as belonging to a 'chopper/chopping tool' tradition of southeastern Asia, in contrast to a 'handaxe' tradition of western Eurasia and Africa.[11] The divide between these traditions has recently been referred to as the 'Bamboo Curtain',[12] based on the idea that the Asian abundance of bamboo that could be made into tools relieved early humans in that area of the need to develop refined tool technologies like those exhibited in European handaxe manufacture. In fact, the strict dichotomy perceived between the traditions no longer obtains. Handaxe-shaped tools are now recognized in East Asian assemblages, though none exhibits the fine and elegant workmanship of some rare examples in the West; and heavy chopper/chopping tools occur throughout East Asian sequences without regard to time.

In any case, the application of the chopper/chopping tool concept to the Mainland in 1949 ignored the data already available from the Zhoukoudian

0   5   10 cm

12 (left) The large-tool inventory of the Asian Palaeolithic as originally described by Movius. Top to bottom: chopper, hand-adze, chopping tool, proto-handaxe.

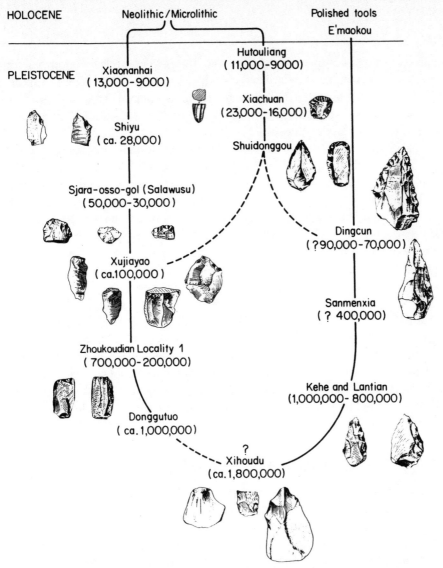

HOLOCENE   Neolithic/Microlithic   Polished tools
                                               E'maokou

                                Hutouliang
                             (11,000-9000)

PLEISTOCENE   Xiaonanhai
                 (13,000-9000)   Xiachuan
                                  (23,000-16,000)

                 Shiyu
                (ca. 28,000)   Shuidonggou

Sjara-osso-gol (Salawusu)
(50,000-30,000)

                                     Dingcun
       Xujiayao   (?90,000-70,000)
      (ca.100,000)

                                 Sanmenxia
                               (? 400,000)

    Zhoukoudian Locality 1
     (700,000-200,000)

                               Kehe and Lantian
                            (1,000,000- 800,000)
         Donggutuo
        (ca.1,000,000)

                       ?
                    Xihoudu
                  (ca.1,800,000)

13 Bilineal development of Palaeolithic tools on the China Mainland. The righthand series comprises large chopper-chopping tools made on flakes and heavy triangular points. It includes relatively few small tools. Conversely, the lefthand series is characterized by the use of small, irregular flakes bearing fine retouch.

excavations of the 1920s and 1930s. These data revealed that the assemblage from Locality 1 consisted almost entirely of small flakes and flake tools – not the large tools predicted. This discrepancy was not fully appreciated until the 1960s, by which time several Palaeolithic sites had been excavated, some yielding assemblages of small flake tools like Zhoukoudian and some yielding large-tool assemblages as at Kehe, Lantian and particularly at Dingcun. The comparative ages of the flake tools from Zhoukoudian Locality 1 (Early Palaeolithic) and the large tools – especially the trihedral points – from Dingcun (Middle Palaeolithic) make it clear that the size of tool was not a product of chronological progression from large to small as expected.

The small-tool flake industry of the China Mainland began in the Early

Palaeolithic as a highly irregular tradition. Flakes were carefully retouched for specific purposes, but standardized tool shapes were just beginning to appear. Among the retouched flake tools are scrapers, points, awls and gravers. Considerable variety and regularity was achieved by the Middle Palaeolithic, and tool types became more systematized.

Flakes were detached from their cores by several techniques: direct percussion with a hard (pebble) or soft (bone, wood) hammer; throwing the core on to another stone; striking two blocks together; and the bipolar technique of setting the core on an anvil stone and crushing it from above with another, thus producing percussion scars at both ends of the resulting flake. It is interesting to note that bipolar flakes occurred by the thousands at Zhoukoudian Locality 1, but not a single example was recovered from Dingcun. Thus, the difference between these assemblages lies not only in the size of tool but also in the method of flake detachment.

fig. 13   To accommodate both types of assemblages, a system of parallel Palaeolithic traditions was proposed for north China in 1972. This system of large-tool and small-tool dominated traditions supersedes the chopper/chopping tool scheme for the Early Palaeolithic, and some Chinese archaeologists have equated the former with warm, humid climates and the latter with cool steppe climates.[13] However, much more regional diversity is now recognized in tool assemblages than is allowed by this scheme, especially for the Late Palaeolithic, and more research is going on into the environmental correlations.[14]

Discovering the Palaeolithic outside China

The excitement of the initial discovery of the Chinese Palaeolithic, in 1929 by J.G. Andersson's crew at Zhoukoudian, is preserved for the English reader in *Children of the Yellow Earth*, written by Andersson himself. It was another two decades before Palaeolithic stone tools were uncovered by an amateur archaeologist in Japan (1949), and over three decades before they were identified in Korea by an American serviceman (1962). It might be said, however, that the Palaeolithic is still in the process of discovery in East Asia as its time limits are constantly challenged in the different regions.

The extent of Pen/Insular Early Palaeolithic occupation is highly controversial. With the recent excavation of *Homo erectus* fossils from Jinniushan in the Manchurian Basin, it is easily imaginable that these early humans could also
fig. 16   have pushed into the Korean Peninsula and on to the Japanese Islands. At the northern Peninsular site of Sangwon Cave, investigators claim that the first stratum above bedrock may be 400,000 years old because of the occurrence of
Box 3   an extinct species of field mouse.[15] There are several weaknesses of dating by faunal assemblages, but Early Palaeolithic layers dated by radiometric methods are rare in Korea. At the Sokchangni site, however, heavy quartzite cores and flakes, choppers and chopping tools occurred at Location 1 below a layer radiocarbon dated to 30,700 years ago. These lower assemblages also contained
fig. 13   bipolar flakes, likened by the excavator to those at Zhoukoudian.[16]

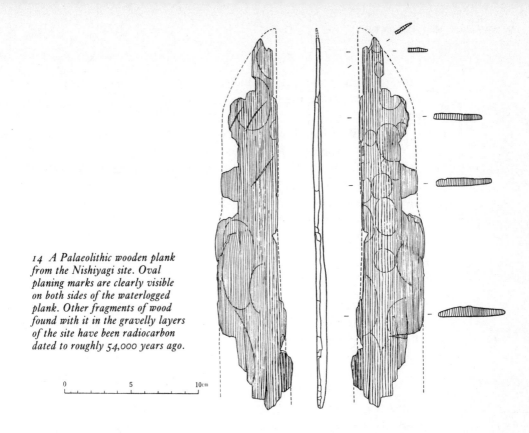

14 A Palaeolithic wooden plank from the Nishiyagi site. Oval planing marks are clearly visible on both sides of the waterlogged plank. Other fragments of wood found with it in the gravelly layers of the site have been radiocarbon dated to roughly 54,000 years ago.

0   5   10cm

Typological similarities in tools have also been used to date the lower level of the Kulpori site to the Early or Middle Palaeolithic. If accurate, this site has produced some of the earliest evidence of a Palaeolithic settlement, since an enclosure 8 × 11.5 m in size marked out by cobbles was discovered in Layer 6. The tools accompanying this enclosure, which has been interpreted as the footing for a tent-like structure, were quartzite flakes belonging to a flake tool industry. Tool maintenance at this site was evidenced by retouched flakes.

In Japan, the excavator of Hoshino and Sozudai thinks these sites represent a Palaeolithic sequence for between 400,000 and 35,000 years ago.[17] Cultural Layer 3 at Hoshino, correlated with volcanic ash known to have been laid down between 130,000 and 65,000 years ago, yielded implements judged to be choppers, chopping tools, picks and proto-handaxes. At Sozudai, a similar range of tools made of quartzite appeared in a layer assessed to have been formed either 200,000 or 400,000 years ago; both the tool types and the sequence are likened to Zhoukoudian. However, no radiometric dates have been obtained for these layers, and the Sozudai lithics themselves are thought by a majority of archaeologists not to be of human manufacture.

Such doubts also plague a whole new series of excavations in northeastern Japan.[18] Amorphous flakes from the Nakamine site, some exhibiting the bipolar technique, were discovered in the fifth cultural layer, dated by thermoluminescence to about 370,000 years ago. These lithics are dismissed by critics as being naturally occurring flakes.[19] At the Zazaragi site, however, points and scrapers recovered from Layer 13 (44,000–40,000 years ago) have been shown by microscopic studies of the tool edges to have been used and are thus undoubted human products. Even sceptics acknowledge that these cultural materials may remain from a Palaeolithic stage commencing as early as 50,000 years ago.

fig. 14 In an exciting new discovery, a clearly worked wooden plank was excavated in 1985 from a site near Osaka which had previously yielded a fossilized human pelvic bone. This site is dated to between 80,000 and 54,000 years ago,[20] and it is only a matter of time before the dating problems for the Early Palaeolithic are solved. It may take longer, however, to recover fossil evidence that makes it possible to determine whether it was *Homo erectus* or modern humans (*Homo sapiens sapiens*) who first colonized the Pen/Insular region of East Asia.

A second peopling?

The appearance of *Homo sapiens sapiens* is not just an East Asian problem but one of worldwide controversy and implications. Basically the same issues as in the first peopling are at stake: were modern humans a product of 'punctuated equilibrium' evolution within one *Homo erectus* group in a corner of Africa or the Middle East who then spread out and replaced *Homo erectus* elsewhere in the world, or did modern humans develop within the whole *Homo erectus* population on a broad geographical scale? These are long-standing questions in East Asian archaeology, and scholars have traditionally taken sides, either supporting the 'replacement hypothesis'[21] or the hypothesis of 'indigenous evolution'.[22] The battle has recently been joined by biochemists, using DNA evidence to support the former hypothesis, which is now alternatively known as the 'Eve hypothesis'.

The 'Eve' or 'replacement hypothesis' follows current evolutionary thinking in requiring the evolution of species to occur only within small, reproductively isolated groups. A 1987 analysis of DNA found within small organelles known as mitochondria in cells of living humans suggested that modern humankind 'can trace their mitochondrial genomes back to a single female founder', and that this founder lived no longer than 150,000 years ago in Africa or middle Eurasia.[23] Based on these data, a second 'Out of Africa' migration was postulated to account for the spread of modern humans and the consequent elimination of local *Homo erectus* populations. This scenario has been hotly *fig. 15* contested by scholars familiar with the East Asian fossils; they see a combination of several facial traits in the *Homo erectus* population of the China Mainland that were genetically passed on to modern Asians and their relatives.[24] A genetic transfer of a complex of such traits would have been impossible if replacement occurred, as the popular hypothesis suggests, because the likelihood of interbreeding is excluded. The propounders of the Eve hypothesis have since had second thoughts about these problems and their own dating calculations,[25] and subsequent statistical studies have exposed serious flaws in their methods.[26] However, the debate over replacement or continuity between *Homo erectus* and *Homo sapiens sapiens* populations in East Asia is far from over.

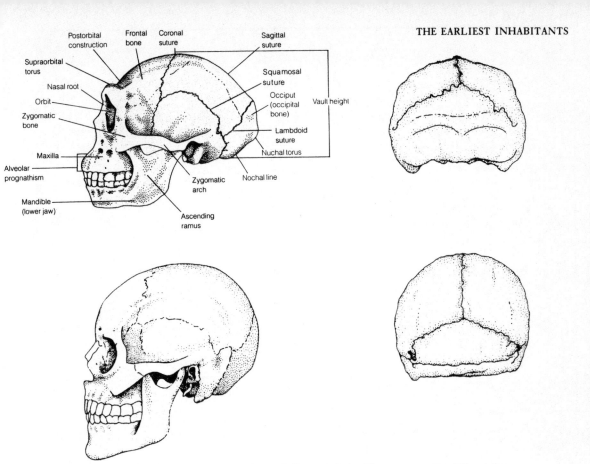

15 Homo erectus *(top) and modern human (above) skull morphologies. Homo erectus was different from modern humans in having a receding chin, pronounced alveolar prognathism, and virtually no forehead; the long, keeled skull sloped back from a very heavy brow ridge – the supraorbital torus. The skull also had thicker walls, more well-developed zygomatic arches for attaching the jaw muscles, a more pronounced nuchal torus for attachment of the neck muscles, and a smaller cranial capacity (775–1225 cc) than at present (mean 1350 cc). The male is estimated to have stood 156 cm and the female 144 cm tall.*

Several fossils identified as 'transitional' between the two species and labelled as *Homo sapiens* have been discovered at the Chinese sites of Dingcun, Maba, Changyang, Dali, Jinniushan, and Quyuanhekou.[27] The remains consist of teeth, face and skull fragments and are sometimes misleadingly termed 'neanderthaloid' by analogy with Europe's own early modern population, the Neanderthals. If *Homo sapiens sapiens* developed outside East Asia as suggested by the replacement hypothesis, there would be no need or reason for the existence of transitional types within East Asia; nor could they properly have been products of interbreeding between *Homo erectus* and *Homo sapiens sapiens* if the assumption holds that these were indeed different species. These data thus argue strongly for the indigenous evolution of modern human populations throughout the range of ancient *Homo erectus*. This scenario is incompatible with evolutionary theory, but some scholars argue that it was precisely because of cultural activities, which separate humans from other animals, that this modification of natural processes could have occurred.[28] Namely, genetic changes could have been spread between regional populations through the mechanism of marriage exchange linked to the trading of raw

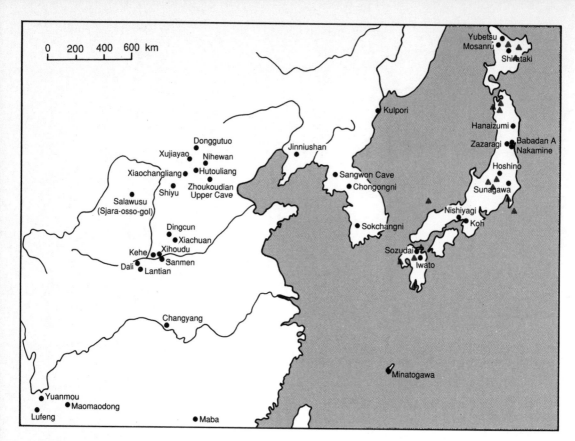

16 Palaeolithic sites in East Asia. Sites dating between 1 million and 10,000 years ago mentioned in the text, particularly in Chapters 3 and 4. Triangles indicate obsidian sources.

materials, a form of artificial intensification of gene-pool sharing which has no corollary in other animal populations.

fig. 22 Long-distance procurement of non-local materials is well known for the Late Palaeolithic and is evidenced in East Asia at the Upper Cave locality at Zhoukoudian (32,000–16,000 years ago), where artifacts made of marine shell were discovered together with *Homo sapiens sapiens* fossils. The shells may have been obtained through exchange with distant coastal groups. Whether similar long-range interaction can be found for the Middle Palaeolithic, however, is another question; and it remains to be seen if such cultural activities can indeed be made to account for the evolution of the human species. Ongoing research promises to clarify the mechanics of the peopling of East Asia as well as to refine many of the assumptions used in evolutionary theory.

Archaeological sites less than 30,000 years old are assumed to have been produced by modern humans. It is noteworthy, though, that very few Late Palaeolithic skeletal remains have been recovered – the most important sites being the Zhoukoudian Upper Cave and the Minatogawa limestone fissure in Okinawa.[29] The latter reflects the intensive colonization of the East Asian littoral in the Late Palaeolithic, a topic to which I shall now turn.

CHAPTER 4

Innovations of Modern Humans
40,000–10,000 years ago

Exploiting East Asialand

The Late Pleistocene, which witnessed the appearance of modern human beings in East Asia, began with a long interglacial of relatively stable warm weather between 130,000 and 75,000 years ago. Subsequent cycling of warm and cold phases of increasing severity led to dramatic fluctuations in the geographical contours of coastal East Asia. During cold phases 70,000, 50,000 and 37,000 years ago and then again during the last glacial maximum at 18,000 years ago, the Yellow Plain and Seto Plain were exposed by lower sea levels, and the Japan Sea became merely a large lake which drained through the present Korea Strait. These increased land areas facilitated the movement of humans and animals among and between parts of East Asia that are now separated by large expanses of water.   *fig. 17*

Since the large plains animals of the Loess fauna are usually considered the primary food resources of Late Palaeolithic hunters, the movement of herds of bison, elephant and woolly rhinoceros and the like might have been of crucial importance in guiding the migration of human groups into the mountainous edge of East Asialand – what is now the Japanese archipelago. The cold-phase dates given above do correspond loosely with the very tentative data for human occupation in the Early Palaeolithic of Japan as discussed in Chapter 3. After about 20,000 years ago, despite extremely cold conditions, Late Palaeolithic populations grew rapidly, as demonstrated by the thousands of known Late Pleistocene sites. Some new groups probably migrated in from the north, as Sakhalin, Hokkaido and Honshu were successively joined to the Siberian mainland.

Elephant bones dredged up from the bottom of Japan's Inland Sea confirm that large game roamed the now-submerged Yellow and Seto Plains. It is quite plausible that many Late Palaeolithic sites were situated on these plains, which are inaccessible in their flooded state today. But one lowland site, Hanaizumi at   *fig. 16* the northern tip of Japan's Honshu Island, provides a glimpse of Late Palaeolithic activities. Consisting of a peat bog formed between 35,000 and 15,000 years ago, Hanaizumi yielded bones of bison, elk (moose), and elephant (*Loxodonta*) at what is thought to have been either a kill site or a bone dump.[1]

Hanaizumi is also one of the few open sites in East Asia to have produced Palaeolithic bone implements. Most have been recovered from caves or rock

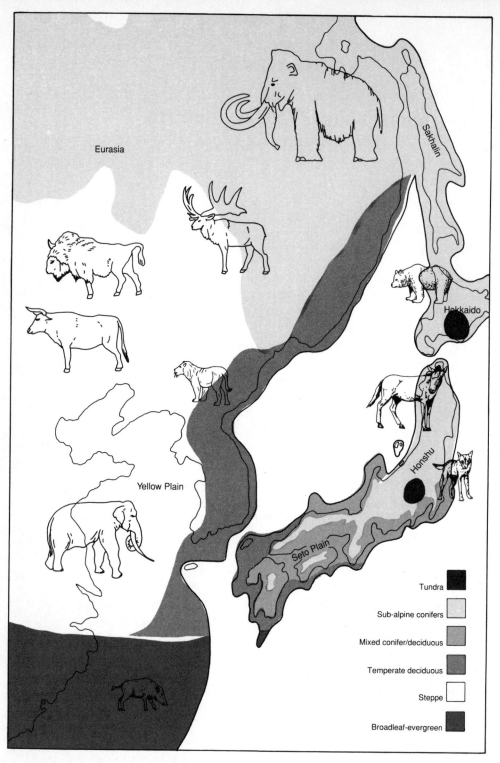

Tundra

Sub-alpine conifers

Mixed conifer/deciduous

Temperate deciduous

Steppe

Broadleaf-evergreen

17 The formation of East Asialand. Chinese scientists undertaking extensive coring in the East China Sea have identified successive beaches corresponding to the rise and fall of sea levels between 130,000 and 5,000 years ago. This map shows the coastline (bold line) at the time of maximum cold during the last glacial period 16,000 years ago, with the Yellow Plain and Seto Plain exposed. Tundra, steppe and boreal coniferous forests characterized the northern latitudes, with temperate coniferous forests spread across the mid-latitude ranges. The steppes and plains were mostly treeless, supporting large herbivores such as auroch, bison, elk and Nauman's elephant. Both the woolly mammoth and woolly rhinoceros extended into the Hokkaido region from the Eurasian landmass, while bison, giant deer, horse, dog and bear remains have been recovered from present-day Honshu.

shelters, as at Maomaodong on the south China Mainland. Just two such sites have recently produced over five hundred bone awls, needles, knives, shovels, clubs and pronged implements.[2] Dating to the end of the Pleistocene, the bone tool assemblage at Maomaodong differs radically from the lithic assemblages found across northern East Asialand, which themselves have been equated with a steppe environment,[3] raising questions as to the possible use of the shovels and pronged tools in the development of southern horticulture.[4]

Most Palaeolithic sites in East Asia have poor preservation of animal and plant remains. The arid steppe of the north China Mainland is one place where faunal remains have been recovered from open sites. From this evidence, it can be postulated that some Late Palaeolithic groups in this region may have concentrated on specific species. Horse and wild ass dominate the assemblages at Shiyu and Xujiayao, but at Salawusu (Sjara-osso-gol) in Inner Mongolia, the remains are almost exclusively gazelle.[5] In other locations, there is little but stone tools through which to investigate the interaction of early modern humans with their changing environment. One avenue for doing so is to analyze the kinds of fatty acids remaining on stone tools after use. These are removed from the artifact in an ultrasonic bath of solvent and then identified and measured with a gas chromatography mass-spectrometer. Artifacts from the Babadan A site (controversially dated to 140,000 years ago) yielded fats very close to those of the Naumann elephant, while fatty acids on artifacts from the Mirikawa #1 site (dated to about 12,000 years ago) were especially close to those of deer.[6] Perhaps this represents a shift in hunting patterns from the megafauna of the Late Pleistocene to the medium-sized game animals pursued in the Holocene.

Another approach is through the investigation of tool use by identifying patterns of wear on tool edges. Whereas most use-wear studies in the West are carried out on obsidian or flint tools, the Japanese corpus consists mainly of tools of siliceous shale. An analysis of several artifacts from the Mosanru site (radiocarbon dated to between 13,000 and 15,000 years ago) suggested the following tool uses: one burin used to scrape bone or antler; a second burin used on the same materials, engraving with one edge and scraping with another; a third burin used for cutting bark with one edge and engraving wood with another; and four end scrapers, one for hide and three for bone.[7] As yet it is impossible to identify from use-wear patterns what kinds of animals or plants were being exploited, but pollen and faunal remains show that the area north of present-day Tokyo was home mainly to boreal forests and northern mammal groups while temperate forest and southern mammals colonized the south-western fringe of East Asialand.

Late Palaeolithic flake technologies

Technological succession
Due to the deep stratification and large areal exposure of Japanese Palaeolithic excavations, researchers there are blessed with an abundance of stone tools with

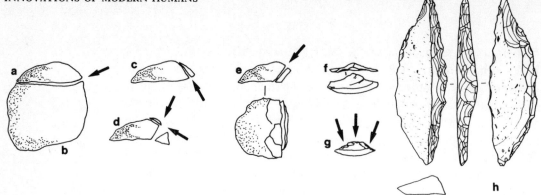

18 The Setouchi technique for flaking sanukite. This is a method of preparing cobbles of sanukite, a fine-grained volcanic relative of andesite, for the production of side-blow flakes; it was named after the Japanese Inland Sea (Setouchi) area where the most abundant rock type was available. The technique seems to have been developed specifically to overcome the rather intractable nature of this rock and its peculiar fracture patterns.

To make a side-blow flake, a large circular flake (a) to be used as the core was struck off a sanukite cobble (b). (The arrows indicate the direction of the blow.) This flake (side-view, c) was covered by the original cobble surface (cortex) on the rounded top surface, but the bottom surface was flat. The circular shape was modified by taking flakes off across one side (c, d) to form a symmetrically bevelled edge. The upper surface of this bevel formed the striking platform where successive flakes were detached (e); in shape, these flakes followed the profile of the lower surface of the bevel – that is, shallow in depth and wide in breadth (f). The platform area was often blunted (g), leaving the blade to be used as it was or sharpened with retouch. A typical artifact made from a sanukite flake was the Ko knife (h, 9.5 cm long). The bulb of percussion occurs on the longitudinal side of the implement, giving rise to the name 'side-blow' flake.

which to reconstruct temporal changes in the methods of tool manufacture as well as in the tool types themselves. The Late Palaeolithic of the Japanese Islands, nominally beginning 30,000 years ago, is currently divided into four major phases, each characterized by a different lithic technology but with notable regional variations. In general, the inhabitants first manufactured rather elongated flakes for tools (Phase I), but in Phase II they achieved the production of true blades – that is, flakes more than twice as long as they are wide with regular, parallel sides. They made some of these blades into so-called 'knives', but for other knives they used side-blow flakes made with the Setouchi technique. As early as 17,000 years ago, they began to manufacture microblades – tiny bladelets which became widely used in Phase III. Usually 3–5 mm long and made of obsidian, microblades were probably used as inserts into composite tools (like a razor blade today). Microblade production represented the refinement and scaling down of the previous blade technology, but an entirely different way of fashioning tools became popular in Phase IV. This was the shaping of both front and back surfaces of a tool through chipping (bifacial retouch) to produce what are now recognized as projectile points (arrowheads/ spearheads) and similar implements. Although this description of successive lithic technologies deals only with flake tools, larger tools such as choppers continued to be made throughout East Asia during the Late Palaeolithic.

On the China Mainland, the lithic traditions have been divided into flake and heavy tool traditions lasting through the Middle Palaeolithic and merging thence onwards. Many of the Late Palaeolithic flake assemblages, such as at Shiyu (29,000 years ago), contain blade-like flakes and cores. The first site yielding true microliths is Xiachuan, dated between 23,000 and 16,000 years

fig. 19

fig. 13

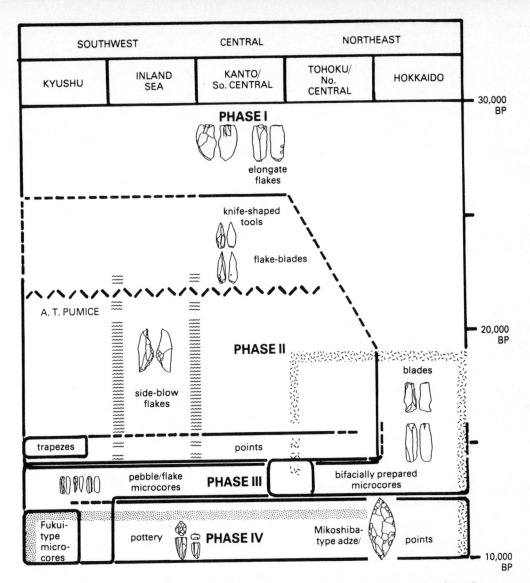

| SOUTHWEST | | CENTRAL | | NORTHEAST |
| KYUSHU | INLAND SEA | KANTO/ So. CENTRAL | TOHOKU/ No. CENTRAL | HOKKAIDO |

19 Periodization of Late Palaeolithic industries in Japan. Phase 1 ended in the Kanto region about 26,000 years ago but continued almost without interruption until 13,500 years ago in Hokkaido; ending dates for other regions are unclear (marked by dotted lines). Phase 2 contains a volcanic ash date marker, the A.T. pumice (zig-zag line), at about 22,000 years ago; knife-shaped tools and flake-blades characterized Kanto and surrounding regions, while the Inland Sea area was belatedly characterized by side-blow flakes. True blades occurred in the northeast from 19,000 years ago or so (dashed mesh). At the end of the phase, trapezes become common in Kyushu, and points appear across the central region. In Phase 3, the central and southwestern Islands boast pebble/flake microcores while the northeast yields bifacially prepared microcores. Phase 4 is characterized in the north by ground-edge adze/axes and stemmed points. Except for Hokkaido, pottery (dotted mesh) enters the sequence at this time.

ago. These dates are compatible with the early microblade occurrences in the archipelago noted above, with the revised date of the Dyuktai microlithic culture of Siberia (18,000 years ago at the earliest),[8] and with the major site of microblade manufacture in the northern Japanese Islands, Shirataki, at 13,000 years ago.[9]

Microblade production was generally confined to the northern half of East Asialand. Two basic shapes of exhausted microcore characterize this vast

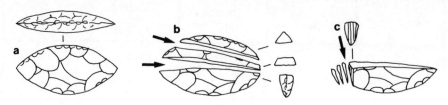

20 *The Yubetsu technique for flaking obsidian. This is one of several methods of preparing obsidian cores for the subsequent detachment of microblades. First, a large biface having an oval shape and thickened centre was created (a). Next, one half of the biface was removed by taking off successive spalls by striking the end of the biface (b). The first spall is triangular in cross-section because it includes the edge of the biface. The second spall consists of two parallel surfaces, giving the piece the name 'ski spall'. These detachments leave a wedge-shaped core with a smooth upper surface forming the striking platform. From one end of the wedge, tiny longitudinal flakes or 'microblades' were detached by applying pressure to the platform, leaving fluted scars on the wedge (c).*

fig. 18

fig. 16

region in the terminal Pleistocene: conical and wedge-shaped. The technology of microblade production on such cores has been studied best in Japan. Several flourishing microlithic traditions, including the Yubetsu technique in Hokkaido and the conical-core tradition in Kyushu, were based near local sources of obsidian, a fine-grained volcanic glass suitable for delicately controlled microblade production. But microliths enjoyed only a very brief lifespan in the archipelago compared with the northern areas of the continent, where microblade production continued well into the postglacial period even within the north-central Neolithic cultures.

A mobile lifestyle

Actual habitation remains for the Late Palaeolithic are extremely scarce and ephemeral in nature, encouraging the view that Late Palaeolithic peoples were mobile hunters.[10] The site of Sokchangni on the Korean Peninsula has produced the most substantial dwelling yet found, dated to 21,000 years ago. A floor measuring 5 m² was edged with rocks, perhaps used to weigh down a roof covering; a burnt spot on the floor indicated a hearth, and several post-holes were in evidence.[11] In Japan, about thirty Palaeolithic sites have yielded evidence of settlement. The most characteristic features at these sites are clusters, 2–3 m in diameter, of burnt cobbles associated with artifact scatters.[12] The cobble clusters might have been locations for food preparation or stone floor linings for large hearths. Some stones are encrusted with charcoal or tar-like substances which have yielded animal lipids, supporting these interpretations.[13] The patterning of lithics at the Shirataki site in Hokkaido, dated to 13,000 years ago, illustrates another possible aspect of settlement organization. Each of the various kinds of scrapers as well as the microcores were recovered from a different area of the site, suggesting that activities using these tools were spatially separated.[14]

That abandoned sites were often reoccupied is known from exercises in core refitting. Where several flakes were struck from a single core – and where many

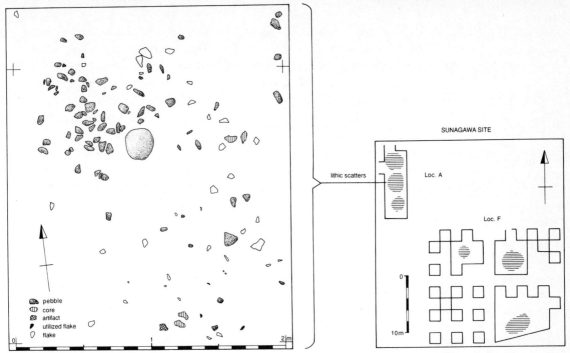

21 Lithic scatters at Late Palaeolithic sites. The Iwato site (left) and Sunagawa site (right) give us different information about the formation of lithic scatters. The internal composition is shown at Iwato, consisting of lithic manufacture debris distributed around a relatively barren central area: was this where the knapper sat? The relative positioning of such scatters is illustrated at Sunagawa. Some of the flakes recovered from the scatters in Locations A and F fit together, indicating the shifting of the manufacturing locus through time.

of those flakes and perhaps the core itself were discarded immediately – it is possible to refit the flakes on to the core to identify the sequence of detachment. Apart from its purely technological interest, core refitting also yields important sociological information about lithic manufacture. Which flakes were chosen for use and carried away (use value)? What percentage of the core debris was discarded (economy)? And did the flaking of one core occur all in one place or was the tool carried around and modified in its lifetime of use (curation)? At the Sunagawa site, cores used to make flakes in one area were first carried away by the inhabitants and then later carried back on to another part of the site for further flaking activity. These successive activities were discovered entirely through reconstructing the sequence and location of flake detachment from the debris in the two areas.[15] Instances are also known of transporting cores to different sites and carrying out successive flaking activities at each.

Palaeolithic peoples could choose to locate their settlements in close proximity to stone resources, as at Shirataki where the river 'provided an inexhaustible supply of water-transported obsidian cobbles for toolmaking'.[16] In other cases they might have travelled relatively long distances to obtain raw materials for stone tools. Three local sources for obsidian used in the Kanto region during the Palaeolithic have been identified through neutron activation and X-ray fluorescence analyses.[17] The people in north Kanto obtained all their obsidian from the inland mountains; the south Kanto populace, however, shifted from a reliance on coastal sources in Phase I, to procurement from both coastal and mountain sources in Phase II, to primary dependence on the mountain sources in Phases III and IV. Meanwhile, as early as 27,000 years ago a small amount of obsidian was apparently transported from the offshore islands,[18] though this source was not exploited heavily until the succeeding Jomon period. The social mechanisms by which they obtained their stone are unknown; most scholars presume some sort of exchange network similar to the 'down-the-line' model developed in the West.[19] Some believe, however, that the people could well have walked the 50–150 km or so overland to the sources – if only once a year – so that there is no need to postulate the existence of trade networks in the Palaeolithic.

Palaeolithic art

The advent of *Homo sapiens sapiens* was not just a biological phenomenon: it was also a psychological revolution, accompanied by the development of self-consciousness and aesthetic appreciation. The suddenly felt need to bury the dead, the use of body ornaments, and the creation of cave and portable art followed from these changes and have been cited as the major attributes of human modernity. In East Asia, these changes manifested themselves in the Late Palaeolithic.

Zhoukoudian once again enters the story here with its exceptional finds from Upper Cave, a different cave from Locality 1. Although a few ashy areas and burnt spots indicate that fires were lit in the cave, there was no extensive tool debris or rubbish characteristic of long-term occupation. Instead Upper Cave

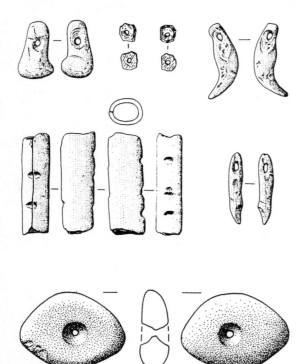

22 *Late Palaeolithic body ornaments from the Upper Cave at Zhoukoudian. Bird bones, pebbles and animal teeth were all pressed into service for the first human foray into the fashion world.*

23 Late Pleistocene art. Palaeolithic rock peckings of deer on the Korean Peninsula (a) contrast greatly with anthropormorphic pebbles found in the Japanese Islands. A pecked face stares out from a cylindrical stone rod (b), and an incised pebble bears the figure of a woman (c), perhaps wearing a grass skirt?

has been interpreted as a burial area where at least five adults, a youth and two children were interred, accompanied by ochre and various personal ornaments.[18] These ornaments comprise the earliest 'jewellery' known from East Asia: perforated teeth of numerous animals; drilled pieces of bone, shell and stone, which were perhaps strung as beads or pendants or sewn on to clothing with one of the bone needles found in the cave; and segments of hollow bird-bone with notches on the exterior surfaces, which also might be beads or clothing decorations. Similar ornaments consisting of bird-bone beads, ostrich-eggshell pendants and perforated shells have been found at the nearby open-air site of Hutouliang.[20]

Artifacts which have been aesthetically transformed but which were probably not meant to be worn on the body are called 'portable art'. The first Palaeolithic examples of Mainland portable art have recently been identified, consisting of geometric carvings on bone.[21] Anthropomorphic stone forms from the Japanese Islands also fit into this category. A 'face' sculpture pecked on to the hilt of a stone rod was excavated from the Iwato site dating between 20,000 and 10,000 years ago, and several river cobbles excavated from the Kamikuroiwa site, dating to 10,000 years ago, bear incised decoration interpreted as depicting female figures. These female forms with heavy breasts (and what look like grass skirts!) foreshadow the subsequent tradition of making ceramic figurines throughout the postglacial Jomon period.

In addition to these portable objects, some rock art on the Korean Peninsula has been ascribed to the Palaeolithic on the grounds that the animals portrayed were Late Pleistocene cold-climate fauna not currently found on the Peninsula.[22] These pecked figures are identified as reindeer and grey deer. It is hypothesized that about 14,000 years ago, with the amelioration in climate, these cold fauna began to migrate northwards together with the recession of the grasslands and forests of their glacial habitat. Korean archaeologists are of the opinion that Peninsular occupants followed the herd animals north, possibly leaving the Peninsula unoccupied in the early postglacial period.

BOX 4
American Connections

Late Palaeolithic East Asia is viewed with great interest in debates over the peopling of the Americas, even though it is not directly on the proposed migration route from Siberia across the former landbridge called 'Beringia' to the American landmass. East Asia's lithic traditions have many analogues in artifacts excavated from early American sites, and possible correlations between them are often cited in debates about the dating of the first arrivals from the Old World.

The currently dominant but much-challenged scenario holds that the first native Americans were large-game hunters who used bifacially flaked spearpoints, called 'Clovis points' after their site of first discovery. These are dated to *c.* 11,000 years ago, comparable with the bifacial flaking technology which arose in the Japanese Islands at about the same time. Microblade technology – which is dated much earlier than bifacial flaking in Eurasia (up to 35,000 years ago on the China Mainland and 14,000 years ago in the Japanese Islands) – also occurs in North America. On the Eurasian side, the Yubetsu technique is common in Hokkaido, the Amur River drainage, the northern Mainland, and Trans-Baikal; the last two regions also host the Campus-type microcores identified first in Alaska. So far, there is no evidence that the Campus technology is as early as its Eurasian counterparts, but researchers are now allowing for interaction in both directions across Beringia so that the Eurasian remains are not automatically assumed to be earlier.

A few sites yielding amorphous cores and flakes in North America date prior to 11,000 years ago. Some researchers dismiss these as mis-dated artifacts or naturally broken stones, believing that the earliest Americans already possessed bifacial technology; others believe these lithics to be the heterogeneous remains of people who made an earlier crossing from Eurasia, taking with them generalized toolkits not yet incorporating bifacial technology. It has already been shown that simple flake technologies co-existed with more formal prepared core technologies late

Harbingers of the Neolithic

The invention of pottery

fig. 43 Just prior to the end of the Pleistocene period, the world's earliest-known ceramic vessels appeared in the southwestern Japanese Islands. The Fukui Cave site yielded sherds decorated with band appliqué and 'fingernail' impressions together with microliths; and at Kamikuroiwa Cave, sherds

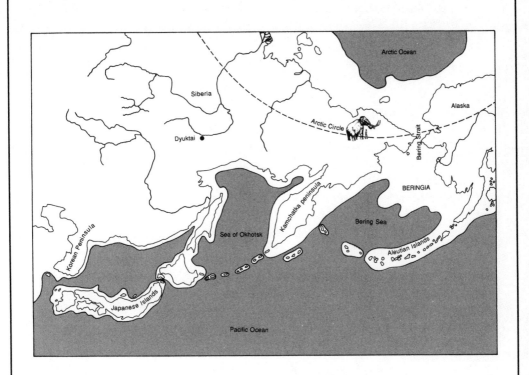

into the Palaeolithic in East Asia, so such a scenario is highly plausible. In any case, earlier migrations would be demanded if controversial datings of sites in Brazil and Chile to 'at least 15,000 years ago and possibly ... 30,000 years ago' were to become generally accepted.

Very little is understood about the environmental adaptations and migratory processes of groups on both sides of Beringia. In fact, the landbridge itself may have been irrelevant if Late Palaeolithic peoples of northeastern Asia had water transport of sufficient quality to make crossings along the Kurile and Aleutian Island chains. The deep-sea fishing capabilities of the early postglacial Jomon peoples of the Japanese archipelago (Chapter 5) thus become relevant to this discussion.

bearing similar raised-band decoration were unearthed along with bifacially flaked projectile points. Both these sites date to about 12,000 years ago, posing two problems for their excavators.

First, Japanese archaeologists are reluctant to accept the idea that the archipelago formed the locus of ceramic innovation in world prehistory, and they look to the continent for precedents. Indeed, clay was used to fashion figurines at much earlier dates (28,000–27,000 years ago) in eastern Europe,[23] and there is a growing body of evidence that pottery occurred quite early on the China Mainland as well; for example, sherds from Pengdoushan in the Yangzi Basin have been radiocarbon dated to 10,000–9,000 years ago.[24] Second, Japanese archaeologists vacillate over whether to include their early ceramic phase in the Palaeolithic, or treat it as the beginning of the long sequence of textured pottery in the postglacial Jomon period of the Japanese Islands.

plates 8–11

Ground-stone tools

Phase IV of the Late Palaeolithic, during which these early ceramics first appeared, also saw the rise to prominence of an edge-ground axe/adze referred to as the 'Mikoshiba adze'. The classic distinction between the Palaeolithic (old stone) and Neolithic (new stone) ages was the difference between chipping and polishing as the means for finishing stone tools. The 'new' technology was judged to have been polishing, which occurred in Europe with ceramics and agriculture. In Australasia, however, there is now a large body of evidence that polishing, first in the form of edge-grinding, began as early as 30,000 years ago.[25] It occurs sporadically on heavy chipped tools throughout the Late Palaeolithic in the Japanese Islands.

These developments in ceramic and ground stone are thus Late Palaeolithic innovations which demonstrate that the European model of technological change cannot be applied indiscriminately to other areas of the world. However, as with any invention, the mere existence of the occasional pottery vessel and edge-ground tool in the Late Palaeolithic may not be as important as the conditions which stimulated their more widespread adoption and use. In East Asia, such conditions might be found in the transformation of the forest regimes in the terminal Pleistocene.

Forest exploitation patterns

Alpine tundra and boreal conifer forests began to recede northwards about 14,000 years ago. According to work done on the Japanese Islands, these might have been succeeded immediately by an open steppe environment,[26] and then came colonizing temperate forests from the south.[27] This involved not only the migration of whole plant communities from south to north but also the establishment of entirely new sorts of forests. By 6000 BC, a warm-temperate evergreen broadleaf forest unique to East Asia colonized a broad strip from the Yangzi Basin across the southern tip of the Korean Peninsula into the western Japanese Islands. Across the northern Pen/Insular region cool-temperate deciduous and mixed forests graded into the alpine coniferous forests of the far north.

The warm-temperate evergreen oak and laurel forests provided acorns from the chinkapin and the evergreen oaks. Experiments have shown that these nuts have low tannin content (c. 1–2.5 per cent) which can be extracted by simple water leaching.[28] In contrast, nuts of the deciduous forest, including acorns and horse chestnuts (buckeye, conker), have a high tannin content (3.7 per cent) which requires extraction through complicated heating and mixing with lye.

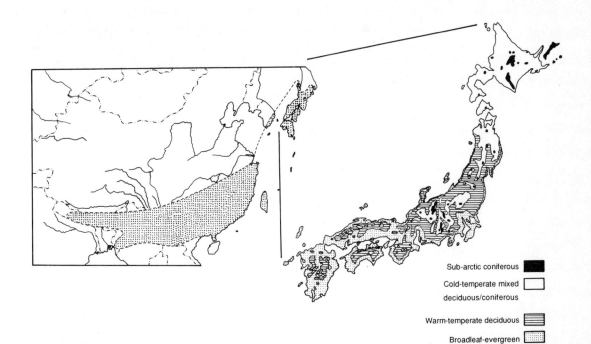

Sub-arctic coniferous

Cold-temperate mixed
deciduous/coniferous

Warm-temperate deciduous

Broadleaf-evergreen

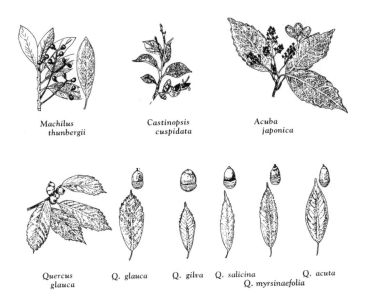

Machilus
thunbergii

Castinopsis
cuspidata

Acuba
japonica

Quercus
glauca

Q. glauca

Q. gilva

Q. salicina
Q. myrsinaefolia

Q. acuta

Ardisia
crenata

Camellia
japonica

Cleyera
japonica

Cinnamomum
japonicum

24 *The distinctive broad-leaf
evergreen forest of postglacial East
Asia: some characteristic species
and forest distributions. Not only
was there a south–north
transformation in forest types,
indicated by the extension (upper
left) of the broad-leaf evergreen
forest (lower left) into the
Japanese Islands, but altitudinal
stratification occurred as well, as
can be seen within the Japanese
Islands (upper right). Cold forest
types which existed in lowland
areas during the glacial maximum
retreated to higher mountain tops
in the postglacial period. Thus, on
a pollen diagram for a
mountainous region, lowland warm
and highland cold species are likely
to occur together, indicating not
temporal change in climate from
one to the other but the
distribution of forest types
according to altitude.*

Nuts were a major food resource of the postglacial period, so it is possible that ceramic pots – though 'invented' in earlier cold-climate environments – found their functional niche in tannin extraction at the time when these forest types were just beginning to form.

The use of polished stone tools might also have been associated with the exploitation of forest resources for supplies of timber. Two characteristic products of the postglacial period not seen in the Palaeolithic are dug-out plate 7 canoes and huts built with posts. With the rise in sea level and gradual flooding of the Yellow Plain during this initial period of climatic warming, coastlines became longer, the sea and its resources became more accessible, and the need to communicate across water became more intense. Boat-building was the obvious solution. It is not clear how Palaeolithic people made earlier crossings of the Korea Strait or how they gained access to the obsidian on the offshore islands of Tokyo Bay or travelled to Okinawa Island. One would assume that rafts or other watercraft were employed, as has been suggested for water crossings in Australasia.[29] However, regular canoe-building by many coastal communities represents a technical application on a completely different scale. Likewise, with the felling of trees for posts. Perhaps Palaeolithic people had the occasional need for a timber or two; but building houses as a matter of course was an activity only seen in the postglacial period when polished stone axe/adzes are abundantly manifest.

CHAPTER 5

Littoral Foragers
10,000–1,000 BC

The early postglacial millennia in East Asia witnessed dramatic changes in regional climate and resources. Such changes had occurred to some extent during every previous interglacial warming period, but they were particularly significant in the early Holocene because they affected modern humans for the first time. With the extinction of many large herd animals at the end of the Pleistocene and the flooding of the Yellow Plain, human groups along the retreating coastlines of East Asialand turned to exploitation of a much broader *fig. 25* spectrum of environmental resources. Fishing and shellfish collection were new strategies, while increased plant manipulation led to the development of two full-fledged agricultural economies on the China Mainland. This chapter will examine the adaptations of the non-agricultural Chulmun and Jomon peoples to the new resources afforded by that portion of the East Asian littoral gradually emerging as the Korean Peninsula and Japanese Islands, shaped by the rising sea levels. The agricultural societies developing on the China Mainland at the same time will be dealt with in Chapter 6.

Regardless of the nature of their subsistence economies, all the early Holocene peoples of East Asia manufactured and used pottery. As noted in *Box 5* Chapter 4, pottery has traditionally been viewed as an attribute exclusive to agricultural societies, but the East Asian data have played an important role in worldwide recognition of what one may now call 'ceramic hunters and gatherers'.[1] Quantities of ceramics in Chulmun and Jomon sites argue for considerable sedentism within their foraging economies, since pots are difficult items to haul around in a mobile lifestyle. Sedentism implies rich resources as well as storage technologies to support stationary populations. A continuing point of controversy, considered below, is whether these 'rich resources' included some reliance on plant cultivation which helped support these sedentary lifestyles, especially since farming was known and practised on the adjacent Mainland.

The Chulmun and Jomon periods were long ones, and it is a mistake to think of them as homogeneous. Numerous regional and temporal variations existed in subsistence technology, social organization, and material culture. Some Jomon groups developed rich material cultures associated with ritually oriented lifestyles. These 'affluent foragers' have been compared to the Northwest Coast American Indian tribes of historic times,[2] which had a similarly rich culture based on sedentary hunting and gathering but are known

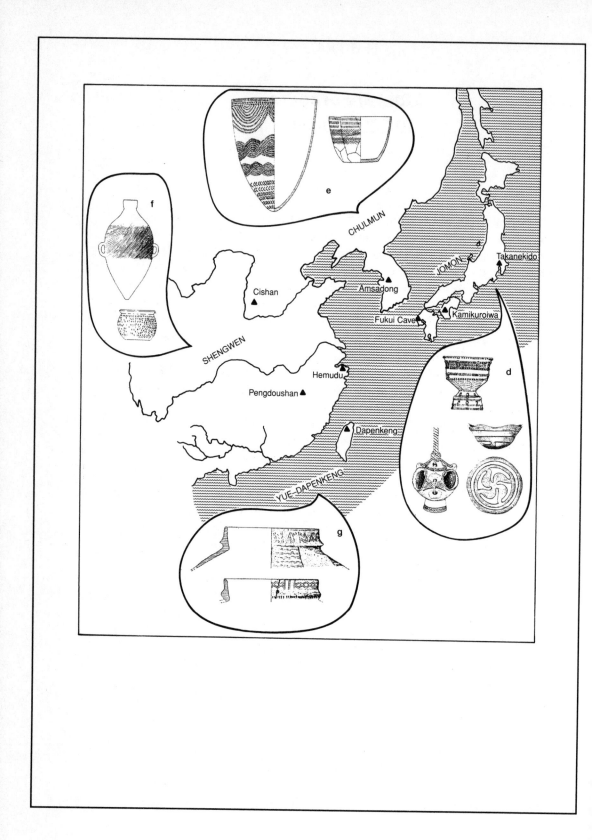

BOX 5
Textured Pottery Traditions

All the main postglacial cultures of East Asia, regardless of their subsistence base, utilized textured-surface ceramics from their very beginnings. In Japan, this type of pottery is referred to as Jomon, which means 'cord-marked' (a), indicating the predominant mode of surface decoration during the long Jomon period (10,000–300 BC). Other decorative techniques, however, were also in use, especially in the earliest and latest phases: raised bands, rouletting (b), incising, nail marking, shell impressing, and appliqué. Archaeologists have identified 254 types of Jomon pottery, each with a particular spatial and temporal distribution, thus forming a framework for relative dating within the Jomon period. These types might be called 'variations on a theme', the theme being a gradual evolution of a variety of complicated shapes – from the simple pointed-base cooking pot in the early phases to exquisite 'teapots', bottles and pedestalled bowls near the end of the Jomon period (d). The middle of the period witnessed the development, in central Honshu, of Umataka- and Katsusaka-type pots with elaborately sculptured rims, the products of highly creative societies.

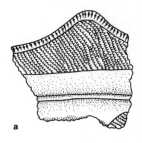

Adjacent to the Jomon tradition of the Japanese islands was the Chulmun ('comb-patterned') tradition of the Korean Peninsula (e), appearing around 6000 BC and lasting until 1500 BC. The main decorative technique was the incising of short parallel lines, but stamping, punching, grooving and pinching were also used. The geometric incising, characteristic of much Chulmun pottery, is strikingly different from Jomon cord marking; both traditions, however, included an early phase of raised-line decoration (c), known as Yungkimun in Korean. Various scholars have proposed competing regional groupings of pottery styles on the Peninsula; but basically, Yungkimun characterized the eastern and southern coastal sites until Classic Chulmun diffused from the central west coast at about 3500 BC, and northern sites were always distinguished by flat bases in contrast to the southern conical shapes.

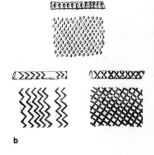

On the China Mainland very early finds of textured pottery (Chapter 4) belong to what has been termed the Shengwen (also meaning 'cord-marked') horizon, due to the predominance of this technique (f). Out of the Shengwen substrate developed the foraging cultures of Yue on the southeastern coast and Dapenkeng on Taiwan at about 4000 BC (g), comparable to Jomon and Chulmun as discussed in this chapter. Mainland pottery continued to be dominated by textured-surface decoration within the early agricultural societies (Chapter 6) and even into the historical periods.

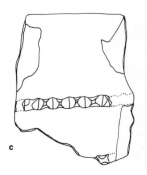

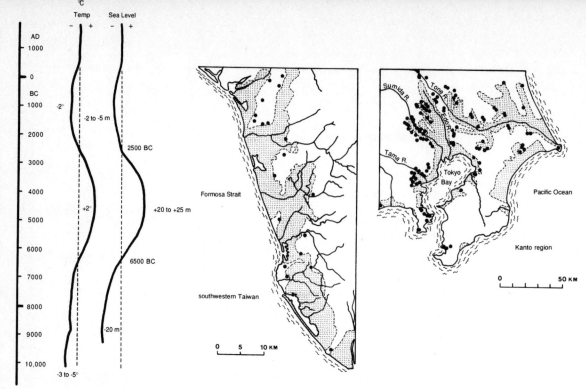

25 *Postglacial climatic changes and rising sea levels. The postglacial climate was marked worldwide by a sudden and major rise in temperature, peaking at average yearly temperatures of 2°C warmer than at present, and then declining again. This brief period between 6500 and 2500 BC is often known as the Climatic Optimum. The accompanying rise in sea level flooded coastal land that is dry today, as shown by the stippled area on maps for the Kanto region of Japan and southwestern Taiwan. Shellmounds (black dots) are positioned at the edges of higher ground on Taiwan. In the Kanto, the maximum extent of this marine transgression was discovered by mapping the oldest Jomon shellmounds (black dots) in the region and then 'connecting-the-dots'! Successively younger shellmounds marked the positions of the coastline as the sea receded.*

to have been organized hierarchically. Thus, a hot topic in current Jomon studies is whether some groups were organized as chiefdoms or not.[3] Focusing on this problem, however, should not lead to a second mistake in thinking that the whole Jomon period can be characterized by a developmental trajectory *fig. 26* from simple to complex society.[4] Changes in population distribution and resources throughout this period of intense climatic change make the fragmentation of social development abundantly clear.

The shellmound databank of Japan will be used here to map the basic resources against which to discuss these interesting problems in forager adaptations.[5]

Anatomy of a shellmound

A sudden turn to reliance on marine resources in the postglacial period is signified by the unprecedented appearance of shellmound sites and the proliferation of fishing implements along the East Asian coasts. This shift, however, might be somewhat illusory since earlier shorelines where such sites and artifacts would have been located in the Palaeolithic are now under water.

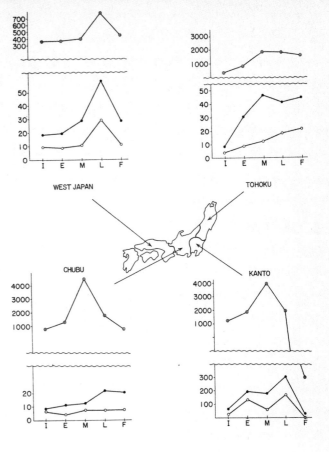

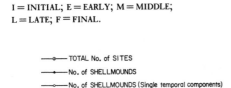

26 *Studies of Jomon site distributions show clear temporal and regional variations. Eighty per cent of Jomon sites are located in the Chubu, Kanto and Tohoku regions coinciding in general with the distribution of deciduous forest and salmon resources. Many fewer are known for the western Japanese Islands. These graphs plot the numbers of sites and shellmounds in each Jomon phase for each region. In the early phases, the western Islands had only about 400 sites, suddenly rising to 700 in Late Jomon. In Chubu and Kanto, the rise was from 1000 to 4000 sites in Middle Jomon. Tohoku shows a steady increase from 1000 to 2000 and then levels off, while all other areas show a dramatic drop in the Final Jomon. These numbers have been translated into population densities and movements, with the final decrease in the west attributed to the arrival and expansion of wet rice agriculturalists.*

I = INITIAL; E = EARLY; M = MIDDLE;
L = LATE; F = FINAL.

————⊙———— TOTAL No. of SITES
————•———— No. of SHELLMOUNDS
————○———— No. of SHELLMOUNDS (Single temporal components)

In fact, peoples on the Australian continent are known to have been eating fish and utilizing shellfish resources as early as 30,000–15,000 years ago, so marine-oriented economies in the Holocene might not be as revolutionary as once thought.[6]

Shellmound sites are accumulations of shells discarded after the extraction of the meat inside. Their calcareous deposits provide excellent conditions for the preservation of additional bony substances and plant remains that would otherwise decay. Though shellmounds account for only a small proportion of archaeological sites, their research value for reconstructing environmental change and subsistence economies is immense. The very locations of such shellmounds in the postglacial Climatic Optimum have enabled archaeologists to reconstruct the successive shorelines of the transgressing sea.   *fig. 25*

The composition of shell species in the mounds tells of both the changing climate and the changing subsistence patterns. One species found in Kanto shellmounds during the Climatic Optimum is the warmth-loving mollusc, *Anadara granosa*. Today only its cold-water counterpart, *Pecten yesoensis*, is found in Tokyo Bay, and *Anadara* is confined to more southerly seas. With the cooling of the climate after 3000 BC which brought about this change in species, the transgressing ocean receded from the Kanto lowlands, and shellmounds which were once on the coast became stranded inland. These were not necessarily abandoned, however, as demonstrated in an interesting study of the Nittano site.[7] This shellmound continued to be used even as it became further   *fig. 43*

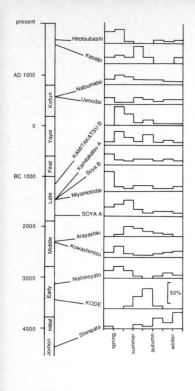

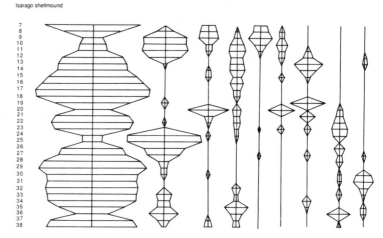

27 *Analyses of Jomon shell-collecting patterns. Graphing the percentages of shells (left) which were collected in each season at different Japanese shellmound sites illustrates the annual patterns of collecting activity at each site. The time scale here also illustrates the fact that shellmounds continued to be formed even into the protohistoric and historic periods in Japan. Seriations (below) of the different kinds of shellfish deposited through successive stratigraphic cuts (7-38) at the Isarago shellmound site show complementary relationships between clams and oysters. When clams decreased, oysters increased – perhaps indicating the depletion of one resource and a shift in reliance to another.*

and further isolated from the shoreline. A change in species occurred as freshwater shellfish from the nearby river came to be collected in place of marine shellfish. By contrast, the species of fish appearing in the shellmound during this environmental transformation remained stable. The shift in shellfish utilization is postulated to have been due to the division of labour between men and women, not mere dietary preference. Women collected shells close to home – regardless of the change in species – while the men travelled the extra distances to continue to fish at the receding ocean's edge.

plate 6 The seasonality of clam collection has been elucidated through counting growth lines in the shell body itself, showing the season in which the clams died (that is, when they were collected for food).[8] Seasonal collection patterns from several sites show considerable variety. The peak season at many sites was spring, but at others the most intensive collecting occurred in summer or winter. In addition to these peak times, the low-level collecting of shellfish apparently continued all year round. These data support the hypothesis of considerable sedentism in the postglacial period.

Shellmounds themselves are not habitation sites but rubbish dumps. In many cases the locations of their associated settlements are not known, giving rise to the idea that the mounds mark shellfish-processing sites on the coast for villages further inland. In other cases, they are integral parts of the settlement

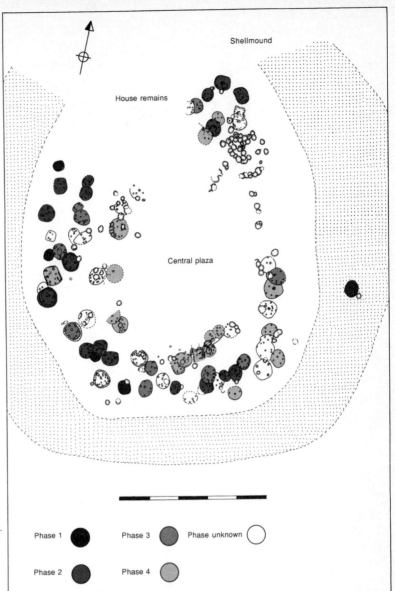

Shellmound

House remains

Central plaza

Phase 1 ●   Phase 3 ●   Phase unknown ○

Phase 2 ●   Phase 4 ●

28 The horseshoe-shaped Takane-kido shellmound. The shellmound itself surrounds a ring of houses and central plaza. Though the site was occupied only during the Middle Jomon, houses belonging to four different pottery phases have been identified.

structure, as with the great circular or horseshoe-shaped shellmounds of the Kanto region. These shellmounds surrounded groups of pit-houses, with anywhere from thirty to over two hundred houses excavated at some sites. Not all of these houses were occupied simultaneously, and the mapping of pottery types occurring in the house features allows the chronology of site occupation to be established. Many sites were inhabited throughout several phases of the Jomon period, over several millennia. The question still remains, however, whether all the villagers lived there throughout the year during those phases. The substantial form of architecture and site stability not seen in the Palaeolithic, together with the seasonality studies on shell contribute to the hypothesis that such sites were permanently occupied. Still, it is likely that during certain seasons some of the population became mobile in order to exploit more distant resources.

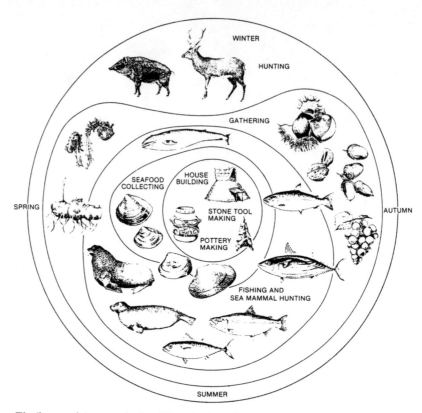

29 *The Jomon subsistence calendar. This calendar reflects a significant shift in Jomon research interests in the last few years, from an exclusive interest in ceramics and their classification to a concern with the environment and subsistence of postglacial peoples. As such, the chart is an accomplishment; but it does not represent regional differences in available resources or differences in emphases in particular subsistence strategies through time even within the Japanese Islands, much less other areas of East Asia.*

Such seasonal activities consisted of fishing, hunting and the collecting of plant food. Japanese archaeologists have recently constructed a Jomon subsistence calendar showing the relative importance of various foodstuffs at different times of the year. Shellfish and young shoots are specified as the dietary staples of early spring; in summer, fishing and the hunting of sea mammals took place; shellfish were again collected for drying in late summer; autumn was the time for collecting nut foods for storage; finally, land and sea mammals were hunted during the winter lean months.

The remains of many of these foodstuffs – and the tools needed for procuring and processing them – are preserved in the shellmounds. Bone fish hooks occur in the earliest middens and detachable toggle-head harpoons in later ones, demonstrating advances in fishing technology. Altogether the remains of fifty or so species of riverine, coastal and deep-sea fish have been identified, and even dolphin oil – adhering to the walls of ceramic vessels – has been identified through lipid analysis.[9] Ocean-going boats were, of course, necessary for some plate 7 of these pursuits, and remains of dug-out canoes have been recovered.

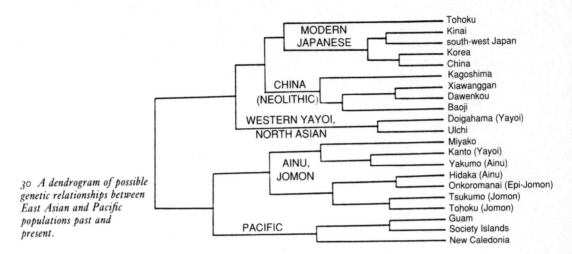

30 A dendrogram of possible genetic relationships between East Asian and Pacific populations past and present.

Of the bones of land animals excavated from shellmounds, over 80 per cent belong to wild boar and deer,[6] suggesting rather specialized exploitation patterns compared with the wide variety of animal remains found in the early agricultural sites of the China Mainland (Chapter 6). Another animal frequently recovered from shellmounds is the dog. Unlike the others, however, it was often buried intentionally, indicating that it was a valued partner in the seasonal rounds. The dog was the only domesticated animal in the Japanese Islands throughout the Jomon period, and its origins might well be sought in the Late Palaeolithic hunting cultures of East Asialand.[7]

What were the Jomon people like, who exploited these seasonal resources? Human burials are also commonly encountered in shellmound excavations, providing us with the skeletal data to reconstruct the Jomon physical type. Averaging 160 cm (5 ft 3 in) tall for men and 150 cm (4 ft 11 in) tall for women, Jomon individuals were quite small compared with Mainlanders. Among the peoples inhabiting North and East Asia both past and present, the Jomon are most similar to the modern Ainu aboriginals of Hokkaido, suggesting that they both derive from an ancient palaeoasiatic stock which may also have included the Chulmun peoples of the Korean Peninsula.[10] The Jomon facial structure is *fig. 82* quite different from that of southern rice-growing peoples of the China Mainland whence the bearers of wet-rice technology ultimately came (Chapter 11). An unusual feature of Jomon skulls is their patterns of tooth modification. The front teeth and incisors were often filed into two or three points, while others were subject to artificial extraction. Recurring combinations of such tooth modifications have been postulated as an identifying feature of marriage groups.[11]

Affluent foragers?

From looking at the Jomon subsistence calendar, one might think that postglacial peoples on the East Asian littoral were living in a Garden of Eden. This is misleading, for some areas were considerably richer in resources than others. In fact, the regionality of subsistence adaptations is quite marked, and several solutions might have been employed to overcome the limitations of restricted resources. One solution, of course, is mobility: the shifting of settlement throughout the seasons to take advantage of the differing abundance of resources. Another solution is the development of plant cultivation, practised together with extensive hunting, fishing and collecting activities. And finally, the problem could have been solved by the development of exchange networks between regions to spread the products of different ecozones among different communities.

In order to investigate regional exploitation patterns, the Chulmun riverine adaptation will be contrasted with the Middle Jomon exchange network of central Honshu. These also represent extremes in social organization and material culture development, clearly illustrating that the term 'affluent foragers' cannot be used to describe all postglacial littoral societies.

Inland Chulmun lifeways

In addition to the many Chulmun-period shellmounds dotting the southern and western coasts of the Korean Peninsula, inland river terraces have yielded Chulmun village remains.[12] The twenty or more pit-house features which were excavated at Amsadong, some of which were reconstructed as a historical park, are thought to be typical of Chulmun settlements. Several similar Chulmun sites nearby, together with Amsadong, might have formed a small community. *fig. 43* Settlement permanence at Amsadong is suggested by the substantial construction of pit-houses and storage pits, some of which were equipped with interior stairs. The overlapping of pits shows at least long-term if not recurrent occupation, and groups of large pots (50 cm diameter on average) are interpreted as storage facilities.[13]

The classic west Peninsular variety of Chulmun pottery was defined on the basis of examples recovered from the Han River drainage where Amsadong is located. The repertoire consists primarily of wide-mouthed, pointed-bottomed pots with bands of simple incised geometric designs. Some of these have perforated rims, perhaps for securing a cover or lid and might therefore be storage jars; most of the pots, however, were used for cooking. Hearths inside the houses at Amsadong were outlined with river cobbles, and four burned-rock features outside the houses might have served as outdoor hearths.[14] The stone tools consist of a limited range of forms including polished arrowheads, chipped 'hoe-axes', a variety of flakes, grinding slabs, grindstones, and boiling stones. These are all thought to have employed local river cobbles. The *fig. 31* traditional interpretation of notched pebbles as 'net-sinkers' has been challenged, and their use as possible weaving weights has been postulated.[15]

The subsistence system of inland Chulmun included riverine net-fishing (assuming the pebbles are net-sinkers), the hunting of small animals, and the grinding of plant foods. Since the fish resources of the inland rivers are subject to extreme seasonality and relatively low productivity,[16] a hypothesis was developed stating that people moved seasonally between inland sites and

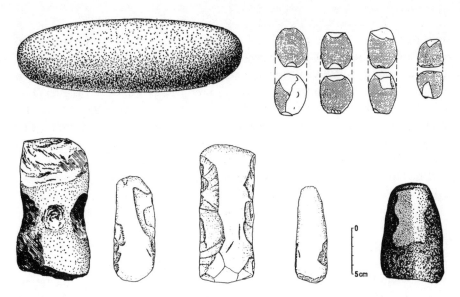

31 Chipped and polished stone tools from Chulmun sites. Top row: a pestle or grinding stone, and notched pebbles; lower row: various axe/adzes.

coastal shellmounds to maximize their foraging potential. Several studies have been undertaken to test this hypothesis, but they concluded that the pottery types at these respective locations are so different that both seasonal migration and trade between inland and coast have to be discounted.[17] Consequently, some archaeologists have hypothesized that the Chulmun were cultivating plant foods to supplement their meagre foraging diet, as discussed below.

Inland Chulmun was not an 'affluent forager' culture, and archaeological evidence of life beyond mere subsistence activities is sparse. One of the rare Chulmun-period cemeteries, at the Hupori site, gives evidence of having contained 'bundle burials' within a stone circle.[18] Accompanying the burials were row upon row of neatly laid out polished stone axe/adzes, including one tool more that 80 cm long. The repertoire of Chulmun ornaments on the Peninsula was limited and, interestingly, confined mainly to the eastern and southern coastal regions. Objects found in these areas consist of some crude clay figurines of people and animals; ceramic, stone and shell beads; and several artifacts interpreted as 'masks', such as a clam shell with three holes punched in it as 'eyes' and a 'mouth'. Long-distance exchange is suggested only by the occasional beadstone artifact, for example jade and marble rings, shell bracelets and 'microcelts', together with obsidian (perhaps from Kyushu). This level of material culture might represent the norm for the postglacial foragers of East Asia, but it is far overshadowed by the atypical richness of the Middle Jomon cultures of central Honshu, a richness which was apparently triggered by the less common solution to resource problems: an exchange network between ecological zones.

A Middle Jomon exchange network

fig. 32

During the early part of the Middle Jomon period, central Honshu supported three different textured-surface ceramic traditions: Umataka-type pottery on the north coast, Katsusaka-type pottery in the central mountains and western Kanto Plain, and Atamadai-type pottery in the greater Tokyo Bay region. The material cultures accompanying these ceramic types were also regionally differentiated, as were the environmental resources in each area. For convenience's sake, each ceramic tradition will be equated here with a certain group of people who were probably exploiting these different resources.

The mountain Katsusaka peoples were very ritually oriented: they lived in fairly large settlements on a relatively permanent basis, and outside some of their pit-houses were altars and large phallic standing stones. Their ceramics are decorated with images of animals such as snakes and frogs that suggest an interest in seasonal regeneration, that is, with fertility in general, and it is possible that ceramic figurines were utilized in ensuring human reproductivity.

The main Katsusaka sites such as Idojiri and Togariishi lay in the piedmont zone, which was favourable for deciduous acorn, chestnut and walnut production, and near a major obsidian source at Wada Pass. Many stone hammers and querns have been recovered from these sites, indicating the processing of plant foods such as might be expected in shelling and grinding nuts. Analyses of obsidian tools throughout the Kanto region have demonstrated that Wada Pass obsidian was widely distributed for tool making.[19]

North of the central mountains on the Japan Sea coast were the Umataka peoples, who lived near beadstone sources of talc and jade. Earrings fashioned of Mount Shiroma talc had been a major trade item from this region in the Early Jomon period, but in the Middle Jomon, jade pendants from the bead-making villages at the head of the Itoigawa River were the favoured trade items. They have been recovered from over a hundred sites along the north coast, through the central mountains and into the Kanto region.

Umataka community organization contrasted with the central mountains in having huge pit-buildings with multiple hearths, such as that found at the Fudodo site. This building had an 8 × 17 m oval groundplan with four interior hearths, two square and two round. The two central hearths also had jars embedded in the ground beside them. Such large pit-buildings are thought to have functioned as community gathering or work places, especially during the long snow-bound winters of the northwestern Honshu coast, which receives all the precipitation of the winter winds from Siberia sweeping across the Japan Sea. The Umataka people also made elaborate pottery characterized by flame-shaped rim projections, perhaps in competition with the central Katsusaka ceramic tradition.

During the Early Jomon, the Tokyo Bay region had supported shellfish collecting on a modest basis. Just before the advent of Atamadai pottery, however, a sudden change in shellmound formation took place there. Many small middens were abandoned, to be replaced by fewer but larger ones, as if populations had consolidated and shellfish collecting had increased. Following

Archaeological investigations past and present

1 *Excavation of a Yayoi-period burial jar by Kyoto University at the Suku site in Kyushu in 1929.*

2 *Rescue excavation along the trunk highway of western Honshu, as Japan expanded its transportation infrastructure in the 1970s. The majority of labourers on site are retired men and women, retrained and highly paid.*

Landscapes of modern East Asia, showing the variety of terrain which has conditioned life throughout the ages

3 *(left) Terraced paddy fields overlooking the Asuka region of Nara Basin, Japan.*

4 *(left below) Thick deposits of loess in the Fen River valley of northern China have been heavily dissected by streams since the Neolithic period.*

5 *(below) The mountainous terrain of the Korean Peninsula gives way intermittently to open basins supporting intensive agriculture and conurbations.*

The rich Jomon material culture was based on the postglacial exploitation of marine resources as well as forest products

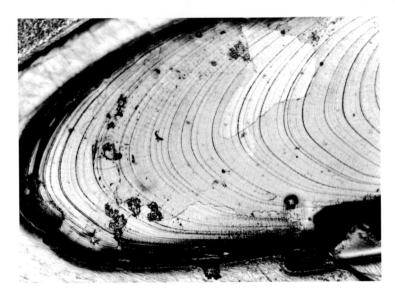

6, 7 *Clam shells and dugout canoes represent estuarine and deep-sea food procurement. The clam shell cross-section (above) shows annual growth rings which, when counted, reveal its age and the season of its collection for food.*

8–11 *Jomon decorative techniques include cord-marking (below left), zoned cord-marking (left), incising (above) and highly sculpturesque rims (below left). Vessel shapes range from the simple 'deep bowl' (below left) to the elegantly designed and surprisingly modern 'teapot'-shaped pouring vessel of Late Jomon (above). Anthropomorphic shapes appear on vessels (left) and as figurines (below right). The female illustrated wears earplugs and perhaps neck ornaments.*

Contrasting artistic traditions
on the China Mainland among
early agricultural societies

12–14 *East Coast ceramics of white (above) and
black finish (right and below) illustrate the
specialist potter's skill in constructing complicated
shapes.*

15–17 *Early art as rock carvings (above) and painted ceramics (below) in the northwestern Yangshao culture, and incised pottery (right) at Hemudu in the southeast.*

Mainland Neolithic jades, from the functional to the cosmologically significant

18 *The perforated disc was used as a symbol of heaven in later Chinese cultures: can a similar meaning be applied to this Neolithic jade disc, or was this artifact more of a utilitarian object like the accompanying macehead?*

19 *This squared tube with cylindrical bore combines the traditional symbols for heaven (square) and earth (circle); deposition of great numbers of them in Liangzhu culture graves suggests their use in elite rituals.*

this change, Atamadai pottery of the bay region began to penetrate into the western Katsusaka region. Nevertheless, none of the ritual aspects of Katsusaka culture diffused eastwards in return.

Given the geographical arrangement of these three ceramic cultures and the obvious terrestrial channelling of human movement through mountain valleys and passes, it is very possible that the Katsusaka peoples acted as a central pivot in exchange relations between the two coasts, bringing in jade from the north and passing it on to the bay region. Its own obsidian and walnut resources were in high demand in the latter region, and these goods were probably exchanged for dried shellfish and/or other marine products.

Many archaeologists in decades past have argued that these Middle Jomon people could not have developed such a rich material culture without some sort of cultivation. They have cited the abundance of chipped stone 'hoes' which, they hypothesized on the basis of ethnographic analogy, would have been used to dig root crops of yam and taro.[20] Though remains of these plant foods are never found in Jomon contexts, more recent arguments have been constructed for nut tree management.[21] Even if the Katsusaka did manage their nut tree stands for maximum productivity, the local environment in the high mountains – subject to heavy winters – was not a Garden of Eden. Their affluence was more probably based on a long-distance exchange system much like the Hopewell 'interaction sphere' documented for North America in the 1st millennium AD.[22] The extensive ritual facilities of the highland Jomon sites might have functioned in regulating both the extraction of local resources and their actual exchange. There is as yet, however, no indication that society was hierarchically organized, with chiefs directing these rituals. Information for such organizational patterns usually comes from rich burials, which occur only in the contemporaneous Mainland Neolithic.

Incipient cultivation?

The arguments for horticulture in the above case studies are based on indirect or circumstantial evidence. For instance, the tools commonly cited as agricultural implements (hoes, reaping knives) could just as well have been used to harvest wild plant foods. The exception might be the so-called stone 'plough shares' found mainly at sites along the Yalu River and, surprisingly, at Amsadong.[23] Here, only direct evidence for cultivation – that is, actual botanic remains of cultigens – is given serious consideration. The remains of millet, rice and barley are now known from Late and Final Jomon sites, and millet has purportedly been recovered from Chulmun contexts. The appearance of these major grain crops speaks of diffusion from the agricultural societies on the China Mainland and foretells the imminent transformation to agricultural regimes in the East Asian littoral (Chapter 11).

Even for the Early and Middle Jomon periods, however, indigenous efforts at cultivation and domestication are now being documented – particularly in Tohoku and Hokkaido where extensive programmes have been conducted for

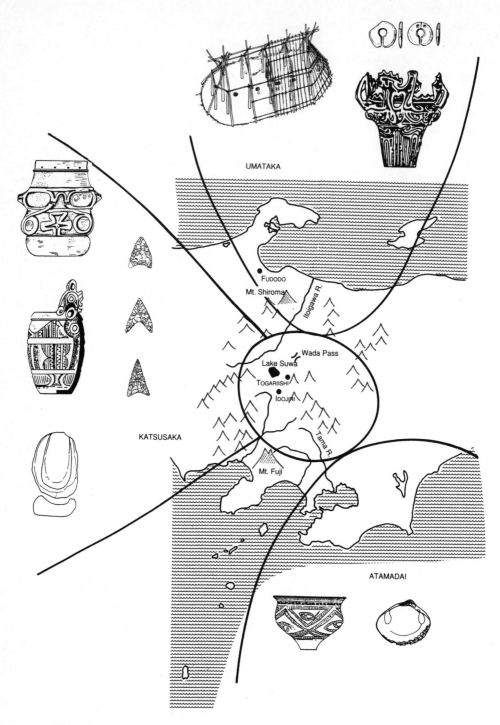

32 Middle Jomon exchange network across central Honshu. Lake Suwa and Wada Pass form the geographical foci for the pivotal Katsusaka people, who might have provided obsidian and nutmeats to the northern Umataka and the coastal Atamadai in return for beadstone and shellfish products, respectively. These hypothetical trading relationships were short-lived, with the central mountains being virtually abandoned in the succeeding Late and Final Jomon periods for as yet unexplained causes.

recovering carbonized remains by floating soil samples in water.[24] Before the importation of the major crops from the continent, it appears that the most important cultigens were two varieties of the beefsteak herb (*Perilla frutescens*).[25] Their seeds have been identified by electron scanning microscopy in the 'bread' or 'cookie' lumps of starch recovered from several Middle Jomon sites.[26] Other sites in northeastern Japan have yielded seeds of barnyard grass (*Echinochloa*); some occurred within a carbonized mass stuck to a Middle Jomon sherd, clearly suggesting that they were considered a foodstuff and not just a weed. Increases in numbers and the size of seeds at sites throughout the Jomon period also support the interpretation that *Echinochloa* was undergoing domestication, resulting in the cultigen *E. utilis* (barnyard millet) of which more than sixty varieties have been cultivated in Japan. Comparing these finds with the early cultigens of Southeast Asia excavated at Spirit Cave in Thailand,[27] it is interesting to note that the plants utilized in both prehistoric sequences continued to be cultivated throughout later history. This is in great contrast to Mesolithic Europe, where most of the plants used experimentally are considered weeds today.[28]

In addition to seed and grain evidence, plant pollen recovered from the geological coring of soil layers has been used to postulate incipient cultivation in the Jomon and in the formative Dapenkeng culture of Taiwan. Pollen diagrams showing considerable forest disturbance around 14,000–12,000 years ago in Taiwan are interpreted as reflecting what is referred to as 'swidden' or 'slash-and-burn' agriculture,[29] entailing the cutting and burning of stands of forest and the growing of dryland crops on the ash-fertilized plots. Extensive burned layers dating from 7700 years ago onwards in the western Japanese Islands have also led to postulations of forest clearance and swidden agriculture, as do large pieces of charcoal accompanied by tentatively identified buckwheat pollen in corings from the Ubuka Bog dating to 4000 years ago.[30]

For Japan, the debate about Jomon agriculture has thus undergone a major shift from 'Was there cultivation in the Jomon period?' (to which the answer is 'yes') to 'How were these plants cultivated' and 'How much did Jomon peoples rely on them?' (the tentative answer to the last question being 'not too much'). The people concerned were still overwhelmingly foragers and there is no need as yet to change the title of this chapter to 'littoral horticulturalists'. However, that time may come as new data emerge and theoretical problems in the definition of agriculture are resolved.

CHAPTER 6

Agricultural Beginnings
7000–2000 BC

Early farming villages

fig. 43

Among the early users of textured pottery in East Asia, at least two groups of people on the China Mainland turned from a foraging way of life to one based on grain production. In the north, millet as revealed at the site of Cishan was the main crop; in the south, it was rice, as known from the site of Hemudu. Sites of these farming cultures appear suddenly in the archaeological record in the late 7th and early 6th millennia BC, and current data allow few insights as to the origins of their already advanced agricultural technologies.

Cishan, Hemudu and their contemporaries were succeeded by several regional Neolithic cultures on the Mainland, many of which are still in the process of being defined. The most recent scheme of cultures posits temporal stages of Initial, Early, Middle and Late Neolithic in the 6th, 5th, 4th and 3rd millennia BC respectively. This chapter begins with a close look at the two sites of Cishan and Hemudu since they represent the two Mainland subsistence economies which were established early and have characterized the agricultural regimes of north and south down to the present day.

Cishan

The site of Cishan,[1] belonging to the Peiligang culture,[2] stands on a riverine terrace at the foot of the Taihang mountains overlooking the Central Plain. Excavations there in 1976 and 1977 uncovered pit-buildings, storage pits and burials, indicating a fully developed village economy by the 6th millennium BC. In addition, the artifacts at Cishan show advanced characteristics. The pottery is mainly plain brown or red with various decorations (cord-marking, comb impressing, incising, and press-and-pick designs). The wide range of shapes – tripods, quadrupods, handled pots, perforated vessels and angled vessel supports – contrasts greatly with the ubiquitous deep, wide-mouthed pot of the contemporaneous textured-pottery forager cultures. The bone tool inventory also shows great variety and functional specificity: tanged and untanged projectile points, some barbed; awls and adzes made of long bones; punches; and several intricately carved or decorated pieces. Stone tools consisted mainly of bifacially chipped or polished axe-hoes, but legged stone querns and serrated reapers suggest that considerable labour was invested in the manufacture of utilitarian tools.

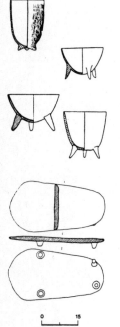

0   15
cm

33 (left) Tripod bowls and legged quern from the northern millet cultures.

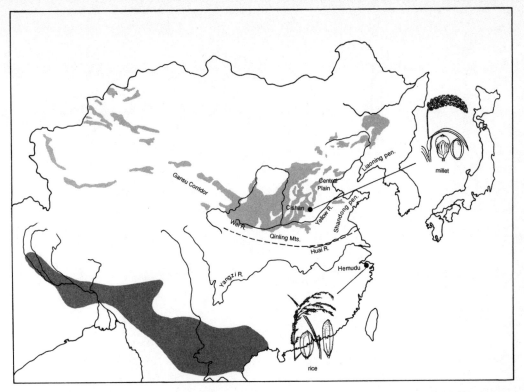

34 Indigenous agricultural technologies of the China Mainland. In the north, the dry, porous loess lands (light tint) necessitated the growing of drought resistant millets, while in the south, abundant water resources encouraged the domestication of rice and other aquatic species. The dotted line marks the modern divide between these two agricultural regimes. Asian rice, Oryza sativa, *is presumed to have originated in the far southwest (dark tint), but the Yangzi Basin might also have been one of the many loci of domestication.*

Such tools together with carbonized foxtail millet found in some eighty storage pits testify to extensive cereal cultivation, while dog, pig and chicken bones similarly provide evidence of animal domestication. These agricultural activities were conducted in concert with continued hunting of forest animals and fishing and collecting from rivers, as attested by abundant wild fauna and mollusc remains.

Hemudu

Hemudu is a coastal site located at the foot of a hill on the marshy edge of a former lake just south of the Shanghai Delta.[3] It is remarkable for the wet-preserved remains in its lowest Level 4: wooden architecture, a red-lacquered wooden bowl, quantities of rice grains and rice plant remains, and thousands of bones and bone artifacts (including flutes!), all dated to *c.* 5000 BC. The early houses built at the site were raised on poles and connected with mortise and tenon joints, reflecting the nature of the surrounding marshy environment and a surprisingly advanced woodworking technology.

The blackish pottery found at Hemudu is mainly plain burnished or cord-marked, but some vessels bear incised designs shared with Dapenkeng textured pottery.[4] Pot shapes are distinctive, with flanges encircling the body and rims *fig. 35f*

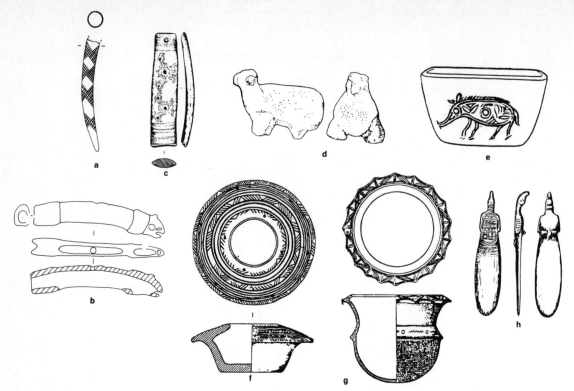

35 Art of the early agriculturalists. Carved bone was a popular medium at both Cishan (a, b) and Hemudu (c). Realistic representations of plants and animals at Hemudu occurred as small figurines (d) or incised motifs (e, plate 16), while ceramics from the site bore elaborate geometric designs (f, g). One of these designs resembles the 'leaf pattern' occurring also on later Jōmon pottery. A spatula-like object bears a three-dimensional carving as its handle (h).

dramatically inverted. Both ceramics and bone materials were vehicles for sophisticated artistic renditions of plant, animal, and human designs during the site's thousand years of existence. Favoured representations seem to have been of birds, petals and leaves; pigs occur both as drawings and figurines.

The economy of the site is evidenced by both wild and domesticated species. The remains of domestic rice consisted of stalks, grains and husks occurring in packed layers up to 50 cm thick. Spades made of hafted scapulae were characteristic cultivating tools. Pig and water buffalo were also tentatively identified as domesticated, in addition to the dog. Quantities of wild fauna, however, suggest continuing heavy reliance on hunting and collecting from the lake, lake edge and hills behind the site. Among these fauna were freshwater fish, molluscs, water fowl, and numerous forest animals.

The domestication of species

Distinguishing between wild and domestic species and determining whether or not societies were 'agricultural' merely on the presence of such 'domesticated' plants and animals are two unresolved issues in archaeology – both in East Asia and in the West. Traditionally, morphological criteria – in other words, changes in shape and size – have been employed for distinguishing wild from domestic. Often, however, these criteria are difficult to measure, show a spectrum of change, and are subject to different interpretations. For example, both the buckwheat pollen and barnyard grass seeds discussed in Chapter 5 fall within the size range of modern-day domestic species – but were they themselves cultigens in that early era, and should the societies with which they are associated therefore be called 'agricultural'?

Lately, there has been a shift in focus away from morphology to investigating the more general relationship between humans and plant/animal communities. The crucial variables here are first, the extent of human control over these communities, and second, the degree to which the manipulated plants and animals were depended upon relative to others whose natural bounty was merely collected. Japanese archaeologists have postulated that Jomon people intervened in the plant communities in order to encourage production.[5] European archaeologists have gone a step further to look at long-term planning, asking whether control over production was related to increasing immediate returns or to ensuring future returns.[6]

These theoretical discussions over the manipulation of indigenous species are complicated by the introduction of domesticates from other areas. For example, does the presence of a foreign species of gourd in Early Jomon sites indicate its cultivation or just a natural expansion of its original habitat?[7] Does a pot full of rice at one northern Chulmun site indicate the grain's local cultivation or its importation?[8] Thus, discussions of domestication issues in East Asian archaeology must be combined with investigations of speculated contact or introductions from other areas – or even introductions between areas within the region.

As for rice, there is only one domesticated species in Asia, *Oryza sativa*,   *fig. 34* which can be divided today into two subspecies: *indica* and *japonica/sinica*,[9] both already present at Hemudu.[10] The wild progenitors of Asian domestic rice still grow today along the southern Mainland coast and in Taiwan, and in Southeast Asia and India. The actual domestication of *Oryza sativa*, however, is thought to have taken place in a more limited region stretching from the Ganges in India eastwards to the Red River delta in Vietnam. The rice at Hemudu is therefore postulated by some to have been introduced from either Southeast Asia or the southwestern Mainland. Those who disagree point out that during the Climatic Optimum, when Hemudu was settled, the geographical range of wild rice could have extended further north into the Yangzi River drainage, so the Shanghai Delta region may have been one of several loci of domestication.[11]

Water was the crucial element in rice domestication, dry rice being a later development.[12] The marshy lakeside at Hemudu would have been perfect for the domestication process. It has also been proposed as a site of experimentation with water crops other than rice, including water caltrop, fox nut, lotus and arrowhead, all of which are exploited in China today.[13]

The wild progenitor of the domestic foxtail millet (*Setaria italica*) grown at   *fig. 34* Cishan is distributed throughout continental East Asia.[14] The question here is,

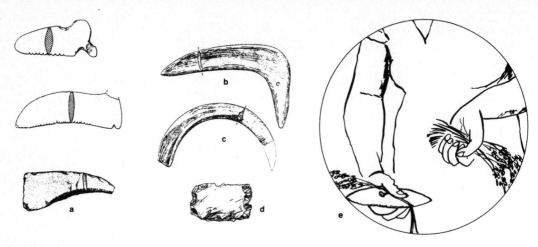

36 Harvesting implements in early East Asian agricultural societies. A variety of materials was used to make sickles and reaping knives: polished stone (a), bone (b) and boar tusk (c), shell, and chipped stone (d). Chipped stone reapers were first developed in the Yangshao millet cultures, but they were quickly adopted in the southern rice economies in polished stone forms. Gripped in the hand by a cord running through perforations or notches, a lunate reaper is used to take only the heads of grain (e), thus allowing the separation of crops from weeds or the selective harvesting of differentially ripening plants. Such selection undoubtedly led to greater genetic control over the crops when the collected grains were used as the next year's seed.

under what climatic conditions would domestication have taken place? Millet thrives in humid climates and is grown in Taiwan even today. It is clear that its plate 4 traditional cultivation in the loess highlands of the north Mainland under arid conditions required special techniques of soil moisture conservation.[15] Again, the warmer postglacial climate could have allowed millet to be domesticated in the north without it needing to be introduced from the south. Regardless of its origins, however, millet's drought-resistant qualities have made it very suitable for northern cultivation in post-Climatic Optimum times.

Within the two subspecies of domestic rice are thousands of varieties with different properties: dry, wet, glutinous, non-glutinous, coloured, aromatic, long-grained, short-grained, etc. These were cultivated in different areas for different reasons – the most important of which was the cool-climate tolerance of the short-grained varieties, allowing them to be cultivated further north. The two species of foxtail and broomcorn millet, both known among the Peiligang cultures, also have several varieties with different environmental tolerances, ripening periods, and so forth, making them extremely flexible crops. A glutinous variety was additionally available and ultimately used to make millet wine, as later documented in the Shang Dynasty oracle bones.

Wild progenitors are known on the Mainland for pigs, dogs, chicken, cattle, horses, and possibly sheep, but it is not yet known when and where these species might have been domesticated. Changes in morphological characteristics are used to identify domestic dog remains at sites such as Cishan and Hemudu,[16] and to suggest that the red junglefowl was in the process of being domesticated at Cishan.[17] The ages of animals at death have also been employed to postulate ongoing processes of domestication. At the Zengpiyan site, 65 per cent of the pig remains show death at between 1 and 2 years of age, a pattern not normally occurring in hunting situations and therefore taken by Chinese archaeologists to indicate pig domestication.[18] Korean and Japanese scholars have also postulated the existence of domesticated boar in the Chulmun and Late Jomon periods.[19]

The identification of sheep, cattle and horses as domestic species in Early Neolithic sites is still open to question, in terms both of morphological change and of the nature of the control exerted over them. But it is significant that by 5000 BC the elements of the present-day southern complex of rice, pig and water buffalo were already in evidence at Hemudu and the 'twin pillars of the ancient civilization of North China',[20] pig and millet, were already present at Cishan. Not until the Late Neolithic, however, did cultures across the northern Mainland rely substantially on herd animals; the subsequent development of pastoral economies in the northern border region after 2000 BC was perhaps related to climatic desiccation (Chapter 10).

In addition to the cereal crops and animals mentioned above, numerous cabbage-type plants, the jujube, peaches, plums, apricots and persimmons were all native to the northern Mainland, forming important additions to the diet; in the southern Mainland, native citrus trees bore oranges and lemons, but more important nutrients were provided by the aquacultured fruit and root crops associated with rice.[21] Several new cultivated species were imported into the north China Mainland and have continued into modern times. Most notable among these are wheat, barley and goats, introduced through the Gansu Corridor from western Eurasia towards the end of the Neolithic period.[22]

Regional Neolithic cultures

The multitude of regional cultures which developed during the Mainland Neolithic are distinguished along two different dimensions: subsistence and craft technology. One provides a north–south grouping of cultures, while the other divides the cultures east and west.

Northern millet, southern rice

The division between the northern millet-growing cultures and the southern rice-growing cultures continued throughout the Neolithic. The divide between the two is reflected in the modern boundary between dry-land and wetland *fig. 34* farming systems. This boundary follows the Qinling mountains in the west – which were mentioned above as marking the general north–south division in Pleistocene fauna – and continues along the Huai River to the east coast. This Neolithic boundary was no more absolute than the Pleistocene one and could be breached by changes in climate or technology.

The southern Neolithic cultures generally following the Hemudu pattern of rice agriculture were Majiabang, Songze, and Liangzhu in the Shanghai Delta region, and Daxi, Qujialing and Qinglongquan in the middle Yangzi Basin. A *fig. 43*

BOX 6
Design and Shape of Neolithic Ceramics

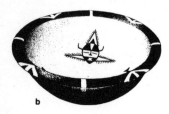

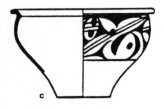

Painted pottery designs of Yangshao

Despite the scarcity of painted vessels relative to textured wares in most Yangshao assemblages, changes in painted designs have been used to demarcate different temporal and regional phases of the Yangshao cultures and their derivatives. Banpo site, in the central Yangshao region, exemplifies the earliest stage of painted pottery when bowls often bore angular geometric (a) or naturalistic designs (b), especially on their interiors (cf. plate 15). Frequent depictions of fish suggest a special niche for this animal in both the subsistence and ritual systems. The Miaodigou and Dahecun successors to Banpo, while retaining animal designs on the bowls, each possessed its own distinctive traits. Dahecun ceramics sport a series of unique celestial symbols, such as stars, whereas the Miaodigou design repertoire replaces the angular geometrics with parallel curvilinear lines, cross-hatches and repetitive 'ribbons'. Some of the Miaodigou pottery designs have been interpreted as flowers (c).

In the far northwest, the Majiayao pottery inspired by Banpo also retained the realistic mode of depicting animals, but curvilinear designs – especially large spirals and thin parallel lines – dominated the geometric aspect (d). In the Banshan and Machang traditions succeeding the Majiayao, large jars were decorated with toothed spirals and bands (e), gourd or leaf-shaped designs, and areas filled with mesh or checkerboard patterns. These tended to be arranged vertically on the vessel shoulder in the Banshan tradition, but horizontally around the jar in the Machang tradition (f). The latter tradition is also noted for its anthropomorphic elements.

The painting of pottery continued in the far northwest long after the transformation of the Yangshao cultures into Longshan cultures in the central region. In the Late Neolithic period, the designs of the Qijia culture reverted to angular geometrics, with panels organized vertically. Contemporaneously with the Bronze

Age Shang and Zhou civilizations, the ceramics of the Xindian culture of the Gansu Corridor were characterized by banded decoration interspersed with twiddle or animal-horn shaped sketches (g).

Distinctive shapes of Dawenkou

The tripod is a vessel shape considered to be peculiarly 'Chinese'. Solid-legged tripods made their appearance early in the Neolithic, as at Cishan where they were typically shaped like deep bowls (h). By the Middle Neolithic they were ubiquitous in the East Coast cultures, tending to occur in a pair of shapes: narrow-necked pots (i) and shallow bowls (j). The beginning of the Middle Neolithic saw the emergence of the hollow-legged tripod (k), perhaps as an East Coast adaptation of the typical mammary-shaped Yangshao water bottle. These new hollow-legged tripods were used to heat liquids; some might have had a perforated bowl set into their openings in order to steam cereals – usually thought to be rice. The Late Neolithic Longshan cultures combined the perforated bowl and tripod to form a composite steamer (l).

In the Middle Neolithic, a variety of pitchers and beakers were developed in the East Coast cultures, suggesting a strong interest in social drinking. Early pitchers had round or flat bottoms or borrowed the three solid legs of the tripod (m, n); in the Late Neolithic, the hollow-legged tripod was adapted into a spouted pitcher equipped with a handle (o, p). Beakers also occurred in a variety of shapes (q, r, s), a particularly delicate version being the pedestalled cup (t, u, v).

The penetration of these Dawenkou vessel types into the southern Mainland has traditionally been viewed as signalling the expansion of interregional contacts in the Middle to Late Neolithic periods. But curiously, these same Neolithic shape-types suddenly appear in the ceramic repertoires of the northeastern Pen/Insular region a millennium later – long after they are assumed to have died out on the Mainland. For this to have happened, it is necessary to postulate their survival, perhaps among Mainland coastal populations that remained out of the mainstream of complex social development but were later in communication with the Pen/Insulae.

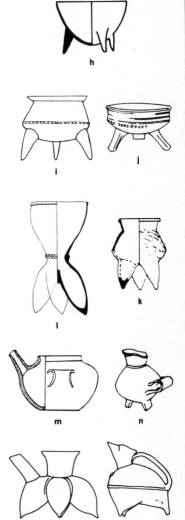

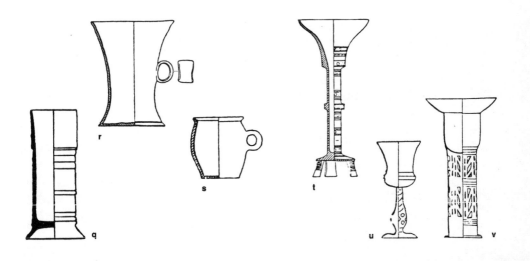

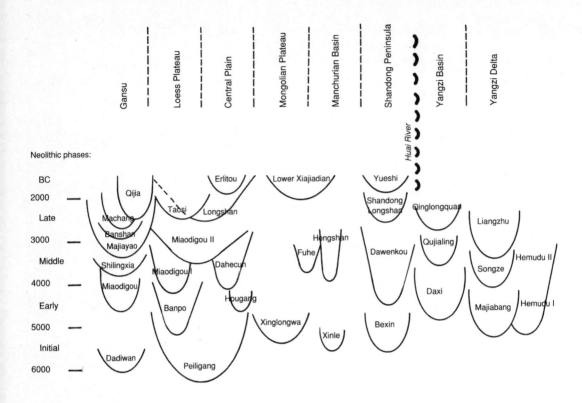

37 *Chronologies of Neolithic cultures on the China Mainland. The bullet shapes cover the timespans of the individual Neolithic cultures as derived from radiocarbon dating. Presented in regional columns, the northern millet cultures are notionally separated from the southern rice cultures by the Huai River.*

noteworthy aspect of southern subsistence activities was weaving, evidenced in the bone shuttles at Hemudu and in the numerous decorated spindle whorls at Daxi and Qujialing sites.[23] It was in the Liangzhu culture that lunate reapers *fig. 36e* became the common rice-harvesting implements.

In the north, the millet-growing successors to Cishan were the Dawenkou culture of the Shandong peninsular region; the Banpo, Miaodigou, and Dahecun cultures of the Yellow and Wei River valleys; and the Majiayao and Banshan cultures of the Gansu Corridor in the far northwest. Given that the Banpo culture was based in the loess highlands and the Dawenkou in the marshy coastal lowlands, they are thought to have had rather different subsistence potentials despite their common reliance on millet. Copious remains of alligators from some Dawenkou sites suggest that these animals were being intentionally hunted for food.[24] The agricultural tools associated with these two cultures differed in part: chipped stone reaping knives characterized the Banpo area, but sickles made of bone, tooth and shell characterized the Dawenkou. The fact that more Dawenkou women than men *fig. 38* were buried with spades and sickles, as well as needles and spindle whorls, suggests that they may have been in charge of cultivation activities.

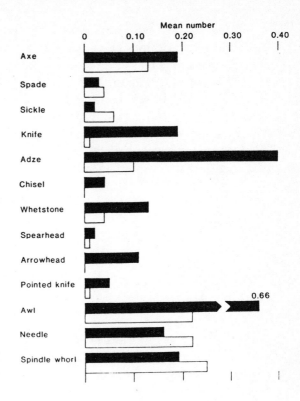

38 Task differentiation from grave goods. Statistical analyses of objects included in 179 East Coast Neolithic sites show that woodworking tools (axes, adzes and chisels), hunting tools (spearheads and arrowheads), as well as whetstones and awls occurred more often with males (filled bars) than females (open bars). But women possessed greater numbers of agricultural tools (spades and sickles) and sewing implements (needles and spindle whorls). Note, however, that few if any of these categories were exclusively associated with one gender.

In the Late Neolithic, the entire north-central area was characterized by the Longshan cultures; a major innovation in the agricultural tool repertoire was a two-pronged instrument, known from impressions in the earth of the Yellow River valley.[25] The far northwestern Machang and Qijia cultures showed a contrasting pattern, moving away from heavy dependence on cropping to animal husbandry (Chapter 10).

East–west ceramic spheres

The north–south grouping of Neolithic cultures based on subsistence is dramatically cross-cut by development in the social sphere, in which the main division is between east and west. Ceramic traditions are the overt indicators of this alternative grouping, but the divide is also maintained in terms of settlement patterning.

Two separate pottery traditions have long been recognized for the Mainland Neolithic: the Yangshao and the Longshan. These used to be conceived in terms of archaeological periods, first as contemporaneous with one another, then as temporally successive, with Yangshao in the Early and Middle Neolithic periods giving way to Longshan in the Late Neolithic. This was at a time, however, when the only Early and Middle Neolithic cultures known were confined to the northern intermontane regions and the far northwest (Banpo, Miaodigou, Majiayao, Banshan, Machang, etc.). The subsequent discovery of the east coast Neolithic cultures such as Majiabang, Dawenkou, and Songze has triggered the realization that the pottery tradition of the Late Neolithic Longshan cultures began in these east coast cultures of the Early and Middle Neolithic.[26] This continuous ceramic tradition acquires a specific name, Longshan, only for the Late Neolithic. In order to reflect its greater time depth, here it will be referred to as the Dawenkou tradition.[27]

The Yangshao and Dawenkou, therefore, were contemporary ceramic traditions which lasted throughout the entire Neolithic period. They cross-cut the north–south distinctions in agricultural regimes, dividing the Neolithic cultures into western (Yangshao) and eastern (Dawenkou) ceramic spheres.

Cultures	Ceramic spheres	
	Yangshao	*Dawenkou*
Late Neolithic	Majiayao, Machang, Qijia	Longshan, Late Liangzhu
Early–Middle Neolithic	Banpo, Miaodigou, Dahecun	Dawenkou, Majiabang, Songze, Early Liangzhu

39   Regional cultures in the Yangshao and Dawenkou ceramic spheres.

In general, the utilitarian ceramics of the Mainland Neolithic were rooted in the textured-pottery tradition of East Asia. Cord-marking, appliqué and incising continued to be important surfacing techniques among the coarse wares throughout the Yangshao and Dawenkou traditions and into the historic periods. Two additional texturing techniques appeared during this time, paddling and stamping, which did not occur in the Pen/Insular textured-pottery traditions until their later diffusion from the Mainland.

One divergence from textured pottery during the Mainland Neolithic was the emergence of smooth-surfaced wares, often highly burnished and/or painted. These fine wares are best known in the West in the form of Yangshao
plates 12–14, 17   painted pottery and the black 'eggshell' ware of Longshan proper. Yangshao and Longshan proper have become known by these fine wares despite the fact that these comprise only a small percentage of the vessels. The eastern and western traditions are better distinguished on a series of other criteria, including shape and method of construction.

Box 6   The differences between Yangshao and Dawenkou pottery are marked. Yangshao vessels are simply shaped with few extraneous projections; double-handled jars are the exception and are distinctive of the Yangshao tradition. Dawenkou vessels tend to be complex, both in design and construction, with more handles, spouts and pedestals.[28] Dawenkou pedestals are further elaborated with perforated cutouts and/or banded incising and grooving. An example of the varying complexity of construction is the Dawenkou hollow-legged tripod; probably inspired by the pointed-bottomed water bottle of the Yangshao tradition, it notionally consists of three bottle tips gathered together to make a new vessel. The increased surface area of the legs is thought to have facilitated the cooking and heating of liquids. It has also been said that whereas Yangshao vessels are made to sit directly on the ground (with flat, round or low-footed bases), Dawenkou vessels are characteristically raised off the ground on high pedestals or feet.[29] This generalization holds fairly well except for the tripod – a bowl or pot elevated on solid legs. The tripod was used throughout the Mainland in the Neolithic, often as a cooking vessel, although its various body shapes may have correlated with a range of functions. Finally, the Dawenkou tradition is noted for its use of the wheel. Already in the Early Neolithic Majiabang and Dawenkou cultures, vessel rims were being finished on slow wheels or turntables, which nevertheless did not use centrifugal force for forming the vessels. There is evidence, however, that in the Middle Neolithic the fast wheel was used, in its centrifugal capacity, to make small vessels. This technique became standard in the Late Neolithic Longshan cultures together with the use of an improved kiln.   Box 8

Settlement studies

Investigations into settlement locations in non-agricultural societies, such as the Late Palaeolithic and postglacial hunting and gathering societies of the previous chapters, usually focus on a site's position relative to the surrounding natural resources. Within agricultural economies, however, the focus often shifts to the relationships among the sites themselves, with the expectation that different sites will exhibit different functions which are integrated into a regional system. The sites may function as resource extraction sites (mining, farming), manufacturing sites (ceramics), storage sites and distribution points (where products of the former are collected and redistributed), and administrative sites (where elites reside and oversee the regional political system).

Chinese archaeologists have yet to deal with the Neolithic settlement patterns, even though thousands of sites are known. The surveys conducted to locate sites have resulted only in distributional generalizations correlated with environment, not in integrated settlement patterns. For example, in the northwestern loesslands, Yangshao sites were usually located on riverine terraces that overlooked the alluvial floodplains of large river valleys; but in the plains regions both north and south of the Huai River, Dawenkou sites usually occupied the alluvial flatlands themselves, though they were situated on river levees or artificial mounds, avoiding the marshes and swamps as much as possible. Rather more informative are the extensive studies based on excavation, not site survey, data. Two topics have been addressed: house architecture and site layout.

Architectural styles
Three different styles of architecture are currently recognized prior to the Late Neolithic. As with settlement position, the distribution of these architectural

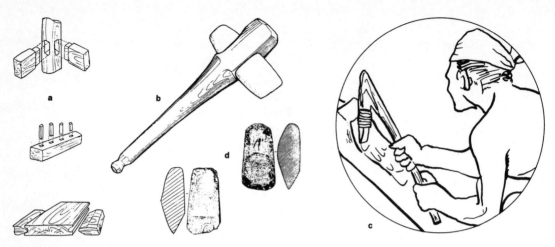

40 *Woodworking tools. Mortise and tenon constructions (a) at Hemudu show precocious joinery skills. Woodworking tools were made of stone. Ideally, artifacts with symmetrically bevelled blades but a slanting edge are termed axes and were hafted with the edge turned perpendicularly to the ground when held upright (b), while those with asymmetrical bevels and a straight edge are termed adzes and were hafted with the edge parallel with the ground (c). Actual artifacts (d), however, are often difficult to categorize – hence the use of the term 'axe/adze'. Adze-shaped tools were used to plane and shape timber as shown, but they could also be used to fell trees with a downward stroke in contrast to the sideswing used with axes. Agricultural activities led to widespread deforestation, but timber rather than stone continued to be used for buildings in East Asia even after the rise of monumental architecture.*

styles was also determined in part by environment. The pit-buildings and storage pits common to the millet cultures of the loesslands would hardly have been useful in areas of high water table. The stilted buildings at Hemudu, raised on piles a metre off the ground, undoubtedly suited the marshy environs of the site; the layers of rice discovered there might have resulted from the collapse of raised granaries. The third type of structure – surface dwellings – was not so environmentally sensitive and occurred from the Initial Neolithic onwards in several culture zones. Most Neolithic surface buildings are one-room wattle-and-daub structures, although multiroom buildings have been discovered at certain sites, including Dahecun. At one Majiabang site, wet-preserved mortise and tenon joints indicate the continuation of Hemudu woodworking skills but as applied to the construction of surface rather than stilt houses.

Site plans
Few village plans are known in entirety. The Yangshao site of Jiangzhai currently serves as an exemplar for loessland Neolithic sites. A circular ditch enclosed a dwelling area of about 2 ha, within which pit-buildings of various shapes and sizes were arranged around a central plaza. Investigators see the buildings falling into five clusters, each consisting of several small structures grouped around a larger one. Outside the ditch were the ceramic kilns to the southwest and the village cemetery to the southeast, where burials were also perceived to have occurred in clusters. This village plan is similar to that at the

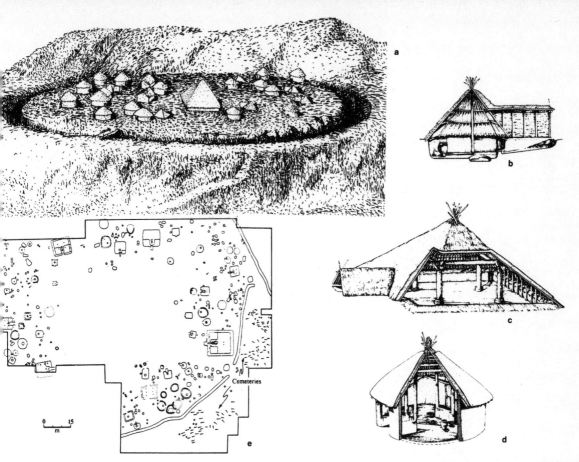

41 *Ditched settlements of the Yangshao culture. A sketch of the Banpo site (a) shows the positioning of different architectural types in the settlement: pit-buildings with sunken floors, both round (b) and square (c) and surface buildings (d). At the Jiangzhai site (e), individual clusters of buildings perhaps indicate the residences of different lineages or clans within the village.*

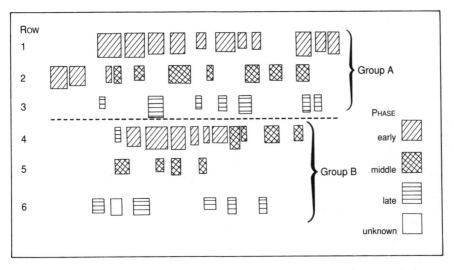

42 *Kin-group burials at Yuanjunmiao. Rows of burials at this Yangshao culture cemetery have been attributed by excavators to perhaps two different kin-groups occupying the site. In an early phase, the two groups buried their dead respectively in rows 1 and 4, then in the next phase in rows 2 and 5, and finally in rows 3 and 6. So rows 1, 2, and 3 represent the cemetery of group A through time, while rows 4, 5 and 6 belonged to group B through time.*

well-known Banpo site; there, however, the cemetery was located north of the dwelling enclosure and the kilns were positioned to the east.

The spatial clusterings of houses and burials in these sites are assumed to represent kin groupings, indicating the organization of Yangshao society into *fig. 42* clans. At the Yuanjunmiao cemetery,[30] archaeologists have discerned two such groupings among the six rows of burials at the site. Each consists of three rows which show parallel development through time, resulting from the systematic addition of burials by each kin group. Major distinctions in the elaboration of burials, however, can be seen between the western Yangshao cultures and the eastern Dawenkou cultures. Female graves were more richly endowed than those of males at the Yangshao cemetery of Yuanjunmiao, and this evidence is used by Chinese archaeologists in support of a matriarchal interpretation of Yangshao society.[31] Conversely, the prevalence of ceramically rich male graves in east coast sites is taken to indicate the emergence of patriarchal society.[32] This is one of the clearest applications of Marxist evolutionary theory in Chinese archaeology.

Shifting villages

An interesting problem in settlement pattern research is the hypothesis that the Yangshao peoples periodically abandoned their ditched villages in order to pursue swidden cultivation.[33] Also called 'slash-and-burn', this cultivation technique requires great reserves of forested land within which trees can be cut and burned *in situ*, thus fertilizing the soil with ash in order to grow a mixture of crops. Ethnographically, it has been shown that yields are good for perhaps the first three years on such a plot, after which fertility drops rapidly and the plot is best left for about twenty years to allow forest regeneration.

This shifting village hypothesis for the Yangshao Neolithic is based on discontinuous occupation layers at sites and the seeming lack of great temporal differences among artifact assemblages within these layers. In addition, pollen profiles from Yangshao sites indicate fluctuating tree and grass cover around the sites. These factors led some archaeologists to posit a cycle of soil exhaustion and forest regeneration, causing the alternate exodus and return of the populace.

This use of pollen diagrams has been criticized for not taking into account the relative amounts or seasonality of pollen production.[34] Other problems arise from comparative ethnographic case studies: although fields are regularly moved in swidden systems, villages – even those without massive construction investment as at Banpo – are moved less often. Thus, it is difficult to imagine that the Yangshao villages would be abandoned lightly. How many village ditches 5 m wide and equally deep (the size at Banpo) would people willingly dig in order to provide a succession of sites for habitation? And how could they protect their empty sites and regenerating forest resources when they were resident elsewhere? Considering that the pollen profiles suggest extensive grasslands developing around the sites, abandonment may alternatively have been due to an imbalance between the cultivation system and the population

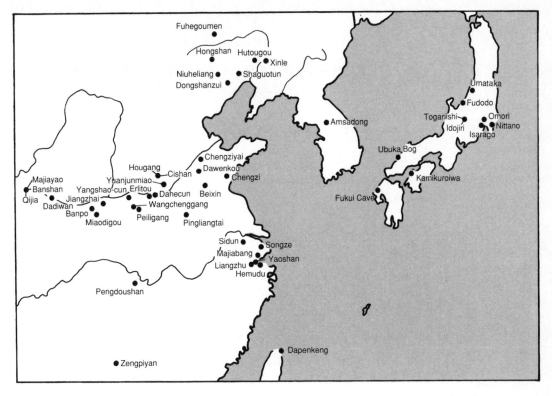

43 Postglacial and Neolithic sites of East Asia. Sites dating between 10,000 and 300 BC mentioned in the text, particularly in Chapters 5, 6 and 7.

which caused the environment to be over-exploited, leading to forest non-regeneration, lower productivity and finally depopulation.

In any case, there is no doubt that the agricultural practices of the Neolithic and later historic peoples contributed to massive deforestation across the eastern loesslands and the Central Plain. In the south as well, paddy fields came to cover the lower flatlands, and the hilly regions were eventually planted with various dry-land crops including tea – destroying the native habitation. Remnants of the original forest cover currently exist only in isolated pockets, for example on the lands of ancestral temples that have great historical depth.[35] This remark brings the discussion to a consideration of social development in the Neolithic, when the clan organization of historic China may have evolved.

CHAPTER 7

The Emergence of Neolithic Elites
3500–2000 BC

Before Longshan

The emergence of complex society on the China Mainland is usually discussed in terms of the Late Neolithic Longshan cultures of the Central Plain. Recent discoveries, however, reveal that sophisticated developments were already under way in the Middle Neolithic across a much broader expanse of the Mainland. From north to south, the host cultures were Hongshan in the western Manchurian Basin, Dawenkou on the east coast, and Liangzhu in the Shanghai Delta region. All these are noted for their amazing jade artifacts. Trends towards status differentiation, craft specialization and public architecture are evident in these societies. These trends continue in the Late Neolithic, but an insidious new addition at that time is violence, especially in the Central Plain region.

Box 7

Although developments in the three cultures named above will be discussed here before turning to Longshan, it is not yet clear how much of their social precocity actually predates the Late Neolithic. Sites in the Hongshan culture have been radiocarbon dated to two phases, early and late; while the jades certainly occur early on, some of the more spectacular sites might be later or even contemporaneous with the Longshan cultures. Liangzhu also overlaps with Longshan and shows a similar degree of social differentiation – more intense than in Hongshan and Dawenkou.

Nevertheless, it is obvious from their archaeological remains that these regional cultures were not secondary spin-offs from the Longshan cultures. In fact, some of them contributed elements to the cultures of the Central Plain, such as the 'face' motif from Liangzhu jades which became integral to the later Shang material culture.

Hongshan happenings

In 1922, Andersson and his survey team recovered painted and black pottery from the Shaguotun cave,[1] located within the sphere of what is now known as the Hongshan culture. In excavations of the past decade, pit-buildings with internal storage pits and hearths, and pottery kilns have been excavated from Hongshan sites.[2] The tool repertoire includes rectangular reaping knives made of shell, presumably for harvesting millet, which is attested even further east in the textured-pottery Xinle culture. Hongshan pottery shows affinities with

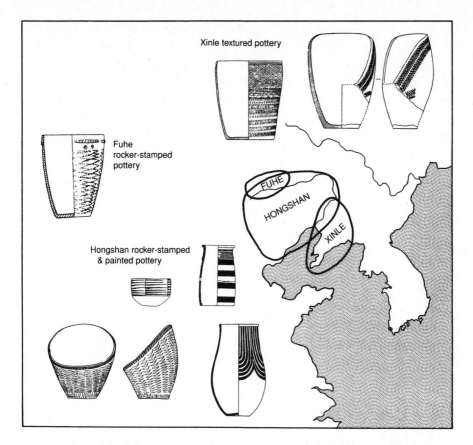

44 Neolithic cultures of the lower Manchurian Basin. Along the northern border of East Asia, the Fuhe, Hongshan and Xinle shared a textured-pottery tradition more similar to the incised Chulmun of the Korean Peninsula than the Neolithic cultures of the China Mainland. Rocker-stamped pottery was popular, as was a curiously asymmetrical bowl. Xinle comprised the easternmost extension of the northern millet regime, while Fuhe is considered a forest foraging culture. Among these, Hongshan stands out for its painted pottery and advanced jade working.

Yangshao in both its shape repertoire (carinated bowls, lugged jars) and its painted designs. An unusual local shape consisted of painted cylinders, used at two sites with exceptional implications for complex social development, Dongshanzui and Hutougou.

The Hongshan culture was centred on the Liao River drainage of the lower Manchurian Basin. Several features dubbed 'temples' and 'palaces' have been excavated in this area, contributing to their citation as the earliest evidence for 'urban' development in East Asia at 3500 BC. These appellations exaggerate the level of social development evident at the sites, but the variety of ritual features recovered and their careful spatial organization illustrate an attention to activities beyond the daily subsistence routine not yet found on the Central Plain at this date.

Two of these special sites are Dongshanzui and Niuheliang. Several round *fig. 43* and square stone-laid features were excavated at Dongshanzui; portions of

Box 7e

enclosing walls and an open area identified as a 'plaza' give this site the illusion of being a compound, though the remains are very fragmentary. Human figurines made of clay, jade animal carvings and painted cylinders are reported from here, but no daily or utilitarian artifacts.[3] One of the circular stone pavements was accompanied by a human skeleton. A house floor has also been identified in the compound interior, while a stone-paved area lay outside the eastern wall. The site of Niuheliang is of an entirely different nature: a structure resembling conjoined vaulted tunnels had interior walls bearing painted decoration. The head of a life-sized unbaked clay statue with inset jade eyes was unearthed inside the structure, as well as body parts of even larger statues and fragments of animal figurines. The building layout and architecture at these two sites is far more elaborate than required for daily subsistence and was probably created for community rituals, perhaps overseen by chiefly figures.

The square, stone-delineated terrace containing the Niuheliang structure is positioned on a wooded hill finger jutting into a valley; several other promontories overlooking the valley support large stone cairns, some with great attention paid to architectural detail of the cairn footings and central burials with jades. Evidence for social status differentiation resides in such Hongshan burial data. The tomb at Hutougou originally consisted of main burials at the centre of a circular enclosure of stones, along which stood painted cylinders. Judging from the site stratigraphy, it is likely that the upper burial was roughly contemporaneous with a multiple-cist surface structure housing at least six burials in five chambers built outside the enclosure. Other burials can be seen to have cut into the upper layers inside the enclosure. It is the spatial distinction and special architecture afforded to the central burial that suggest differences in social status among those buried (and not buried) there. These kinds of burial data, missing from the contemporaneous Middle Jomon sites of central Honshu, for example, allow some degree of social hierarchy in Hongshan society to be hypothesized, with the central burial belonging perhaps to a chiefly figure.

Dawenkou developments

The Dawenkou culture originated earlier than the Hongshan, and its long burial record shows clear trends towards richer, more elaborate furnishings and structures through time.[4] Graves with so-called 'ledges', resulting from infilling the grave pit up to the level of the coffin lid and then depositing goods on the packed-in earth, were a local innovation. Burials equipped with such ledges averaged twice as many grave goods as those without, indicating both increased labour investment in building the grave and wealth in furnishing it. Another structural elaboration was the use of log chambers; grave goods were twice as abundant in later log-chamber burials than in earlier phases, illustrating increasing 'conspicuous consumption' of material objects through time.

At the Chengzi cemetery, spatial segregation is added to this brew of increasing differentiation. There, 62 per cent of the burials had no grave goods

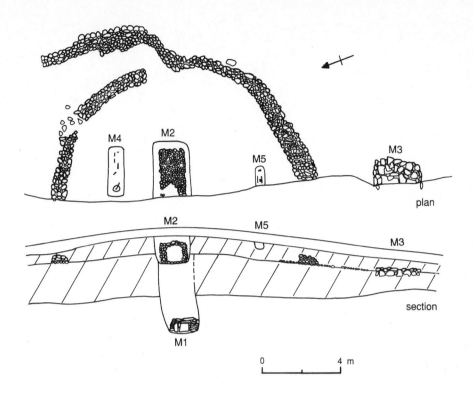

45 *Differential burial practices at Hutougou. Two burial phases can be discerned in the stratigraphic superimposition of the central graves and mound fills at Hutougou. Those buried at the centre of the mounds are believed to have been more privileged than those buried in the multiple cist chambers built outside the stone enclosure.*

and were positioned in the eastern part of the cemetery. Of the remainder, 5–7 per cent of the burials were extremely well equipped with large pits, caskets, abundant finely made ceramics, and pig mandibles, and they were located together in the northern part of the cemetery.[5] One may reasonably hypothesize that what is being seen here is the emergence of a social elite – not just one chief accorded special privilege in death but a whole segment of society that was both figuratively isolated from the others by access to otherwise restricted goods and literally isolated in separate burial grounds.

The grave deposits yielded a bewildering variety of prestige goods, including jades, incised turtle shells, specialized drinking vessels, and painted pots echoing the Yangshao tradition. Some of these were products of specialist craftspeople while others, like the turtle shells, were valued for their scarcity. Given the variety of materials represented and the different sources from which they must have been procured, it is very likely that the Dawenkou elite participated in a far-flung interaction network. This provided them with exotic goods which simultaneously signified, legitimized and bolstered their status in the community. The painted pottery might represent the first breaching of the

46 *Prestige goods from Dawenkou. Burials in phase III included many greenstone and bone ornaments and tool imitations as well as fine ceramics.*

east–west divide among the Middle Neolithic communities, while the jades illustrate a value system held in common with other coastal communities, such as those of the Liangzhu culture to the south.

Lessons of Liangzhu

Boxes 6, 7

A precocious member of the east coast cultures was the Liangzhu culture of the Shanghai Delta region. Sophisticated jades and advanced ceramic technology imply the presence of specialist craftspeople, perhaps the first to appear in East Asian prehistory. It was noted above that Liangzhu pottery was part of the Dawenkou ceramic tradition of the east coast, and a high proportion of Liangzhu vessels were constructed on the wheel. Many of these were refined blackwares, carefully constructed and polished to a high lustre.[6] It appears that these distinctive Liangzhu ceramics may have predated the similar but more renowned 'eggshell' wares of the Shandong peninsula by more than a millennium.

Liangzhu jades are mainly recovered from burials which show tremendous resource investment and 'religiosity'.[7] Rich graves were often clustered into burial precincts, such as the square earthen 'platform' excavated at the Yaoshan site, which was mounded over with earth. One rich grave at the Sidun site was that of a young man, buried under a mound 20 m high with over a hundred jade objects. His thigh bones and some of the jades had been burned – as had bones, artifacts and earth at other Liangzhu burial sites – giving rise to speculations about cremation or at least fiery funerary rituals. Extra immolations around the primary burial are interpreted as human sacrifices.[8]

Little is known about Liangzhu settlements, but the above burial data suggest that the Liangzhu social system was hierarchical, as signified by the extreme spatial demarcation and wealth. Among the cultures dealt with here, Late Liangzhu was unquestionably the most advanced, rivalled in its day only by the Longshan cultures of the north.

Competition and conflict in the Late Neolithic

The Late Neolithic of the north China Mainland is heralded in the archaeological record by ceramic changes. The east–west division in ceramic traditions is irrevocably breached, and Longshan-type pottery is incorporated on a large scale into the Yangshao cultures of the central Yellow and Wei River valleys. Painted pottery declined in both frequency and quality, the dominant colour turned from red to grey, and textured surfaces occurred in hybrid mixture with Longshan shapes. From this point onwards, cultures of the Yangshao ceramic tradition (except for Qijia in the far northwest) shared their general social trajectories with the Longshan cultures of the Central Plain.

The Late Neolithic Longshan cultures were characterized by advanced ceramic and jade technologies; an increased reliance on domestic animals, especially sheep and cattle; varying degrees of social differentiation, including stratified clans; and the utilization of exotic items such as jades, ivories, and turtle shells in ritual and exchange. This particular cultural mix had been brewing since the middle of the period; the outstanding additions in the Late Neolithic were social conflict and the resulting emergence of new settlement forms.

Conflict and social control

The occurrence of headless and footless corpses in less than auspicious burial circumstances (stuffed down a well!), the appearance of walled settlements, and a sudden proliferation of projectile points all suggest an increase in social conflict in the Late Neolithic Longshan cultures.[9] Enclosing a settlement with a wall of tamped earth no doubt required many labourers, much co-ordination and greater technical knowledge than, for example, digging a ditch around a Yangshao village. We might, therefore, see this development as a reflection of the extension of chiefly authority and organization over the local population. The initial motive for such construction might have been community defence, but the labour conscription and building technology were soon directed towards a task of less universal benefit: the construction of earthen foundation platforms for elite buildings. At this point, sacrifice seems to have shifted from animals to humans and moved out of the cemetery into the town, for many foundations incorporate human interments thought to be of a ritual nature.

BOX 7
Jade, a Neolithic Valuable

Jade occurs naturally along the northern fringe of East Asia and far to the southwest in Southeast Asia. Known sources exploited in prehistoric times include the Itoigawa area in the Japanese archipelago (*fig. 32*). The slit earrings of jade produced by the Jomon (a) suggest that the central Honshu trading network may have connected to the Mainland, where slit earrings are known along the east coast down to Southeast Asia. These body ornaments are complemented on the Mainland by bracelets (b), beads (c) and arc pendants (d).

Two major traditions of jade-working flourished on the Mainland between 3700 and 2000 BC: the northern, Hongshan tradition and the eastern, Liangzhu tradition. The recent discoveries in the Hongshan culture of the southwestern Manchurian Basin have been a great surprise: not only are they much earlier than expected, but also they show a high level of jade technology. The products are mainly flattish animal figures with back perforations to allow suspension or attachment. The shaping of these figures involved abrasive sculpting, a very labour-intensive technique. Bird and turtle shapes are common (e), and may have been two totemic symbols adopted by different Hongshan groups.

The Liangzhu tradition is renowned for its ritual jades: the long tubes called *zong* with cylindrical bores and squared sides (f), perforated discs called *bi* (g), and flat openwork plaques which may have been used as head-dress ornaments (h). Technically, these were simpler to produce than the sculpted Hongshan jades, since they focused on flat rather than three-dimensional surfaces; but their standardized shapes and elaborate methods of decoration called for supreme skill and sophistication. Fashioned from slabs or blocks of jade that were sawn with abrasives, they required little laborious shaping – only planar finishing of edges and perhaps the incising of superb designs. Judging from the systematic variations in shapes and sizes, deriving from standardized blocks of raw materials, these ritual jades were being mass-produced by specialists in the Liangzhu culture. The surface designs form a 'face motif' (f), giving rise to the protohistoric *taotie* mask pattern used on later bronzes. Similar incised face patterns are found on the jade axes characteristic of the Dawenkou culture (i).

The Liangzhu face motif appearing on the head-dress ornament (h) can be interpreted in two ways. The face at the top has a torso underneath, with bent elbows. Below is the primary face (eyes, nose and tabular mouth) with the crooked elbows from above forming eyebrows; the upper face is incorporated as the design of another head-dress (cf. fig. 53d).

In the early historic periods both *zong* and *bi* were used as ritual offerings, and their shapes related to the current cosmology: the *bi* signified heaven (a circle), and the *zong*'s circular bore and square exterior have been equated with the traditional Chinese geometrical symbols for heaven and earth, respectively. Whether these meanings can be projected back on to Neolithic jades is doubtful, but given the jades' skilled production and prominence in elite burials, one certainly cannot say that they were devoid of symbolic meaning altogether (plates 18, 19).

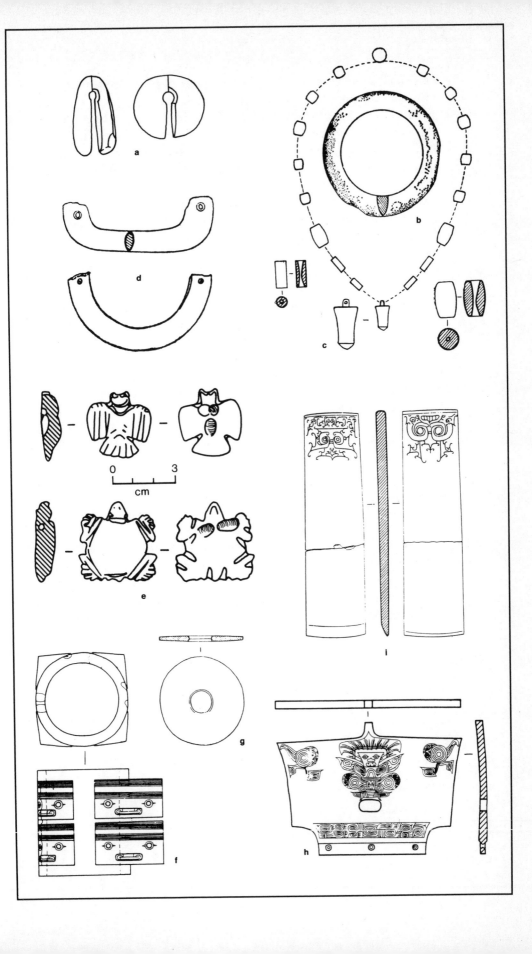

0   3
cm

This trend represents the systematic assertion of power over human life and death on behalf of the lifestyle of emergent rulers.

Human sacrifice can be manipulated towards various ends. As a means of demonstrating and reaffirming power, whether of an individual or of a regulating belief system, it is unsurpassable. It is also useful as a method of social control, since victims are often transgressors of rules or customs. Even sacrificed prisoners of war serve as reminders to the local populace of the power that can be turned on them should they fall into disfavour. The appearance of human sacrifice in the Late Neolithic cultures, particularly in conjunction with the building of monumental structures, no doubt reflects the efforts of regional elites not only to aggrandize their status in competition with other elites but also to consolidate control over their own populace.

Another means of control potentially available to the emerging elites was the custom of heat-cracking animal scapulae for divination purposes. Already in *fig. 44* use in the Fuhe culture of the eastern Mongolian Plateau in 3700 BC,[10] this custom was adopted by all the Longshan cultures and also Qijia in the far northwest during the 3rd millennium BC. A variety of animal bones were used: pig, sheep, cattle and even deer. These were the forerunners of the inscribed oracle bones of the Mainland Bronze Age, although the Longshan divination bones had no inscriptions. Whether divination was a practice limited to Longshan chiefs or of general use later to be co-opted by the elite is not yet known, but its full potential for ritualizing and controlling decision-making came to fruition in the succeeding Bronze Age.

Walled enclosures

Chengziyai – the type site for the Longshan culture,[11] discovered in 1928 on the Shandong peninsula – is only one of several walled settlements now known for the Late Neolithic. These vary greatly in size, but all seem to have encompassed dwellings and some craft facilities, with pottery and stone tools among their artifact repertoires. This form of settlement layout and defence stands in stark contrast to the village patterns preceding it (Chapter 6).

The walled settlement at Pingliangtai had guard houses on each side of its southern gate and more than a dozen dwellings in its interior, all built of adobe

Site	Wall length (m)	Area (ha)	Walls (m)		
			height	width at base	width at top
Chengziyai	390 × 450	17.5	6	10	8
Hougang	250 × 400	10.0	2–4		
Pingliangtai	185 × 185	3.4	13	8–10	
Wangchenggang	82.4 × 92	0.75	4.7		

47   *Walled sites of the Longshan cultures.*

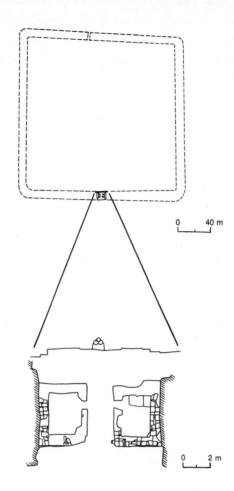

48 The Late Neolithic (Longshan) walled site of Pingliangtai. One of the earliest walled sites yet discovered, Pingliangtai was the size of a large village covering about 3.5 hectares. An elaborate gate structure, magnified here, restricted entrance to the site.

bricks. Some of these houses were distinguished from others by being raised on tamped-earth platforms. Scattered among similar earthen foundations within the Wangchenggang enclosure were found several underground pits, filled with skeletons of both adults and children, sandwiched between tamped-earth layers. The Chinese excavators of the site interpret these pits as being related to the rituals of laying the earthen foundations.[12]

Social stratification

Interestingly, these Late Neolithic trends of conflict and warfare were resolved with the ultimate stratification of Longshan society, which was facilitated by the application of a new technology – bronze casting – to the prestigious activity of elite drinking rituals. The most widely adopted definition of social stratification in anthropology emphasizes 'differential access to basic resources' among members of the population.[13] This definition refers mainly to agricultural resources, but in the case of the China Mainland the crucial ingredient appears to have been bronze. The presence of bronze-working alone, however, will not cause society to develop a class structure, as attested by

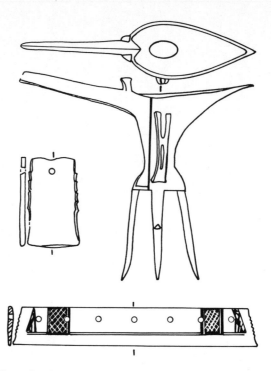

49 The earliest bronze vessel, from the site of Erlitou. This three-legged wine vessel had solid legs, a flat base, a slotted handle, rim knobs and a long slender pouring spout. It was discovered with two jade renditions of blades – one an axe blade and another with seven perforations.

the Bronze Age record of Europe. More important was the social context into which bronze-working was adopted; on the China Mainland, it was applied to the traditional drinking rituals of Longshan elites.

plates 12–14   The east coast ceramic repertoire from the Middle Neolithic onwards included many vessels for the pouring and serving of liquids. The occurrence of these in rich burials confirms that they played a role in elite activities. Feasting or the ritual sharing of food and drink is generally recognized as an important stage for political manoeuvring, and to have one's rivals convert to and participate in one's own rituals is a strategic *coup d'état*. This seems to be what happened at the end of the Neolithic, when one particular group of elites in the Erlitou culture co-opted bronze for the production of their ritual vessels. The cult that developed from their activities was widely adopted throughout the north China Mainland, integrating competing elites into what is now recognized as the Shang cultural sphere.

The advent of bronze vessels in the archaeological record signals the beginning of the Shang period, during which class society characterizes the Central Plain. Investigations into the degree of social development throughout the rest of the China Mainland, however, are just beginning.

CHAPTER 8

The Mainland Bronze Age
2000–1500 BC

The advent of bronze-working

Neolithic bronze?

The origins of bronze-working on the China Mainland are obscure. An alloy of copper and tin, bronze was thought by foreign scholars earlier this century to be unique and therefore it could not have been invented more than once. They postulated that the technology had diffused from Western Asia,[1] where it was present earlier; more recent discussions have suggested Southeast Asia as the source.[2] These views are eschewed by Chinese archaeologists.

Bronze was not totally unknown during the Mainland Neolithic: occasional fragments of small bronze and copper objects like rings and knives have turned up at sites belonging to several Neolithic cultures in a broad band across the northern Mainland.[3] It is not known where they were manufactured, and it is obvious that the mere existence of these metals in such small quantities – whether locally produced or imported – did not change the character of Neolithic society. The real changes occurred with the initiation of large-scale bronze production in the early 2nd millennium BC, and by the end of the millennium several regional bronze-working traditions had emerged. The Shang was only one of these, albeit the earliest, and it was certainly the most significant, since it was within the Shang cultural sphere that the most complex social developments took place, leading into historic Chinese dynastic organization.

Shang bronzes and their contemporaries

The wine vessels of the *jue* variety excavated from Erlitou are currently the earliest locally produced bronzes known in East Asia. Although Erlitou itself is often assigned to the local Xia culture, these vessels are the first manifestation of what was to become the Shang bronze tradition, which eventually encompassed the entire Central Plain. Their manufacture was extraordinary, using a piece-moulding system unknown anywhere else in the world at the time. Speculating on the origins of this full-blown technology, some scholars have postulated an earlier phase of sheet metal-working – a suggestion hotly debated.[4] Others have seen no need for a more primitive bronze-working technology to precede piece-moulding; instead they assign a critical role to the Longshan ceramic specialist, who had the expertise to 'invent' the piece-mould

fig. 49

fig. 50

BOX 8
Advances in Kiln Technology

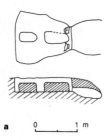

a

Beyond the potter's contributions of piece-moulds and crucibles to the incipient bronze industry, changes in kiln technology also had far-reaching ramifications for metal-working. Much Middle Neolithic pottery on the China Mainland was unusual in East Asia for being fired in updraught kilns (a), while most textured pottery of the surrounding peoples was presumably fired in open bonfires. By the end of the Neolithic, several innovations in kiln structure allowed the production of the high-fired earthenwares seen in the east coast tradition. These refinements included a chamber set more directly over the firebox to form a vertically organized kiln structure which provided a better draught (b). Among Shang wares are some miscellaneous vessels that were fired at such a high temperature (over 1200°C) that they achieved stoneware quality – that is, some minerals in the vessel body vitrified to form a hard glass causing the vessel walls to ring if tapped, and a particular mineral called mullite formed within the glassy phase. Such stonewares also occasionally bore streaks of natural glaze, formed by ash from the firewood fuel settling on the vessel in the kiln and melting into a hard glass on the surface.

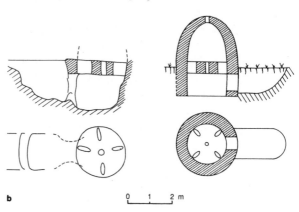

b

That such stoneware vessels were not produced systematically in the Shang and Early Zhou periods suggests that they were not valued as a distinct product. In the Late Zhou period, a kiln with a sloping floor was developed in the south-central Mainland in which temperatures of 1300°C could regularly be achieved (c). From then onwards, stonewares were consistently produced in this area. It is interesting to note both that this type of kiln was apparently developed in order to utilize the local silaceous stoneware clays with their high proportion of iron, and that this technological advance came soon after the perfection of iron smelting technology in the same general region (Chapter 9). There may have been some feedback between the iron and stoneware industries, just as there was between the ceramics and bronze industries a millennium and a half earlier up north.

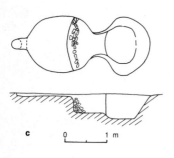

c

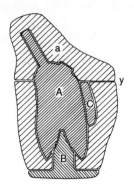

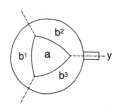

50 A clay piece-mould for making a bronze vessel. The inner cores for body (A) and handle (C) are surrounded by a three-piece assembly mould (b¹, b², b³), capped by a top section (a) and supported by an inter-leg core (B). Spacers were used to keep the mould and core sections apart, allowing a thin space into which the molten bronze was poured through the opening at (y).

and could contribute much knowledge and experience on high-temperature kiln firings, which could have been brought to bear on the smelting process.[5]

Slightly after Erlitou comes evidence of bronze production at several other locations across the China Mainland: at Wucheng,[6] Sanxingdui,[7] Xin'gan[8] and Haimenkou.[9] The bronzes found in the southern Mongolian Plateau – previously referred to as 'Ordos bronzes' but now included in the 'Northern Bronze Complex' – are also thought to extend back to near the beginning of the Shang period.[10] In the past, most scholars have assumed that all other Shang-period bronze traditions were stimulated into existence by the Shang tradition. This argument may work well for the Lower Xiajiadian bronze culture in the area of the former Hongshan culture of the Bohai Corridor region, but others such as Sanxingdui or the Northern Bronze Complex vary from the Shang in significant ways. The first difference is the widespread use of single or bi-valve stone moulds and/or the use of the lost-wax process instead of clay piece-moulds. Second, other regions often produced very different types of objects from those of the Shang tradition. Even when they incorporated Shang-type ritual vessels, as did Sanxingdui, neither that tradition nor the Northern Bronze Complex placed as much emphasis on ritual vessels as the Shang and its successor tradition, the Zhou. Third, the outlying traditions showed a greater tendency to depict realistic forms of animals and humans in preference to the abstract *taotie* designs of the Shang.

Such differences pose a challenge to the diffusionist argument for the origins of bronze-working from Shang to beyond. In particular, the Northern Bronze Complex is now suspected to have arisen from the Eurasian steppe bronze tradition; and even the other Mainland bronze traditions, which are generally acknowledged to have been stimulated into existence by Shang, developed very differently thereafter. To discuss the Shang period entirely in terms of Shang

fig. 59

plates 30, 32–34

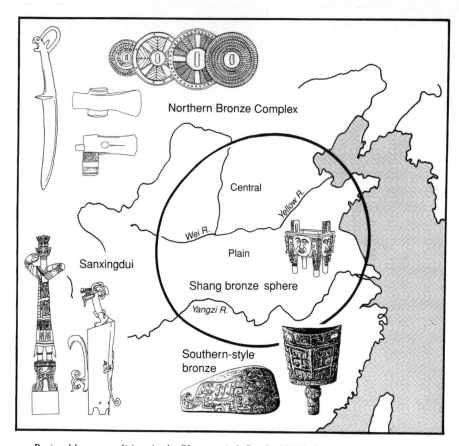

51 Regional bronze traditions in the Shang period. By the Middle Shang period, the Shang bronze tradition had spread into the Wei River valley to the west and encompassed the entire Central Plain. Along its northern border stretched the Northern Bronze Complex, comprising short daggers and curved knives – many with animal head pommels – tube-socketed battle axes and mirrors. These were imported into the Shang cultural sphere, and mutual influences can be traced. The Sanxingdui bronzes of the Middle Shang period in the southwestern Sichuan Basin include a very unusual emphasis on the human form (plate 30); this tradition is postulated to be the beginning of the bronze traditions of the Shu state in the succeeding Zhou period. The Haimenkou bronzes in the far southwest (not shown) are similarly viewed as the beginning of the Dian bronze tradition of the Han period (fig. 93, plate 31). The Yangzi Basin tradition of the Late Shang period placed great emphasis on musical instruments, especially bells and sounding stones as shown here, though these examples were excavated from Anyang.

bronze development, therefore, is extremely reductionist. Nevertheless, the common approach – though increasingly unsatisfactory – is to rely on Shang-period phases as defined on the basis of technical advances ascertained at certain excavated sites.

Among the metropolitan (central Shang) bronzes, the thread-relief decorations of Style I were produced by incising patterns into the inner mould surface. Incising was never common on Mainland Neolithic ceramics, but it was developed to perfection in jade-working. Moreover, the incised motif produced for the bronzes was the *taotie*, foreshadowed by the superbly executed

Period	E. Shang[11]	M. Shang[12]	L. Shang[13]
Site	**Erlitou**	**Erligang**	**Anyang**
	● *bossed decoration*	Style I ● *mould-incised thread relief*	Style IV ● *background/foreground distinction* ● *seam flanges*
		Style II ● *mould-incised ribbon relief*	Style V ● *foreground relief*
		Style III ● *model-incised design*	

52   Shang bronze styles of the Shang-period phases.

'face motif' on jades, especially in the southern Liangzhu culture of the Late   *fig. 53*
Neolithic. Erligang bronze technology thus suggests the incorporation not only
of a non-local symbolism,[14] but also perhaps of some secondary jade-
decoration techniques. This is appropriate to a model of elite interaction across
the landscape, which predicts the transmission of symbols and technology
resulting in the mutual reinforcement of the position of elites in their respective
societies.[15] Style II comprised a widening of the incised area to form a broad,
smooth, raised band on the finished vessel (ribbon relief). Style III represents a
rather different technique: the decoration is incised on to the clay model rather
than directly into the mould, so that the finished bronze bears concave rather
than raised designs. Styles IV and V incorporate a distinction between the
major motifs and a background design.   plate 26

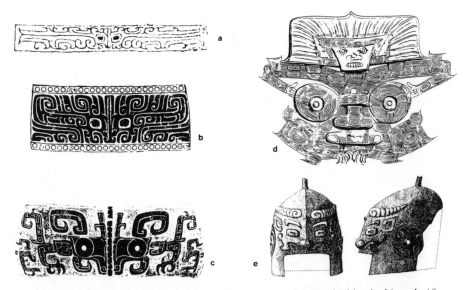

*53 The taotie 'beast' motif and its relatives. Thought to have been inspired by the Liangzhu 'face
motif' (d), the taotie (a–c) is nevertheless usually interpreted as a beast with horns, fangs, claws,
and quills down its back. On Shang bronzes within the Erligang phase, the raised line relief of
Style I (a) was replaced by the ribbon relief of Style II (b). In the Anyang phase, background
and motif were clearly separated, as in Style IV (c). Some of the earlier styles were revived in
Late Shang and Early Zhou, making quick attribution on stylistic grounds difficult for the
uninitiated. The independent 'face' image was retained on bronze helmets of the period (e).*

Within the Shang cultural sphere, bronze vessels of Shang shapes but local design motifs are called 'provincial' by art historians, as opposed to the 'metropolitan' bronzes of central Shang.[16] This is an art historical distinction that is based on the analysis of *taotie* motif development, but it does not account for the actual geographical distribution of bronzes of known provenance. Furthermore, the term 'metropolitan' does not presume a centralized production and distribution network for bronzes. Metropolitan-style bronzes could be and were made in outlying areas, and very few bronzes in these areas have been identified as having been imported from the Shang centres.[17]

Central Plain cultural development

The trends in the Mainland Late Neolithic towards defended settlements, social hierarchies, and forceful methods of social control all accelerated in the Early Shang period to produce a Central Plain society fully divided into elite and commoner strata. The accompanying transformation of the material culture was phenomenal, resulting in urbanization, industrial craft production and monumental burials. The bronzes were perhaps the most significant

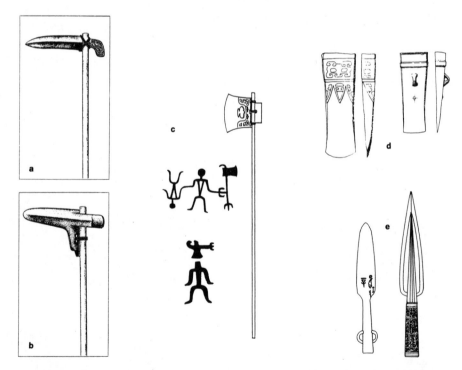

54 Shang bronze weapons. Among the weaponry, ge dagger-axes are a unique type, meant to be hafted perpendicularly to a long pole and used with a chopping motion (a). Over time, a flange was extended down the shaft to provide for more secure hafting (b). The executioner's tanged axe was also hafted like the ge, and emblems cast into the bronzes vividly show their use (c). Socketed axes (d) and spearpoints (e) have brought into question possible contact with the West, whence came the charioteer complex.

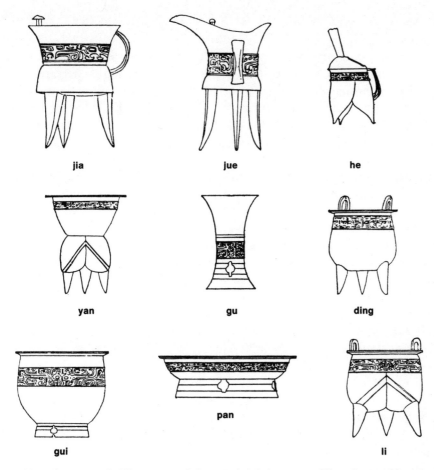

55 *Shang bronze vessels. The main vessel shapes included the unspouted* jia *and spouted* jue *wine goblets, the ewer* he, *the steamer* yan, *the slender* gu *wine goblet, the solid-legged tripod* ding, *the deep bowl* gui, *a shallow basin* pan, *and the hollow-legged tripod* li.

material element. Consisting mainly of ritual vessels with a secondary emphasis on weapons, they illustrate the dual power base on which elite domination was established. Their mass production implies a centralized ability to obtain large amounts of metal and to mobilize the labour for casting.[18]

plates 38, 39

These bronzes are usually assumed to have been used in ancestral rites, through analogy with the historically documented use of bronze vessels in the Zhou period. Presumably by claiming that communication with the ancestors was possible only through the use of the precious sumptuary bronzes (to which only the elite had access), the elite were able to create and maintain their status separate from the masses. The fact that the bronzes used were vessels to hold food and drink suggests that the Longshan tradition of elite feasting had been upgraded with a major investment of resources, skills and labour in the adoption of bronzes over ceramics for ritualistic activities.[19] In the northern Zhou states of the succeeding period, possession of such ritual vessels (the 'Nine Bronze Tripods') was the tangible evidence of the right to rule.[20]

plates 27–29

Urbanism

Only a few major sites of the Shang culture have been excavated; of these, the Late Shang site of Anyang is said to provide 'perhaps 90 per cent of all the basic data, archaeological and textual, on Shang civilization, and the researches of these data account for perhaps 99 per cent of all scholarly publications on Shang'.[21] Three other important sites are Erlitou of the Early Shang, and the Middle Shang sites of Zhengzhou and Panlongcheng.[22] All of these illustrate developing urbanization entailing the interdependency of the elite and the craft specialists in their employ.

fig. 59

Early in the Shang period at Erlitou, there developed a use of walled enclosures quite different from the fortified villages of the Late Neolithic: foundation platforms themselves were enclosed and a building constructed in the interior precincts on an additional earthen foundation. This double-deck construction with an enclosing corridor running around the edge of the lower foundation platform is interpreted as palatial architecture.[23] Accordingly, two 'palaces' are known at Erlitou 150 m apart from each other; their lower foundation platforms measure 100×108 m (1 ha) and 58×73 m (0.4 ha) respectively. The tamped-earth walls at the edges were only 0.5 m wide for the first and about 1.1 m wide for the second. Both had rows of post-holes at different points paralleling the walls, indicating the construction of a corridor – possibly open at least to the interior of the compound. Both walls also showed evidence of gates on the southern side, while the building foundations were located in the northern interior; the same positioning of these facilities is well attested in later, historically known palaces. The northern building foundations measure 25×36 m (900 m^2) in the first case and 12.5×33 m (412.5 m^2) in the second. The building on the latter foundation seems to have had an exterior veranda whereas the first did not.

Zhengzhou is the name of a modern Chinese city where remains of a Middle Shang-period earthen wall have been identified. It incorporates almost twice as much area as the present city walls, for a total of 3.25 sq. km. Inside these ancient walls, earthen foundation platforms for buildings formed part of a palace where bronze hairpins were recovered. Outside the walls stood several

fig. 64

bronze, bone and pottery workshops in which objects were manufactured for elite use. A ditch at the bone workshop containing human skulls, many with their crowns sawn off for conversion into bowls, hints at control over life even within the production process. Here in the Erligang phase of the Shang period, interdependency between craft specialists and the elite is for the first time institutionalized into a recognizable pattern of urban layout. Zhengzhou has been used as the model for the theoretical construct of the 'ceremonial centre', which has been proposed as the earliest form of urbanism in many early state societies.[24] In this model, the wall is not so much defensive as serving to exclude the masses, who were neither privy nor privileged to participate in the esoteric rites of elite politics.

Northeast of the modern city of Anyang spread the extensive remains of a Late Shang site. This site, sometimes referred to as Yinxu but more often as

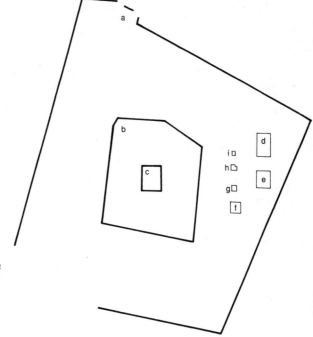

a. Xiadu (Z) 2,300 ha
b. Zhengzhou (S) 360 ha
c. Chengziyai (L) 17.5 ha
d. Hougang (L) 10 ha
e. Panlongcheng (S) 7.5 ha
f. Pingliangtai (L) 3.4 ha
g. Erlitou-a (S) 1.1 ha
h. Wangchenggang (L) 0.76 ha
i. Erlitou-b (S) 0.4 ha

56 Scaled comparisons of walled sites in the Longshan (L), Shang (S), and Zhou (Z) periods. From these comparisons it is clear that there are major differences in size that can be assigned to town and city enclosures.

Anyang, is so large that it encompasses districts known by modern village names. Dotted across a broad area of countryside are a royal Shang cemetery, a palace and temple complex, many housing areas for aristocrats and commoners, and craft workshops. Testimony of the exalted and powerful status of the Shang elite is provided by the royal cemetery of shaft tombs and sacrificial burials near the village of Xibeigang. The excavated portion of the cemetery consists of a western section containing seven shaft tombs and a large rectangular pit, plus an eastern section with five more shaft tombs. Eight of the tombs had cruciform plans with four ramps leading into the centre shaft; three had two ramps and one had one ramp. The longest ramp was 31.4 m and the deepest shaft was 12 m. Nearly 1200 small pit-graves of individuals, which are thought to have been sacrificial burials, occur across the cemetery site. Sacrificed monkeys, deer, horses and elephants were also buried in the Xibeigang cemetery. The scale of wealth in the top-ranking Shang tombs is so much greater as to be incomparable with the 'rich' burials of the Late Neolithic. Unfortunately, most of the shaft tombs at Anyang had been plundered before excavation, but the inventory of grave goods in the untouched tomb of a royal consort named Fuhao included over two hundred bronze ritual vessels, seven thousand cowrie shells and almost six hundred jade and jade-like objects.[25]

At the Anyang temple complex near the village of Xiaotun, the tamped-earth foundations and adjacent grounds of a series of building compounds contained many more sacrificial burials of humans and animals – particularly the central and southern areas. The palace buildings have been analysed as to function, with the residential area postulated in the north, the Temple and Hall complex

fig. 57

plate 20

cf. plates 21–24

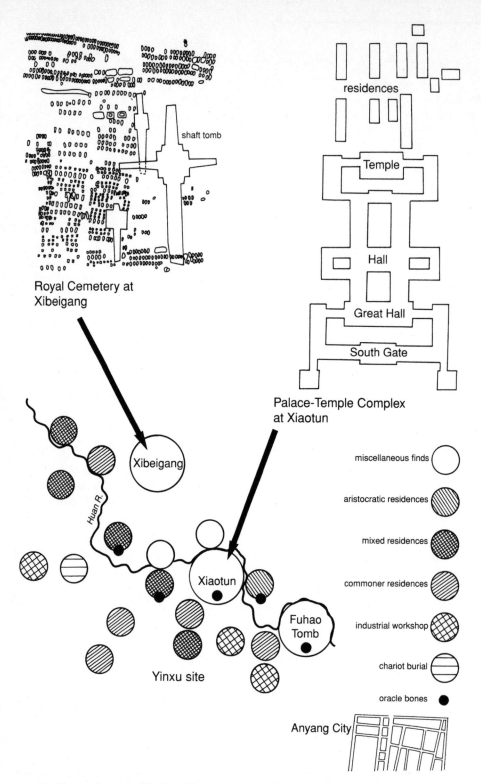

residences

Temple

Hall

Great Hall

South Gate

shaft tomb

Royal Cemetery at
Xibeigang

Palace-Temple Complex
at Xiaotun

Xibeigang

Huan R.

Xiaotun

Fuhao
Tomb

Yinxu site

Anyang City

miscellaneous finds

aristocratic residences

mixed residences

commoner residences

industrial workshop

chariot burial

oracle bones

*57 The Yinxu urban area. The Late Shang capital stretches over 5.8 km along the Huan River
northwest of modern Anyang, a gridded city. Yinxu's urban nature is encapsulated in the diversity
of functions at the site, which included workshops for manufacturing bone and bronze goods as well
as residential areas for both commoners and elite.*

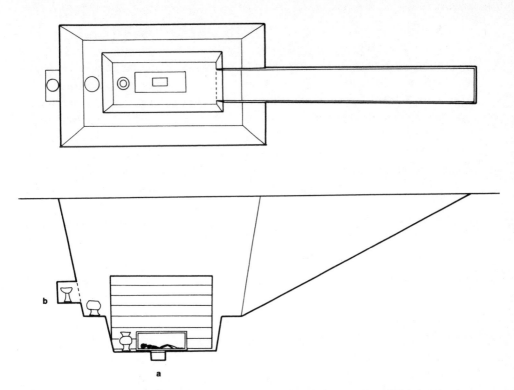

58 *Construction details of a shaft tomb with single ramp. A 'waist pit' under the coffin (a) and a niche at the head end (b) are common additions to the shaft. The 'double coffin' construction indicates a coffin (often of nested layers in later periods) placed inside a timber 'chamber'. The 'ledges' on which objects were placed often resulted from the infilling of the pit around the chamber up to the level of the cover and the placing of objects at that level before completing the infilling of the pit.*

in the centre, and the Great Hall in the south, flanked by the Eastern Hall and Hall of Ritual Vessels. Between these Halls and the South Gate stood two multi-storey towers and two independent altars.[26] Pit-house remains, which are interpreted as servants' quarters, stood between and among the building compounds across the site. Oddly enough, this temple complex was not surrounded by an earthen wall, as was the custom of the times, though new excavations have reportedly uncovered some kind of wall at the site.

Zhou architectural contributions

The remains of the alleged predynastic 'capital' of the Zhou – the Fengchu remains at Qishan, contemporaneous with Anyang – reveal the beginnings of two very important aspects of subsequent elite architecture in East Asia: the use of ceramic tiles and stone. All buildings in the Shang period were constructed of perishable materials, with wooden pillars and thatched roofs. Only the tamped-earth foundation platforms manifested their 'monumentality'. At Qishan, the thatched roofs of the Fengchu buildings were capped by semi-cylindrical tiles along the ridge poles; and by the Late Zhou period, the roofs of elite buildings were fully tiled.[27] Fired bricks were an invention of Early Zhou. It seems that they were initially affixed to the face of tamped-earth structures,[28] but in the Han period they came to be utilized for building burial chambers in earth-mounded tombs. Stones were first used in elite architecture as pillar footings or for drainage. At Qishan, pebble-paved areas around the foundation platforms served to catch and drain off water. In the Early Zhou period, pillars were often footed on cobble pavements to provide a firm foundation; this practice was later augmented by the provision of a single large foundation stone as a pillar base.

The discovery of tamped-earth platforms, tiles, or bricks at a site is thus irrefutable evidence of elite presence, whether the structures in question were residences, temples, state halls or tombs. The monumentality of much of the protohistoric architecture from the Zhou period onwards in East Asia is also indicated archaeologically by auxiliary components such as stone footings and pavements.

Cities versus capitals

The above sites possess characteristics that define them as urban: they display functional differentiation in their structure and layout, and they were densely occupied by a mixture of elite and commoners – the latter serving the former. Such concentrations of craft workshops around elite residences have long been interpreted by anthropological archaeologists as evidence of political centralization; and Chinese archaeologists have gone so far as to equate some of the archaeological sites which have Shang remains with the historically named 'capitals' of the Shang state.[29] It is difficult, however, to assign 'capital' status to an urban site in the absence of unambiguous documentary evidence, and identifying the extent of the 'polity' using material culture alone is one of the most challenging exercises in protohistoric archaeology (Chapter 9).

Membership in the Shang cultural sphere is assumed to denote the sharing of ritual practices, and it is often assumed that all members belonged to the same political unit. However, it can be argued from documentary sources that the Shang state was far more restricted in extent than the reach of the Shang bronze culture. By analogy with historically known stratified societies and incipient states, it is likely that regional groupings participating in the elite Shang culture shifted in their political loyalties or affiliations through time. Any of the bronze *cultures*, including the Shang, must not be confused with *polities* themselves. More often than not in human societies, cultural boundaries cross-cut political boundaries, so a one-to-one correlation between polity and culture cannot be assumed.

CHAPTER 9

Early Mainland States
1300–220 BC

Political development

The Shang elite are commonly described as the rulers of the first East Asian state. Knowledge of the Shang-period political situation is gleaned from the inscriptions on the oracle bones. Such inscribed oracle bones have so far been recovered from only two locations: the Late Shang site at Anyang and the contemporaneous predynastic Zhou 'capital' at Qishan. The identification of protohistoric oracle bones in early 20th-century medicinal shops and the tracing of their source to Anyang is one of the most exciting and important archaeological detective stories of modern times.[1] Their discovery led to the excavation of the Yinxu site at Anyang (Chapter 8), with its oracle bone archives. The scapulae and plastrons had been carefully scraped down on the back side, and oval cavities about 1 cm long were hollowed out in rows; a heated metal rod was inserted into the cavities to produce cracks on the front surface. The cracks were then read by a diviner in answer to 'charges' put to him by the Shang king: was it auspicious to go hunting? Would the harvest be good? In contrast to Neolithic divination bones, the successful oracle bones were inscribed with the charges and then stored in an archive.

Box 1c

Some of the Shang inscriptions concern hunting or military campaigns and receipt of tribute; these can be looked upon as rudimentary administrative records and histories – material evidence of state organization. It is important to emphasize that almost all the information on Shang as a state derives from such inscriptions; other archaeological remains from the Shang period are of neither the quantity nor quality to reveal much about political organization at the time. And although other named groups mentioned in the inscriptional material are increasingly referred to as 'states' contemporaneous with the Shang state, they are difficult to identify archaeologically and lack detailed textual description. At the moment, therefore, Shang is still treated as the first East Asian state, though it did not exist in a vacuum and is now thought to have been surrounded by other, subsidiary states.

The Shang state
Since few Shang occupation sites other than at Zhengzhou and Anyang have been excavated in any detail, it is difficult to deduce the territorial organization or overall pattern of settlements from archaeology alone. Discussion of Shang

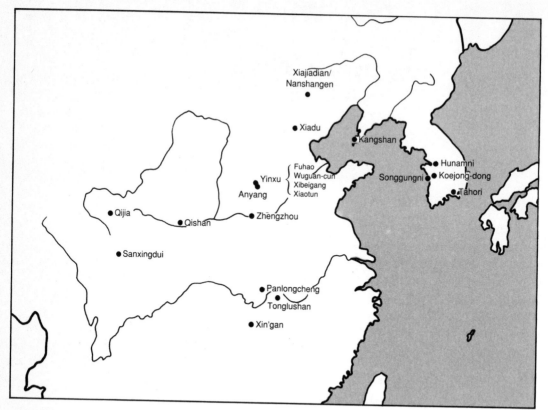

59 *Protohistoric sites mentioned in Chapters 8, 9 and 10.*

state organization is usually textually based and heavily biased towards an Anyang perspective. It might be noted here, however, that the Shang never referred to themselves or any other group as a 'state'; this term is a modern one, applied retrospectively.

The areal extent of the Shang 'state' was much more circumscribed than was the Shang culture sphere. Oracle bone inscriptions provide names of Shang 'enemy' and 'friendly' groups which have been used to reconstruct the approximate territorial limits of the Shang state.[2] These were not fixed boundaries, however; political allegiances with or against the Shang could change through time,[3] and many of the court diviners were members of some of the 'enemy' groups,[4] indicating interactive relations despite apparent hostilities. Moreover, the existence of Shang sites in far distant areas, such as Panlongcheng and Xin'gan in the south, has led some historians to include these in the Shang state (as colonies or outliers) rather than just members of the Shang cultural sphere.

The inscriptions also mention the division of Late Shang territory into an inner 'capital' and an outer 'domain'.[5] The capital apparently extended far enough beyond the Anyang remains for three statelets to be carved out of it in the succeeding Zhou period.[6] This textual concept of the 'capital' has been

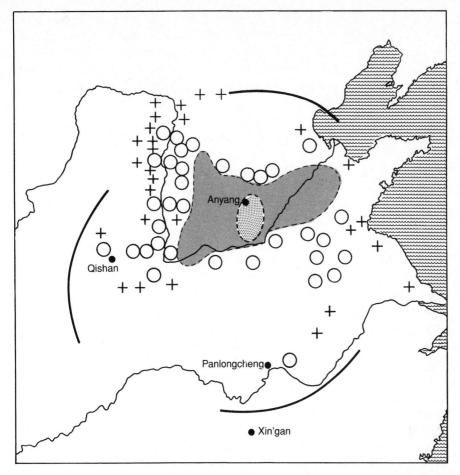

60 *Shang state territory and surrounding lords. Between the nuclear Shang area (dotted) and the territories of the hostile (+) and friendly (o) lords associated with Shang is a natural buffer zone (tint) consisting of the Taihang mountains, the Huanghe Corridor and the Yellow River flood zone. Does the term 'outer domain' apply to this area or to the territories of the 'friendly lords'? Was the Shang state administrative structure confined to the 'inner capital', or did it extend to the outer domain? How are we to understand the Shang culture remains at Panlongcheng and Xin'gan vis-à-vis the early state? As we know from the Zhou at their predynastic capital of Qishan, those who shared the Shang bronze traditions were not always allied with the Shang kings.*

equated with the heavy distribution of Shang archaeological remains southward from Anyang over a distance of 165 km.[7] Thus the Yinxu site at Anyang represents only a tiny fraction of the active sites in the core area of Late Shang.

The inscriptions mention two units basic to Shang socio-political organization: town and kinship group (commonly referred to as 'lineage' or 'clan').[8] The towns are assumed to be walled, and Panlongcheng – one of the rare excavated Shang settlements[9] – is given as an example. It is tempting to equate this walled site with the 'lord' assigned to this area on textual grounds, although the former

Box 1b

belongs to the Erligang phase and the latter to the Anyang phase. Why more Shang towns are not known archaeologically is an enigma, given that at least a thousand town names have been identified in the inscriptions.[10] Any particular town is understood to have included people from more than one kinship group; and some of the towns were assigned to court officials, princes and royal consorts, becoming their power strongholds and perhaps providing for their economic well-being. Only one of the ruling clan's lineages supplied the 'kings'; this lineage was in turn divided into two groups, with kingship probably alternating between the two.[11]

Although the Shang 'kings' 'lay at the core of a vast kinship organization, based on actual and legendary blood relations and coupled with the state structure',[12] it is not at all clear how the various 'lords' named in the historical documents were integrated into this organization. Two possibilities, both of which probably occurred in greater or lesser degrees, present themselves: 1) the centripetal attraction of outlying elites to the Shang caused them to submit to the king and receive a fictive kin bond that was reinforced through emulation of Shang ritual practices; and 2) the centrifugal fissioning of the royal clan and the establishment of members in outlying districts widened the Shang network through space. Whatever the case, the lords were directly 'enfeoffed' by the Shang king, owing 'services and grains' in return.[13] This implies a highly personalized and semi-autonomous relationship between centre and subcentre, an impression sharpened by the fact that the lords of neighbouring towns could engage in armed conflict with each other.

fig. 60   The Shang state can thus be interpreted as entailing considerable organizational differences between the inner capital and outer domain, with the former centrally controlled through hierarchically organized court officials and princes but the latter ruled through fealties on a semi-autonomous basis. It remains to be explained how these historical terms 'inner capital' and 'outer domain' relate to the distribution of archaeological materials and regional lords. At the least, Shang 'state' administration should be understood as limited to the 'capital' area only, since the outlying domain was under the rule of semi-autonomous lords.

Early Zhou states

The Zhou are acknowledged to have been a different ethnic group from the Shang, occupying the Wei River valley to the west of the Huanghe Corridor. They did, however, share the bronze material culture of the Shang and interacted with them on an equal if sometimes hostile basis. Describing the Zhou conquest of the Shang in 1027 BC, historical texts mention the destruction and/or subjugation of 750 'states' associated with Shang.[14] These 'states' must have been quickly absorbed into larger entities (or the number exaggerated by Zhou historians), since only between twenty and seventy-one names of Early Zhou states are known subsequently,[15] one of which was Royal Zhou.

The Early Zhou period is often characterized as one of increasing 'bureaucratization' within Royal Zhou, entailing the rise of ministerial families,

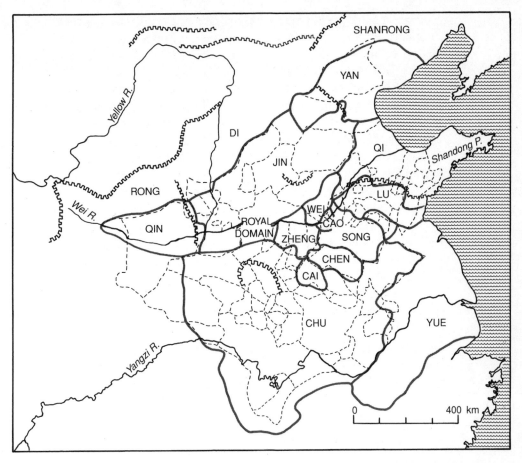

61 *Early and Middle Zhou states and Late Zhou defensive walls. The multitude of small states (dotted outlines) that paid homage to the Royal Zhou in the Early Zhou period were soon consolidated into a few large states (solid outlines) in Middle Zhou. The state of Lu, just south of the Shandong peninsula, was the home of Confucius (see Box 2). In the Late Zhou period, long walls were built as buffers between the states; still standing today are the Wei wall in Shaanxi built of sun-dried brick, the Qi wall of stone or pounded earth in different locales in Shandong, the Chu wall in Henan, the Zhongshan wall between Hebei and Shanxi, the Yan wall in Hebei (334–311 BC), and the Zhao wall in Henan (333–307 BC).*

but of 'feudal relations' between it and its satellite states,[16] very much resembling the organization of the Shang state but on a much larger scale. The rulers of these satellite states were enfeoffed, hierarchically ordered, aristocratic lineages, which raised armies and conducted sacrifices in their own ancestral temples.[17] If the rulers were related by blood to the Zhou kings, their states were known as a state of Zhou surname; if they were not, their states fell into the category of non-Zhou states. The relative uselessness of this classification, however, is exemplified by the northern state of Yan.

Yan is said to have been founded by a branch of Royal Zhou and is thus considered a 'true' Zhou state rather than a non-Zhou state such as the southern states of Wu or Chu. Nevertheless, the material culture of the local populace derived from the preceding Xiajiadian cultures (Chapter 10), and it has been argued that Yan was so isolated from the centre of Zhou politics that it developed its own regional culture and political interests.[18] If anything, Yan was a true 'melting pot', a description which becomes important in understanding the nature of its influence to the northeast in the Late Zhou period.

The Zhou concept of 'state', which continued through the early historic period, focused on the walled city, or *guo*. This term applied both to the urban conurbation and to the polity of which it formed the centre. The walled site as capital was accorded an important place in Zhou political ideology as the proper location for aristocratic residence. The ideal layout of the Zhou city, exemplified by the Royal Zhou capital, was 'a square with sides of 9 li [3744 m],[19] each side having 3 gateways. Within the capital there were 9 meridional and 9 latitudinal avenues, each of the former being 9 chariot-tracks in width.'[20] When new states were established, or elites enfeoffed, a new walled town was built and its ruler was granted by the Zhou king a clan name, a local supporting population, a name for the polity, and all the 'ritual paraphernalia and regalia befitting his new political status and that of his town'.[21] This kind of investiture was also conducted within polities for local ministers. For example, an inscription on a bronze vessel from an Early Zhou tomb in Yan reads 'Marquis Yen [Yan] bestows on Fu ceremonial caps, robes, servants, shells. ...'[22] Excavations of these new towns show that they were built over Neolithic remains without a preceding Shang conurbation, indicating the creation of a fresh elite settlement pattern. Nevertheless, archaeological remains of Early Zhou walled sites are as rare as those of the Shang.

Zhou warfare and sacrifice

The Middle Zhou witnessed a consolidation of states into fewer and larger units than in the Early Zhou, and the centrality of the Royal Zhou, who had conquered Shang, declined as power shifted outwards from the Zhou king to his feudal lords and then to the ministerial lineages.[23] Several states, particularly Qi and Jin,[24] became extremely powerful in their own right, forming hegemonies with their lesser neighbours. A major source of power for the individual states, and indeed for individual lineages, was warfare in the service of their ancestors. A recent analysis has made clear the integral relationships between Zhou warfare, hunting and sacrifice:

> These activities, symbolically linked through the ceremonial exchange and consumption of meat, reached their common culmination in the offering up of living beings at the altars. Thus the noble was above all a warrior and sacrificer, a man who took life in order to feed the spirits who gave him power.[25]

The Early Zhou bronzes used in such ceremonies were often inscribed with passages detailing for and by whom the sacrifice was given and in commemoration of what event. Sacrificial vessels were the tangible remnants of this practice of ancestor worship, but the intangible legacy was Confucianism.

Box 2

20 *In testimony to the emerging elites' command over life and labour, a monumental shaft tomb of the Mainland Shang at Wuguan-cun, near Anyang, yields its sacrificial victims to the excavators' trowel. The bodies of the funeral victims were laid on the ledges above the coffin chamber.*

21–24 *Shang jades are mostly flat with sometimes recognizable (top) but often alien forms (above and below); three-dimensional sculptures are less common (right).*

Intricate designs played out on the stone and bone artifacts of the Shang period

25, 26 The fine surface carving on a bone jug (right) resembles Late Shang bronze decoration, even to the extent of foreground and background differentiation. Tigers were popular motifs, one forming the handle base of the jug and another decorating the stone chime (above), which shows wear marks at the hole for its suspension.

27–29 *A Shang tripod (left) and an Early Zhou square container (right), showing the clear distinction between background and foreground casting of the decoration. In the Zhou period, such vessels were used for food offerings on ancestral altars (below), and this function is extrapolated back in time for Shang bronzes.*

The Central Plain bronze vessel tradition, challenged by the unique products of regional centres of bronze manufacture on the protohistoric Mainland

30, 31 *Unusual human figure representations (right) marked the bronze industry of the Sichuan Basin in the southwest (right), while bronze drums (below) similar to those of the Dongson culture of Southeast Asia characterized the Dian culture further to the southwest during the Han period.*

Animal art of northern steppe and southwestern montane regions of the China Mainland in the 1st millennium BC

32, 33 *Bronze ornaments from the Ordos Desert, north China, depicting (above) men wrestling in a forest between two horses, and (left) a stag.*

34 *(below) A bronze ornament, possibly a harness mount, with wolves attacking a deer. From Yunnan province, ht 13.5 cm.*

Later Zhou bronzes illustrating the proliferation of forms and functions in the metal's employment beyond ritual vessels used in ancestral rites

35-37 *Could the 'teapot' shape of Late Zhou (above left) have influenced Jomon ceramics (cf. plate 9), or vice versa? Human representation was a latecomer to the central bronze tradition (above, cast bronze wrestlers or acrobats), and the mirror for reflecting the human visage (left), adopted from the northern steppe cultures, secured a major place in the bronze repertoire at this time.*

Tools of violence in the Mainland's evolving polities

38–41 *The executioner's axe and the spearhead (above) played important roles in the elite politics of Shang. The spearhead has a jade blade and inlaid bronze handle. Sword (right) and dagger-axe (below) were the weapons of choice for Zhou's developing armies.*

Of horses and chariots

Warfare was mostly conducted by chariot. This vehicle probably originated in the southwestern steppe region of Eurasia, diffusing from there into both Mesopotamia and the north China Mainland.[26] The earliest excavated examples in East Asia occur at Anyang (c. 1300 BC). From Shang times onwards, the role of the chariot changed dramatically.[27] It is mentioned as being used for the hunt in Shang oracle bones, and the burial of splendidly fitted-out chariots, complete with horses in harness, in pits at the mouths of the shaft tombs at Anyang suggests that they also functioned as royal prestige items. Chariots continued to be an important component in Zhou-period burials. When used in battle during the Late Shang and Early Zhou periods, they seem to have functioned as mobile command stations and are cited as possibly having been the crucial factor in the Zhou conquest of the Shang.[28]

By the Middle Zhou period, the number of chariots fielded in warfare became the major means of competition among the Zhou states. Chariot warfare, however, had a short lifespan: infantry armies, increasingly employed after the mid-6th century BC, took over the role of the aristocratic warrior, and the adoption of mounted cavalry in the 5th century BC gave superior mobility to charging forces. The chariot reverted to being an aristocratic accoutrement and was eventually transformed into a sumptuous two-wheeled carriage for the nobility (*fig. 68*).

The creation of infantry armies constituted a major advance in state organization during the Late Zhou period. Such armies were an innovation that

62 (right) Characters for 'chariot' occurring in the oracle bone inscriptions. All drawn as seen from above, each shows differing amounts of detail: yokes, axles and wheels, and carriage.

63 An Early Zhou chariot burial with horses in place, and an idealized reconstruction.

plates 40, 41

undercut the status and authority of the old aristocracy, which had defined itself in terms of its exclusive prerogative to wage war in service of the state.[29] Moreover, their formation was integrally related to the development of taxation methods and land grants, since all of these features required the state's direct control over the peasantry.[30] One stimulus for the shift in the 5th century BC from reliance on charioteers to mass infantry was the need to combat increasingly hostile groups on the northern frontiers who fought entirely on foot – until the advent of the Hu tribespeople and the adoption of mounted warfare.[31]

The formation of the Hu ethnic group in the Mongolian Plateau, which later split into three peoples (including the infamous Xiongnu), seems to have been predicated on horseback riding for long-distance raiding. The technique of riding horses was no doubt known to the Shang and Zhou elite, having been received from western Eurasia in association with chariotry. However, riding was not the favoured form of transportation in the core areas; it seems rather to have developed in concert with nomadic pastoralism in the steppe areas (Chapter 10). Thus the adoption of mounted warfare from the late 5th century BC by Zhou armies represents a self-protective response to mounted incursions by the Hu, which became more prevalent throughout the Late Zhou period.

Defensive architecture

In contrast to the dearth of known settlements for the Early Zhou period, remains of walled cities abound in the mid-1st millennium BC, when a drastic reorganization of facilities in and around the typical walled compound appears to have taken place. Differing from the Shang model site as manifested at both Zhengzhou and Panlongshan, where most craft facilities are scattered around the outside of the walled compound, the Late Zhou walled site is self-contained. It incorporates within its walls the community's workshops and markets as well as administrative and elite residential buildings. The tendency towards exhaustive enclosure increased towards the end of the Zhou period, when hostilities among the 'warring states' and with their tribal neighbours probably demanded such enclosure on defensive grounds. This recalls the settlement layout of the violence-ridden Longshan society during the process of social stratification.

fig. 64

Mainland polities thus had long experience in building walls to embrace their settlements, and such technology was extended to long-wall construction as early as the 7th century BC.[32] Many of these were of tamped–earth construction, but other local materials were often employed: in desert areas, layers of tamarisk branches and reeds were used to strengthen walls made of sandy soil.[33] Wall-building was a response to increasing internecine warfare among the Zhou states in the Middle Zhou period, and remains of walls separating those competing states still exist in central China today. But most important were the walls built by the northern and western states against the steppe nomads, whose raids on settled agricultural society began in earnest in the 4th century BC and became a cyclical menace to the Chinese dynasties

fig. 61

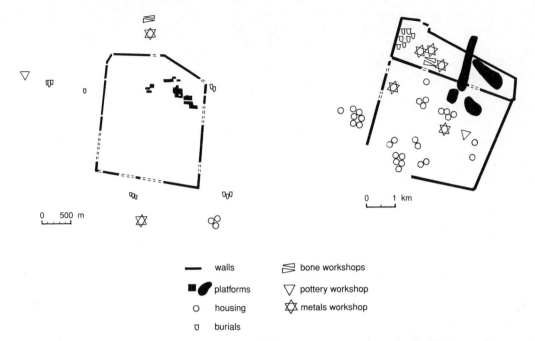

walls   bone workshops

platforms   pottery workshop

○ housing   metals workshop

burials

64 Changing patterns of urban organization. The Middle Shang capital at Zhengzhou (left) consisted of a walled compound enclosing tamped-earth foundations for elite buildings; outside the wall were scattered various industrial workshops, commoner housing and burials. At the Late Zhou site of Xiadu (right), capital of the state of Yan, almost all facilities lay within the walls – which enclosed more than twice the area of Zhengzhou (see fig. 56).

throughout subsequent history.[34] Yan and Zhao built their northern walls, now located in the southern Mongolian Plateau, between 311 and 279 BC. The western ones built by Qin and Wei effectively walled out the Ordos region, which was later incorporated into Qin territory by a portion of the 'Great Wall' between 221 and 206 BC.

Commercial endeavours

The Zhou states competed not only militarily but also economically. Different coinages of the various states are the visible remains of the latter, making early Chinese numismatics a rich field of study. The initiation and expansion of iron production also provided a new basis for economic competition, which resulted in the formation of a *nouveau riche* among the Late Zhou aristocracy. Although Confucian mores distained mercantilism, the development of a true marketing system and the rise of a merchant class provided the necessary infrastructure for imperial consolidation at the end of the Zhou period.

Markets and coinage
During the Shang period, cowrie shells were used in royal gifting practices, but since these are often deposited in hoards in tombs – effectively taking them out

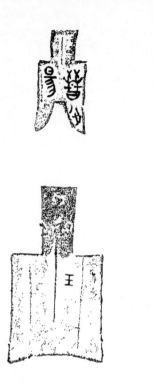

*65 Zhou-period currencies.
Production of metal coinage began in
the Middle Zhou period. Coins shaped
like spades (left) and knives (lower
right) are assumed to have developed
from their utilitarian analogues.
Round coins with round holes (upper
right) were also known in Late Zhou.*

of circulation – they probably did not function in a true market economy. Not
until the Middle Zhou period did markets flourish. From that time on, each of
the Zhou states minted its own coins, with spade- and knife-shaped coins and
stamped metal plates being the most distinctive. Spade-shaped coins were in
use in the north-central Zhou states, while the knife-shaped coins were found
in the eastern Shandong peninsula region. These two types of coin perhaps
developed from the use of actual iron spades and knives in economic
transactions. After 500 BC the practice of using knife money spread into the
north-central Mainland; this expansion has been attributed to the establishment of a monopoly over coastal fishing and salt-making by the state of Qi on
the Shandong peninsula, which then traded with the interior states.[35] In the
Late Zhou period, several eastern states were manufacturing knife-shaped
coins in distinct styles.

Stamped-plate coin manufacture was carried out particularly in the realm of
the southern state of Chu. The predominant metal used was gold, but stamped
silver, copper and lead plates are also known. Some gold plates hold two, six,
fourteen or sixteen individual stamps, and it is not clear whether these are
varying denominations or whether the plates were meant to be broken apart for
use in fragments of one stamp each. The stamping was in the nature of a seal
application to soft metal and clearly derived from the manufacturing
plate 60   techniques of the stamped pottery of the region.

Not only are the shapes and styles of coins useful in determining
chronological sequences, but coins often bear inscriptions that give their locus

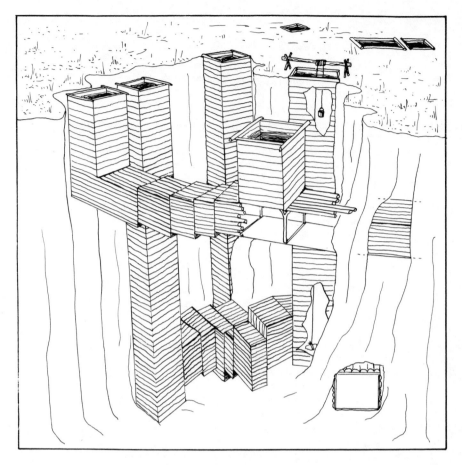

66 The Tonglushan copper mine. The scale of the Zhou-period bronze industry is well illustrated by the copper mine shafts at Tonglushan, discovered and excavated in 1973–4.

of manufacture or their value. Numismatic research on these coins, however, is still in the beginning stage of mapping out their distributions chronologically and spatially. Nevertheless, it should be noted that they are very important indicators of the economic transformation in which exchanges of goods among elites in prestige systems were no longer the dominant economic form, having been supplanted by widespread market transactions.

Manufacture of iron

The major technological advance during the Zhou period was the development of iron-working. The first use of iron on the China Mainland was the rare hammering of meteoritic iron into service as parts of Shang and Early Zhou bronze implements.[36] Despite this knowledge of meteoritic iron and the fact that iron was a common inclusion in copper ore, the mining of iron ore for its own sake and the production of iron artifacts did not occur until the Middle Zhou period.

BOX 9
Chinese Iron Technology

The carbon content of iron is significant in two ways: carbon added to the furnace lowers the melting point of the ore, but the carbon is also absorbed into the smelted iron, making the metal brittle. Because of its brittleness, such molten high-carbon iron must be cast in moulds rather than forged into shape (unless the carbon is removed or 'decarburized' by other means). If iron ore is smelted at relatively low temperatures without added carbon, a spongy mass (a 'bloom') rather than molten iron is obtained. The bloom, however, is not brittle and can be hammered, or wrought, into shape. Thus, the metallurgical terms 'cast iron' and 'wrought iron' refer to their carbon content (high and low, respectively), which determines the method of forming articles from them.

Bloomery iron was the only kind produced in the West until the 13th century AD, when the adoption of the blast furnace made possible the high temperatures needed to produce molten 'cast' iron. Meanwhile on the China Mainland, both wrought iron (that is, low-carbon iron) and cast iron (high-carbon iron) were present from 500 BC onwards. Moreover, steel (medium-carbon iron) was common after 300 BC. The earliest blast furnaces, such as the one shown here, have been dated to the 1st century BC and so were used at least 1200 years before they were known in the West. Although many Chinese archaeologists believe that only the bloomery furnace was used in the pre-Han period, the estimated output of 'several hundred tons of iron per year' argues instead for the early existence of the blast furnace (illustrated below).

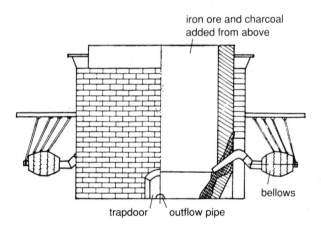

iron ore and charcoal added from above

bellows

trapdoor   outflow pipe

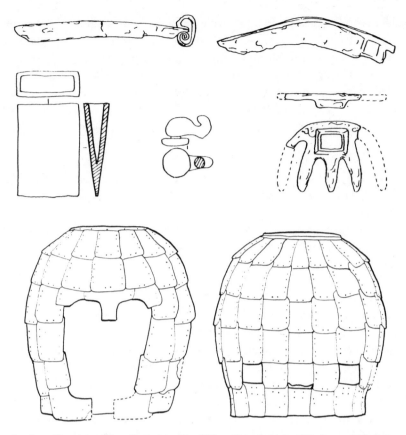

67 *Late Zhou iron objects from the state of Yan. Excavations at Xiadu, capital of Yan, have yielded iron knives, belt buckles, socketed axes, forked hoes, and a unique iron-plate helmet. Yan appears to have been one of the major iron producers of its time.*

Current estimates for the onset of iron-smelting fall between the 7th and 5th centuries BC, and a recent review of the evidence argues cogently for 500 BC as the date by which iron artifacts are clearly in existence.[37] The earliest are a lump of iron and an iron rod excavated from two elite graves in the territory of Wu, a southern 'state on the periphery of the area of Chinese culture'.[38] Wu is proposed as the initiator of regular iron-smelting because it was one of the areas in which bronze was used extensively to make agricultural tools; this resulted in the production of a bronze with a high iron content (one excavated bronze ingot contained 34 per cent iron), perhaps in order to extend the bronze supply to meet the demand for goods.[39] These conditions are thought to have stimulated the development of iron production separate from bronze production perhaps as a cheap bronze substitute – something that would never have happened in the ritual setting of bronze among the northern states.

As with Mainland bronze, the technology employed from the very beginning of iron-smelting appears to have been unique within its time period. However, due to the differences in lay and specialist terminology employed, there is considerable confusion as to just what these techniques were. Iron is often categorized by the lay person as 'wrought' or 'cast' when speaking about how the metal was shaped into implements. In ferrous metallurgy, however, these terms are more appropriately applied to the smelting process and have very different meanings in that context, being indicative of the amount of carbon in the iron. Zhou-period iron technology is outstanding in that high-carbon 'cast' iron was produced from the inception of iron use, with steel appearing almost as early.

Box 9

In its organizational aspects, the integration of iron production into Late Zhou society very much resembles the place of bronze production in Shang society. However, in contrast to bronze production, which was conducted by and for the elites, the establishment of the iron industry provided a competing basis for wealth which may have led to the rise of a new elite.[40] Both industries were highly centralized and geared to copious production in their respective periods. Iron foundries were apparently located on large-scale 'iron plantations' positioned in remote areas to take advantage of the forest resources necessary to produce the quantity of charcoal needed.[41] Mass production and distribution of iron articles virtually guaranteed the transformation of the agricultural, economic, and military spheres in the Late Zhou states.

Though considered the weakest of the seven major Late Zhou states,[42] Yan produced a greater abundance of iron artifacts than Qin, the strongest state, and iron foundries have been excavated at several Yan sites.[43] The earliest-known iron armour is also from Yan, and this state may have played a major role in initiating the Korean Iron Age around 400 BC – only a century after iron production became a viable industry on the Mainland itself.

fig. 67

CHAPTER 10

The Northern Frontier
3000–300 BC

In the Late Zhou period (475–221 BC), mounted warriors burst upon the stage of Chinese history, harrassing the northern Zhou states to the extent that they each erected long defensive walls along their northern borders. Who were these mounted warriors? The answer to this question lies in a complex interaction of several factors: the development of pastoralism; the invention of transport systems superseding human bipedalism; and the distinctions between simple pastoralists, mounted hunters, and mounted nomads. The changing ecology through time in the modern steppe region is particularly important for tracing the development of nomadism.

In cultural terms, the emerging herding societies of the early 1st millennium BC across the northern frontier shared a distinctive bronze repertoire which derived from the Eurasian steppe bronze tradition and incorporated many animal motifs (Chapter 8). The Upper Xiajiadian culture, located in the area of the former Hongshan culture of the Bohai Corridor region, was one manifestation of this new Northern Bronze Complex. Nomadism appears to have developed about this time and is associated with a particular 'Animal Art' style of bronzes. Much has been written about the supposed Scythian affinities of this art,[1] suggesting continuing cultural contact and exchange across the Eurasian steppes.

plates 32, 33

In the Late Zhou period, soon after the onset of iron manufacturing in the central Mainland, iron began to appear across the north in the form of utilitarian horse trappings such as bits and stirrups – even while more decorative items were still made of bronze or, more elaborately, of gilt bronze after 300 BC. The state of Yan expanded into the lower Manchurian Basin, creating a cultural synthesis from the various elements of nomadic, agricultural and state-level societies.

During the 1st millennium BC, the Korean Peninsula benefited successively from these bronze and iron cultures. Aspects of the non-nomadic Upper Xiajiadian tradition reached down into the Korean Peninsula, giving rise to the Korean Bronze Age from about 700 BC, and Yan is thought to have been instrumental in initiating the Korean Iron Age from 400 BC, through the export of iron objects from its own production centres.

Although there was considerable continuity in the bronze and iron repertoires of the societies across this region, their economic bases differed radically – from nomadic pastoralism to cereal agriculture. The occurrence, therefore, of metal objects bearing steppe Animal Art in non-steppe locations, for example, cannot be used as evidence of nomadic pastoralists in alternative environments. These objects carried with them their own prestige value and were highly desirable to emerging local elites operating in their own economic systems.

Nomadic solutions

Steppe adaptations

The Eurasian steppe, like the North American prairie and the African savannah, is a series of broad, arid stretches of grassland suitable for the grazing of large ungulates. At its eastern end, the steppe descends through the Mongolian Plateau to meet the loess highlands of the China Mainland. As was described earlier, Palaeolithic hunters along the plateau's southern edge stalked herds of wild horses, donkeys, bison and gazelle;[2] and in historic times, the Mongolian steppe has been home to nomadic pastoralists herding flocks of sheep and horses.

In the early Holocene, the Mongolian Plateau was environmentally much richer than either today or in Palaeolithic times, and was able to support a greater variety of livelihoods than just large-game hunting or herding. The plateau edges were heavily forested during the Climatic Optimum, and textured pottery found there belonged to microlithic postglacial hunters and fishers, such as those who occupied the Fuhegoumen site. The central plateau, on the other hand, supported agriculture – assumed from the presence of Yangshao and Greater Longshan-type potteries. The important question here is when and how nomadic pastoralism became the dominant subsistence patterns along the northern Mainland border.

fig. 43

Increasing aridity has long been invoked as the reason for this development.[3] Using climatic change to explain human behaviour, however, is always risky: the deterministic nature of environmental explanations denies the possibility of human creative response to the limitations imposed by climate. With a given level of technology, it is true that only certain solutions are possible within given climates; but humankind has often found the ability to change its technology to conquer those environmental limitations. The appearance of *pastoralism* around the edges of the Mongolian Plateau might have been just such a response to the establishment of steppe environments caused by the decrease in glacial melt watering the area in the 3rd millennium BC. But environmental factors do not account for *nomadism* as a strategy for exploiting the great steppe expanse.

It has been argued that the crucial factor in the development of nomadic pastoralism was the invention of *transportation* – carts and horses that could carry groups and their possessions in the constant searching out of sufficient pasturage for large herds.[4] Simple pastoralism can be integrated with settled village life if forage can be provided from harvest by-products or by transhumance – the seasonal movement of flocks and herds to green pastures.

68 Rock-engravings of vehicles in modern Mongolia. Contrasting representations of the four-horse chariot (left), presumed to be Early or Middle Zhou in date, and the two-wheeled carriage (right) of a later age.

Nomadic pastoralism, on the other hand, requires a continuously shifting pattern of settlement with domestic animals serving as draught or pack animals and as mounts. This secondary use of domestic animals for their labour, milk and wool – beyond their provision of meat, horn, bone, tusks and teeth for food and tools – constituted the 'secondary products revolution' after the first revolution of domestication itself.[5]

The secondary products revolution occurred not in the Mongolian Plateau but far to the west, in Central Europe and the Near East. Most important was the invention of wheeled transport, which allowed full exploitation of the steppe. Rock engravings of animal-drawn vehicles occur across the steppes, and our earliest excavated examples of wheeled vehicles are the chariots at Anyang, their easternmost destination.

Herding economies

Mainland agricultural societies were never completely devoid of domestic animals: as mentioned above, dogs, pigs, chickens, and water buffalo were integrated into the earliest northern and southern farming economies. In the Late Neolithic cultures of the 3rd millennium BC, these animals were joined by substantial numbers of cattle, probably as native domesticates, and sheep/goats were introduced from the west.[6] The latter may have arrived through the Gansu Corridor together with wheat from the Middle East.

As yet, the degree of reliance placed on animal resources in the Mainland Longshan cultures of the Late Neolithic is not known; but at least on the southern Mongolian Plateau, Neolithic sites yield the bones of domestic as well as wild animals: dogs, pigs, bovines, and sheep/goat,[7] alongside various kinds of deer, rabbit and fish. Horse bones have been recovered from at least two Neolithic sites, but it is not clear whether they were domesticates.[8] Among the faunal remains, the bones of dogs and pigs are abundant. They have turned up in houses and hearths, suggesting not only a settled existence but also a possible affinity with the millet agricultural regimes of the northern Mainland.

This picture is modified in the Shang period with the development of mixed

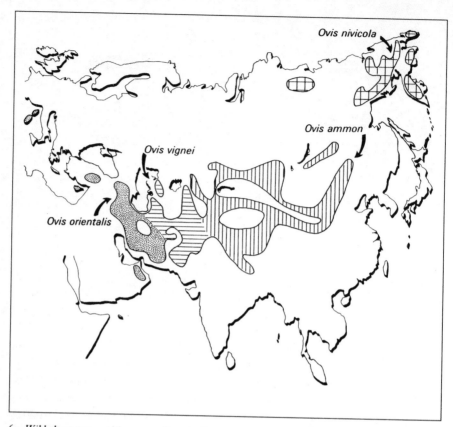

69 *Wild sheep communities across Eurasia. Domestic sheep, descended from the Mouflon breed (O.* orientalis*) of present-day Iran, were apparently introduced into Mainland China in the 2nd millennium BC. With the expanding means for exploiting the steppe regions during the Zhou period, sheep became one of the major herd animals of the Mongolian Plateau.*

economies with a heavy reliance on herding. Sites of the Lower Xiajiadian culture on the southeastern Mongolian Plateau yield the same range of domestic animals as in the Neolithic, but bovines and sheep/goats are increasingly abundant. These faunal remains were excavated from house, hearth and burial sites, indicating the continuation of a relatively settled existence. Caches of bovine scapulae, and sacrificed dogs and pigs are also *fig. 59* characteristic of Lower Xiajiadian culture sites; in conjunction with the occurrence of Shang-style bronzes, these materials indicate that Lower Xiajiadian was related more closely to Mainland agricultural regimes than to the northwestern, incipient pastoralists.

At Qijia culture sites (2500–1500 BC), located in the northwest near the base of the Gansu Corridor, a similarly large quantity of animal bones has been recovered: dogs, pigs, cattle, and sheep/goat but with the addition of domestic horses. Interestingly, all but the dog bones also occurred as divination bones, and burials of sacrificed animals were found.[9] Both house remains and cemetery burials occur at Qijia sites, indicating that the herding of animals was carried out within the constraints of a settled society. By the end of the 2nd millennium BC, the Shang oracle bone inscriptions name the inhabitants of this region as the Qiang people, who were said to be especially familiar with horses and whose name is written partly with the Chinese character for 'sheep'. Moreover, goat horns have been recovered from sites in this area dating to about 1000 BC.[10]

By the end of the Shang period, therefore, the evidence suggests that the cultures across the northern frontier of the Mainland were heavily involved in animal husbandry but maintained cultural ties to the Mainland bronze traditions. Though certainly present by this time on the steppe, pastoralism had not yet encroached upon the northern edges of East Asia.

In the Early Zhou period, two innovations are apparent in Upper Xiajiadian culture sites: the presence of animal-style bronzes and the addition of the domestic horse to the faunal repertoire. The scope of sacrificed animals was widened to include the horse as well as sheep/goats. In further contrast to Lower Xiajiadian sites, which fail to yield any wild animal bones, hunted fauna are again part of the excavated assemblages. One incised bone plate illustrates two horse-drawn chariots, two deer and a hunter with bow and arrow; another decorated Upper Xiajiadian bronze item depicts a mounted horseman and running rabbit. The latter is the first evidence for horse-riding in East Asia, and it is significant that horses, both ridden and draught, were employed at this time for the hunt but not necessarily for warfare. That the Upper Xiajiadian

70 The horse and the hunt. Pictorial representations from steppe and capital attest to hunting from horseback and by chariot. The crudely incised bone plate (upper), excavated from a Middle Zhou-period stone cist burial at Nanshangen, contrasts with a sophisticated rendition on a bronze mirror found at the Late Zhou capital of Luoyang (lower).

peoples were, nevertheless, militarily oriented is evidenced by the bronze weapons and helmets interred in their stone cist burials.

An Early Zhou bronze vessel inscription dated to 979 BC states that the Zhou did battle with named ethnic groups from the Ordos region, from whom they captured 355 oxen, 38 sheep and 30 chariots.[11] From the head counts of animals, Chinese archaeologists believe that the Ordos groups were fully nomadic by that time. Significantly, however, the first evidence of horse-riding in warfare, superseding chariot use among these nomads, is not documented until 484 BC.[12]

Thus, current data from the southern Mongolian Plateau indicate that domestic livestock herding was common to settled cultures on the northern frontier throughout the Late Neolithic and Shang periods. During the latter, horses were known among the western Qijia and the Shang themselves, but not to the Lower Xiajiadian in the east even though it shared many aspects of the Shang bronze culture. This suggests that the southeastern Mongolian Plateau remained isolated from the northern steppe cultures until the Zhou period when the main cultural affiliation of the southeastern plateau shifted to the northern steppe rather than being with the Zhou states to the south.

Thus it was in the Early Zhou period that the 'steppe/sown' dichotomy appeared, resulting in friction between the agricultural and nomadic ways of life from the Han period onwards.[13] Nevertheless, this dichotomy may have been overemphasized by Chinese historians. Cultivation, though disdained by the mounted warrior ethic, appears to have been practised at various times and places on the steppe when environmental conditions permitted and social necessity demanded.[14] It may have been carried out by temporarily settled groups or by non-warrior segments of society. Data from modern Mongolia suggest tremendous variation in subsistence practices across the Plateau. The one constant factor is and probably also was reverence for the horse.

The techniques and customs of horse-riding were probably transmitted with chariotry, but at first riding was limited to transportation and hunting. Only belatedly did the horse come to be used as strategic equipment in mounted warfare. This development was roughly simultaneous with the advent of fully nomadic society and was accompanied by the development of specialized horse trappings. It is still unclear, however, what the exact relations were between the elements in the emergence of nomadic pastoralism. Did horses come to be herded for warfare purposes and secondarily enable nomadism, or did the necessary use of horses in long-distance grazing lead to herding horses themselves and encourage horsemanship?

Questions of ethnicity

Chinese archaeologists and historians, past and present, have always made a strict distinction between groups of ancient people thought to be ancestral to the 'true' Chinese (*huaxia* or Han people) and non-Chinese. In ancient texts, the latter are referred to as 'barbarians' because they did not exhibit the

Archaeological remains	Northern Bronze Complex	Upper Xiajiadian	Coastal dolmens
Locations	Ordos	southeastern Mongolian Plateau	Yellow Sea Basin
Ethnic groups	the Di	the Shan-Rong, Rong, and Hu	the Dongyi

71   Matching archaeological remains with historically known ethnic groups.

'civilized' standards of living defined by the literate, ritualized court societies. First mentioned of such peoples are the 'enemies' of the Late Shang state and the 'barbarians' of the eastern coastal regions,[15] suggesting considerable ethnic diversity and differential levels of political development across the Shang-period landscape. Curiously, there is no specific documentation of the identity of the bearers of Northern Bronze Complex bronzes and chariots to the Late Shang site of Anyang, but northern groups mentioned in Early and Middle Zhou-period documents and inscriptions are now being equated with particular archaeological cultures: the Di with the bronze culture of the Ordos region; the Rong, Shan-rong and Hu with the Upper Xiajiadian culture; the Dongyi with the circum-Yellow Basin occurrence of dolmens, etc. The opposite emphasis also occurs with the named group taking precedence over the archaeological culture – for example, Xiongnu archaeology of the major group of mounted nomads in the Qin and Han periods. These identifications are potential pitfalls of protohistoric archaeology, for it is not at all certain that an archaeological culture (in the sense defined by Gordon Childe)[16] was the exclusive product of a single ethnic group; several ethnic groups might have shared the same material culture and distinguished each other in non-material ways such as language.

The most widespread characteristics of northeastern frontier archaeology in the 1st millennium BC are stone cist burial and bronze dagger distributions across the Manchurian Basin into the Korean Peninsula. Not only do they

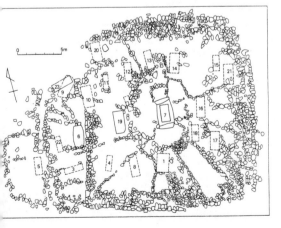 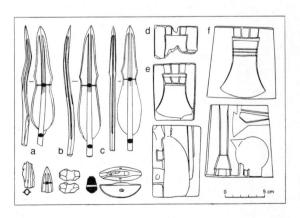

2 Northeastern cist burials and weaponry. Liaoning-type bronze daggers (a–c), stone moulds for casting axes d–f), and bronze horse trappings were recovered from this well-planned burial site spanning several centuries t Kangshan.

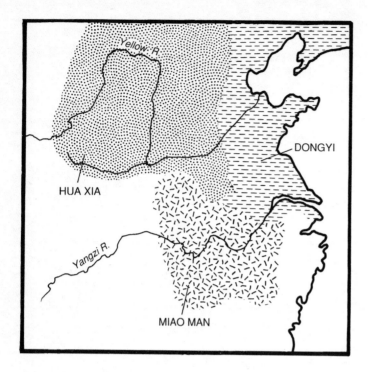

73 *Protohistoric ethnic groupings in the Central Plain region. This modern reconstruction places the Dongyi, who were perhaps related to the Bronze-Age population on the Korean Peninsula, in the coastal areas, with the Yellow River drainage occupied by the 'true Chinese' (Hua Xia). These distributions are strangely reminiscent of the split between the East Coast and Yangshao ceramic cultures of the Neolithic period on the China Mainland.*

transcend the boundaries of several archaeological cultures (including the Upper Xiajiadian), but also interpretations of these remains in terms of ethnic groups are problematic. Attempts at such interpretations illustrate the extreme sensitivity of modern nationalism to the need for locating the ethnic 'roots' of modern nations in the prehistoric past, as seen in the 1978 writings of a South Korean archaeologist:

> Among Chinese archaeologists the idea is strong that . . . the stone coffins . . . in the Liaodong area, belonged to the Donghu ethnic group. The term Donghu is an ambiguous label for an ethnic group; it is used to designate the people who lived to the east of the Xiongnu people. [However, the Liaodong area] was inhabited by the so-called Dongyi ('Eastern Barbarians' in the Chinese documents) or the Ye Maek and was the place of origin for people who were ethnically the same as Koreans. This seems to be proven by the distribution of the Liaoning bronze dagger, which is directly connected to the Bronze Culture of the Korean peninsula.[17]

The Peninsular Bronze Age

On the Korean Peninsula, the shift from the Chulmun period to the Bronze Age is first manifested in a change in settlement pattern, accompanied by the emergence of Mumun pottery, perhaps as early as 1500 BC,[18] and new cist-like burial facilities. In contrast to Chulmun villages, which are always located at the sea's edge or on riverbanks, Mumun pottery settlements occur almost exclusively in upland or inland areas – on hilltops, hillsides and terraces. The locational difference in settlement has been explained by some as reflecting a change in subsistence emphasis, with Mumun pottery users relying mainly on grain production and no evidence as yet of animal husbandry.[19] An ecological interdigitation is envisioned until the Chulmun population was peacefully absorbed into or converted to the Mumun way of life – an idea which will be examined further below.

Paradoxically, bronzes are almost non-existent in Mumun pottery sites until the 8th or 7th century BC.[20] Thus this early period from 1500 to 700 BC should perhaps be termed the Proto-Bronze Age, although most South Korean scholars give 1000 BC as a nominal start for the Korean Bronze Age *per se*. (North Korean scholars give it as 2000 BC.) It was during this early period that the infrastructure of the mature Bronze Age society was laid, such as can be seen at the Hunamni site.

Proto-Bronze Age Hunamni

The site of Hunamni spreads up the gentle slope of a hill, bordering directly on the left bank of the Southern Han River in the central Peninsula. Fourteen rectangular dwellings were excavated between 1972 and 1977 at 90–115 m altitude. Four of these have been radiocarbon dated to between 1570 and 270 BC, indicating occupation throughout the Bronze Age.[21] Houses No. 8 and 12 belonged to the Proto-Bronze Age as defined here, and their contents are representative of the simple ceramic and stone tool repertoires of that era: Mumun pottery; clay net weights; polished stone projectile points, disc maceheads, and spindle whorls; and irregularly ground stone axe/adzes. Two further types of stone object are of outstanding significance: polished stone sword imitations and reaping knives.

figs 59, 74

The polished stone swords from House No. 12 are of the three main varieties found on the Peninsula: tanged blades with blood-letting grooves running down both sides of the central ridge, and smooth-bladed swords equipped with flared hilts with or without a grooved grip. The hilted types were probably modelled on bronze swords of the Zhou period, one of which has been discovered on the Korean Peninsula.[22] Together with the polished stone projectile points and maceheads, these swords represent the development of a weaponry in the Proto-Bronze Age which may indicate that the relations between the Chulmun and Mumun pottery people were not as peaceful as had been envisioned. The initial ecological interdigitation documented for the two groups quickly dissolved in favour of a universal Mumun occupation. The fate of the Late Chulmun peoples is unknown and not yet modelled in theoretical terms as has been done for the hunter-gatherer/agriculturalist interface elsewhere in the world.[23] This same problem surfaces in trying to understand the relations between the Jomon and Yayoi peoples of the Japanese Islands a millennium later (Chapter 11).

It is questionable whether the upland locations occupied by the Mumun pottery people provided greater opportunities for farming than the flat alluvial

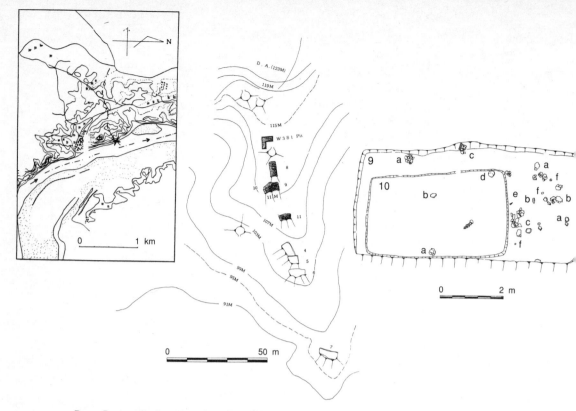

74 Proto-Bronze Age houses cut into the hillside site of Hunamni. X marks the excavated area along the river. Inside houses no. 9 and 10 were found coarse brown pottery (a), stone anvils (b), black pottery (c), fine brown pottery (d), a polished stone projectile point (e), and ceramic fish net sinkers (f).

and coastal plains of Chulmun occupation. The land within a 13 km radius of Hunamni contained only 15–30 per cent flat land, the remainder being hills with a slope of 2–15 per cent. That agriculture was practised by the Hunamni inhabitants is not in doubt, however. The stone reaping knife was accompanied by copious botanical evidence, recovered from House No.12 by flotation. The remains included barley, foxtail millet, sorghum and short-grained rice. The first three are dryland crops which were probably cultivated in hillside plots. The discovery of rice at this site, however, was a great surprise and has revolutionized the thinking about its introduction into the Korean Peninsula from the southern Mainland (Chapter 11).

Early Bronze Age Songgungni

The Peninsular Bronze Age *per se* is defined by the intrusion of the Liaoning

fig. 72a–c dagger from the Manchurian Basin.[24] This unusually shaped tanged dagger derives from the Upper Xiajiadian culture. Several individual examples are known on the Korean Peninsula, but only one so far has been found in association with other artifacts. This was excavated from a cist burial at the site

fig. 59 of Songgungni, where a 5th-century BC Bronze Age village occupied rolling countryside in the Kum River drainage of the central western Peninsula.[25] At least twenty-one round and rectangular pit-buildings, an open pottery kiln, one

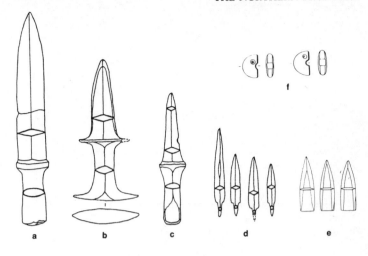

75 Polished stone articles of the Peninsular Bronze Age. Polished stone swords (a, b, c) might have been copied from Zhou-period iron swords of the China Mainland. Long thought to be ceremonial, the identification of some with sharpened blades stimulates the view that they were actually functional and subject to wear. Polished stone arrowheads (d, e) of very different shapes point to competing manufacturing traditions. Was the half-moon shaped perforated bead of amazonite (f) related in concept or use to the curved jade bead of the protohistoric Japanese Islands?

stone cist burial and several jar burials have been excavated there since 1975. In addition to the standard Bronze Age artifacts as found at Hunamni, Songgungni is further distinguished by red burnished pottery, a stone mould for casting bronze implements, many whetstones and a total lack of fishing equipment. The whetstones testify to the home production of the numerous axes and reapers found at the site, while the mould suggests the beginning of local bronze production in the south – though the mould itself is of a Manchurian style and could have been imported.

Late Bronze Age Koejongdong

A Late Bronze Age cist burial discovered at Koejongdong,[26] in the western Peninsula, illustrates the major changes which occurred in the bronze repertoire in the late 1st millennium BC. The broad Liaoning dagger has been

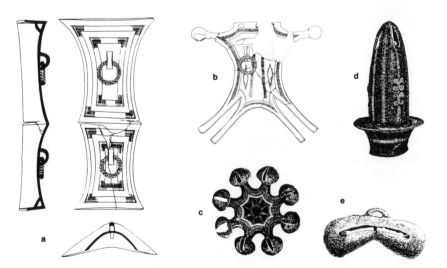

76 Enigmatic bronze shapes from the Bronze-Age Korean Peninsula. The strange flared artifact (a) excavated from the Koejongdong cist burial is now known to be the front cover panel of a sheath for the slender bronze sword. Its twisted-rope rings are repeated on a spread-eagled bronze rattle (b), a popular type of object taking many forms (c, d, e).

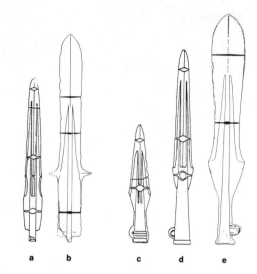

77 *Broad and slender bronze weaponry. The slender Peninsular dagger-sword (a) and socketed spearhead (c, d) were recast in Japan as broad, flat implements (b, e). Were these functional or ceremonial weapons?*

78 *(below) Bronze mirror design on the Korean Peninsula. Growing out of the Northern Bronze Complex, the bronze mirror tradition of the Peninsula became (from top to bottom) increasingly refined and technically demanding.*

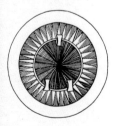

transformed into a slender stabbing sword; flaring-bladed socketed axes have become narrower with a rounded blade; and the short, stubby socketed spearheads have become long and slender. The Koejongdong assemblage also includes some typical Peninsular products: ground slate arrowheads, semi-circular amazonite beads, and very unusual dagger sheaths made of bronze. The function of these latter objects was unknown for a very long time, until the recent discoveries of lacquered sheaths of the same shape at Tahori site.[27]

The mechanics and organization of bronze production at this time are unknown, except for the recovery of numerous stone moulds. Chemical analyses of artifacts show both that zinc was a common additive to copper to form a zinc-bronze alloy, and that in tin-bronze the amount of tin increased as the Bronze Age progressed.[28] In one category of artifact – bronze mirrors – a change in style from coarse design to very fine design was accompanied by a change in casting technique. No stone moulds are known for the fine-lined geometric mirrors, so it is assumed that their designs were so delicate that they had to be engraved on clay. No two mirrors are alike, supporting the notion that the clay moulds were destroyed in a single casting.

The higher tin content of the slender swords has been interpreted as indicative of their 'ceremonialization'; being more brittle, they were thought to have been replaced in real use by iron weapons. This is ironic because it is these very swords, taken across the Korean straits into Kyushu, that Japanese scholars regard as the true functional weapon that was later 'ceremonialized' by the contemporaneous Yayoi peoples (Chapter 11). Much work has yet to be done on these concepts of utility and ritual.

Dolmens

The existence of dolmens on the Korean Peninsula has excited many a scholar's imagination, resulting in hypotheses of their diffusion from Europe or Southeast Asia.[29] Recently, however, they have been viewed as an indigenous

BOX 10
The Tungusic Speakers

The gradual infiltration of bronzes into the Korean Peninsula and their clear derivation from Manchurian and steppe precedents have suggested to many Korean archaeologists that they arrived with an influx of Tungusic-language speakers. The Korean and Japanese languages today are both generally thought to be related to the Altaic language family rather than the Chinese language family, even though they incorporate many Chinese loanwords. In the case of Japanese, the Altaic elements are suspected to overlie an earlier language perhaps of Polynesian affinities. This is due to Japanese having an open syllable structure, with each syllable consisting of consonant plus vowel, except for the independent vowels and the syllabic consonant 'n'. The syllabic structure of Korean has been heavily influenced by the Chinese language, with many more final consonants and consonant clusters than Japanese. Nevertheless, its pronunciation structure shows a tendency towards forming open syllables.

The question is, when were the Altaic elements introduced into the Pen/Insular region? The hypothesis that the proto-Eastern Altaic languages spread into the Korean Peninsula during the early 1st millennium BC is compatible not only with the appearance of bronzes from the Northern Bronze Complex but also with the theoretical location of the Tungusic homeland being somewhere in south-central Siberia. Moreover, the Rong ethnic group, associated with the Upper Xiajiadian culture, is also thought to have consisted of Tungusic speakers. If this language group did become established on the Peninsula during the Korean Bronze Age, it would then have been transmitted to the Japanese Islands during the spread of rice agriculture, replacing (with some incorporations) whatever previous languages were spoken there.

Thus, during the transition from the Chulmun period to the Bronze Age on the Peninsula and from the Jomon to Yayoi periods in the Islands, not only were there dramatic changes in subsistence technology and material culture, but language may also have been involved. Without written records, however, the exact timing and mechanics of language change are impossible to recover with archaeological methods.

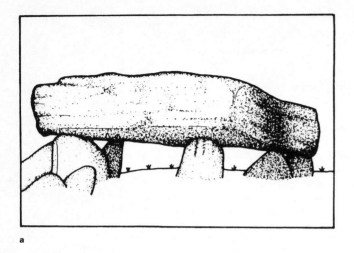

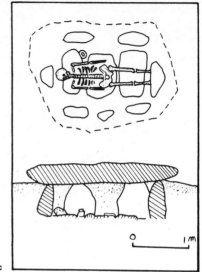

79 Pen/Insular dolmen structures of three varieties. Table-like dolmens of the northern Korean Peninsula (a); capstone on supporting stones in the southern Korean Peninsula (b), and a capstone over a cist burial (c) in Kyushu, across the Korea Strait.

Bronze Age development, perhaps as megalithic burials built in response to the alien phenomenon of cist burial. Cists[30] are now recognized to be an imported tradition of Siberian derivation;[31] but if cist burial was a custom brought by Tungusic speakers from the north, then the indigenous Peninsular population might have reacted by constructing their own megalithic burials. The two main types of dolmens are the northern table type (huge slabs and capstone forming a cist-like chamber above ground) and the southern 'go-board' type (a large capstone resting on several smaller stones at ground level with the burial in the ground underneath). A third type, prevalent mainly in the south, has recently been added; in these, the capstone rests directly on the ground. The burials under the last two types may take any number of forms, from jar burials, cists or stone chamber burials to plain pit burials.

The dating of the northern-type dolmens, which are mainly distributed from the Han River basin northwards, is very difficult since their above-ground chambers have long since been emptied. They are generally acknowledged to have emerged earlier than the southern type, perhaps in the Late Chulmun period. The few whose surroundings have been excavated yielded Bronze Age pottery and stone implements and some small bronze articles but no iron, so dolmen-building is thought to have been discontinued by 300 BC.[32] Table-type dolmens are often found in groups or rows, but unlike the contemporary cist burials of some Early Bronze Age sites, they do not occur in association with settlements. Thus it is difficult to form an integrated picture of their role and function within Early Bronze Age society; it has been suggested that cists and dolmens represent different ethnic groups or different levels of social status or both.[33]

Southern-type dolmens occur in clusters of scores to hundreds along the main river valleys of the southern Peninsula. They date almost exclusively to the Late Bronze Age, and many can be related to village sites nearby. Settlement pattern studies in the southwest show that villages continued to be located on hillsides while the dolmen fields occupied the flat alluvial plains below.[34] Such dolmen cemeteries are taken to indicate the 'existence of clan-based village communities' and the 'chiefdom stage of political evolution',[35] although a recent study has challenged these interpretations by finding no evidence of hierarchy in the southern dolmen culture.[36] Whereas chiefly figures might be postulated in conjunction with cist burials such as that at Koejongdong, which is rich in bronzes, the southern dolmens have proven to be relatively poor in contents. Thus the societies associated with the dolmen cemeteries might have had less hierarchy and more of a segmentary organization – analogous to those which built the long barrows of Neolithic England.

CHAPTER 11

The Spread of Rice Agriculture
1000 BC–AD 300

The Peninsular bronze cultures discussed in the preceding chapter are assumed to have been supported in part by rice agriculture, and rice grains have indeed been recovered from a few sites. Nevertheless, there are no varieties of wild rice indigenous to the Peninsula, so it is commonly agreed that wet-rice technology must have spread there from the Shanghai Delta region of the China Mainland. This technology was then passed on to the Japanese Islands, as attested by the many Peninsular artifacts recovered in northern Kyushu in association with the Islands' earliest paddy fields. These fields are dated by their associated Jomon pottery types to the first half of the 1st millennium BC, so wet-rice agriculture must have been established before that time on the Peninsula.

The story of this technological diffusion is so far known only piecemeal. Local scholars hotly debate the various possible routes of diffusion, while virtually ignoring the social contexts and conditions for the adoption of rice. However, research on the spread of rice agriculture has been especially productive within Japan, touching on many of the important problems associated with technological diffusion: the role of migration of peoples, interaction networks and cultural preferences.

The establishment in *c.* 300 BC of the Yayoi culture, the first fully agricultural society in the Japanese Islands, set the stage there for the development of complex society. Within a mere six hundred years, society became stratified into elite and commoner social classes, with state formation following on in the subsequent Kofun period from AD 300. In this chapter we shall examine the subsistence base of the Yayoi peoples, while a review of their political development will be saved for Chapter 13.

Subsistence transformations

From Mainland to Peninsula

From the time of Hemudu (*c.* 5000 BC) onwards, wet rice is assumed to have been a major crop of southern Mainland cultures in suitable alluvial locations. Alas, very little is known about this early agricultural technology aside from the tools used in cultivation (Chapter 6). No prehistoric paddy fields have yet been excavated on the China Mainland, or even on the Korean Peninsula. Thus current knowledge about the field system and irrigation technology of

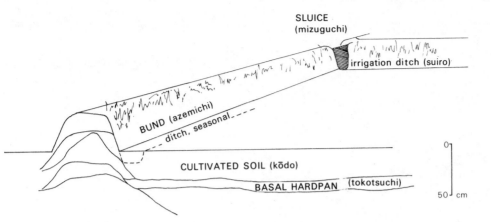

SLUICE
(mizuguchi)

irrigation ditch (suiro)

BUND (azemichi)

ditch, seasonal

CULTIVATED SOIL (kōdo)

BASAL HARDPAN (tokotsuchi)

0

50 cm

80 Historic paddy field construction in Japan. The construction of paddy fields and their feeder canals demands extreme ingenuity to keep the growing rice plants continuously and evenly inundated. Field-building is heavy labour, involving ground-levelling, tamping in a leak-proof base if soils are porous, and surrounding each field with bunds and canals to control the water supply. Fields must be absolutely level so that water does not collect in one corner or stagnate and ruin the crop; this restriction has traditionally limited field size by comparison with dry-land cultivation.

Paddy-field construction is highly significant for archaeology for two reasons. First, although it destroys many cultural materials in the upper layers, those that are below the impermeable base are effectively sealed off and protected. Second, the field system itself is of much greater substance and durability than mere ploughing; hundreds have been excavated in Japan, though none yet in China or Korea.

prehistoric wet rice is based mainly on Japanese data. The requirements of wet-rice technology can be summarized from modern experience as well.   *fig. 80, plate 3*

Diffusion of wet-rice technology from the southern Mainland northeastwards into the Pen/Insulae had already occurred by the end of the Zhou period. Of the two main varieties of rice (long-grained and short-grained) present on the eastern China seaboard, it was the latter which was more cold-resistant and therefore transmitted outwards from the Shanghai Delta. The social causes for this spread are poorly understood. A reasonable hypothesis might see the warfare and territorial expansion of the predatory Zhou states as forcing coastal peoples into increased interaction or migration – incidentally leading to the diffusion of wet rice. But this would depend very much on a clear dating of the transmission, which does not exist as yet.

Another major problem in tracing this diffusion is determining whether rice-growing spread first to the northern Mainland and Bohai Bay region and was then transmitted overland to the Pen/Insulae, or whether it was transmitted by sea from the Shanghai Delta region directly to the southwestern coastal regions of the Pen/Insulae. Studies of stone tool typologies argue for a northern, land-based route of wet-rice diffusion;[1] so too do the recent discoveries of harvesting tools and rice grains on the northern coast of the Shandong peninsula and the northwestern Korean Peninsula. Still, caution must be exercised with both these forms of data. Tools do not have to be used in one culture in the same way

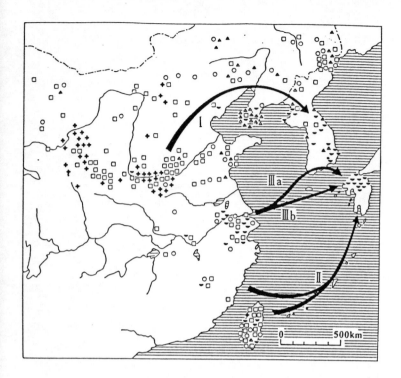

81 Postulated routes of rice expansion in East Asia. I. overland, II. via Taiwan and the Ryukyu Islands, and III. direct from the Shanghai Delta to Kyushu (b) or via the Korean Peninsula (a). The distributions of different shaped stone reaping knives are thought by East Asian archaeologists to be important in determining the route. Cross: chipped stone; Square: polished stone, rectangular in shape; Circle: polished, half-moon shape using the straight edge as blade; Lunate: polished, half-moon shape using the curved edge as blade.

as in another: for example, the stone reaping knife was developed in the Yangshao millet cultures but subsequently found its major employment in rice-harvesting. The crop reaped with a particular knife-type cannot be inferred from shape alone but requires more specific contextual information. Further, the discovery of rice grains at a site does not prove local cultivation, rice being an ideal commodity for exchange and storage. What is needed is clear evidence of both rice cultivation and processing.

The current best estimate is that rice technology was introduced into the Korean Peninsula in the late 2nd millennium BC[2] – after Chulmun pottery had been replaced by Mumun pottery but before bronze had appeared in the area (Chapter 10). With the exception of the data from the few sites which have yielded rice grains, however, no specific information on actual rice-growing is yet available. Still, it is assumed that the Late Bronze Age society of the southern Peninsula was founded on a rice economy – mainly in order to account for the evidence that rice was introduced from there into the Japanese Islands.

Peninsular bequest to Kyushu

Rice grains have been recovered from several Late and Final Jomon sites dating between the late 2nd and middle 1st millennia BC, but documentation of actual Jomon cultivation of rice occurs only with the recovery of paddy field remains associated with Final Jomon Yamanotera-type pottery. The Korean Peninsula is assumed to have been the source of this technology because a whole series of Peninsular artifacts, features and manufacturing technologies were also introduced into north Kyushuan groups from Late Bronze Age society.[3] These did not arrive as a package but intermittently over a millennium; thus the rise of the Yayoi culture must be viewed as a synthesis of north Kyushuan Jomon and Peninsular Bronze Age elements.

For example, Peninsular red burnished pottery – as found at Songgungni and commonly included in Late Bronze Age burials – most probably inspired the burnished storage jar which accompanied early rice production in Kyushu. *fig. 83a*, plate 54 Iron objects were imported from the very beginning of the Yayoi period, suggesting that iron must also have been present in the southern Peninsula at that time (Chapter 13). Nevertheless, iron finds in both areas between 300 BC and AD 1 are exceedingly rare. Several types of polished stone tools and cylindrical beads, which can be traced stylistically and/or petrographically to the Peninsula, were also received into Kyushu. Among the tools were handled and tanged stone daggers, polished untanged arrowheads of triangular cross-section, disk axes, laurel leaf-shaped and triangular reaping knives, grooved reaping knives, and grooved adzes. Other adopted technologies were spinning and weaving, lathe-working, and bronze-casting. In short, the transition from Box 11 Jomon to Yayoi was not just a change in subsistence pattern but an entire restructuring of the material economy in the Japanese Islands.

Yayoi excavations in western Japan have revealed the existence of two distinct skeletal types, identified as belonging to the indigenous Jomon genotype and an immigrant population from the continent. Jomon-type people were shorter, more robust and round-faced than the immigrants who were taller, gracile and long-faced.[4] Quantifying the scale of immigration at this time has been most difficult, since few bones are preserved in burials and this was only the beginning of several migratory waves through the ensuing millennium.[5] In any case, physical anthropological studies of modern Japanese show that continental effects on skeletal genetics rapidly diminish as one travels eastwards from Kyushu – except for the Kinai region, which received many Peninsular immigrants directly in the 5th century AD.[6]

82 Contributions to the modern Japanese genotype. The tall immigrants from the continent during the Yayoi period (left) intermarried with the shorter indigenous Jomon peoples (right), producing the modern mix of Japanese physical types. Archaeologists in Japan today often classify themselves in jest into one of these two types.

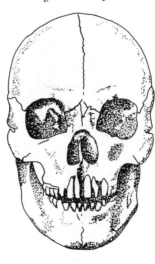
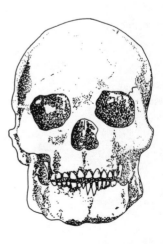

Yayoi   **Jomon**

BOX 11
Weaving Implements and Textiles

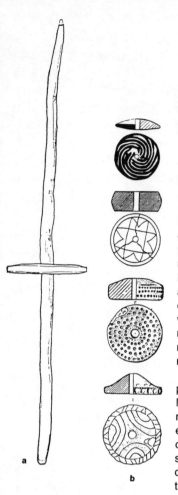

Spindle whorls are the ubiquitous archaeological testimony to the fabrication of cloth. Used to weight the spindle rod during the spinning of thread (a), whorls are often *ad hoc* adaptations of ceramic sherds or they are purpose-shaped (and sometimes decorated) artifacts of clay or stone (b). Even precious beadstone whorls of jasper and jade are known from elite graves. Spindle whorls first appeared in the early agricultural societies of East Asia such as Hemudu, Yangshao and Yayoi; they also occurred infrequently in the postglacial Chulmun culture, but not the Jomon. However, the cord-marked pottery of many of the postglacial cultures, including Jomon and Dapenkeng, attests to the use of plant fibres in cordage from early in the Holocene. The weaving of mats and baskets (c), and therefore even matted clothing, might have preceded the spinning and weaving of cloth. Indeed, arguments have been made for interpreting the notched stones occurring in Chulmun sites as weaving weights rather than net weights. Rather than acting as loom weights, however, such notched pebbles were probably used in seaming reed blinds or mats, an activity still extant today although wooden spools are now used as weights.

The early weaving technology represented by spindle whorls probably employed either the simple backstrap loom (d) or ground loom. The wooden loom parts, along with the spindle rod itself, are not normally preserved in the archaeological record except in especially wet or dry conditions, such as at the waterlogged sites of Hemudu, Toro and Karako, where thread and fabric beams and shuttles have been recovered (e). The rough cloth products created on these early looms used bast fibres from ramie, hemp or the *kuzu* vine. The earliest extant fragments of these fabrics date to the Middle and Late Neolithic on the China Mainland, and some

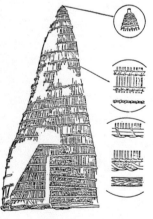

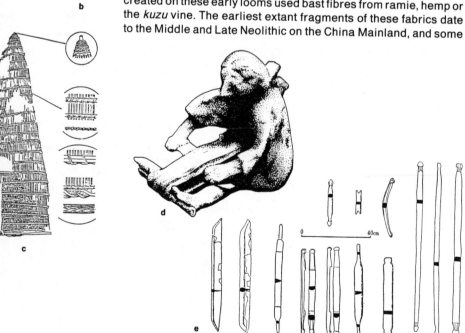

0   40cm

examples are known from Yayoi sites.

By the middle of the Han period, loom technology had advanced considerably. In contrast to the West, where a vertical loom equipped with weft weights was in use, the Mainland solution was to thread the warp horizontally in a wooden frame, with the weaver sitting at one end. The increasing complexity of the woven pattern, especially the development of brocades (f), was related to the use of silk. That most famous East Asian textile came into production as early as the 3rd millennium BC. Fragments of a tabby weave were excavated from a Liangzhu culture site on the Mainland, and half of a silkworm cocoon surfaced at a Yangshao site further north. Interestingly, most of the silk recovered from the Shang period has not been clothing but rather traces of cloth used to wrap precious bronze objects.

'Sericulture', or silkworm breeding, was fully developed by Shang times. It also involved the cultivation of orchards – as depicted on this bronze object – to provide the silkworm caterpillars' favourite food, mulberry leaves (g). The caterpillars begin spinning their cocoons a month after hatching and after having eaten about 20 g of mulberry leaves. From two glands they exude silk threads made of protein; these are bound together with a gum as the cocoon is built up (h). The threads, which can be up to 800–1000 m long in one cocoon, can be unwound by first degumming the cocoon in boiling water and then winding the threads on to a reel.

Silk was a precious commodity, frequently demanded as a tax-in-kind from peasant households as early as the Middle Zhou period. It was also widely used for gifts, tribute, and exchange along with other bolts of cloth, leading to the development of the 'Silk Roads' in the Early Han period. With fragments of silk appearing at several Yayoi sites in northwestern Kyushu, it is suspected that sericulture was being practised there by the Middle Yayoi. Its adoption was only a small part of the influence from the expanding Han empire, which was so actively sought by the Yayoi peoples of Western Seto.

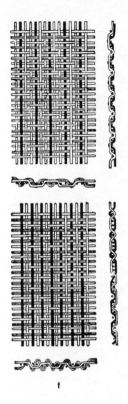

f

g

h

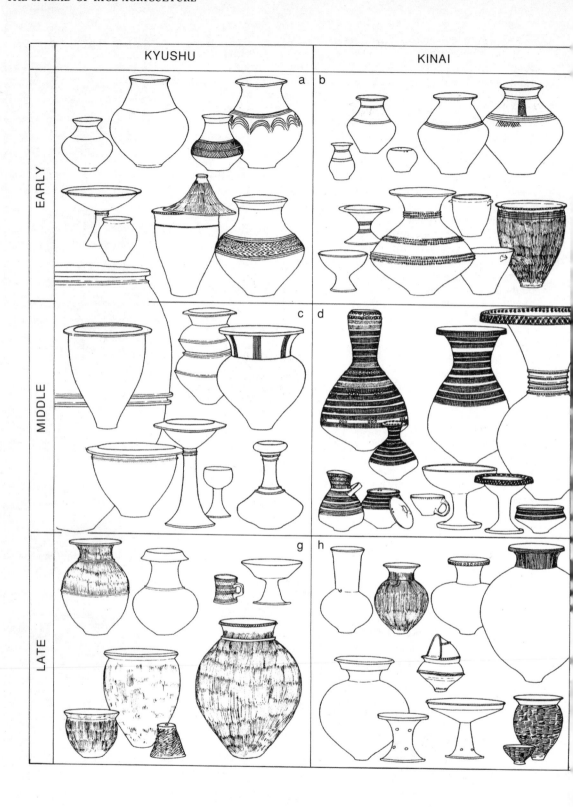

	KYUSHU	KINAI
EARLY	a	b
MIDDLE	c	d
LATE	g	h

83 Yayoi potteries from southwest to northeast. Early Yayoi pottery (a, b) occurs throughout the western Japanese Islands as the first widely distributed Yayoi ceramic style; it is contemporaneous with Final Jomon pottery in the northeast. In the Middle Yayoi period, regional varieties were developed: ribbed and coloured surfaces characterized Kyushu (c), where large burial jars were also manufactured; the Kinai is noted for its combed decoration (d); while Tohoku potters adopted Yayoi shapes but retained Jomon decorative techniques (e, f). Marked by a general decrease in surface decoration, Late Yayoi ceramics in Kyushu and Kinai often bear tell-tale textures of their manufacture (g, h); decoration on the Yayoi ceramics of eastern Japan is sparse but elegant (i), and Jomon traditions persist in the north (j).

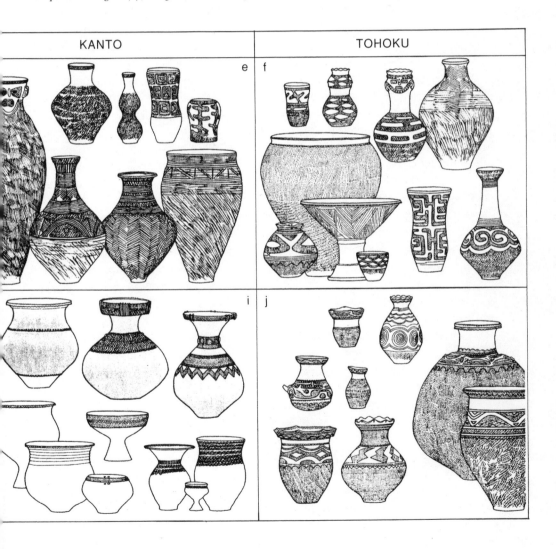

KANTO TOHOKU

From Kyushu to Hokkaido

North Kyushu acted as an incubator for the formation of the Yayoi culture. The transitional period was initiated through the adoption of wet-rice technology by the Final Jomon peoples of north Kyushu using Yamanotera-type pottery; and it ended about 200 BC with the development of a new ceramic style, Yayoi I, as known from the Itazuke site in northern Kyushu.[7] Subsequently, both this new pottery and the agricultural way of life soon expanded explosively throughout the western Insular lowlands. This diffusive process is usually understood by archaeologists in terms of actual migration of Yayoi people out of Kyushu – a reasonable hypothesis since the new agricultural technology surely triggered a population boom on the circumscribed plains of north Kyushu. Nevertheless, how these Yayoi people interacted with the Jomon people already ensconced in the western Islands in the 3rd and 2nd centuries BC is as yet a little-explored topic.[8] The continuation of Jomon patterns of shell-collecting and hunting through the Early Yayoi period, alongside the initiation of paddy field construction, suggests a rapid but not instantaneous change in lifeways. Although Jomon pottery was replaced by Yayoi ceramics, the occurrence of Jomon motifs on Early Yayoi pots implies both the continued valuation of Jomon symbolic patterns and the actual acculturation of Jomon people to wet-rice cultivation.

One hypothesis explaining the ready receptivity to this complex, structured and intensive form of agriculture is that the western Jomon were already well aware of the advantages of cultivation and familiar with plant needs through their own efforts at horticulture (Chapter 5).[9] This basic receptivity, coupled with the assumed low population densities in the Seto region, facilitated the rapid spread and adoption of an agricultural way of life. The situation, however, was far different for Jomon groups in the northeast. There, a formidable resistance to agriculture has been demonstrated – not on climatic grounds as once thought, but due to a thorough commitment to a productive and efficient marine-based way of life which the people actively chose to continue.[10]

During the century of Early Yayoi expansion in the west, northeastern Honshu was occupied by peoples who shared a fairly homogeneous Final Jomon material culture known as the Kamegaoka (or Obora) culture. It is renowned for its elaborately decorated objects made of organic materials, fortunately preserved at the eponymous lowland peat site. Excavations there since the 19th century have produced lacquered red and black baskets, lacquered ceramics, and bone and wooden objects. The ceramics of the Kamegaoka culture are highly refined and very unlike the heavy, high-relief pottery of some earlier Jomon phases.

Coastal fishing villages and shellmounds in the northeast reached their highest densities during the Final Jomon period.[11] Shell-collecting along the rocky coasts and deep-sea fishing formed the inhabitants' main livelihood, and an elaborate tool technology comprising toggle-head harpoons and detachable-shaft bone hooks complemented their advanced abilities at seafaring.

fig. 100

plates 54, 55
fig. 83e, f

42 *The Qin Emperor's soldiers, given everlasting life in clay, were instrumental in unifying China in 221 BC by conquering Qin's rival states.*

45 (right) The Great Wall of China originally consisted of individual segments built by the late Zhou states, which were linked together between 221 and 206 BC. Later dynasties built subsequent walls further north, and the one tourists visit today is of Ming-period construction.

43, 44 *Greater than life-sized soldiers (left) and horses (right) were found by the thousands stationed in regimented lines within large pits near the tomb of the First Emperor of Qin.*

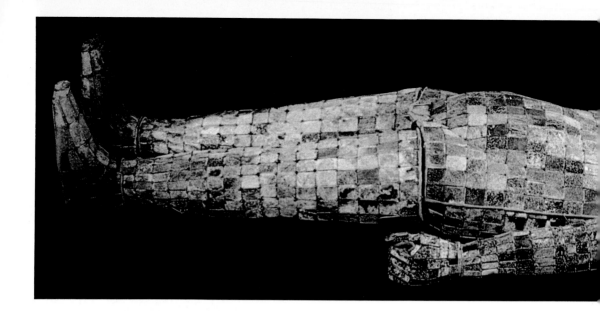

46, 47 *Exquisite lacquerware (left), and jade suiting (above), excavated at Mancheng, expedited the Han elite to the next world.*

50, 51 *(opposite) Increasingly graceful bronze sculptures bring new life to the medium in the Han period. A gilt bronze oil lamp (above) takes the form of a servant girl; from the tomb of Princess Douwan, Mancheng, c. 2nd century BC. A cast bronze horse (below) comes from Gansu, 2nd century AD.*

48, 49 *Gold seals such as this one (near right), with titles inscribed on the bottom (far right), were given by the Han court to tributary polities.*

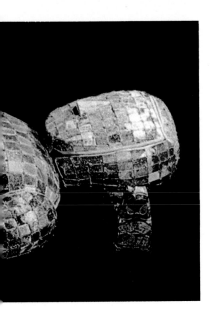

The sophisticated court
culture of the Han dynasty

52 *Raised-floor granaries (see also incised image, plate 56), a Southeast Asian form of architecture, were part of the introduction of wet rice agriculture into the Islands from the continent.*

53–55 *The shape of Yayoi pottery in the west (centre) derives from Peninsular types, but the decoration and formation of pots in the east (right) show continuity with Jomon. Stone moulds (left) for casting weapons of the Peninsular type are a rare find.*

Life on the Korean Peninsula
and Japanese Islands at the time
of Han

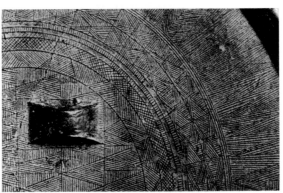

56, 57 *Yayoi bells (top) and Peninsular mirrors (above) have fine raised-line decoration in common.*

58, 59 *New technologies of silk spinning, reconstructed here at the Suwon folk village near Seoul (right), and iron working, as depicted in this painting displayed at the Masan site (below), were adopted from Han by protohistoric societies on the Korean Peninsula.*

60–62 *Surface stamping of pre-Han paddled stoneware (above) from the southern Mainland recalls the surface texture of bronze vessels, in great contrast to the painted and incised hard-fired earthenwares (below) of Han. The Pen/Insular stoneware traditions (right) synthesized many Han elements, including paddled and combed surfaces as well as miniature sculptures of vessels, humans, and animals placed on jar shoulders, etc.*

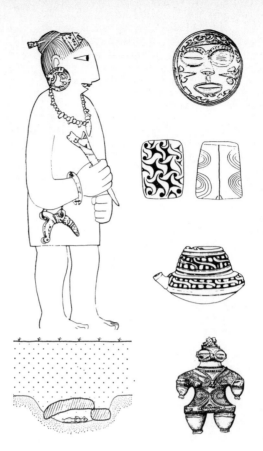

84 The richness of Final Jomon material culture. A 'shaman' wears personal ornaments of carved bone, lacquered wood and beadstone. Underneath the ground is a ceramic figurine, shown large-size on the side, buried in a ritual possibly related to child-bearing. At top right is a ceramic mask with carved stone plaques below, all presumably used in Jomon ceremonies, and an Obora-type spouted pot.

So productive was this subsistence economy that the inhabitants could not quickly be induced to become farmers. Indeed, the northeast resisted the adoption of rice technology until late Middle Yayoi, forming the last holdout of Jomon culture on Honshu.

A two-stage model for the spread of rice agriculture in Japan puts the limit of the first wave of diffusion through the western coastal areas at the waist of Honshu Island at about 100 BC. Since the publication of this model,[12] Early Yayoi sites have also been identified on the far northern tip of Honshu, indicating that some pioneers exceeded this limit by sailing up the Japan Sea coast to try to colonize the northwestern lowlands. At the site of Tareyanagi, near Kamegaoka, paddy field structures have been recovered through excavation. Some archaeologists take these remains as evidence of the wholesale transition to rice agriculture in the northeast at this time.[13] However, these northern Early Yayoi sites were short-lived, and the full adoption of rice agriculture came belatedly, as postulated by the second stage of the model. Rice did not reach Hokkaido at that time, leaving the Jomon way of life to continue on the island until the 8th century AD in what is called the Epi-Jomon period, contemporaneous with the Yayoi, Kofun and Nara periods to the south.

Insular rice regimes

More than two hundred sites containing ancient paddy fields and their attendant canals have been excavated in Japan.[14] These range in date from the

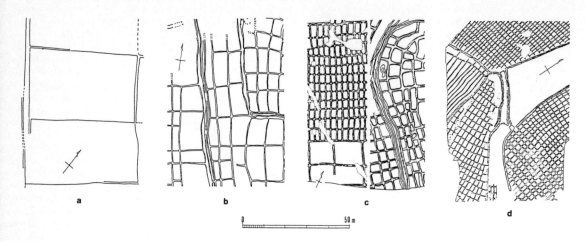

85 *Two strategies of Yayoi-period paddy-field layout. Large undivided fields were excavated in 1948 at the Toro site (a), but at other Yayoi sites excavated since then, most large field areas are internally divided into many small paddies of varying dimensions (b, c, d). Note the accommodations made to the natural topography in field layout.*

Final Jomon (*c.* 500 BC) to the medieval periods of Japanese history (12th–16th centuries AD). In the Kanto region north of Tokyo, deposits of ash from historically active volcanoes have buried many field systems, acting both to end their economic usefulness at the time and to preserve them in the stratigraphic record. Flood deposits are another agent of preservation for entire field systems, especially in western Japan. Through broad-scale exposure in modern rescue excavations, enough prehistoric field systems have been laid bare to enable generalization about their size and extent. Two types of prehistoric fields are distinguished (though why they differed is not known): rare large ones (*c.* 30 × 50 m) without subdivisions, and numerous grids of very small fields (*c.* 3–4 × 6–7 m).[15] The latter are often fitted into irregular sections of the landscape. The paddy fields at the well-known Late Yayoi site of Toro,[16] averaging 2000 m², are of the large variety and are thus not representative of most prehistoric field systems.

The importance of the reaping knife in this agricultural regime was that it was used to harvest only the individually ripened heads of rice. Analyses of phytolithic remains (silica bodies occurring in motor cells of the grass family) from paddy fields in Japan indicate that pure stands of rice were not characteristic until the medieval period.[17] In earlier times, fields contained many companion weed plants or wild plants such as reeds, which shared the same growing conditions as rice. Harvesting individual grain heads allowed the rice plants to be sought out from other plants growing in the fields. Even more importantly, the early-ripening grains could be harvested separately from the late-ripening ones; this probably led to the storing of the former for use as seed grain, resulting in the development of better strains of rice through differential selection.

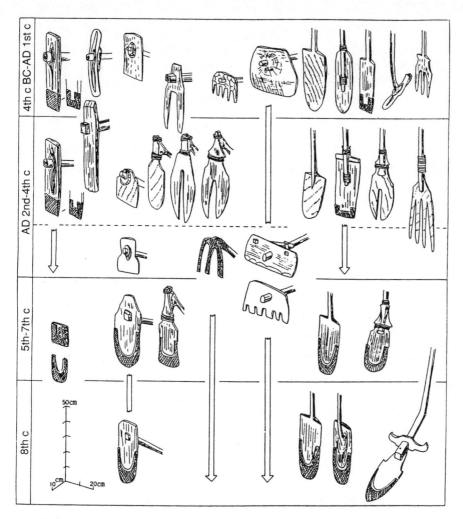

86 *Iron blades for wooden agricultural tools through the ages. Single-bladed and pronged hoes and spades accompanied primitive foot ploughs before the use of ox-drawn ploughs.*

A major architectural advance accompanying wet-rice technology was the raised granary made of wooden boards. Components of such structures were preserved in the waterlogged conditions at the Toro site. The stilted granary is thought to be a southern form of architecture which was transmitted directly to the Islands from the south China Mainland. It stood in contrast to the typical Yayoi pit-house, which had no or only low-standing walls and whose thatched roof extended almost to ground level. At Toro, the digging implements peculiar to wet-rice cultivation were made entirely of wood; but further west in the Late Yayoi period, these began to be fitted with iron edges, increasing their productivity and allowing greater agricultural development through the digging of large-scale irrigation systems.

plates 52, 56

Yayoi culture

Descriptions of Yayoi culture tend to present the progressive aspects of the southwestern Islands as representative of the entire archipelago. In fact, there is marked variation in the levels of political, social, and material culture development between the northeast and the southwest. Moreover, within southwestern Yayoi, two contrasting spheres can be discerned, focusing respectively on the eastern Seto and the western Seto regions.

The customs and beliefs operating behind these archaeologically recognized differences might even argue for different organizational identities: ethnic groups, tribes or polities. As with the Jomon, soon it may be more appropriate to speak of several Yayoi 'cultures' rather than a single one. Historical documents do support the inference for several political groupings (Chapter 13). Given the current state of knowledge, however, describing the Yayoi in all its variational glory in a few pages is as difficult as dealing briefly with the regional and temporal variations seen in the Jomon.

Northeastern Yayoi

The character of the northern Yayoi during and after the second stage of rice diffusion is controversial. Majority opinion has it that the Kamegaoka Jomon people were eventually converted to the agricultural way of life through the diffusion of technology alone, without the massive immigration of Yayoi people from Kyushu that is thought to have occurred in the west. Once the Jomon communities incorporated agricultural technology and Yayoi ceramic shapes, they are considered by archaeologists to have 'become Yayoi'. Yet, there is considerable divergence of opinion as to whether rice did or did not dominate the crop repertoire as it did in the west, since millet and other northern grains also played important roles.[18] Many cultural elements were also retained from the Jomon period, such as cord-marking applied to Yayoi-shaped vessels. Moreover, the extensive sets of bronze implements used by Yayoi people in the west were never adopted in the northeast at all. Finally, secondary jar burial was practised in the northeast; this custom required that only the bones of the deceased – after the flesh had been removed in an initial burial event – be interred in the jar, and several jars were often buried together in the same pit. In the west, the whole body was interred, whether in a jar, in a coffin or just in a pit. Based on these facts, it is clear that the northeastern Yayoi comprised a distinct sub-culture within Honshu, one whose local socio-political complexity almost certainly did not rival that of southwestern Yayoi.

Southwestern Yayoi

Settlements of western Yayoi agriculturalists are found in two distinct topographical locations: lowland flood plains and hill promontories. Those in either location were often surrounded by large ditches. The function of these ditches, and indeed the significance of choice of location, remain obscure; the ditches have been interpreted as village boundaries, drainage facilities to

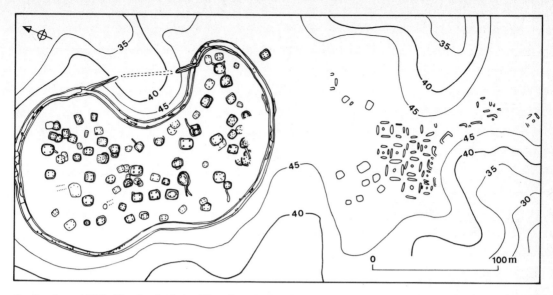

87 *Otsuka, a Middle Yayoi upland site. The village on the left is surrounded by a large ditch, while the cemetery of 25 squarish moated precincts on the right is unbounded. Each precinct contained one central pit-burial, while other pit- and jar-burials occurred within the moats. The total population of the village over time is calculated at 500 persons, so only a small number of them were given preferential burial in the precincts.*

protect lowland settlements from flooding, and defensive fortifications – a variety of opinion recalling the differing interpretations of Yangshao village ditches of the north China Mainland. Among these, defence is a good possibility, given the Mainland dynastic records of Insular strife (Chapter 13).

An important example of an upland site now fully excavated is the ditched village at Otsuka, measuring 130 × 200 m, accompanied by an adjacent cemetery of moated precincts. Over ninety pit-houses dot the site's interior, although probably no more than thirty were in use at any one time. A distinctive aspect of this site is its apparently undifferentiated function. There is no evidence of craft production or of differential status among the inhabitants, in contrast to some lowland sites.

Moated precincts are only one of several Yayoi burial systems, prevalent in eastern Seto. The precincts usually contain several burials of adults and children and are viewed as family burial grounds. Grave goods are rare – maybe a pot or two, in contrast to the jar and cist burials of western Seto, which often contain many bronzes and other exotic objects. Jars are used throughout the

	Western Seto	Eastern Seto
	dolmens	moated precinct
Coffin		
adult	large jar or cist	wood coffin or pit
child		small jar
Grave goods	bronzes	some ceramics
No. persons	individuals	families

88 *Different burial facilities in eastern and western Seto.*

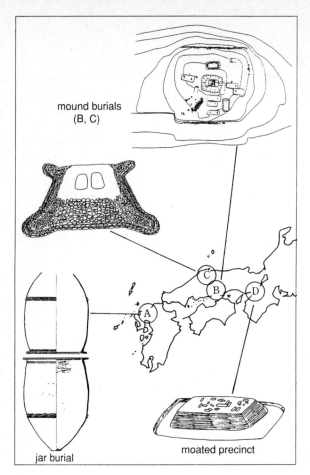

mound burials
(B, C)

jar burial

moated precinct

89 Regional burial traditions among the Yayoi.

plate 1

Islands for burial but in very distinct ways. The Kyushu jar burial tradition entailed the production of jars specifically for use as coffins and large enough to receive a whole body rather than just the bones. Even the moated precincts of eastern Seto also contained some jar burials but these were exclusively for children, wooden coffins or just plain pits being used for adults.

Much of Yayoi craft production was also regionalized. Bead-making, for example, was a specialization of the northwestern Honshu coast with its ready sources of hard beadstone such as jasper and jade. Stone tool workshops are known from north Kyushu at the Monden and Tateiwa sites. The former has yielded stone anvils, polished arrowheads, stone copies of Mainland-style dagger axes, and reaping knives. At Tateiwa, which is actually a cluster of several sites, a similar range of artifacts was manufactured from a local source of volcanic tuff; the products were distributed throughout the region. A mould for casting a bronze weapon also turned up at Tateiwa. Many bronze daggers and spearheads were imported from the Peninsula, and some of these were subsequently melted down and recast into local styles of weapons – perhaps in a mould like that from Tateiwa. Both imported and recast weapons were plate 53 deposited in western Seto burials. In particular, the broad sword cast locally is thought to be a ceremonial rendition.

The significantly different distributions of bronze artifact types between

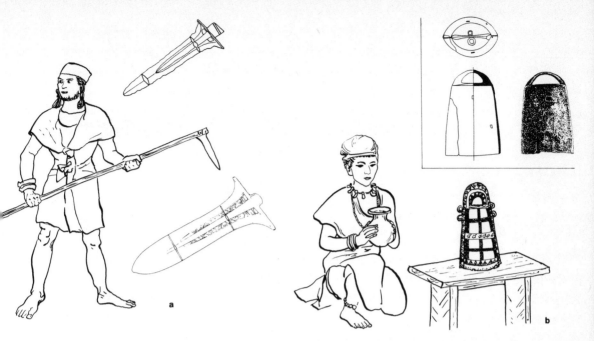

90 *Yayoi bronze cultures and their Peninsular antecedents. Weaponry (a) characterized Western Seto; narrow Peninsular dagger-axes (upper) contrast with broad Insular types (lower). Bronze bells (b), stimulated by small simple Peninsular types (upper), functioned in Eastern Seto rituals.*

western Seto (weapons) and eastern Seto (bells) argue for contrasting systems of social control. Since bronze weapons are usually found in individual graves, they must represent either the real or ceremonial invocation of force. Bells, on the other hand, are always found in non-burial contexts, usually in caches on isolated hilltops. They are perceived not as individual possessions but as ceremonial objects belonging to and benefiting the whole community, perhaps through use in agricultural rituals. Metallurgical analyses have revealed that the eastern bells were cast from melted-down imports of continental bronzes;[19] thus it was not that weaponry was unavailable to eastern Setoites, it was that they chose not to use the objects but to recast them in another form more suitable for their values and ideals. This distinction between the eastern and western bronze repertoire echoes the different burial systems of the two areas, both in the construction of burials and in the fact that one required the deposition of grave goods while the other did not.

Thus for the Middle Yayoi period, at least, it is probably safe to discuss Yayoi social development in terms of three major spheres: the non-rice agricultural areas of northeastern Honshu as opposed to the rice-based economies of southwestern Honshu, and the split within southwestern Honshu between eastern and western Seto on the basis of material culture and social organization. A significant aspect of this ordering is that western Seto, which for at least a millennium had shared in the culture of the southern Korean Peninsula, was drawn further into interaction with the continent than the other regions. Many of the archaeological differences between eastern and western Seto, despite a common subsistence base, are thus due to differential contact with societies in the Yellow Sea Basin (see Chapter 13).

CHAPTER 12

The Making and Breaking of Empire
220 BC–AD 500

Unification

By 221 BC, just before the Yayoi expansion and after a decade of warfare on the continent, the Late Zhou state of Qin had conquered its six major rivals and proclaimed a unified dynasty. Qin's advantage might have been due to its adoption, around 350 BC, of 'county' administration as developed in the Zhou state of Chu. This consisted of dividing the state 'into small and approximately equal administrative districts, each governed by an official appointed by and obedient to the ruler'.[1] The system brought local districts under the direct control of the ruler instead of the semi-autonomous feudal lords, greatly increasing the centralization and power of the central government.

The era of 'warring states' thus ended, and with Qin and its successor dynasties in the Han period, it is possible for the first time to talk in terms of a unified 'China' (the name itself being derived from Qin). The territorial nucleus of this newly consolidated and expanded state occupied the whole of the north China Mainland above the Yangzi River, with its capital at Xianyang. The First Emperor of Qin, however, continued to expand his authority to the south by building roads through to the coasts and establishing local administrative centres referred to as 'commanderies'. Expansion to the northwest was undertaken in the name of defence against the steppe peoples, and the First Emperor is credited with consolidating the northern defences into a Great Wall that extended over 5000 km in length.[2] This was accomplished both by linking together existing wall fortifications built by the earlier northern Zhou states and by building new segments.

plate 45

The military preparedness of the imperial forces is extravagantly illustrated by the ceramic statues that were buried *en masse* in orderly rows in pits near the First Emperor's mounded tomb outside the modern city of Xi'an. As one of the most spectacular archaeological discoveries of the century, this 'terracotta army' is now well known to Westerners through several books and many exhibitions abroad.[3] These figures facilitated the first large studies of the styles and construction of body armour,[4] of which only miscellaneous fragments made of leather or metal had previously been recovered.

plates 42–44

Box 14a

Strategies for economic unification were pursued in parallel with military conquest and administrative consolidation. Some of the most familiar and numerous united-Qin artifacts are sets of graduated bronze or ceramic measuring cups and bronze or iron weights. These usually bear inscriptions of edicts by the First Emperor, including his exhortation for standardized

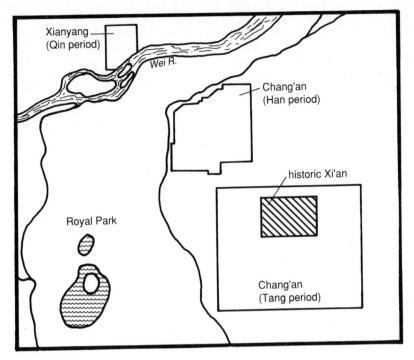

91 The countryside around modern Xi'an is home to several ancient Chinese capitals. North of the Wei River sits the Qin capital of Xianyang, while to the southeast are located the two cities of Chang'an – one dating to the Han period and the other to Tang. The Royal Park of the Qin emperors is focussed around an artificial lake which was used in the Han period both as a reservoir for Chang'an and as a naval training ground.

measurements: 'When they are not uniform or are in doubt, make them clear and make them uniform.'[5] He also banned the spade and knife coinage issued by the previous Zhou states and unified the currency by minting a single type of round coin with a square central hole. (The significance of imposing standard measures and coinage for centralized control is highlighted by the difficulty of getting the metric system and a common currency accepted in today's Europe.)

Overzealous taxation and exploitation of peasant labour led to local uprisings that cost the First Emperor his throne. Though his reign was short, nevertheless he managed to establish the infrastructure for a united China. The reforms instituted by the First Emperor underlay development and expansion in the economic, military and administrative realms in the succeeding Han period.

Territorial expansion

The Han capitals

The Han period as defined here entails three dynasties: Western or Former Han (206 BC–AD 8) and Eastern or Later Han (AD 25–220) with the very short Xin Dynasty in between (AD 9–23). For simplicity's sake, these will be referred

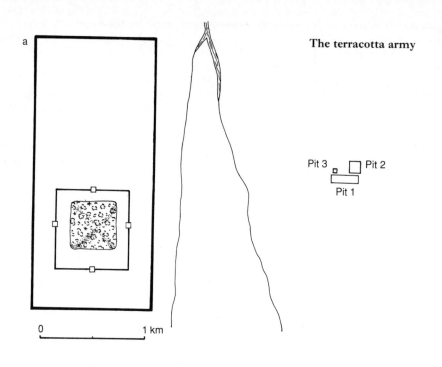

a

The terracotta army

Pit 3 Pit 2
Pit 1

0   1 km

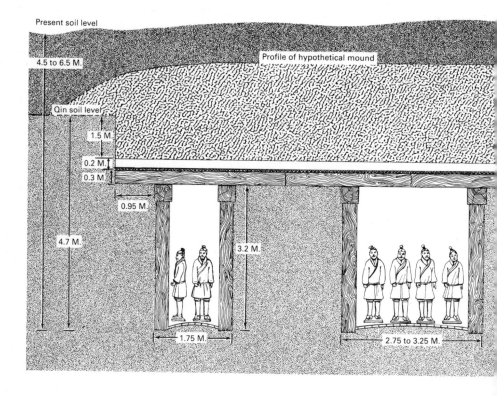

Present soil level

4.5 to 6.5 M.

Profile of hypothetical mound

Qin soil level

1.5 M.

0.2 M.
0.3 M.

0.95 M.

4.7 M.

3.2 M.

1.75 M.

2.75 to 3.25 M.

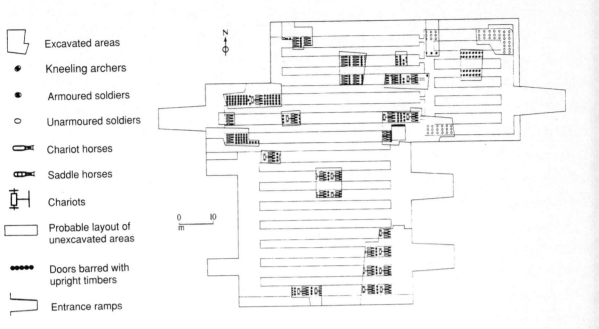

Excavated areas

● **Kneeling archers**

◐ **Armoured soldiers**

○ **Unarmoured soldiers**

Chariot horses

Saddle horses

Chariots

Probable layout of unexcavated areas

●●●●● **Doors barred with upright timbers**

Entrance ramps

0 ____ 10
m

KEY

tilled soil

undisturbed soil

earth fill

plaster

woven fiber mat

timbers

bricks

92 (Above left) The tomb and accompanying 'terracotta army' pits of the First Emperor of China. Forty kilometres east of Xianyang, Qin Shi Huang Di ordered the erection of an enormous mounded tomb nearly half a kilometre square, enclosed in two nested compounds (a). Legend has it that the tomb chamber contains a model of the palace with rivers of mercury flowing around it, while cocked crossbows guard the entrances. Recent investigations have indeed documented traces of mercury fumes at the site – a danger to archaeologists as well as prospective thieves. The tomb remains unexcavated, but well-digging a couple of kilometres east of the tomb complex in 1974 brought up fragments of ceramic statues, leading to the uncovering of the spectacular 'terracotta army', one of the greatest archaeological discoveries of all time. Pit no. 2 (above right) contained a wide variety of soldiers, horses and chariots – in contrast to Pit no. 1 (left), which contained only orderly rows of statues of foot soldiers but in alarming quantities. The pit measures 210 m by 60 m and contains an estimated 3,210 statues. Excavation of the site will carry on well into the next century.

to here as the Early, Middle and Late Han periods. Chang'an, the Early and Middle Han capital, was built on the opposite side of the Wei River from where the previous Qin capital of Xianyang had been located. In AD 25 Chang'an was thoroughly sacked during the overthrowing of Wang Mang, the ruler of Xin, and a new, much smaller capital was established further east at Luoyang. These ancient cities have been subjected to considerable archaeological research, so that their layouts are known in fair detail.[6] Both Chang'an (6 × 7.6 km in size) and Luoyang (2.7 × 3.4 km) followed the Zhou ideal in being oriented to the compass and having twelve gates in their walls. However, their plans were rectangular (notwithstanding the effect of the river on northwestern Chang'an), and thus deviated somewhat from the Zhou ideal of squareness. Perhaps because it was built piecemeal during three phases of construction, Chang'an evinced less attention to interior zoning than did Zhou-period cities. The interior grid of avenues was seriously disrupted by the placement of several palaces, but the main markets remained in the north as in the Zhou capitals. In Luoyang, the palaces lay on a north–south axis, and the shift of the main market to the middle of Luoyang between the palaces along the western wall was a major change in urban layout.

Territorial administration

These capitals stood at the apex of a territorial administrative system that consisted of two different kinds of provinces: 'kingdoms', of which there were twenty, and 'commanderies', numbering eighty-three by the end of the period. After an initial transitional period, the former were ruled by relatives of the Han Dynasty founder, and the latter were administered through governors or generals appointed by the central court. In time, however, the imperial kin were dispossessed and all areas came under central court appointments.

At the beginning of the Han period, the southernmost Mainland still eluded central control. Texts state that the far southwest was occupied by the Dian people, who are known archaeologically to have possessed a bronze culture with affinities to the Southeast Asian Dongson culture.[7] The southern coasts were populated by the Yue peoples. However, discoveries of Han-style solid-brick tombs at Lei Cheng Uk in Hong Kong and in northern Vietnam indicate that by the Late Han period, Han culture had penetrated the far south.[8] Debate rages as to whether Han tombs in the peripheral regions represent an acculturated local population or whether they belonged to Han commandery personnel. I shall return to this question when examining the remains of the Lelang commandery on the northern Korean Peninsula (Chapter 13).

plate 31, fig. 93

fig. 102

Expansion to the northwest

The great Han thrust to the northwest took place between 153 and 90 BC with wars waged against the Xiongnu.[9] Commanderies were established through the Gansu Corridor to Dunhuang between 104 and 67 BC, and the Great Wall was eventually extended westwards to the Tarim Basin. These installations did not incorporate the surrounding areas under firm administrative control but served

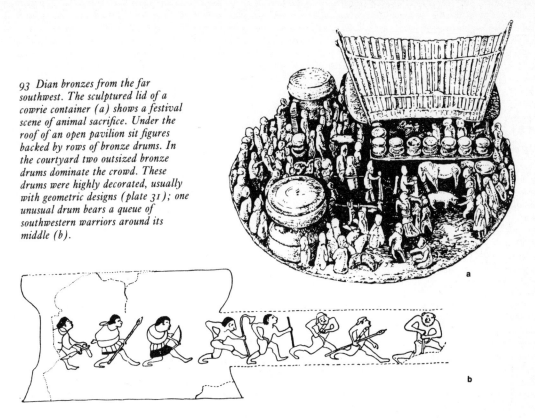

93 *Dian bronzes from the far southwest. The sculptured lid of a cowrie container (a) shows a festival scene of animal sacrifice. Under the roof of an open pavilion sit figures backed by rows of bronze drums. In the courtyard two outsized bronze drums dominate the crowd. These drums were highly decorated, usually with geometric designs (plate 31); one unusual drum bears a queue of southwestern warriors around its middle (b).*

more as a line of defence and communication, the maintenance of which was dependent on the fortunes of the central Han court. The physical remains of these Han defences were first introduced to the Western world by explorers such as Stein, Bergman and Hedin in the early 20th century.[10] Towers perhaps 10 m high, square or rectangular in plan, punctuate the Great Wall at intervals. Like the Great Wall itself in the desert region, these towers were often built of layers of tamarisk branches and reeds sandwiched between rows of sun-dried bricks, the whole then being plastered and whitewashed.[11] Signals were transmitted from tower to tower by smoke, flag or torch fire. The defences were accompanied by storehouses for military and maintenance equipment as well as grain. Some units of conscript troops were assigned agricultural work in an effort to make the garrisons self-supporting. The military establishments thus were not heavily dependent on supplies from the distant capital.

Although few of the remains in the northwest have been properly excavated, we are none the less well supplied with information about the accoutrements and lifeways in the area, thanks to the preservation by the arid desert climate of numerous wooden strips with ink inscriptions. These are administrative artifacts comprising the daily record-keeping files of these outlying posts. Their contents concern postings of mail, inventories of equipment, guard duties, salaries and taxes, etc. Thousands of these wooden strips were extracted from the desert ruins by Western scholars, the largest collections being those of Bergman (now housed at Academia Sinica in Taipei) and Aurel Stein (now in the British Library in London).

94 *The earliest example of a tomb 'spirit path' sculpture. Stone sculpture began in the Han period in order to provide large figures set before tomb entrances. This crude but powerfully sculpted horse straddling a Xiongnu warrior commemorated the exploits of a Han general and guarded the gate of his tomb at Xingping into modern times.*

Han expansion can perhaps be explained by the intertwining of two needs, not mutually exclusive: defence, mainly along the northern border, and trade, particularly to the west and south. In the early 2nd century BC, the Han court instituted a tributary system to appease and pacify the border peoples, especially the Xiongnu.[12] Giving gifts of precious silk materials to aggressive foreign leaders in return for acknowledgement of Han sovereignty was thought to be less costly than maintaining standing armies in strategic areas. This tributary system was revamped in the mid-1st century BC, becoming much more successful than envisaged and putting great stress on the court's finances. First, contraband materials such as iron weaponry passed out of the garrisons via private exchanges by soldiers. Second, eventually many regional peoples came to the commanderies or directly to the central Han court or its Wei Dynasty successor in voluntary submission, hoping to receive great bounty. In this way, much artifactual material of Han and Wei origin flowed in significant amounts into the surrounding areas, particularly bronze mirrors, lacquerware, silks, wine and grain, etc.

Of mirrors and seals

Mirrors and seals are perhaps the most enduring objects which provide evidence of the integration of surrounding regions into the Han (and later the Wei) tributary system. Both objects were given to emissaries to the court from foreign parts; in the court's eyes, seals were the material manifestation of the holder's submission to Han and positioned him or her within the empire's territorial hierarchy. The inscriptions on archaeologically recovered examples can sometimes be matched with references in the dynastic histories to the bestowal of seals on the heads of regional groups.

The style of mirror is an important clue to the dating of many phases of interaction with the Han and Wei courts.[13] Bronze mirrors were initially a product of the Northern Bronze Complex (Chapter 8), but production among the Zhou states began in earnest in the Middle Zhou period. The designs cast on the reverse surface are usually laid out in concentric bands, and the dominant motifs are used to identify the mirrors typologically. Inscriptions were first added to the design pattern at the end of the Zhou period. 'TLV'-

95 *(left) Inscription on a silver seal recovered from the northern Korean Peninsula. The inscription reads 'Pujo Yegun' (in Korean), possibly the name of a local figure who was acknowledged by the Mainland Han bureaucracy through the gift of the seal.*

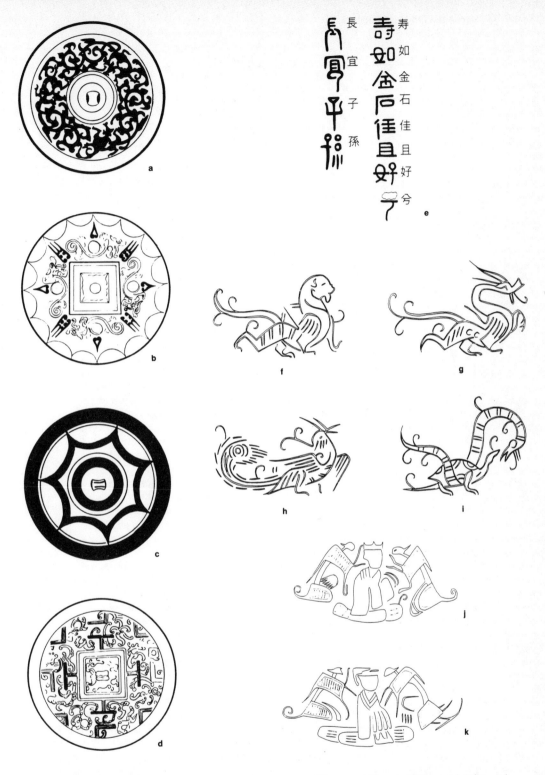

寿如金石佳且好兮
長宜子孫

96 Early Chinese mirrors. The most popular motifs during Late Zhou were 'Shattered Mountain' (plate 37) and 'Intertwining Dragons' (a), which lasted into Early Han. These were augmented from the middle of Early Han by bossed mirrors decorated with star and cloud patterns (b) and 'Inner Petal Ring' types (c); the latter often bear a standard inscription (e) around the central knob reading 'May your family line be longlasting.' TLV mirrors (d), so called because they carry designs resembling these letters, are thought to originate from a board game of the Han period that had cosmological referents. The animal symbols of the four directions occasionally occur as part of mirror decoration: (f) White Tiger of the West, (g) Green Dragon of the East, (h) Red Bird of the South, and (i) Black Warrior (snake and turtle) of the North. Especially popular in Late Han were mirrors bearing the pair of figures, Immortal King of the East (j) and Queen Mother of the West (k).

BOX 12
Han Tombs and Art

In contrast to the vertical shaft tombs such as Mawangdui which continued in popularity from earlier periods, new Han types of tombs were characterized by horizontal access. (a) Chamber tombs were dug like caves into rock cliffs as at Mancheng with its carriage burials and jade suiting (plate 46), or constructed of hollow bricks as at Luolang (b) or of solid bricks as at Lei Cheng Uk in Hong Kong, or built of cut stone. Different kinds of roof corbelling and arch construction reveal great strides in engineering, while a shift in beliefs in the afterworld is implied by the chamber shape, often resembling a house, and its furnishings.

Later Han tombs are noted for the sudden proliferation of flat art in their interiors: impressed bricks and tiles (c), stone panels carved in bas-relief (d), and painted murals (e), which depict scenes in the lives of the elite. These are complemented by a whole new series of ceramic figurines and models (f) of everyday objects such as houses, granaries and models of paddy fields and ploughing. The non-valuable nature of these tomb furnishings suggests a move away from the inclusion of wealth *per se* towards the abstract representation of the secular lifestyle and status of the deceased. Needless to say, this art is extremely informative regarding daily life activities, and it is partially for this reason that it is said that 'of all the historical dynasties of imperial China, the Han is without question the most archaeologically dependent'.

The creation of monumental earthen mounds over the horizontal chambers was another Han civil engineering feat which required great investments of time and labour. From the early 2nd century BC onwards, large stone sculptures of animals began to be placed outside these mounds, giving birth to the 'spirit path' leading up to the tomb in which realistic and semi-mythical animals and even humans were represented (*fig. 94*). A late example can be seen at the Ming Tombs outside modern Beijing. These stone figures contrast greatly with Buddhist sculpture, which has been described as 'profoundly foreign to the Chinese genius'. Three-dimensional animal sculptures were also incorporated into funerary pillars and stelae, with turtle- and lion-shaped bases being favoured in the mid-1st millennium AD.

d

type mirrors, popular during the Middle Han, sometimes incorporate depictions of the Directional Deities. The 'TLV' components themselves might relate to patterns on astrological divining boards.[14] In the Late Han, a major change in design execution occurred. Previous mirrors bore fine linear relief decoration, often with contrasting areas of raised, flat relief such as were characteristic of the distinction between foreground and background on Late Shang bronzes. The adoption of high relief on mirrors in the Late Han allowed for the casting of more realistic portrayals. The 'Queen Mother of the West' is a common sculptural element in Late Han mirror design.

It is debatable how much of a cosmetic function mirrors had in East Asia. In the Zhou period, it was believed that the mirrors themselves had magical powers to ward off evil and ensure a fruitful life. Han-period mirrors, whose cast designs were often of cosmological significance, not only had religious importance to individual owners but also functioned as valued political gifts.[15] Such mirrors, however, were often kept as heirlooms, passed down for generations before finally being deposited in a burial. Like coins and other clearly datable heirloom objects found in burials, they thus provide only a *terminus ante quem* – a 'date before which' the deposit could not have existed.

Economic expansion

State monopolies

Perhaps the greatest stimulus for Han expansion to the south was the potential for trade and industry, that area being an important production zone for lacquerware, iron and salt, and of course, rice. Rice production in particular skyrocketed during Han times with the invention of the mouldboard plough. The wealth of some rulers of Han kingdoms involved in both production and long-distance trade is revealed in lavishly constructed and richly furnished tombs, such as those of the Marquis of Dai (who died in 186 BC) and his family. He, his wife and a son were buried at Mawangdui near modern Changsha City, each in old-fashioned shaft tombs *c.* 15 m deep covered by earthen mounds 50–60 m in diameter. The wooden chambers held nested lacquered coffins filled with sumptuous grave goods, and the body of the wife was so perfectly preserved that an autopsy was recently performed on it.[16] Included were many kinds of silk, hundreds of lacquerware vessels and vanity boxes (one of which contained a cosmetic mirror along with other toilet articles), ceramics, musical instruments, game boards, bronzes with gilt surfaces and jade inlay, weapons inlaid with gold, bronze and silver belt hooks, beads, maps and paintings on silk, bamboo and wooden strip texts (including an important astronomical treatise), plus a multitude of food offerings with exotic spices. It is significant that only ceramic replicas of coins – not the real thing – were deposited in this tomb; indeed real coins were rarely included in Early Han tombs.[17] This suggests that money did indeed function in a market system and was not subject to hoarding. In contrast, coin numbers increased in Late Han burials. It has been noted that the fief of the Marquis of Dai included only seven hundred

Box 12f

fig. 100

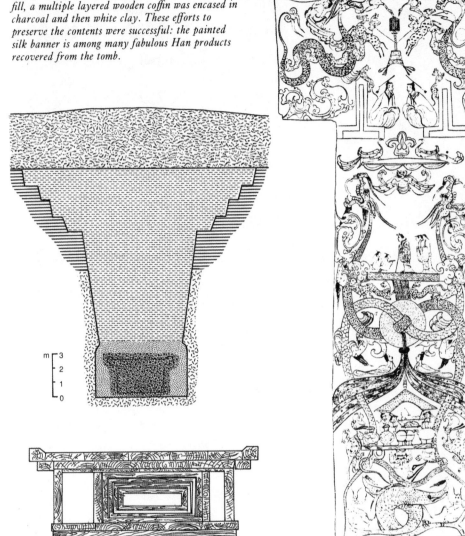

97 *The Mawangdui shaft tomb and silk banner. At the bottom of a deep shaft, under tamped-in earth fill, a multiple layered wooden coffin was encased in charcoal and then white clay. These efforts to preserve the contents were successful: the painted silk banner is among many fabulous Han products recovered from the tomb.*

households – not nearly enough to support such luxury;[18] he must therefore have accumulated most of his fortune through economic transactions.

In 117 BC, iron and salt became state monopolies.[19] The former was crucial to agricultural and military success. Documentary sources indicate that iron armour became common in the Han period, though few examples remain.[20] The organization of labour in the salt industries is perhaps illustrated on a brick tile from a tomb in the Sichuan Basin. Then in 112 BC, the central court monopolized the minting of coins. Two types of coin that are of particular significance in the archaeology of East Asia are the common *wushu* (minted from 73 BC) and the *huoquan* (minted by Wang Mang in AD 14). With strong

98 The Han-period salt industry. A pictorial brick from the 2nd-century AD tomb in the Sichuan Basin illustrates the drawing of water from a well, evaporating it at a hearth, and transporting the salt across the mountains.

central control over the currency and such a basic subsistence item as salt, the Early Han court fostered the rise of a middle class of aristocratic managers. The positions of private entrepreneurs and merchants were undermined in the Early Han period by both of these official monopolies and by the Confucian ethic placing artisans and tradespeople below farmers on the social scale. The governmental stranglehold on private economic development did not change until the Late Han period, when foreign merchants from western Eurasia took up residence in the Luoyang capital.

Beginnings of the silk trade

Around 110 BC, Han intervention was extended west beyond the Dunhuang commandery across the Tarim Basin, leading to the establishment of trade routes into Central Asia. The impetus for this expansion was ostensibly to acquire a new breed of horse for the Han emperor.[21] Whether this story is apocryphal or not, the thrust westwards opened the doors to the influx of many Central Asian products through both tribute and trade: raisins, peaches, clover, furs, woollen textiles and rugs, jade, lapis lazuli and garnet. Later, myriad other products followed from further west (India, Persia, Byzantium): pearls, coral, turquoise, glass objects, gold and silver wares, and perfumes, fragrances and incense. The major commodity exchanged for these materials was silk in the bale, stimulating the 19th-century German geographer Ferdinand von

plate 51

Richthofen to refer to the routes crossing the Takla Makan desert in the Tarim Basin as the 'Seidenstraßen' or 'Silk Roads'.[22]

fig. 100

An incidental import which accompanied goods from South Asia was Buddhism – an import which in time changed the very nature and philosophy of Chinese life, more than could mere material objects. In contrast to Confucianism, which was very much tied to this world through its function of regulating interpersonal relations for the good of the state, the essence of Buddhism was a rejection of this world and its trappings in order to break out of what was believed to be the cycle of rebirth caused by karma. Developed from the teachings of Siddhartha Gautama, who was born in 563 BC to an aristocratic family in northern India but gave up his position and status to seek enlightenment, Buddhism took hold within the small states of northern India and Central Asia in the later 1st millennium BC.

In the Han period, Buddhist monks who accompanied the trading caravans, especially from the state of Kushan in the upper Indus River drainage, established places of worship *en route* and in the foreign merchant communities of the Han capitals. Buddhist cave temples, like those at Bamiyan in Afghanistan, were first constructed along the northern desert route in the Tarim Basin in the Late Han period. Stone Buddha carvings on the east coast of the China Mainland suggest diffusion of the religion through the heart of Han

99 An 8th-century silk brocade. By the Tang period, woven silks as well as Sassanian silver, Persian glass and a hoard of exotic craft goods were transferred from the West through China to Japan. This fabric, preserved in the Shosoin (plate 81), is a weft-figured brocade of bold, large-patterned design – a newer type of silk weaving than warp-brocades.

territory,[23] though Buddhist traditions could also have been brought to the eastern coastal regions by the 'sea silk routes',[24] passing around Southeast Asia from the Indian subcontinent and the Persian Gulf.

Dissolution of the empire

Han successors

The suggestion, often found in the scholarly literature, that the Late Han Dynasty finally succumbed to foreign invasions along its northern border is in fact inaccurate. Rather, the Dynasty was felled by a series of rebellions within its own central provinces starting in AD 187.[25] Within a year, a group of regional warlords was governing through a puppet emperor. When the Dynasty was formally dissolved in 220, the territory of Han was divided up among three ruling houses: Wei in the north, Wu in the south, and Shu (Minor Han) in the southwest. These 'Three Kingdoms' were short-lived, as a *coup* in the Wei territory led to brief unification under the Jin Dynasty (Western Jin AD 265–317, Eastern Jin AD 317–419). The Jin government controlled the northern frontier by holding the Xiongnu leader hostage at court. His long residence there and resultant sinicization had important effects on the subsequent political organization of the northern China Mainland. In 311 and 316, steppe nomads destroyed successive Western Jin capitals and captured the emperors, leading to a century of extreme political fragmentation (the Sixteen Dynasties). At the end of the 4th century, they established the first state on the Central Plains to be run by a northern ethnic group, the Toba Wei Dynasty (386–532).[26]

Buddhism embraced

At the beginning of the 4th century AD, Buddhism suddenly gained favour as a solace to the literati who struggled to survive in those times of extraordinary political turmoil. Since its introduction during the Han period, it had remained confined mainly to foreign merchant enclaves in the Han capitals, although there are records of the establishment of Buddhist communities elsewhere and the building of Buddhist temples in palaces of certain emperors and princes. By the end of the 5th century, however, the existence of almost 8500 temples and over 100,000 monks and nuns bears witness to a remarkable expansion of religious communities and devotees.

fig. 110   The Jin rulers became patrons of Buddhism, which eventually led to the construction of large cave temples at Dunhuang, Yungang and Longmen. The earliest cave at the Mogao grottoes in Dunhuang was dedicated in AD 366.[27]

plate 75   Today Mogao boasts 492 surviving caves identified in a 1.5 km stretch of cliff, dating from the 5th to the 14th century AD. Many have a rectangular floor plan with a central column, on the model of two types of Indian cave temples: one with an anteroom and/or a corridor leading into the main chamber, the other with numerous niches or small rooms leading off from the main chamber. These caves are carved into cliff rock unsuitable for sculpting; thus the walls of

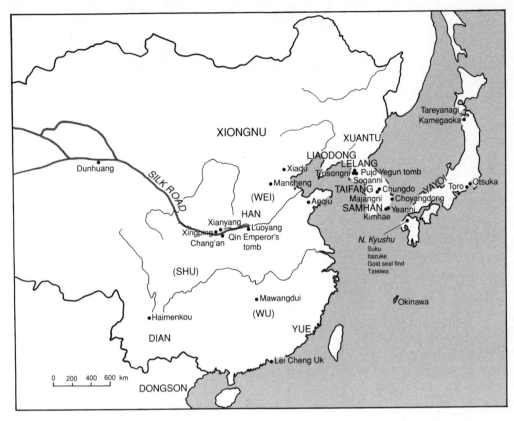

100 Early historic sites of East Asia and contemporary populations, dating between 300 BC and AD 300.

the rooms were plastered with clay and brightly painted with murals which now cover more than 45,000 sq. m of wall and ceiling space. The frescoes portray individual Buddhist deities or scenes from Buddhist literature. Buddhist images were also installed in niches or on pedestals in the caves; constructed with clay modelled over straw-covered wooden frames, they were then painted in brilliant colours. Numbering more than two thousand, some of these astonishing figures seem to merge into a wall as if carved in high relief. The Yungang and Longmen caves, on the other hand, show the magnificence achieved in rock sculpture where the material was available. These caves in sandstone and limestone cliffs were commissioned respectively in AD 460 and 494 by the militant Toba Wei rulers of the north China Mainland near their successive capitals. In addition to the rectangular cave room, these sites also favoured a type of shallow hemispherical niche. Each such niche contained a large central sculpture. *In toto*, the statues at Longmen number 97,300.[28]

CHAPTER 13

The Yellow Sea Interaction Sphere
500 BC–AD 500

During the millennium 500 BC–AD 500, the eastern coastal areas of the Yellow Sea were drawn into an exchange network originating in Zhou state economic expansion and continuing under the Han Dynasty tributary system.[1] The distribution of knife coins as far south as Okinawa indicates the scope of early economic contact, and as mentioned in Chapter 9, the Zhou state of Yan was probably responsible for the introduction of iron into the northern Korean Peninsula. The entire Bohai Bay region was affected by Yan political expansion, which had knock-on effects down the Korean Peninsula. Historical sources give an intriguing picture of emergent political organization in the northern Peninsula: a polity named Choson, documented by 194 BC, came into conflict with Han Dynasty tributary policy in 108 BC. This incited an invasion which changed forever the nature of socio-political development in the region by bringing even the western Japanese Islands into the Han tributary system.

Choson

In the 2nd and 1st centuries BC, the Liaodong peninsula and northern Korean Peninsula were known to the Han court as the Chaoxian region. The *Shiji* implies that Yan actually ruled this region between 300 and 195 BC. At the latter date, an official of Yan named Weiman is said to have fled to Chaoxian and 'founded a principality with its capital at Wang-hsien, a town which apparently occupied the site of modern P'yongyang'.[2] This polity, known by the Korean pronunciation Choson, was ruled by Weiman's grandson when it was invaded and destroyed by Han troops in 109–108 BC. At that time, the Choson 'king' had subordinate to him several 'prime ministers', 'high ministers' and 'generals'. One general was also referred to in the *Shiji* as an 'assistant king'.

One problem in protohistoric archaeology is the interpretation of such documentation. Being written from a Chinese point of view, it is possible that the titles of the offices were applied to the case by the historians. A different problem concerns Wangxian: most scholars assume it to have been an earthen-walled town, but none have been dated to this period on the Korean Peninsula. It is also not clear whether Choson was a city-state or a large territorial entity.

These questions, unanswered by the texts, have stimulated heated debate among Korean scholars, many of whom use nationalistic arguments to classify

Choson as an incipient 'Korean' state rather than a Yan-derived entity. Instead, it is fair to say that Choson was a small polity, hierarchically organized and with centralized leadership, which drew on the developing cosmopolitanism of the place and time. Pit-burials containing horse trappings and carriage fittings form the dominant material remains of the Taedong River basin at the time of invasion.[3] These clearly link the local elite with Yan and the values of state society, regardless of the Choson people's exact ethnic identification.

Because the name Choson survives in the historical documents, most archaeological remains of this time period are assigned to this entity; yet one of the reasons for the Han invasion was that the Choson elite tried to bar communications between other regional chieftains and the Han court. It is thus very likely that the Choson elite were only one group among several vying for political and economic supremacy on the northern Peninsula, just as the contemporaneous Late Bronze Age society of the southern Peninsula might have consisted of several regional aggregations, some with competing chiefly figures (Chapter 10).

The Lelang commandery

Upon the defeat of Choson in 108 BC, five Han commanderies were established in the eastern Manchurian Basin and the northwestern Peninsula. Only three of these remained viable – Liaodong, Xuantu, and Lelang – and a fourth, Taifang, *fig. 100* was created in the 3rd century AD. The *Shiji* states that some Choson personages were enfeoffed within the initial commanderies as a reward for helping to topple Choson,[4] so some continuity with the local elite was apparently maintained.

Ironically, the commandery headquarters of Lelang were revealed archaeologically through yet another colonization of the Korean Peninsula – by the Japanese nearly two thousand years later. In 1934–5, Japanese archaeologists excavated nearly 1200 m² in the walled enclosure at T'osongni that is thought to have served as the late headquarters for the Lelang commandery.[5] The walls enclose approximately 42 ha of uneven ground on the south bank of the *fig. 101* Taedong River near modern P'yongyang. Seven trenches and a large area of 700 m² were excavated in the northern and northeastern portions. Disturbed soil told of previous plunderings, though some features were still recoverable. Brick-paved lanes and covered drainage culverts attested to the well-planned nature of the commandery town. On the higher terrace in the northeastern section, excavators uncovered rows of foundation stones for the pillars of a wooden building; inscribed roof tiles identified it as the 'Lelang Ceremonial Palace', presumably one of the administrative offices of the commandery. An abundance of Han-period bronze coins and clay sealings indicated the headquarters' central economic and administrative functions.

In the hills to the southeast of the walled site are scattered nearly 1500 earth-mounded tombs for the commandery's occupants. The earlier tombs, dating to the late 1st century BC, are Han-style wooden-chamber tombs with internal

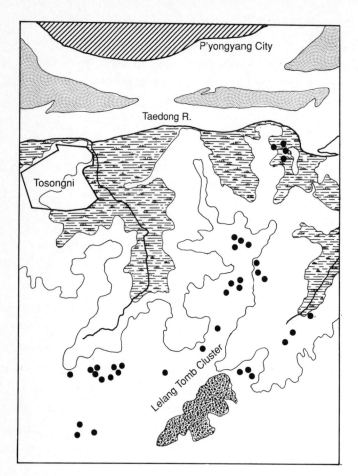

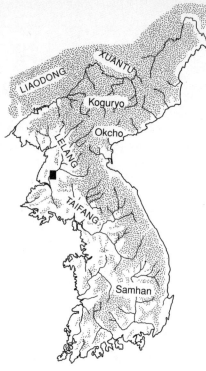

101 The Korean Peninsula in the 1st century BC. The Tosongni walled site, on the south side of the Taedong River near modern P'yongyang, served as the Lelang commandery headquarters for several centuries. Mounded tombs in the hills behind the site contain the remains of the commandery's elite.

partitions separating coffin and grave-good areas. Later tombs, following the styles of Late Han, consisted of brick-chamber (less commonly stone-chamber) tombs in addition to the wooden-chamber ones. These later examples often contained double-encased coffins.

fig. 103   Soganni tomb No. 212, whose mound was 30 m in diameter and 5 m high, had an internally partitioned wooden chamber, one section of which held two wooden coffins, presumably for a husband and wife who were dressed sumptuously and wrapped in silk for interment. The man wore a silk sash, beads, two bronze belt hooks and two silver finger rings, and he carried a wooden seal and iron sword. The woman wore beaded earrings and bracelets, beads in her hair, nine finger rings, and a tortoise-shell decoration in the shape of a round coin hanging from her silk sash. The western compartment held an assortment of ceramics, lacquered wood and bronze vessels, weapons, horse trappings, and carriage fittings. A bronze mirror – accompanied by wooden combs, bundles of silk cloth and a lacquered table – bears an inscription dating it to the 1st century BC.[6]

The bronze vessels and lacquerware items deposited in the tombs, many inscribed with dates, were imported from the China Mainland. The famous painted lacquer basket, for example, excavated from one of the Lelang wooden-chamber tombs in 1931,[7] is presumed to have come all the way from the Sichuan Basin in the far southwestern Mainland, a well-known area of lacquerware manufacture. Furthermore, many of the wooden coffins of the Lelang tombs are made of *Chamaecyparis*, a variety of fragrant wood imported from south of the Yangzi River. The provisioning of the commandery with luxury goods illustrates that Lelang was well integrated into the Han market system, at least in its prosperous years.

The identities of some of those interred in the Lelang tombs are known from the personal seals buried with them. The first intact wooden-chamber tomb excavated by the Japanese in 1925 was found to have belonged to someone called Wang Xu, as attested by his wooden seal. Other individuals are known only by their titles inscribed on administrative seals made of bronze, silver or jade. Two silver seals inscribed with the characters 'Buruo Zhang' (in Chinese), *fig. 95* excavated from a tomb in P'yongyang in 1961, are assumed to have belonged to the *zhang* (a governor of a district with less than 10,000 households) of Buruo, one of the twenty-five known counties of the Lelang commandery.[8]

The identity in ethnic terms of the tombs' occupants, however, is a much more controversial issue. Wang Xu is assumed to have been a member of the

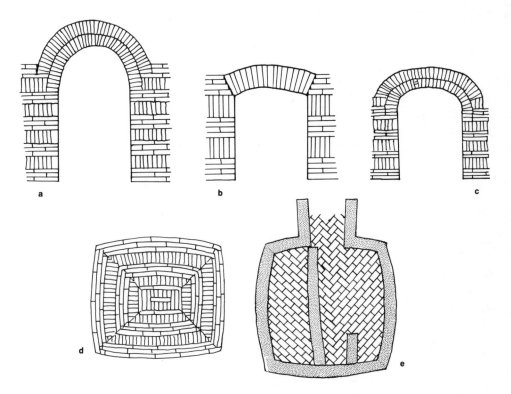

102 Brickwork in Han tombs at Lelang. Arches (a, b, c) and vaulted ceilings (d) taxed the Han bricklayers' ingenuity. Brick floor paving (e) in several patterns added attractively to the finished tomb's appearance.

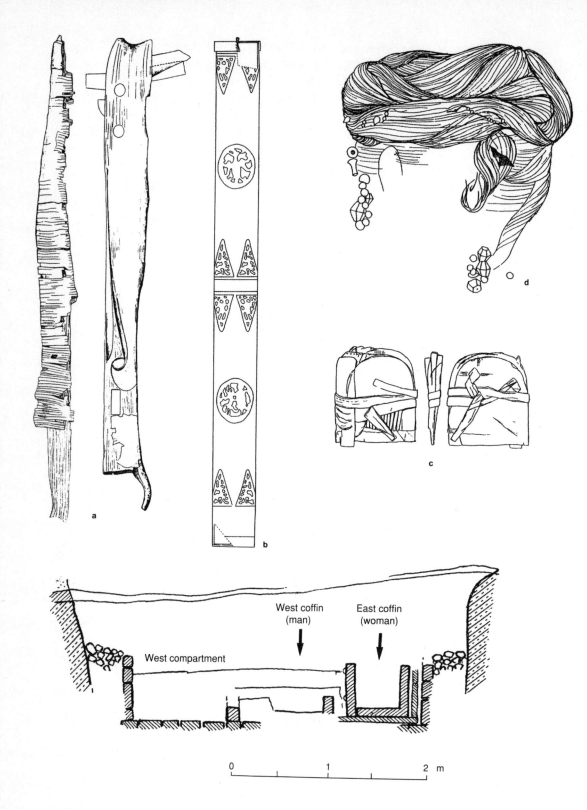

103 Man and wife together forever in tomb no. 212 at Soganni. Grave goods included a wooden crossbow (a), lacquered quiver with appliquéd silver medallions (b), and silk pouch containing wooden combs (c). The woman's hair (d) was miraculously preserved, ornamented with silk-strung beads, her earrings in place below.

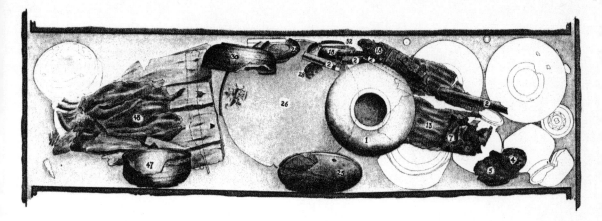

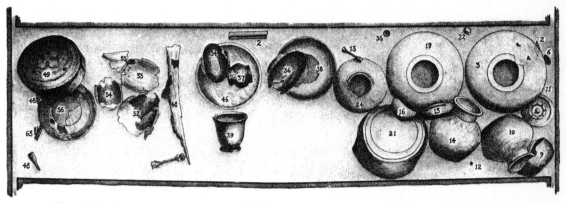

104 Watercolour illustrations of the Lelang tomb finds. These exquisite reproductions show the skill and care devoted to the original Japanese excavation reports. The grave goods are illustrated at two levels of discovery: the top layer above, the underlying layer below.

Chinese immigrant population, both from his name and from the many Chinese-style grave goods and three women interred with him. Buruo Zhang, on the other hand, is considered a Peninsular native because of the more indigenous nature of his grave goods: slender bronze daggers, a mirror, horse trappings and carriage fittings, very similar to the contents of the pit-burials attributed to Choson. The acculturation of native elites to Han material culture was perhaps to be expected, but a recent study also shows a modest adoption of local ways by the commandery elites.[9]

The fortunes of Lelang waxed and waned with the fluctuations in the political stability of the central Han government. During its first two centuries, the commandery headquarters appears from its tomb remains to have been a prosperous community, whereas by AD 190 the local administration was bankrupt due to the decline of the Han court. At this time, many of the Mainland residents of the commandery appear to have fled, their places taken by an influx of local peoples. Such deterioration stimulated the warlord of the Liaodong commandery further north to intervene and re-establish Lelang as part of his private holdings. In AD 220, upon the fall of the Han Dynasty, he carved out a new commandery called Taifang from Lelang's southern districts.[10] The successor state to Han in north China, the Wei Dynasty, tolerated this appropriation until AD 237 when Wei armies attacked the Liaodong, Lelang and Taifang headquarters and reintegrated these regions under central control. These conquests marked the re-imposition of commandery influence on the eastern coasts of the Yellow Sea, setting the stage for further tributary contacts with the Yayoi peoples of the western Japanese Islands in the mid-3rd century AD.

The southern Peninsula

With the Lelang commandery controlling most of the northern Korean Peninsula, what was happening in the south? The archaeological record and historical documents tell very different stories for the early centuries AD, commonly known as the Proto–Three Kingdoms era or Iron Age II (AD 1–300). Dolmen burials, as described for this area in Chapter 10, ceased in the south at this time, but the tradition of Mumun pottery continued and was joined by new ceramic forms of Mainland derivation. Local manufacturing of iron only began during this period, despite iron being known in the north since 400 BC.

The 'Three Han'

According to the *Weizhi*,[11] the Korean Peninsula south of the Taifang commandery was divided into three areas known as the Samhan, or 'Three Han':[12] Mahan, P'yonhan and Chinhan. Today these are generally understood to correspond respectively to the southwestern Peninsula, the Nakdong River valley, and the southeastern Peninsula. Each of these areas was further subdivided into small polities: Mahan harboured fifty-four polities, P'yonhan and Chinhan twelve each.

Each of these seventy-eight small polities is said to have been ruled by a chieftain, whose title varied depending on whether the polity was small or large. At least in Mahan, priestly duties were apparently entrusted to a second, independent figure. The commandery administrators acknowledged the positions of some of these chiefs by giving them titles and seals, thereby increasing their status and authority. This practice, however, also served to set chiefs against each other. Some local chiefs or lords were appointed – or bribed into co-operating – by Lelang officials without having a local power base. As commandery agents, these appointees are seen by some historians as having undermined the indigenous structure of authority, thus retarding the natural political growth of the Samhan polities through a policy of divide and rule.[13]

Scholars tend to interpret Iron Age II archaeological remains in terms of these small political units named in the historical documents. An outstanding feature of these remains, however, is their paucity and lack of hierarchical structure. Thus from the archaeological point of view, the southern Peninsula looks less well organized than the texts imply. In fact, a decline in hierarchical organization from the Late Bronze Age society of this region can be postulated, perhaps bearing out one historian's assessment that interaction with Lelang destroyed the indigenous social order.[14]

Contact with Lelang is evidenced in regional graves furnished with exotic goods. Near the modern city of Kyongju, pit-burials in the Choyangdong *fig. 100* cemetery have yielded several Han mirrors and an abundance of iron weapons, some with lacquered sheaths.[15] The excavation of this site in 1981–2 caused a sensation among archaeologists, for few Han Dynasty tribute goods had previously been recovered from the southern Peninsula. Choyangdong burial No. 38 is described as having belonged to a powerful local chieftain who involved himself in 'brisk economic activity' in the Yellow Sea trading network.[16] Another unusually informative site on the southern Peninsula is Tahori, a cemetery of jar and coffin burials spanning Iron Age II into the Three Kingdoms era. Burial No. 1, the best preserved, shows considerable influence from China Mainland funerary traditions.[17] It was a pit-tomb with wooden coffin and a separate hole within the pit for the deposit of grave goods. Scores of objects were found beside and inside the coffin, and the interior pit yielded bronze and iron spearheads, Star-and-Cloud bronze mirrors of mid-Early Han date, an animal buckle, a small bronze bell, *wushu* coins, a lacquered brush handle, and a lacquered sword sheath. The brush suggests a literate and therefore politically powerful person, and the iron and lacquerware indicate a high level of local craft development.

The presence of Lelang apparently stimulated the development of a Peninsular iron industry.[18] During Iron Age I (400 BC–AD 1), the iron artifacts in evidence in the north are assumed to have been imported; but as the commanderies established themselves, they demanded raw materials both for their own provisioning and for sending back to the central Mainland provinces. This demand apparently led local societies on the Peninsula to initiate iron manufacturing in both the Han River basin and the Nakdong River delta region. Scholars disagree as to whether the raw material utilized in local production was obtained from iron sands in the southern region or from the extensive outcroppings of iron ore in the major river valleys. Analyses of iron objects reveal disparate production methods: Chinese-style goods of wrought iron and white cast iron evince rather sophisticated techniques (carburization, folding-forging, and quenching, heat treatment, and parching), whereas indigenous shapes such as flat and oval-socketed axes were products of a simple smithing technology.[19] The obvious conclusion is that the more sophisticated Mainland-style goods were imported.[20]

Typical of production sites in the Han River drainage is Majangni near Seoul, originally discovered by American troops digging foxholes in 1952.[21] A rectangular pit-house contained a circular hearth 1.2 m in diameter constructed with river cobbles and clay mortar, positioned towards one corner of the 6 × 7 m room. Embedded in the soil near the hearth were clay bellows nozzles, refining slag and two fragments of iron, one perhaps ready for forging.[22] The type site for Iron Age II is the Kimhae shellmound, located west of Pusan on the southern Korean coast.[23] It is one of several shellmounds in the region to

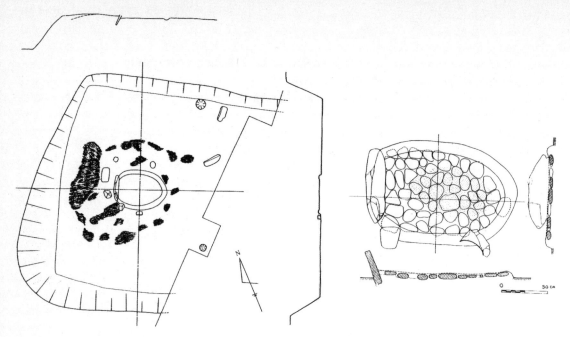

105 An iron workshop at the Peninsular site of Chungdo? Located upriver from Majangni on the Han River, this late Iron Age site yielded a cobble-paved hearth (right) positioned inside a pit-building (left). The floor was covered in places by charcoal deposits several centimetres thick. Various iron objects including knives, an arrowhead and sickles were recovered from the interior.

yield evidence of iron-working in the form of slag and utilitarian iron articles such as knives and axes. The Kimhae shellmound, positioned on a hillock, now overlooks alluviated coastal plains of recent formation; in the Late Iron Age, it would have been a coastal site well situated for commercial access. This site provides the name of the dominant ceramics of this period, though their nature is much disputed.

The *Weizhi* states that the Samhan polity called P'yonhan sent iron to Lelang and Taifang as tribute. Additionally, it records that the peoples of 'Wa, Ye and Han' (in the Japanese Islands, northeastern Korean Peninsula, and southern Korean Peninsula respectively) all converged on the southern coast of the Peninsula to obtain iron for use in their own markets. The Yellow Sea trading network thus consisted not only of commandery trade but also much indigenous regional trade. Any implication, however, that these Pen/Insular peoples had a market system as well developed as that of Han China is doubtful. Such textual references must be used with care when assessing indigenous social, economic and political organization.

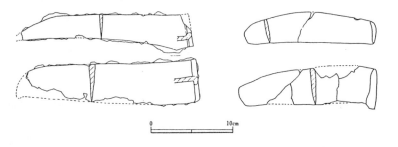

106 Iron sickles in Yayoi-period Kyushu. In the Late Yayoi period, stone reaping knives disappeared altogether, being replaced by iron sickles. The iron trade with the southern Korean coast must have been crucial in supplying such tools to the Insular polities.

BOX 13
Stoneware Production

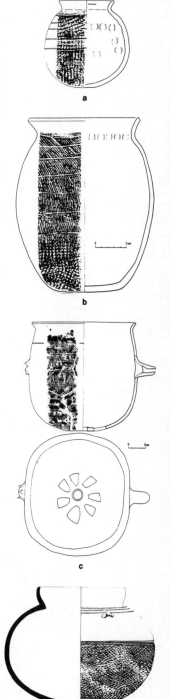

The advent of stoneware production on the Korean Peninsula is a hotly disputed topic. The resolution of the debate will have important ramifications both for the dating of Iron Age sites and for understanding the mechanisms of technological transfer from the China Mainland to the Pen/Insular regions.

The non-Mumun pottery of the Korean Iron Age has traditionally been called 'Kimhae ware', a category which includes red and grey earthenwares as well as so-called 'stonewares'. Recently, a new earthenware category has been defined called 'Wajil ware', potentially overlapping with the Kimhae earthenwares. Certain Kimhae and Wajil vessels owe some debt to Mainland-style ceramics in their surface finishing and decoration: the paddled surfaces and incised lines drawn around the shoulders of Kimhae pots (a, b), including the new-style steamer (c), imitate Late Zhou and Han greyware vessels (d); and the incised cross-hatched bands on the shoulders of some Wajil basins (e) echo southern Mainland ceramics of the 2nd–3rd centuries AD (f). The kiln technology for firing these wares at high temperatures was probably introduced into the Peninsula either via Lelang or directly from the southern Mainland where stoneware production was in full swing.

Whereas the traditionalist users of the Kimhae ware category believe that stoneware production on the Peninsula commenced in the 1st century BC or so, revisionist proponents of the Wajil category insist for various reasons that the date must be brought forward to the late 3rd or early 4th century AD. As a result, a site yielding 'stoneware' could be dated by the traditionalists to any time after the 1st century BC, but the same site would be dated by the revisionists to no earlier than the 3rd century AD. These dating problems have yet to be resolved, but when they are, the archaeological sequence for the Korean Peninsula is due to undergo some drastic revisions.

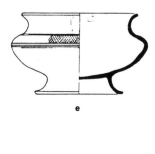

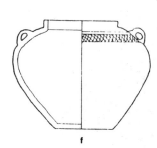

Western Yayoi interaction

Tribute from Wa

From recorded instances in the dynastic histories, the *Houhanshu* and *Weizhi*, it is known that the Wa peoples from the Japanese Islands sent envoys to the Han Dynasty court, probably through Lelang, in AD 57 and 107.[24] Also, between AD 238 and 247, four envoys were sent from Wa to Taifang. The envoys submitted tribute consisting of local products: cloth with woven designs, jade, pearls, cinnabar, bows and arrows, and 'slaves'. They returned with gifts from the court consisting of brocade, silk, gold, swords, bronze mirrors, jade and red beads.[17] Of course, these extensive contacts through the Yellow Sea and across the Korea Strait required well-made boats and considerable navigational skills (Chapter 16).

On the Japanese Island of Kyushu, the Middle Yayoi jar burial cemetery at plate 1   Suku reveals the wealth of materials gleaned from the commandery trade by the Wa peoples. Twenty-nine of more than two hundred burials were excavated in 1929 and 1962, producing Early Han mirrors, glass *bi* disks, bronze and iron daggers, spearpoints and halberds. Many newly excavated sites around the Suku cemetery have yielded moulds and other evidence of the manufacture of bronze and glass objects. This area of the north Kyushu coast was a locus of elite activity, possibly corresponding to the country of Nu mentioned in the inscription on a gold seal discovered in 1784 under a rock on an island in modern Fukuoka Bay. The *Houhanshu* states that: 'In the second year of the Chien-wu Chung-yuan era (AD 57), the Wa country Nu sent an envoy with tribute who called himself *ta-fu*. ... Kuang-wu bestowed on him a seal.'[25]

Political development

The *Weizhi* describes the political organization of Wa as being much like that of Samhan: more than a hundred small polities (*guo*) scattered through the

107 A snake-knobbed gold seal from north Kyushu. Could this be the exact same seal mentioned as being bestowed on the King of Nu by the Han dynasty in AD 57? The inscription on the bottom reads, in modern Japanese, as 'Han no Wa no Na no Kokuoh', possibly translatable as 'The King of Na of Wa, affiliated with Han.'

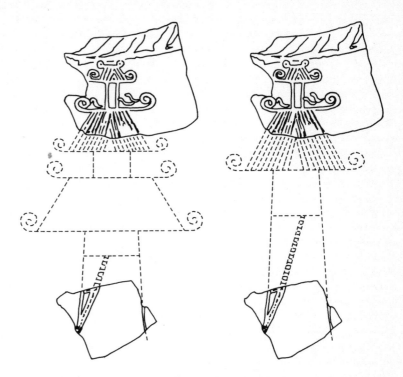

108 Picture sherds from a Yayoi jar in Nara. The recent excavation of these picture sherds, illustrating a multi-storied tower, is taken by some Japanese archaeologists as confirmation of the Kinai hypothesis of Yama(t)ai location. Reconstructed here in two different ways, the architecture is thought to conform to the descriptions of structures at Queen Himiko's capital.

western Islands, with several under the hegemonic rule of a country called Yamatai. The exact location of Yamatai within Japan has been debated for over one thousand years, due to the fact that the navigational instructions for reaching it as described in the *Weizhi* are hopelessly inadequate.[26] There are two schools of thought concerning its location: the Tokyo school, which places Yamatai in Kyushu; and the Kyoto school, which places it in the Kinai region. The Kinai hypothesis has come to dominate this controversy, but recently debate has been reopened by the recognition of transcriptional variations in the name of the country. 'Yamai' is now proposed as the original name by those who believe the country was located in Kyushu.[27] This is a controversy that will never be settled unless direct inscriptional material is discovered. Nevertheless, a tremendous amount of energy is expended in trying to equate archaeological remains with Yama(ta)i.

The *Weizhi* further states that Yama(ta)i was ruled for a time by an older woman called Himiko, who apparently employed shamanistic skills in her reign. She is said to have lived in a stockade protected by guard towers; and though she had a thousand servants, no one but her brother ever saw her. In AD 238, Himiko sent tribute to the Wei court via Taifang. In accordance with the policy for voluntary submissions, she was granted the title 'Queen of Wa Friendly to Wei' and was sent in return a gold seal and many sumptuous gifts including one hundred bronze mirrors.[28] When Himiko died a few years later, it is recorded that for her burial place 'a great mound was raised, more than a hundred paces in diameter'.[29] This passage in the *Weizhi* has captured the imaginations of generations of Japanese scholars, and many sites including the

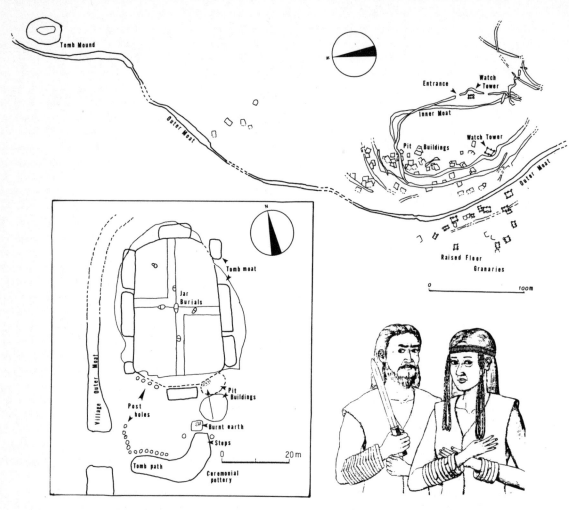

109 The double-moated Yayoi site at Yoshinogari, north Kyushu. The best-preserved lowland Yayoi site in Japan, Yoshinogari's architecture and organization conform to descriptions in the early Chinese texts of the chiefly capitals of Yayoi society. The central jar-burial in the northern mound (inset), dating to the early 1st century BC, contained blue glass beads, and an unusual bronze dagger and hilt cast in one solid piece. The beads are 'Chinese' glass, the dagger was imported from the Peninsula, and the mound technology is non-indigenous. In contrast to these continental-type goods, Yayoi men and women wore arm bracelets of different kinds of shells imported from the southern seas around Okinawa Island.

Middle Yayoi jar burials of Kyushu have been nominated as her grave. Proponents of the Kinai hypothesis prefer to believe that Himiko was interred in the Hashihaka tomb in Nara Prefecture – an interpretation which partakes of the Kinai hypothesis of Yama(ta)i location – but this leaves unexplained the hundred-year gap between her recorded death and the estimated date of construction of the tomb.

The recent discovery of the double-moated Yayoi site of Yoshinogari[30] in Kyushu has also fuelled interest in Yama(ta)i, though it has no direct link with

Himiko. The Late Yayoi component consists of features that can be related to architectural structures named in the *Weizhi*: large post-holes supported pillars for tall buildings interpreted as watchtowers; the interior precinct may have been an elite residence; and an adjacent fenced-off structure is interpreted by some scholars as a temporary burial palace.[31] The fortified nature of the site   *fig. 87* recalls other Late Yayoi moated sites, in sharp contrast to the unbounded agricultural village of Toro (Chapter 11). The mound-burials at the northern and southern edges of Yoshinogari entail the first indications of elitist intercourse with the continent that would become quite considerable later on.

Undoubtedly, competition and conflict in the western Japanese Islands was endemic during this period. Two further lines of evidence support this claim. One is the actual mention in the *Weizhi* of a 'Wa disturbance' lasting seventy to eighty years in the late 2nd and early 3rd centuries AD. Another is an analysis of changes in stone arrowheads during the Yayoi period, demonstrating their sudden increase in size and weight – changes which are interpreted as a shift in their function from game hunting implements to weapons.[32]

These indications of increasing strife in the Late Yayoi period are accompanied by the construction of mound-burials which have been interpreted as the graves of chiefs. Mound-burials vary considerably in shape   *fig. 89* and size but generally contain few grave goods. Though quite extensive in plan, they are too low in height to permit considering them as monumental constructions, like the mounded tombs built from the 4th century onwards (Chapter 14).

The trend towards institutionalized violence in the Yayoi period, followed by the emergence of an elite material culture in the Kofun period, echoes the transition from the Late Neolithic to the Shang period in Chinese protohistory and marks the beginnings of local state formation in the Pen/Insular region.

CHAPTER 14

The Mounded Tomb Cultures
AD 300–700

Both historical and archaeological sources reveal phenomenal changes in the Pen/Insular region upon the decline of the Wei Dynasty in AD 265 and the demise of Lelang in AD 313. In the material record, several 'mounded tomb cultures' emerge, characterized by earthen or stone mounded tombs containing rich grave goods in bronze, gilt bronze, gold, jade, jasper and ceramic. In the historical records appear the names of strong polities which are usually equated with regional manifestations of the mounded tomb cultures: Koguryo, straddling the modern border between China and Korea, Paekche and Shilla on the Korean Peninsula, and Yamato in the western Japanese Islands. There was also a group of small polities known collectively as Kaya in the centre of the southern Peninsular coast.

These historically known polities co-existed during the Korean Three Kingdoms period (AD 300–668) and the Japanese Kofun period (AD 300–710). From the 4th century AD onwards, the infrastructure of state administration was assembled and elaborated in each polity, leading to competition between them for territorial domination. Aspects of their internal organization and the nature of interaction between the polities are known from the contemporaneous Chinese dynastic histories and the native historical records, the *Nihon Shoki* and *Samguk Sagi*, which cover these periods retrospectively.[1]

The *Samguk Sagi* gives traditional founding dates of Shilla, Koguryo and Paekche respectively as 57, 37 and 18 BC. These dates are at odds with the mounded tomb evidence for social stratification – manifested only around AD 300. Thus the historical and archaeological data offer vastly different criteria for recognizing the appearance of state level organization in the Pen/Insulae. The criteria adopted here are that the mounded tombs signify social stratification and that stratified society is the foremost prerequisite for state formation; so whatever forms the Peninsular polities took prior to the 4th century cannot be termed 'states' according to this reading of history.

Rise of the regional elite

Mounded tomb burial
As was mentioned in Chapter 7, the erection of large burial-mounds began on the China Mainland in the later 3rd millennium BC. These were more common

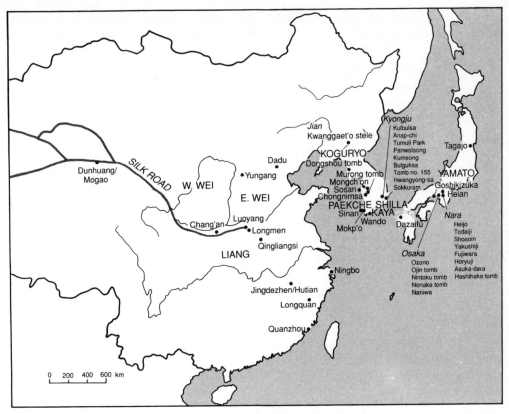

110 Protohistoric and early historic sites from AD 300 onwards mentioned in the text.

in the south than the north, and the regional traditions probably had different origins. For example, in contrast to the mounded platform burials in the Late Neolithic Liangzhu culture, the mounds of the northern Zhou state of Zhongshan supported funerary palaces, suggesting that they developed from earthen foundation platforms.[2] The Han Dynasty tradition of mounded tomb-building was transferred to the Korean Peninsula with the establishment of Lelang. Surrounding peoples passing through Lelang on tributary missions must have seen the mounded tombs, but the intriguing fact is that the constructions were not generally copied once the missions returned home. The two large mounds dating to the 1st century BC at Yoshinogari are an exception.   *fig. 109*

As far as is known, such large earthen mounds were not built again outside of Lelang in the Pen/Insular region for another three hundred years. It is unlikely that there was a sumptuary restriction on such constructions that could be enforced by the Chinese. More likely, the indigenous chieftains did not have control over the necessary labour resources. This is not to say, however, that mounds were not used at all over burials. The cist-burial cemetery at Late Iron Age Yeanni on the southern Korean coast might have had a very low mound covering each burial,[3] while in the Islands, both moated precincts and mound-burials had low mounds. But virtually none evinced monumentality and rich furnishings on a par with the mounded tombs built from the late 3rd century onwards.

It was the construction of very large mounds, worthy rivals to their Mainland predecessors, that marked the emergence of a Pen/Insular political elite in the early 4th century. These mounds are monumental in size, rich in contents, and positioned in separate, isolated cemeteries – emphasizing the social distance between elite and commoner strata. There were three main mounded tomb traditions in the Pen/Insular region. These correspond somewhat to the polities named in the historical documents, but as was the case with the Shang, the boundaries of material culture distributions cannot be strictly equated with political boundaries.

The first tomb-building tradition of the northwestern Peninsula focused on the use of stone. Cairns made of heaped river cobbles prior to 300 AD gave way in the 4th century to pyramids of hewn stone blocks containing an elevated burial chamber. Both types of burial facilities are traditionally identified with Koguryo in the north, but the latter type also occurs as far south as the Han River drainage in early Paekche territory – perhaps supporting the historical ideology that the Koguryo and Paekche elite were related to each other.[4] Very few grave goods have been recovered from these tombs because they were easily looted; however, historical references to gold objects and horse trappings substantiate their elite attribution, and intact tombs have been excavated by Chinese teams in Jilin Province.[5]

The second mounded tomb tradition of the southeastern Peninsula was characterized during the 4th century by multiple stone-lined pit-burials covered with a single mound. This tradition spans what subsequently became the territories of Kaya and Shilla, though Shilla later distinguished itself by developing a unique tomb structure incorporating elements from both Koguryo and the Mainland. This structure is evident in the royal tombs of 5th- and 6th-century Shilla in Kyongju City, which contain a wooden coffin and chamber structure at ground level, heaped over with river cobbles and then covered with a thick layer of earth. This structure has prevented looting, and the gold and glass objects recovered from these tombs are incomparable.

In the Japanese Islands, the third tradition of mounded tomb building began in the late 3rd century in the Nara Basin – the traditional homeland of the Yamato state[6] – and spread westwards. The early tombs had several shapes: round, square and keyhole. Prior to the late 5th century, the main burial was set into the summit of the main mound. Throughout the Kofun period clay cylinders and funerary sculptures called *haniwa* were erected on the tomb surface around the burial pit; the sculptures might owe their inspiration to the stone-figure 'spirit paths' of Mainland mounded tombs. Early *haniwa* included sculpted representations of houses (for the deceased's spirit?), parasols as a badge of rank, and shields to ward off evil. A distinctive aspect of the Insular tradition is the striking homogeneity of grave goods in tombs throughout the western Islands. These consisted of objects with primarily ritual or ceremonial

plate 63

plates 64, 65

fig. 112

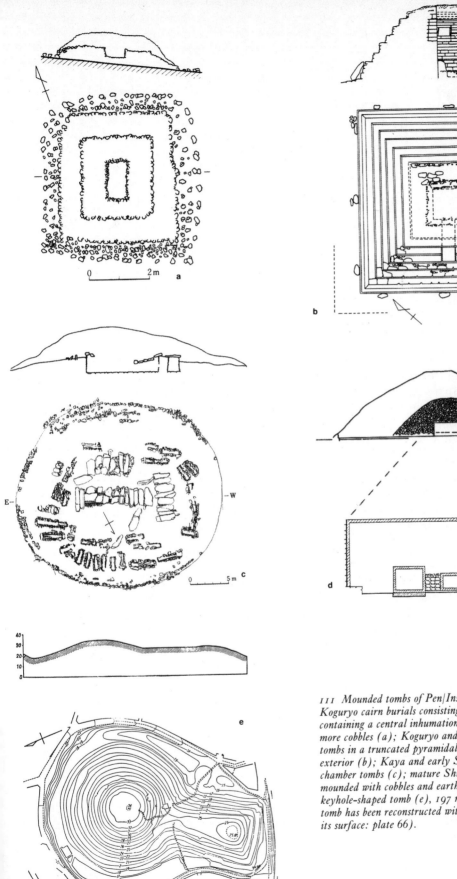

111 Mounded tombs of Pen/Insular cultures. Early Koguryo cairn burials consisting of a bed of river cobbles containing a central inhumation then mounded over with more cobbles (a); Koguryo and Paekche hewn stone tombs in a truncated pyramidal shape with a stepped exterior (b); Kaya and early Shilla multiple stone pit-chamber tombs (c); mature Shilla wooden chamber tombs mounded with cobbles and earth (d); and Yamato keyhole-shaped tomb (e), 197 m in length (this keyhole tomb has been reconstructed with replicas of haniwa on its surface: plate 66).

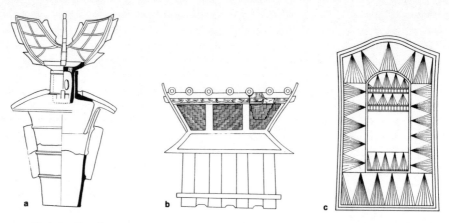

112 Early haniwa *funerary sculptures. A 'parasol' symbolizing elite status, equipped with finials and set into a finned cylinder (a), an upper-class house with hipped and gabled roof and panel walls (b), and a decorated shield to protect the grave (c) are some of the objects in the Early Kofun-period* haniwa *repertoire.*

significance: bronze mirrors, jade and jasper beads, and so-called 'bracelets' made of jasper or green tuff.

In the late 4th century these regional traditions of tomb construction began to be superseded by simplified versions of the Mainland-style horizontal tomb chamber equipped with an entrance corridor and covered by an earthen mound. Such tombs first appeared in the northern Peninsula in the old territory of Lelang and the capital area of Koguryo on the Yalu River. Built either with natural boulder or hewn stone walls, many of these even have formal architectural features such as antechambers, pillars, and corbelled ceilings – constructed with varying degrees of sophistication. A rare few bear interior wall paintings which are sketched directly on to bare walls (in the case of hewn stone construction) or on to plaster (covering natural stone surfaces), then coloured and finally detailed with heavy black brush strokes.

fig. 114

The earliest motif in the Koguryo tomb murals,[7] in common with those on the China Mainland, is the official portrait showing the deceased in a formal pose. A Koguryo adaptation is the genre mural, showing the deceased involved in various activities such as hunting and feasting. These genre paintings are especially informative on Koguryo lifestyles and customs of the 5th and 6th centuries. Finally, there is the motif of the Directional Deities, most popular in the early 7th century. Subsidiary designs include heavenly fairies riding dragons and playing musical instruments, floral scrolls, and miscellaneous guardians and beasts. Almost 80 per cent of the Koguryo mural tombs contain some Buddhist motifs, suggesting the degree of elite interest in this new religion. The fame of the mural tombs overshadows the fact that they account for less than 1 per cent of the known Koguryo tombs (66 out of *c.* 10,000)[8] and are even rarer in the other Pen/Insular cultures.

The corridor tombs of the southwestern Peninsula occur in a greater variety of shapes although they are mostly of stone. The most famous is the unusual

113 Corridor-type stone chambers across East Asia. Mainland-style chamber architecture (a); Koguryo corbelled roof tomb (b); Shilla stone chamber with offset entrance corridor (c); horizontal stone chamber of Yamato equipped with two stone sarcophagi.

brick tomb of King Muryong (d. AD 523) of Paekche.[9] Whereas the structure was modelled on the Mainland tombs of the southern Liang Dynasty (AD 502–56), the grave goods were local products.[10] This tomb is one of the rare ones recovered intact, and its contents demonstrate not only kingly wealth but also the wide variety of specialist craft products – including lacquered coffins and footrest, painted wooden pillows, gold hairpin, silver and gold bracelets and other ornaments, silver wine cup, and bronze chopsticks, comb and bowl – that were being produced in 6th-century Paekche.

The horizontal chamber tomb was introduced into the Japanese Islands by Paekche elite in the early 5th century. Its adoption there coincided with the breakdown of mounded tomb culture homogeneity and the rise of regional variations. In 6th-century eastern Honshu, *haniwa* were reoriented on the tomb surface to emphasize the corridor entrance, while also taking on new forms representative of the Kanto frontier culture: lively figures of nobles, warriors, entertainers, shamans and commoners as well as animals, farmyard scenes, and the like.[11] Concurrently in Kyushu, the mounded tombs bore not

plates 67, 68, 72, 83

114 Tomb mural types found in corridor-tomb chambers. Genre murals of Koguryo style (a); portrait murals of Mainland style (b); directional deities as wall murals (c); Buddhist lotus motifs (d); Kyushu style showing boat-bird-sun motif (lower left) and three quivers (e).

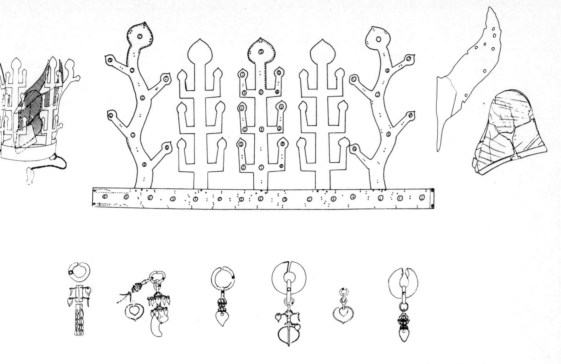

115 Shilla gold crowns and jewelry. A gold crown, cap and diadem and a reconstruction showing how they were worn together; a row of gold earrings, often including a jade curved bead (second from left).

haniwa but stone sculptures on their surfaces, and many of the tomb chambers were decorated inside with wall paintings reminiscent of continental murals.[12]

Box 14e
fig. 114e

Prestige goods production

The precious goods deposited in the tombs were products made on elite demand or obtained for their exclusive use. As with Shang bronze-working, several new industries or products came into being with elite intervention; it is very likely that itinerant or immigrant craftspeople were pressed into service for these purposes.

plates 69–71

For example, Shilla is renowned for its gold-working, which was technologically related to that of the Han Dynasty as evidenced at Lelang. The name of Shilla's capital, Kumsong, and its ruling clan, Kim, both refer to gold.[13] The Kim clan is one of three that are believed to have migrated into Shilla territory and taken over rulership. The date and reality of this event are unknown, but if the Kims were actually connected with gold-crafting, they might have migrated from Lelang upon its demise, bringing with them gold technology and the wooden chamber form of burial. In the 5th century, gold ornaments of Shilla style, including earrings, bracelets, finger rings, and crowns, were imported into or influenced local production in all the other Pen/Isular states.

plate 84

In the Japanese Islands, two characteristic artifact types occur in the early mounded tombs which indicate very different relationships of rulers to prestige good producers. The foremost artifact is the bronze mirror. Although bronze-

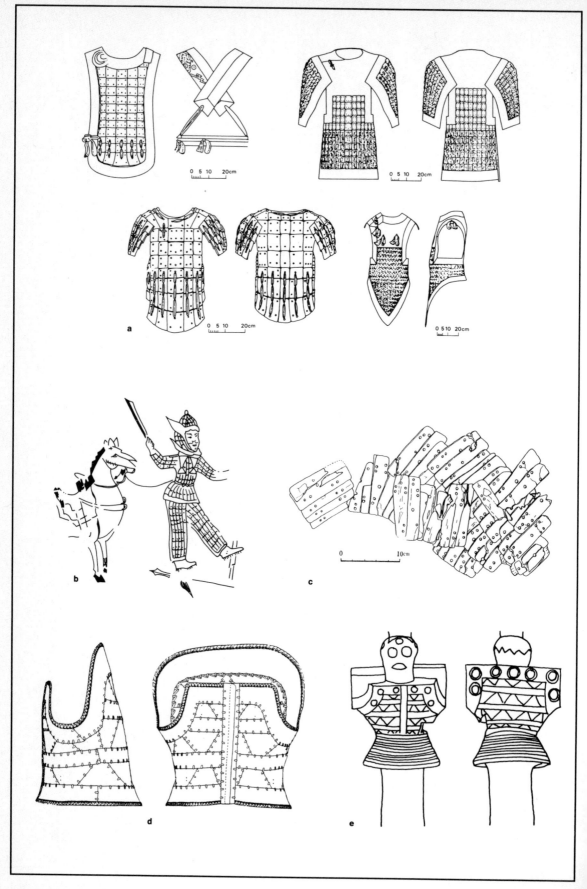

a

b

c

d

e

BOX 14
The Warrior Aristocrat

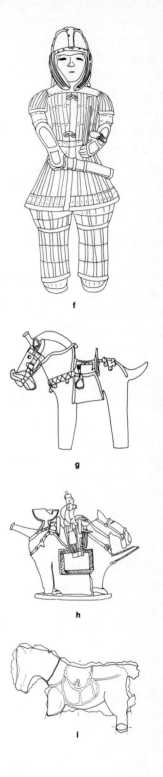

f

The terracotta army of the first Qin emperor provides the earliest substantial examples of body armour. Several types were in use in the late 3rd century BC: vests with longer or shorter aprons in front depending on whether the soldier was mounted, driving a chariot, or on foot (a). All were constructed of rectangular overlapping plates, probably of leather, but there is controversy over whether these were joined with leather thongs or whether some had rivets. This general kind of lamellar armour apparently continued into the Han period with the addition of neck protectors, though finds of Han armour are few. Carrying through the technology of lamellar body armour, suits made of jade plates sewn together with gold thread were worn by the deceased when they were buried in the Han-period cave tombs of Mancheng (*plate 46*).

The armoured, horse-riding warrior became a common image with the late 4th-century rise of the Toba Wei in the north China Mainland. Trained in the steppe traditions of horsemanship and clad in full body armour of Western derivation, the Wei aristocracy made its influence felt in elite circles throughout the Pen/Insular region. Mural tombs depict Koguryo counterparts (b), while armour made of bone (c) and iron (d) has been excavated from early Paekche and Kaya sites respectively. Yamato tombs have also yielded short and long iron body armour and helmets, while the stone figures of Kyushu (e) and Kanto-region *haniwa* (f) depict fully armoured warriors.

The horse was a valued possession, lavishly fitted out with gilt bronze harness ornaments and filigree saddle decorations – all replicated on 6th-century *haniwa* (g) and Shilla effigy vessels (h). In the 7th and 8th centuries, smaller figurines of horses became popular in Shilla, made of iron (i), and in Yamato, made of clay. Excavations in Japan are beginning to provide hard evidence for horse sacrifice (j), an act specifically prohibited in the *Nihon Shoki*, which states that it was carried out at the owner's death.

The adoption of horse and armour as part of the Pen/Insular aristocratic order marks the fruition of trends begun on the steppe more than a millennium earlier. The sharing of the mounted warrior ethos across northeastern Asia was a phenomenon brought about as much by competitive emulation as by actual military necessity.

g

h

i

j

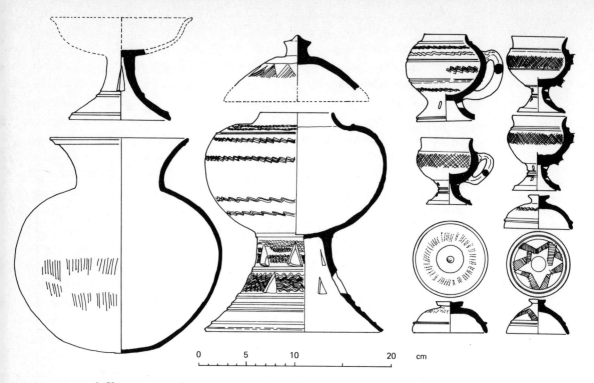

116 Kaya stoneware from an early 5th-century Yamato tomb. Evidencing importation of these elite products before stoneware production began in the Japanese Islands, these Kaya vessels bear surface designs of both wave and punctate motifs, incised or drawn with a comb.

casting had been carried out throughout the preceding Yayoi period (Chapter 11), no full-sized mirrors were made in the Islands, they were all imports from the continent. Beginning in the 4th century, however, a specific type of mirror was produced locally, having a rim triangular in cross-section. The craftsmanship is close to that of Mainland mirrors, yet no mirrors of that type have been found there, so it is suspected that the casters were continental immigrants. Simultaneously, the local rulers developed relations with village producers of greenstone objects – 'bracelets', ferrules, staffs, and beads – in communities located near the sources of jade, green tuff, and jasper along the northwestern coast of Honshu. It is not yet known what exchange mechanisms operated to supply these village-crafted materials only to the western elites.

As noted in the previous chapter, the Kaya area was famous for its iron production, exploited by Lelang and other Yellow Sea societies. Upon the demise of the commandery, the iron resources seem to have become the focus of competition, leading to actual military conflict among Pen/Insular polities in the late 4th to early 5th centuries. Tombs of this era in both Kaya and Yamato

Box 14   yield iron armour and weapons; it is not at all clear yet what these finds signify in terms of whose army was where and which polity dominated which areas. These archaeological finds feed into the debate over the 'Horserider Theory' and the 'Mimana Problem' as described below.

The 4th century also saw the emergence of a distinct Peninsular stoneware

Box 13   tradition, although the quality of firing did not always ensure the attainment of

63 *Shilla tombs (above), restored and offered for public consumption as a historic park in modern Korea. The tomb chamber of Chonmach'ong is open as a site museum.*

Mounded tombs of the emerging states in 5th-century Korea and Japan

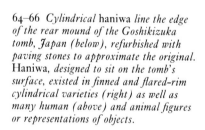

64–66 *Cylindrical* haniwa *line the edge of the rear mound of the Goshikizuka tomb, Japan (below), refurbished with paving stones to approximate the original.* Haniwa, *designed to sit on the tomb's surface, existed in finned and flared-rim cylindrical varieties (right) as well as many human (above) and animal figures or representations of objects.*

67, 72 *The costume of a fully armoured clay* haniwa *warrior (left, ht 1.35 m) contrasts with the fine detail of an elite lady's court dress (far right, ht 1.28 m).*

68, 69 *The caparisoned* haniwa *horse (above) illustrates the placement and use of many bronze trappings, such as these horse bells (below) interred as grave goods.*

Elite dress and accessories of Kofun-period Japan

70, 71 *Gilt bronze crowns (above) and shoes (below), items of status among early state rulers on the Korean Peninsula, were adopted by the Yamato elite and preserved in their tombs.*

73 (left) Small gilt-bronze statues of Buddha (here, ht 40 cm) were portable icons, facilitating the proselytization activities of monks as they travelled from country to country.

74, 75 Buddhist stationary art consisted of rock cut sculptures, as at the Kulbulsa Temple in Kyongju, Korea (above), or frescoes and stucco sculptures at Dunhuang, China (below).

The imported Indian religion of
Buddhism, monumentalized and
immortalized in sculpture and
architecture of the mid-1st
millennium AD

*76 (right) The wooden pagoda, developed in
China from the Indian stupa, only survives in
present-day Japan. Housing Buddhist relics
under its central pillar, this 5-storied pagoda at
the Yakushiji temple appears as 3-storied.*

*77 (below) Pagodas surviving from the initial
Buddhist period in Korea are made of brick, or
of stone as at the Bulguksa temple in Kyongju.*

Urbanization in protohistoric Korea and Japan: Chinese urban planning tempered with indigenous architectural features

78, 79 Recently reconstructed pavilions overlook Anapchi Pond at the Unified Shilla capital in Kyongju (above). Excavated in the late 1970s, the pond yielded thousands of objects used by the palace's courtiers. Ceramic paving tiles (below), popular in the early state capitals, were adopted into historic Korean architectural traditions.

80–82 One building of the 8th-century Heijo capital of Japan, the Shosoin treasury of the Todaiji Temple (top), still stands; others are reconstructed at the Nara palace site (centre and below). Chinese-style roof tiles (top and below) contrasted with native cedar shingles (centre), while wattle-and-daub was put to new use in sophisticated structures (centre) and stuccoed walls of immense proportion (below, c. 3 m high).

Faces of East Asian civilization, the female countenance

83–85 *A* haniwa *comes to life (above left), the glory of a Shilla queen (above right), and a lady of the Heijo court dressed in Tang style (below), watching a croquet-like game. Ball games were popular with the court in the early historic periods (see fig. 128b, c).*

stoneware bodies. This tradition had several regional variants corresponding generally with the different states – principally Koguryo, Paekche and Kaya. The hard-fired grey pottery of Kaya was exported to the Japanese Islands early on, followed in the early 5th century by the immigration of Kaya craftspeople themselves, who established kilns in Yamato to supply the demands of the Insular elite. Their products, assigned the name Sué ware by Japanese archaeologists, were treated completely differently from the native Haji pottery, which up till then was never deposited in tombs. Following the burial customs of the Peninsula, Sué became the major funerary ware, suggesting a dramatic shift in the belief systems of the Yamato elite. Instead of burying quantities of precious goods or tools and weapons with the deceased as in the Early Kofun period, from the late 5th century onwards family members provided abundant food and drink in these Sué vessels for the deceased, who took only the ornaments and accoutrements they were wearing into the next life.

plate 61

Secondary state formation

Creative response

The Pen/Insular polities are secondary states, which – by definition – arise in situations of contact with already extant and operating states.[14] Thus, they have at their disposal ready-made models for polity administration and the means to create and maintain elite status through interaction with the 'higher court', as it may be called. Nevertheless, the Pen/Insular polities that arose in the late 3rd and 4th centuries were neither mere extensions of Wei Dynasty power through Lelang nor copycat borrowings of the dynastic system. They arose in a power vacuum when Mainland influence in the region was on the wane. Exposure to Mainland empire practices in the preceding centuries had led to a useful familiarity with highly organized political systems.[15] But consider two facts: 1) that the strongest states (Yamato, Koguryo, and Shilla) developed in areas which had the least contact with the dynastic courts, and 2) that their internal organization was highly variable. This suggests that the hierarchical systems of these states represent local solutions with their own creative (rather than externally imposed) choice of rulership components.

Kingship and administration

Like the Shang nearly two millennia earlier, the mounded tomb cultures are protohistoric in nature, with written documents supplying details on internal organization inaccessible to archaeology. For the major states, there are not only lists of kings but also the names of the prominent clans.[16] Kinship ranking was desperately important in Shilla, where the royal lineage in the ruling clan held the rank of 'hallowed bone' (analogous to 'royal blood'), and other lineages and clans held graded ranks below them. This 'bone rank' system was borrowed by Yamato in a modified form.[17] Analyses of 5th-century succession patterns in Yamato suggest further similarities with the Peninsula. Fraternal

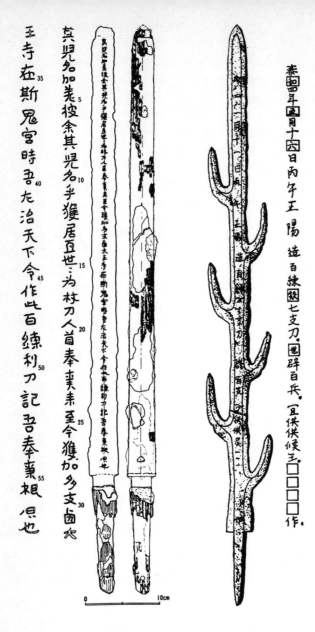

117 Inscribed swords used to cement political alliances. A 7-branched sword (right) was allegedly given as a gift to Yamato by Paekche in the late 4th century. Approximately a century later, a Kanto ruler was buried with a sword (left) bearing a description of his service to the Yamato paramount.

succession was practised, with kingship passing from brother to brother before devolving on to the next generation;[18] this, of course, led to fierce succession disputes among the families of the brothers' children. Also, recent studies on the composition of Shilla clans have demonstrated that women were equally allowed to rule;[19] Yamato likewise had several empresses, though they attained their status by succeeding their husbands rather than inheriting rights from their fathers or brothers.

State formation is marked by the divorcing of administration from kinship ties, and this process is accelerated in secondary contexts. Whereas nearly a thousand years passed between the emergence of the primary state of Shang and the institution of non-kin governors in the Late Zhou polity of Qin, Paekche accomplished this in less than a century. Ministers were appointed for short terms of three years each in managing the six spheres of government: the royal household, finance, education, security, internal affairs and defence.[20] In the late 4th century, the Koguryo kings used imported Confucian concepts and institutions to systematize the administrative structure.[21] Persons could rise through the Confucian examination system on merit, though then as today, members of the elite would have had preferential access to the educational system preparing them for those exams. In Yamato, the appointment of managers to oversee the production and collection of tax goods not only stabilized and routinized state financing but also drove an administrative wedge into the territorial regimes of local patriarchal rulers.[22] As both Shilla and Yamato expanded to incorporate the territories of previously autonomous polities, local chieftains were integrated into the status systems of the central court. Inscribed swords discovered in the Kanto region and north Kyushu indicate the material means by which these feats of integration were accomplished by Yamato.[23]

Box 2

In the space of two hundred years, Buddhism was received and adopted in all the Pen/Insular states, becoming the state religion in several. It was introduced by proselytizing monks into Koguryo (by AD 366), Paekche (in AD 384) and Shilla (in AD 417–57), but the religion had little effect on these societies until taken up by the ruling elite. More importantly, it is possible that writing – in the form of the Chinese script – was introduced into these fledgling state systems by the sutra-bearing monks, supplying the basic tool with which to begin administrative consolidation and refinement. Tradition has it that this writing system was transmitted to the Yamato court in AD 405 by two Paekche scribes who served as Yamato treasury accountants. It was another 150 years before Buddhist practices were separately introduced, via gifts of sutras and Buddha images from the king of Paekche to the Yamato paramount in AD 552. This resulted in violent clashes between those clans (mainly of Peninsular derivation) who supported Buddhism and those clans with vested interests in the indigenous ritual system. The former won, and eventually the Buddhist hierarchy that arose from this introduction came to compete with political rulership, having a profound effect on state organization.

plate 73

Regional interaction

Relationships between the Pen/Insular states consisted of patterned shifts in alliances and hostilities, as known from the early chronicles and embodied in many archaeological monuments. In AD 313, Koguryo was strong enough to attack and demolish Lelang, though it did not move its capital from its location on the Yalu River down to the commandery headquarters on the coast until AD 427. Pushing further southwards, it came into conflict with Paekche, which was forced to retreat from its own capital on the Han River into the Kum River drainage of the southwestern Peninsula. From there, Paekche opened negotiations with the Liang Dynasty of the southern Mainland in its search for allies against Koguryo, resulting in the adoption of chambered tomb styles (as

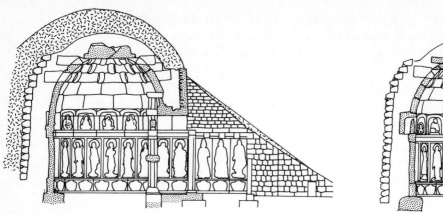

118 Sokkuram Buddhist grotto near Kyongju City, Korea. Not a real cave, this grotto is constructed in the manner of a mounded tomb with the inner stone chamber dedicated to an image of the Buddha.

plate 74   noted above) and Buddhist stone carving techniques. The Sosan Buddhist triad carved high on a cliff overlooking the Yellow Sea is thought to have protected the sea routes between Paekche and the southern Mainland.[24]

In AD 581, the politically fragmented landscape of the China Mainland was once again united, this time under the rule of the Sui Dynasty. Koguryo's forays into the Liaodong peninsula in AD 589 invited reprisals by Sui troops, but their unsuccessful attacks against Koguryo's well-fortified cities between AD 611 and 614 bankrupted the Sui.[25] The succeeding Tang Dynasty formed plate 5   an alliance with Shilla, and Shilla began its expansion from the Kyongju Basin towards unification of the Peninsula.

fig. 119   Scores of mountain fortresses built in the central Peninsular mountains mark the hostilities among the Peninsular states. Similar fortifications were built in the western Japanese Islands in the 7th century as Shilla threatened to extend itself overseas.[26] Conversely on the defensive in AD 751, Shilla built a Buddhist monument, the Sokkuram, at the highest point on its eastern border overlooking the Eastern Sea as protection from marauding 'pirates' from the Japanese Islands.[27] Interestingly, Sokkuram is a grotto containing Buddhist sculptures, but it is entirely artificially constructed in the manner of a chambered mounded tomb for an area lacking in caves.

Turning to the Islands, in the 5th century petitions from 'Five Kings of Wa' were submitted to the Mainland dynasties, particularly to the Song (AD 420–78), for recognition as a regional power. They asked the courts, albeit unsuccessfully, to bestow on them imposing titles that implied their political dominance over all other Pen/Insular entities.[28] The Kwanggaet'o stele of Koguryo, erected in AD 414, concomitantly records several 'invasions' by the 'Wa'. Although it has previously been assumed by scholars that these historical citations refer to Yamato, the uncritical identification of Wa with Yamato is currently being scrutinized, partly because ideas have been revised on the extent of Yamato power in different centuries. The 4th-century mounded tomb culture of Japan was initially interpreted by scholars as the extension of Yamato power throughout the western Islands; now this is properly recognized as a cultural phenomenon, with Yamato state power only developing in the 5th century and limited to the Kinai region in eastern Seto. This leaves many other areas outside Yamato proper, including the southern edge of the Korean Peninsula as implied in some historical documents, as the possible sphere of Wa occupation.[29]

The role of Kaya in this sphere raises many difficult questions, particularly pertaining to Yamato involvement on the southern Korean Peninsula. There is little doubt that this area was producing iron for Insular consumption, and the transfer of stoneware technology from this region to Yamato in the early 5th century is an archaeological fact. The 'Horserider Theory' of Japanese state formation suggests that the southern Peninsular coast was a staging point for the Peninsular conquest of Yamato;[30] conversely, the *Nihon Shoki* suggests that the region was a colony named Mimana belonging to Yamato.[31] Problems abound with both interpretations: the archaeological data for 'horseriders' in Yamato are too late to fit the theory,[32] and textual criticism has revealed distortions in the use of the Mimana name in the *Nihon Shoki*.[33] Nevertheless, recent excavations in Kaya burials have yielded much iron armour and weaponry of kinds also present in Yamato, so relations between the two areas – whether marital, economic or political – almost certainly had a military gloss.

Such close interaction with the Peninsula caused the coastal area of Osaka Bay to be developed as Yamato's window on the world. Here are located the Ojin and Nintoku mausolea (the two largest tombs in Japan), the Suémura kiln site, the Nonaka tomb with its iron armour and Kaya ceramics, and the recently excavated state storage facilities at Naniwa, consisting of sixteen large storehouses with an average 90 m² of floor space each. These were probably used for storing grain as well as whatever tribute goods Yamato was able to extract from outlying Pen/Insular communities. These developments partook of an indigenous trend towards urbanization that was cut short by the adoption of Mainland models in the ensuing period.

fig. 116

Box 14d

CHAPTER 15

East Asian Civilization

AD 650–800

Box 2   The archaic states of Shilla and Yamato matured and survived by adopting many aspects of the Tang Dynasty administrative system, incorporating at the same time a Confucian outlook on state management.[1] The Tang system, however, should not be looked upon as a perfectly organized and fully developed bureaucracy that served as an ideal model. It too matured gradually and barely preceded the centralizing efforts of the Pen/Insular states, which also drew to a great extent on the governmental system of the Sui Dynasty before it. Though Sui collapsed in AD 616, the Tang founder did not restore civil order until 624 when he promulgated the system of administrative law underwriting the dynasty; the prefecture-county system of territorial administration was not regularized until after 630.[2]

The year 645 is the historically transmitted date for the Taika Reforms of the Yamato state in which a number of these political and economic reforms were said to have been carried out. Research shows, however, that the crucial reforms bringing about a state based on Tang administrative law (referred to in Japanese as *ritsuryo* law) took nearly a century, from 603 to 701.[3] Unified Shilla likewise achieved its major reforms during the 7th century, with 685 named as the year in which the territorial administration was revised using traditional Mainland concepts transmitted through Tang.[4] In both cases, the reforms of archaeological significance were the adoption of the gridded city plan, centralized provincial administration, and land reallocation and taxation.

Cityscapes

Incipient urbanization

Pen/Insular state capitals during the Kofun and Three Kingdoms periods took on surprisingly divergent forms. On the Peninsula, walled sites were the norm, whereas a pattern of 'shifting palaces' obtained in Yamato.

fig. 119   Among the hundreds of walled sites located throughout the Peninsula, it is difficult to determine which might have served as a political capital. For example, Mongch'on T'osong in the Han River basin has proved through excavation to have been an urban locus for a variety of productive and administrative activities during its occupation between *c.* 350 and 475.[5] But one can only speculate that this particular walled site – one among the dozen or so

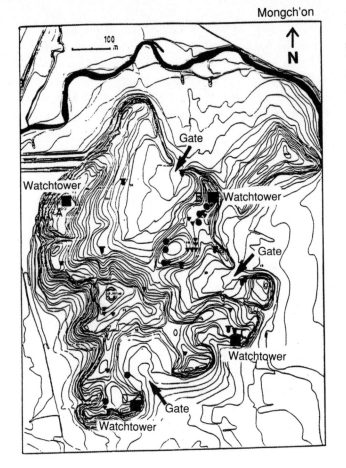

Mongch'on

Gate

Watchtower

Watchtower

Gate

Watchtower

Gate

Watchtower

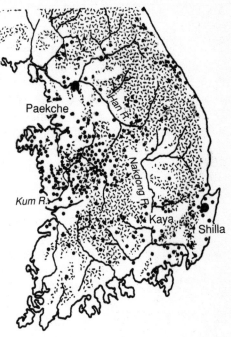

Paekche

Han R.

Kum R.

Nakdong R.

Kaya

Shilla

119 Walled sites on the southern Korean Peninsula. Mongch'on, in the Han River basin near modern Seoul, belonged to early Paekche; while Panwolsong, in Kyongju, is thought to have been the capital of Shilla during the Three Kingdoms period. Other walled sites dotted across the Peninsula (above) served as mountain forts, military centres, and barriers to movement across the landscape.

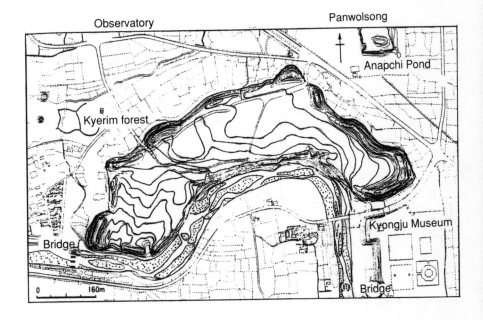

Observatory

Panwolsong

Anapchi Pond

Kyerim forest

Kyongju Museum

Bridge

Bridge

0   160m

known either archaeologically or historically in the Han River basin – was the early Paekche capital named as Hansong in the *Samguk Sagi*. As with the early Mainland capitals, without inscriptional data, the identification of a political capital is almost impossible from archaeological remains alone.

As for the Insular 'shifting palaces', the *Nihon Shoki* records that each successive ruler frequented one or more, which were often newly built and usually used for less than a generation. Given their apparently temporary nature, it is difficult to conceive of their architecture on a scale much more elaborate than a residential unit. Perhaps the earlier ones followed what seems to have been the elite settlement form in the Islands at the time: the housestead, a self-contained multi-building unit enclosed by ditches and fences and spatially isolated from peasant villages. It seems that 4th to 6th-century palaces were built near areas of already flourishing settlement and important economic activity;[6] though these areas might be termed 'urban', they functioned as 'capitals' only briefly due to the transient presence of the ruler.

fig. 122 Nine of the latest palaces of Yamato paramounts prior to the construction of the first gridded city are located in the small confines of the Asuka valley in the southern Nara Basin. Excavation of five of these reveals that they were generally built in the indigenous architectural style with unfooted embedded pillars and thatched or shingled roofs. However, a new architectural use of stone is seen at these sites: paved plumbing facilities included stone-lined ditches, eaves catchments, and well surrounds. These features were probably borrowed from Peninsular Buddhist temple architecture. This trend is *fig. 110* particularly apparent at the Naniwa Palace site which, however, was located outside the basin at the edge of Osaka Bay.

120 A possible 'housestead' at the Ozono site, Osaka Prefecture. This late 5th-century site is internally divided by ditches into compounds, each populated by several buildings (2–5; 6, 8, 9, 11) and one raised-floor storehouse (1, 7). Such compounds are thought to have belonged to middle- or lower-level elite.

121 The stone pagoda of Chongnimsa. Erected in the second half of the 7th century, this is the second oldest Paekche pagoda on the Korean Peninsula; its form resembles the wooden pagoda. When repaired in 1967, it was found to contain a glass sarira bottle and a gilt-bronze box holding 19 gilded plates inscribed with the Diamond Sutra.

Gridded cities

Excavations in Kyongju are just beginning to reveal details of the Unified Shilla capital of Kumsong. A new gridded city was laid out during the 7th century just north of the Panwolsong walled site, which is identified as the Shilla capital during the Three Kingdoms period. Several very large stone-footed building plans oriented to the grid have been recovered, indicating the siting of administrative buildings. To their northeast is a garden pond named Anapchi, faced by pavilions associated with the royal palace. Excavated in 1975, the pond mud yielded a wealth of objects illustrating life at the palace: wooden dice, Buddhist images, gilt-bronze scissors, stoneware pottery, roof tiles, etc. To the east of the ancient city, excavation is proceeding at a large temple, the Hwangyong-sa, so far revealing a linear sequence of buildings within a corridor enclosure. Other halls and a bell tower flank these main buildings. Hwangyong-sa's celebrated nine-storey wooden pagoda is said to have been built under the direction of a Paekche craftsman.[7] It stood in great contrast to pagodas of shorter stature constructed in stone or brick.

plate 78
fig. 119

plate 77

In Yamato, the first gridded city was Fujiwara, built in 694 just north of the Asuka valley. Positioned between the three landmark peaks of the southern basin, the palace alone measured 1 km² and contained numerous ministerial offices and ceremonial halls in addition to the imperial residence. The Fujiwara capital was linked to the northern Nara Basin and Osaka Bay by government roads, which were also laid out on a grid pattern corresponding with the *jori*

fig. 127

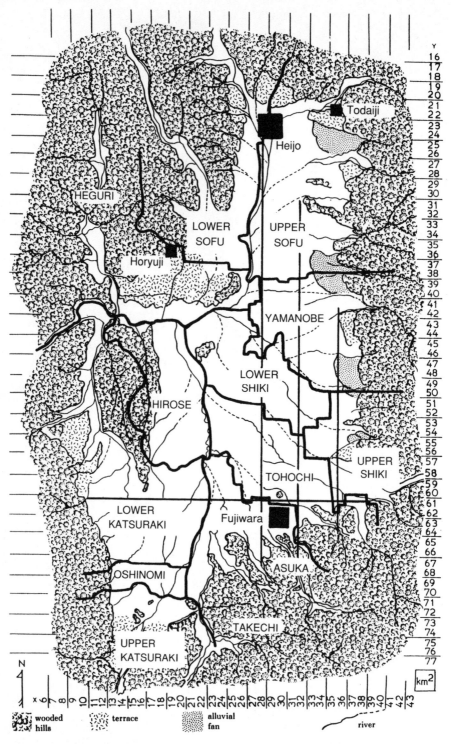

122 The early ritsuryo *landscape of the Nara Basin. Gridded roads served the Fujiwara capital Asaku in the far south and its successor, Heijo, in the far north. The named county divisions followed old clan territories.*

land-divisioning system instituted about this time. Huge labour levies were required to build the roads and rechannel the rivers along the rectangular grid, imposing lasting changes on the natural landscape of the lowland areas. The one-hectare field divisions of the *jori* system are still in use in some parts of Japan today.[8]

Temples and tombs

Integral to the layout of these capitals were their Buddhist temples. Though not a state religion by law, Buddhism was patronized by many of the rulers and aristocrats and could be an influential lever in political affairs. Priests often served as informal court advisors or even spies, since they frequently travelled among the states – especially to the China Mainland – and consequently were important sources of information on contemporary politics. In material terms, both temple plans and sculptural styles document the routes of communication between the different states. For example, although Buddhism was introduced to Yamato by a Paekche king, the first temple to be built, Asuka-dera, followed a plan only found in Koguryo at the time. Paekche architects and sculptors are historically known to have worked personally on Shilla and Yamato temple construction, helping to create a pan-East Asian religious basis for state operation.

The adoption of Buddhism gave rise to the new practice of cremation burial, which was more popular in Shilla than in Yamato. Numerous cremation urns with typical stamped decoration are known for Unified Shilla. In Asuka, *fig. 123* however, mounded tomb burial continued for the highest elite, with several imperial tombs in the area. Interestingly, the largest tomb in Asuka – Ishibutai, a square moated tomb housing a stone chamber with capstones weighing 70 tons each – belonged to the founder of the earliest temple in Japan, the Asuka-dera. In time, however, it proved too expensive for the aristocrats to erect both temples and tombs, so temple-building alone became the standard means for aggrandizing one's status.

Analysis of the evolution of temple plans reveals a great deal of variation in arrangement of the different buildings.[9] The function of the pagoda was to house sacred fragments of the body of Buddha: pieces of bone, teeth, etc. These were buried under the central pole in the case of a wooden pagoda or deposited in a container in a chamber within brick or stone pagodas. The wooden pagodas were stunning, being the highest human-made structures at the time. *plate 76* Moreover, they had an ingenious internal construction whereby the central pole was entirely unconnected to the surrounding wooden bracketing which filled the interior. This allowed the building to shake during earthquakes without falling down. Alas, the wooden architecture was exceptionally vulnerable to fire. Still, the oldest wooden structure in the world – at the Horyuji Temple in Nara – dates to the 8th century. *fig. 124*

In 710 the capital was moved to a new site in the northern Nara Basin. The new capital, Heijo, had its own complement of temples, but the relationship *plates 81, 82* which evolved between state and temple was totally different from that at

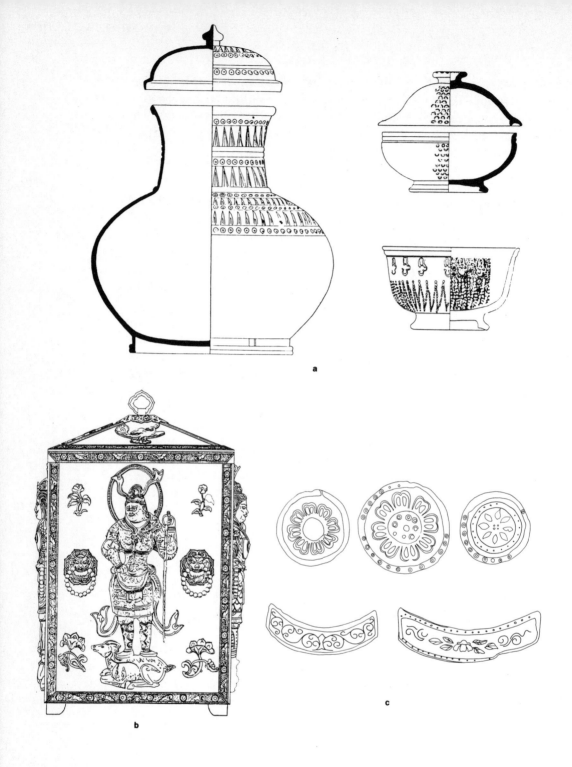

123 *Early Buddhist material culture. Stamped stonewares of Unified Shilla were often used as cremation urns* *(a). Relics of the Buddha merited more precious containers, such as this gilt bronze box protected on its four* *sides by guardian figures (b). Temple roof tiles had both circular and arched eaves ends decorated with various* *plant designs (c).*

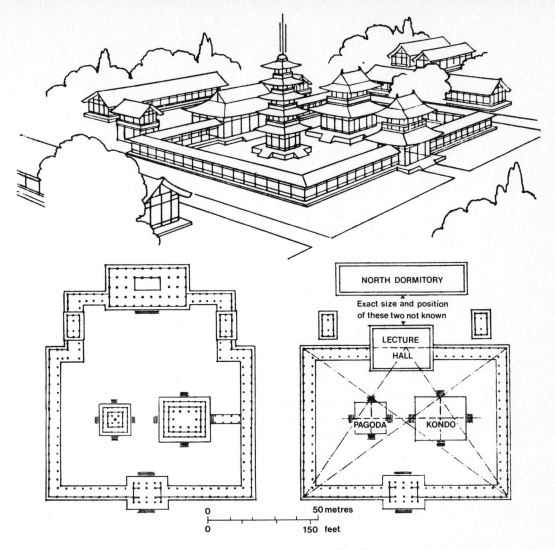

124 The Horyuji Temple of Japan. Together with the Asuka-dera, the present (left) and original (right) placement of buildings within the main Horyuji compound follow the sideways layout characteristic of early Koguryo temples. Other early Japanese temples followed the Paekche or Shilla compound layout in which buildings were ordered vertically, in line with the front main gate towards the back hall.

Fujiwara, with parallel territorial hierarchies headed respectively by Heijo and the temple of Todaiji.

Territorial administration

Provincial systems

The unification of the Peninsula forced Unified Shilla to devise an expanded system of territorial administration. For this it drew partly on the traditional Mainland urban forms transmitted through Tang. In 685, it created nine provinces, echoing the Zhou system, each with its own provincial capital, plus

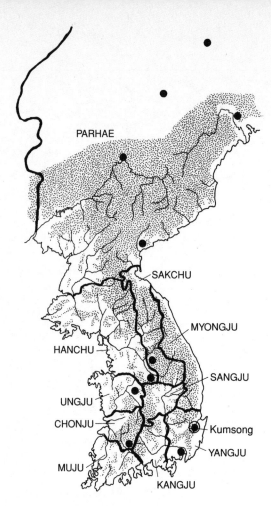

125 The territorial system of Unified Shilla. Kumsong, the capital of Unified Shilla, was accompanied by five regional capitals as well as the provincial centres. Parhae, with its five capitals, bordered Shilla on the north. The boundary between the two states ran just south of P'yongyang, the present-day capital of North Korea.

five additional regional capitals scattered across the country. The aristocratic families of the conquered states were forcibly resettled in these regional capitals.[10] An important point to note about Shilla territory at this time is that though Koguryo was defeated by Shilla, most of the area of old Koguryo was not incorporated into the Unified Shilla state. Instead, it became the locus of the Koguryo successor state, Parhae. The border between Parhae and Shilla ran east from the Taedong estuary. This divisioning perpetuated the cultural split between the northern and southern Peninsula, which is notable from the Iron Age onwards and which is accentuated again today by the demilitarized zone. The centre of Parhae was located in the Sungari River drainage of the northern Manchurian Basin, and the state was governed from a series of five regional capitals.

fig. 126 Yamato also used a Tang model to create provinces and counties and group them into regional administrative districts which focused on trunk roads but had no regional capitals.[11] These roads passed through most provincial centres and were also supplied with 'stations' at which government couriers could have their horses serviced or changed. The increased efficiency in communication and transport ensured greater control over the provinces, especially facilitating the transfer of tax goods to the capital. In the Nara Basin, the county boundaries established at this time surprisingly conform to earlier distributions of clans and to even earlier tomb clusters spaced across the landscape, suggesting considerable continuity in local political organization from the 4th century onwards.

fig. 122

The provinces of the *ritsuryo* state were created from the territories of regional leaders who had submitted to the Yamato court during the 5th and 6th centuries and received the title of *Kuni-no-miyatsuko*, integrating them into the central court hierarchy. With the reforms of the late 7th century, provincial governors were dispatched from the court to administer the provinces, bringing them under direct central control. The *Kuni-no-miyatsuko* were demoted to county heads and were given the task of collecting and forwarding the newly instituted state taxes. Thus their activities were closely monitored by the state. Shilla also placed central functionaries in all provincial administrative posts, and it implemented a 'hostage system' in which members of all powerful local families were 'required to undertake low-level military or court duties in the capital on a rotation basis'.[12]

plate 85

In the consolidated Yamato territory, excavations have demonstrated that most provincial and county administrative centres were newly built in areas separated from previous loci of power. The provincial centres were generally one-hectare fenced or walled enclosures containing three embedded-pillar buildings arranged in a U-shape inside. The walls, however, were nothing like continental earthen walls but narrow and tall, built up with mud and stones or tiles and plastered on the exterior surfaces. Although they were specialized and highly sophisticated constructions, they represent a far smaller labour investment than the continental tamped-earth walls. Outside the walls of the administrative centres were other activity areas, including large granaries for surplus storage.

During the 8th century these provinces were administered from the new capital at Heijo. East of the Heijo palace stood the great Todaiji Temple, for which a gigantic bronze Buddha figure was cast, using in part bronze mirrors donated by the ladies of the court. In 742 the emperor decreed that each provincal centre should have a nearby monastery and nunnery which became linked to the Todaiji. Like the great Todaiji itself, many of these subsidiary temples still function today. This temple network duplicated the regional administrative structure without directly threatening it. However, the long-term effects undermined the basic tenets of administrative law, since the temples were granted tax-free status and were allowed to own estates to provide maintenance income.[13] Although this practice violated the *ritsuryo* philosophy of state ownership of all land and taxation of the populace, tax-free estates were also increasingly granted to aristocratic families during the ensuing Heian period. Thus both individual families and temples were able to develop local power bases, allowing them to challenge the central government's rule. This eventually caused the downfall of the *ritsuryo* system and the rise of feudalism

fig. 126

126 Heijo at the centre of a new territorial system. Based on trunk roads passing through new provincial centres, the regional administrative system solidified the territorial hierarchy, provided for speedy communications, and routinized tax deliveries. Dazaifu and Tagajo served as gateways to the continent and to the northern frontier respectively. Administrative centres and forts established successively northwards served to bring the Emishi territory under central control. At the apex of the regional hierarchy sat the Nara Palace in the Heijo Capital, organized as a grid city on the model of Tang Chang'an.

in the medieval period. In Unified Shilla as well, private estates in the form of tributary villages belonging to the aristocracy were the bane of government efforts to maintain control over the local population and the revenue they generated.[14]

Frontier facilities

Unlike Shilla, whose northern border with Parhae was fairly clearly drawn, Yamato's administrative hold gradually faded into the northern Honshu frontier. The early texts indicate that the Tohoku region was occupied by a people called Emishi. The Emishi were once thought to have been hunters and

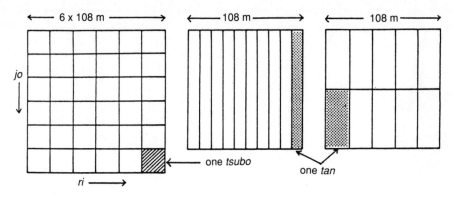

127 The gridded field system. Land was measured in jo *north to south and in* ri *east to west. The intersection of* jo-ri *produced 36* tsubo *per one* cho *(c. hectare) of land; each* tsubo *was divided into ten* tan, *two of which were allocated by the state to each male, and 1.33* tan *to each female, for the production of rice.*

gatherers – perhaps the forerunners of the Ainu, the presently recognized indigenous peoples of Hokkaido. However, recent archaeological analyses of subsistence remains have revealed a variety of crop plants at northern domestic sites in the early historic period,[15] so the Emishi are now considered to be descendants of the northeastern Yayoi agriculturalists. In extending the administrative reach of the state, central troops waged sporadic military campaigns against this local population in pursuit of what might be termed the 'manifest destiny' of Japan to control the entire archipelago. Several forts were built in Tohoku, their founding dates showing the progress of expansion up the island.

In the far west, the threat of Shilla's expansion in the 7th century led to the construction of several Paekche-style mountain-top fortresses, with either stone or tamped-earth walls, and a military headquarters on the plains of north Kyushu. This installation, Dazaifu, served as the bureaucratic gateway to the continent, much as the site of Naniwa had done on the Osaka Plains. Both Dazaifu and Tagajo, the major fort in the northeast, were built on plans similar to the provincial centres.

State finance

Taxation

The Anapchi garden pond of Unified Shilla and many administrative sites in Yamato, especially in the Heijo palace and capital, have yielded an important new source of documentary evidence about palace operation and state administration: wooden tablets with inked inscriptions, like those which saw their heyday of use on the China Mainland during the Han period.[16] Called *mokkan* in Japanese, these tablets provide contemporaneous information for comparison with the transmitted histories, the *Samguk Sagi* and *Nihon Shoki*. Since these tablets were often used in Japan as baggage tags for tax goods being

cf. Box 1f

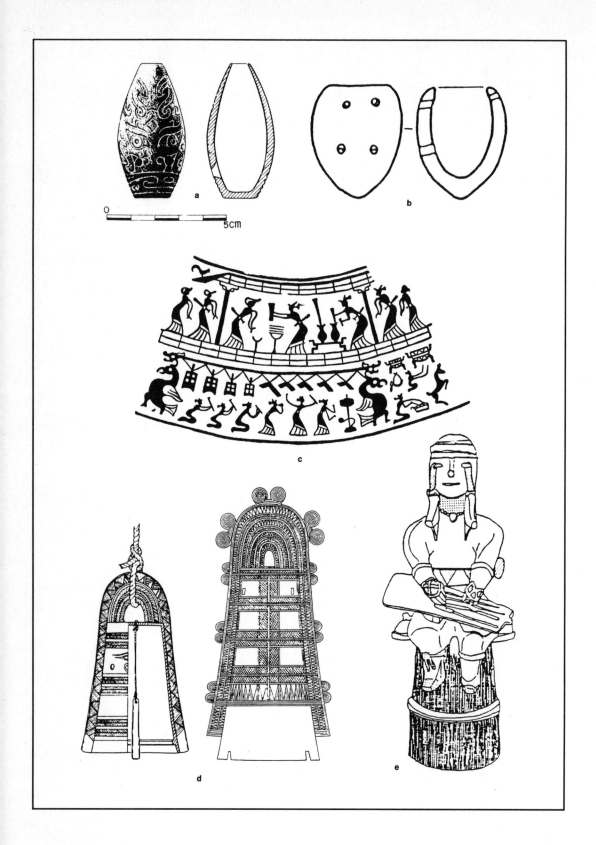

BOX 15
Music Archaeology

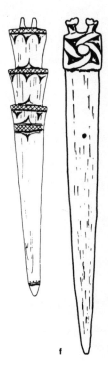

Within Confucian political traditions, music played an extremely important role, regulating the harmony between ruler and heaven. It is no wonder then, that in the Meiji Restoration of 1868, the Japanese government adopted German marching music along with reform of the army on a Prussian model! The importance of music to government may even predate Confucius himself, since some of the earliest musical instruments have been excavated from the Shang site of Anyang (a). These are ocarinas carved in the manner of Shang white ware. These egg-shaped vessel flutes are one of three classes of musical instrument, all clearly of continental derivation, that appear in the archipelago for the first time during the Yayoi period. This is no coincidence, given that Yayoi was a period of intense continental influence in general. But all three types – the others are bronze bells and long zithers – differ significantly from their Mainland precursors, in ways suggesting that only a visual memory rather than actual specimens of those instruments reached the Islands. For example, the Yayoi ocarinas (b) differ from their Shang and Zhou predecessors both in shape (the 'egg' is inverted) and in finger-hole placement. This type of instrument disappeared from the Islands after Yayoi but survived on the continent. Even today such ocarinas are used in Confucian ceremonies in South Korea.

Ranks of tuned bells and boomerang-shaped gong stones (cf. plate 25) were spectacular inclusions in Zhou-period aristocratic burials; here a set is depicted on another bronze object (c). The bronze bells of Yayoi (d) are said to have been made originally as 'bells to listen to', thereafter gradually losing their musical function and becoming highly decorated 'bells to look at'. These bells, too, disappear from use after Yayoi.

Long zithers are well represented in the tomb figurines of Han and Tang as well as *haniwa* (e). As part of elite ensembles, these sophisticated instruments stand in great contrast to indigenous spatulate zithers developed by the Final Jomon peoples (f). When continental-style zithers first appear in the archipelago in Yayoi, the variety of their shapes, sizes and workmanship precludes their having been parts of standardized ensembles.

f

Lutes are unknown from archaeological excavations, but ornately decorated Tang examples are among the principal masterpieces in the Shosoin and here one is depicted on a Tang figurine (g). A number of other Tang instruments were adopted and adapted by the Pen/Insular courts; indeed, through the process of marginal survival, many Tang tunes and dances are now known only in their Pen/Insular loci of preservation, Japanese court music (*gagaku*) and dance (*bugaku*) being the prime examples.

g

fig. 127

shipped to the capital, a great deal is known about the distribution of tax levies throughout the Islands.

Tang administrative law provided for the allocation of small parcels of partially heritable land to all adult males; in return for this they paid a grain tax and also owed corvée labour. Cloth was another tax good, provided almost exclusively by female family members. In Yamato, land grants were also made to females, who thus bore a double tax burden. It was through such taxation laws that control was first extended to the level of the individual, signifying the maturation of the state. In both Nara-period Japan and Tang-period China, however, administration of the individual was apparently too much for these early systems to handle successfully. Tang changed its tax policy in the mid-8th century by giving each province a tax quota and the freedom to raise it as it could.[17] In Yamato, peasants escaped from the heavy levies by taking refuge on tax-exempt temple and aristocratic estates.[18]

Trade

After disruptions during the long period of political fragmentation between Han and Sui times, trade along the Silk Road picked up again with Tang unification. Tang aristocrats partook of many fashions in food, clothing and music from points west, particularly Persia, and some of these were transferred to the courts of Unified Shilla and Nara. Many Tang objects have survived to this day in Japan's Shosoin storehouse, located on the grounds of the Todaiji

plate 80

Temple.[19] This extant storehouse is of unique construction: squared logs set edge-to-edge rather than side-to-side. It was believed that the logs expanded during humid periods and contracted in dry periods, maintaining a fairly constant humidity inside, but scientific studies disprove this. The dense grid pattern of underfloor pillars, found at the Shosoin and other post-6th-century storehouses, is much easier to recognize in excavation than the four or six pillars of their predecessors, the Yayoi granaries.

The Shosoin preserves a stunning variety of goods, both domestic and foreign-made: 8th-century documents, including census records from Shilla; Persian glass and Sassanian silver vessels; an ivory foot ruler (29.6 cm in length divided into 10 'inches'); ceramic models of pagodas glazed as Tang three-

fig. 99

coloured ware; costumes and silks of various weaves; inlaid and ornamental bronzes; musical instruments lavishly inlaid with ivory and mother of pearl; lacquered and marquetry wooden furniture; dance masks, and so forth. Though these were the possessions of the Nara ruler and not accessible to the populace, they do represent the participation of the Nara court in the shared elite culture that also gave present-day East Asia its common philosophical, legal, and administrative base.

CHAPTER 16

Epilogue
AD 800–1800

With the emulation of Tang Dynasty (618–906) government and culture by societies surrounding China during the 7th and 8th centuries, for the first time East Asia became a coherent regional entity based on common aesthetic values and philosophy, literary tradition, and state structure. These societies, however, were by no means carbon copies of Tang, and the elements they shared ensured neither peaceful relations nor parallel development thereafter.

China itself was subsequently subject to two 'foreign' dynasties: the Yuan Dynasty of Mongol origin (1279–1368) and the Qing Dynasty of Manchu origin (1644–1911). These northern peoples who were able to usurp the throne brought to the Chinese court a commitment and sensitivity to their homelands. Rather than imposing a northern brand of government on their Chinese subjects, however, the foreign rulers 'became Chinese' in the sense that they fitted themselves into the traditional mode of rule instead of re-casting the system in their own image. Koryo (918–1392), the successor to Unified Shilla on the Korean Peninsula, also experienced Mongol incursions in the 13th century, after having dealt with the hostile Khitan and Jurchen polities along its northern border throughout the 10th–12th centuries. Unlike continental peoples, the Japanese escaped the attempted Mongol invasions in 1274 and 1281, partly through the intervention of a 'divine wind' (*kamikaze*), a fortuitous typhoon which destroyed the Mongol fleet as it tried to cross the Korea Strait to conquer the Islands. In compensation, the medieval Japanese were wracked by warfare among their own warlords and their samurai retainers. The warrior class had gained power through the privatization of land-holdings, which also deprived the *ritsuryo* state of its tax base and led to the dissolution of bureaucratic government after 1185 in favour of a shogunate.

The archaeology of these historic periods is very poorly developed as yet, with documentary and geographical research providing most of the data on the prevailing socio-political structures, economic trends and lifeways of the people. Still, there are several areas where archaeological data become paramount, and progress is being made in the excavation of historic sites.

Porcelain production

One of the largest areas of historical archaeological research concerns the development of porcelain manufacture and trade. Following hard on the heels

128 *Artifacts from the historical Song Dynasty of China. Lively portrayals of everyday activities graced ordinary objects, such as the woman making tea carved onto a brick (a), or football games depicted on a ceramic pillow (b) and bronze mirror (c).*

a

of regularized production of stoneware on the southern China Mainland from the 3rd century AD, green-glazed celadon wares were developed and then true porcelains using porcelain stone and, later, kaolin clays. Three areas in the southeast are particularly known for these wares: Yue stonewares were produced near Ningbo during the Tang period; green-glazed celadons were produced at Longquan during the Song Dynasty (960–1279); and at Jingdezhen, both Qingbai porcelains and blue & white wares were produced during the Yuan Dynasty.

Formerly the exclusive province of art historical analysis and appreciation, these Chinese ceramics now play a ubiquitous role in the excavation of sites of the late 1st and early 2nd millennia. And not only in East Asia: with the maturation of export economies in the Song and Yuan Dynasties, many of these ceramics – particularly celadons and blue & white wares – were shipped to and exchanged at locations throughout Southeast Asia and even across the Indian Ocean to the eastern African coast, where Chinese trade ceramics are a common resource for dating archaeological sites.

On the China Mainland, investigations have been undertaken at some kiln sites in order to source these various wares. The 'Discovery of Ru Kiln' at *fig. 110* Qingliangsi in Henan Province was just such a field project, identifying through surface survey and test excavation the location of the kiln site where 'official' Ru ware was produced for imperial consumption during the early Song Dynasty. Ru ware was the acme of northern celadons, having an exquisite bluish-tinted glaze, and its development was intimately connected with Korean celadons during the contemporaneous Koryo period.[1]

Another project is located at the site of Hutian near Jingdezhen, a modern city still very much involved in ceramic production and the locus of the Yuan

b   c

Dynasty Fouliang Porcelain Bureau between 1278 and 1352.[2] Hutian was designated an 'Important and Protected Cultural Unit' in 1959 and consists of 40 ha of medieval ceramic factories and waste heaps.[3] Excavations began in 1972 and in 1978, a late 13th-century kiln was revealed, measuring 2.9 m wide and 13 m long with a sloping floor of 14.5°.[4] The Mongols were apparently interested in the Qingbai white wares produced at Jingdezhen for reasons of ritual purity.[5] Their patronage, however, stimulated production for both domestic use and export. More than a third of the cargo of the Shinan shipwreck off the coast of Korea, for example, consisted of Qingbai wares presumably produced at Jingdezhen.

Underwater archaeology

Advances in underwater archaeology have allowed the excavation of several shipwrecks around the East Asian coasts. At Ningbo and Quanzhou, ships dating to the Five Dynasties (907–60) and Southern Song (1127–1279) were found to be carrying spices, medical supplies and porcelains.[6] Ningbo, just south of Shanghai, was the point of departure for sailing east to the Pen/ Insulae. The heavily indented coastline of the southwestern Korean Peninsula, where east–west and north–south routes intersected, seems to have claimed its share of shipwrecks. In 1976, after fishermen brought up numerous celadons and porcelains in their nets near the town of Shinan, a Yuan Dynasty ship was located at a depth of 20–23 m. An underwater diving team from the Korean Navy, joined by several international underwater archaeologists, was recruited to rescue the cargo. They salvaged almost 17,000 ceramic vessels and 18.5 tons of Chinese coins as well as other metal, stone, wooden and lacquered objects.[7]

fig. 110

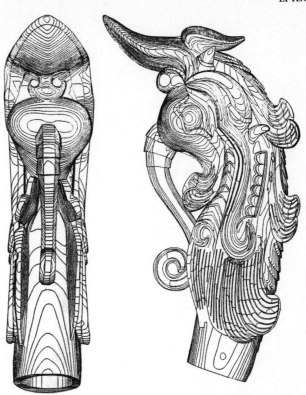

131 Photogrammetric reproduction of a bronze finial. Excavated from a ritual deposit on Oki Island, this appears to be a dragon shape of some sort; 22 cm long. Photogrammetry records surface contouring without the need for shading.

the contrasting tonnage of the vessels, with the Wando ship's 10-ton capacity dwarfed by the Shinan ship's 200 tons.

People put faith in rituals for safe passage, conducted both at sea and on land. In the hull of the Shinan ship, plugged with a block of wood, was a tiny recess containing a bronze mirror 13 cm in diameter. It was decorated with several bosses which seem to form the shape of the heavenly constellation, Ursa Major. With the Pole Star thus guiding its way, this ship was obviously well equipped to navigate the seas, but the insurance bought with the magical mirror was not enough to weather the typhoon which sent the ship to its final resting place. From the 4th to the mid-10th centuries, similar ritual objects were deposited under rock overhangs on Oki Island off Kyushu by ship crews wishing safe passage across the Korea Strait. Offerings dating from the 4th to the 6th centuries consisted of the kinds of goods found commonly in tombs: bronze mirrors, weapons, personal ornaments, horse trappings, etc. But in the 7th–8th centuries, a specialized repertoire of miniature bronze or ceramic replicas of everyday objects (weaving tools, musical instruments) was developed for deposit. Chinese coins and imported and indigenous pottery also turn up in these later assemblages, mirroring the cargo carried back and forth.

Mortuary studies

Historical archaeology in China is dominated by the excavation of elite tombs. The burial places of nearly a hundred emperors, princes and nobles have been excavated for the Ming period alone (1368–1644).[10] The Imperial Ming tombs, located just north of Beijing and on every tourist's itinerary, are the most prominent examples. Among them, the tomb of the Ming Emperor Wanli (d. 1620) was excavated in 1957, and its five spacious subterranean stone chambers now constitute a museum.

Many of the architectural styles and furnishings are carry-overs from the traditions developed in the early periods. For example, the spirit path leading up to the gate of the Imperial Ming cemetery is composed of larger-than-life-sized statues of human figures and various animals, providing continuity with the Han Dynasty tradition. An earlier tomb, belonging to the son of the Prince of Shu (d. 1389), was furnished with over five hundred 30 cm high glazed figurines depicting warriors, banner-bearing attendants and musicians, in the manner of the Tang tradition. The continued use of Han-style decorated bricks in Northern Song times (690–1126) provides resources for assessing contemporaneous lifestyles. Chinese archaeologists are particularly interested in tomb furnishings providing pictorial representations of customs, some of which were otherwise known only from texts.

fig. 128a

Cremation gained popularity with the conversion of the masses to Buddhism. Jars or boxes that held the ashes were buried in temple cemeteries in Japan and in small mound cemeteries in Korea that are still actively maintained. Such cemeteries are seldom intentionally disturbed for archaeological research, though excavations within the precincts of a medieval temple in Japan have uncovered cremation facilities. In Korea, the modern relocation of family tombs from areas scheduled for dam construction has triggered considerable grief and resentment.

Reburial and preservationist issues

Relocation of modern populations in connection with government projects occurs occasionally in East Asia as elsewhere, as in the case of Korean dam construction noted above. The situation differs, however, from that in other countries where there is friction between the politically dominant group (which usually includes the archaeologists) and an indigenous people of ethnically different origin. The politically sensitive issue of reclamation and reburial of human remains by the indigenous group is not (yet) part of the East Asian archaeological scene, even though the government of China, for example, recognizes fifty-five ethnic minorities living within its boundaries. Among the Ainu of Japan, a recent surge of ethnic consciousness has led to efforts to preserve their traditional material culture through museum construction, videotaping projects and social networking. Efforts in China to promote the traditional cultures of the ethnic minorities have a heavy ideological component, but on the whole, relations seem to be going smoothly.

This does not mean, however, that there is no friction between government and people. The 1960s Preservation Movement in Japan is a case in point.[11] In the early phases of the post-war construction boom that led Japan to economic recovery, many mounded tombs were razed to provide earth for landfill in road and rail projects. The perpetrator.of this destruction was the government, which – according to the 1954 amendments to the Law for the Protection of Cultural Properties – was also responsible for guarding the nation's archaeological heritage. To force it to fulfil its own legal obligations, the citizens of Japan rallied in a grass-roots movement to petition and lobby the government and even to boycott its activities in their neighbourhoods. The result was a massive response that has built the most comprehensive state archaeological bureaucracy and excavation programme anywhere in the world.

Archaeological remains are undergoing similar destruction in China today, for example in the Shenzhen economic zone, as development programmes take precedence over protectionist legislation. Hopefully the Chinese populace will respond with equal force and effectiveness to save its material heritage from wanton destruction.

Urban archaeology

This subdiscipline of archaeology includes both the excavation of ancient conurbations and excavations within modern cities. Researchers in East Asia are pursuing both avenues with increasing vigour. Investigations of the Yuan Dynasty capital of Dadu (1271–1368), now the city of Beijing, and of Heian-kyo, the capital of Heian-period Japan (794–1180) and now the city of Kyoto, combine the two approaches.

Despite the razing of Beijing's city walls earlier this century, the northern wall of Dadu still stands. Excavations in the city have provided data to correct *fig. 132* certain historical misconceptions or even missing conceptions: the axis of Dadu was found to run from north to south straight down the centre of the city, not slightly to the west as formerly believed; and the ancient Jinshui River, whose course had been a mystery, was confirmed to have run diagonally through the city. These examples illustrate the valuable 'challenger' and 'elaborator' roles which historical archaeology might perform in correcting and expanding knowledge beyond documentary evidence.

The Heian capital is researched through the Kyoto City Research Institute for Cultural Properties, established in 1976. Heian (later renamed Kyoto) was chosen as the site for the Japanese capital in 794 and remained the imperial capital until 1869, far beyond the end of the Heian period. Thus, urban archaeology in this city is deep and rich, and 65 per cent of the underground remains are estimated to be undisturbed by modern urban development.[12] Nevertheless, the original gridded street plan, similar to that of Heijo, had become obscured by historic construction, and excavations have helped clarify the city's early layout. The Kyoto City Institute does not, however, limit its investigations to the area of the original gridded capital: excavations are also conducted at known temple, castle, and other historical sites throughout the Kyoto Basin.

In organizational terms, the Kyoto City Institute resembles the Xi'an

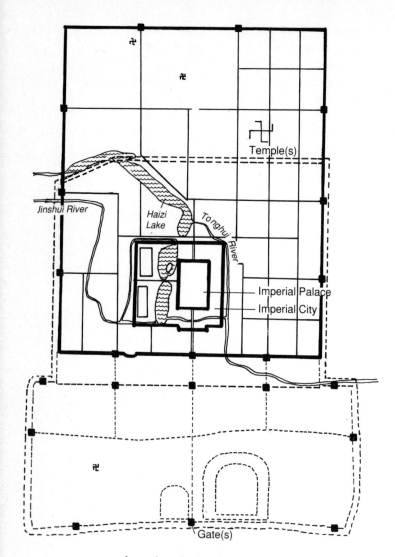

Jinshui River

Haizi
Lake

Tonghui River

Temple(s)

Imperial Palace

Imperial City

Gate(s)

*132 Plan of the Yuan Dynasty
capital of Dadu, now modern
Beijing. Built on the Zhou ideal of
three main avenues north–south
and east–west, the 13th-century
capital of the Mongols was
enclosed by walls and a moat
(heavy line). Subsequently the
city shifted slightly southwards
(double dashed line). Modern
Beijing embraces both areas. The
Forbidden City (central square)
continues from the Imperial Palace
at Dadu, and its Royal Park is
now open to the public.*

branch of the Institute of Archaeology in China, which oversees all archaeological activities in Xi'an City. This geographical catchment approach contrasts greatly with that of the Excavation Group for Metropolitan Schools, which undertakes rescue excavations exclusively on school grounds in greater Tokyo. Interfacing directly with the public, this Group publishes within the year of discovery preliminary report pamphlets with full-colour photographs and multi-colour graphics in both English and Japanese to explain fully the content and significance of the finds.

Shifting from archaeology within urbanized areas to the archaeology of ancient conurbations, major progress has been made in Japan in the excavation of medieval and feudal mansions,[13] forts, administrative sites and castles. One definition of 'urban' offered in delimiting the subject matter of urban archaeology requires a site to exhibit a central function, as for example a centre of distribution or a gathering spot for traders or manufacturers.[14] A major focus of this research is the towns which grew up around the bases of castles in order to provide the goods and services to keep the castles running. Another theme is the development of industrial craft production, including ceramics, and many historic kilns have been excavated. Archaeological studies of the Edo period (1603–1868) have demonstrated how complicated the marketing system had become by that time, with ceramics from production sites virtually anywhere within Japan and China turning up at almost any site, causing minor nightmares in identification and classification. As with the advent in Britain of the archaeology of the Victorian era, the Japanese are becoming more and more sensitive to Meiji-period (1868–1914) remains. Strata which were once bulldozed away to get down to the ancient layers are now being meticulously dug and recorded, causing excavation schedules and budgets to balloon.

Future pathways

Some say that at the present rate of excavation in Japan (nearly 15,000 digs a year and still increasing exponentially), the country's archaeological resources will be exhausted in thirty years' time. Japanese archaeologists are inundated with data which they have little time to analyse. Perhaps when they have finished digging in 2020, they will turn their attention to the outstanding problems. But by then it might be too late, for data collected without reference to a specific research problem can never be fully useful in solving that problem.

Meanwhile, the non-imperial archaeology of China through its many centuries of existence has barely been touched. There is a tremendous amount to learn about the relations of the state with local communities and peoples as evidenced by material remains. These new research directions add to an already full agenda of traditional problems in the prehistoric and protohistoric periods. With increasing excavation in the provincial areas, there will soon be a picture of the tremendous variety in regional lifestyles conducted under the imperial umbrella. Perhaps most fascinating is the potential for understanding adjacent neighbours in Southeast, Central and Northeast Asia. This will take the focus off the imperial centre and illuminate the debt which Chinese civilization owes to interaction with the surrounding areas.

Archaeology in Korea is still a young discipline, so we can look forward to many revisions and refinements in our understanding of the Peninsula's development. With the dating of periods and the contents of successive material cultures still undergoing definition, the reader will have to work hard to keep up with the new insights and discoveries that will surely alter the present synthesis.

In view of such prospective changes due to new discoveries and new interpretations, a book such as this can only provide a baseline for study of the region's past. Hopefully it will serve to structure future enquiries as the reader learns to challenge the data and syntheses presented here. The search for new answers to old questions and the posing of new questions to be asked are part and parcel of the developing field of East Asian archaeology.

Notes to the Text

Preface

1 North and South Korea, both of which are included by the use of the singular term 'Korea' in the rest of this book.
2 This is also commonly spelled 'Silla'.
3 The South Korean government uses a modi-fied McCune-Reischauer system in which initial 'shi', as in Shilla, is used contrary to common practice, and the structural components (e.g. Songguk-ri) are retained with a hyphen in administrative unit names. Here we have also been somewhat eclectic in our choice of pre-ferred spellings: the initial 'shi' is used, but site names (usually administratively derived) are spelled according to their pronunciation, not structure (e.g. Songgungni), to correspond to the major new English-language textbook on Kor-ean archaeology (Nelson 1993).

Chapter 1: Orientation

1 See Sherratt 1980: 53; Chang 1986a: 23.
2 See p. 12 in Preface for an explanation of the term Pen/Insular.
3 Thomsen 1848. K.C. Chang (1986a: 4) notes that materially defined stages were also proposed for Chinese social development by Chinese historians in the 3rd century BC.
4 Service 1975; Fried 1967, 1975.
5 Morgan 1877.
6 In addition to the sexist nature of the term 'handmaiden', the word does not convey an accurate image of the nature of the relationship, so it is avoided here.
7 Andersson 1934.
8 These are comparable to European 'archaeo-logical cultures' as defined by Childe 1951; for regional variations among the Chinese cultures, see Chang 1986a.
9 Bowen 1979.

Chapter 2: Archaeology Emergent

1 Chang 1986a: 8.
2 See entry on 'Yusoku Kojitsu' in Kodansha Encyclopedia of Japan [KEOJ] 1983.
3 See entry on 'Protohistoric Archaeology' in KEOJ 1983.
4 Kim, W.Y. 1981: 22.
5 Bleed 1986.
6 Daniel & Renfrew 1988.
7 Daniel & Renfrew 1988.
8 Chang 1986a: 4.
9 Lubbock 1865.
10 E.g. Hamada and Umehara 1923.
11 KEOJ 1983.1: 77.
12 KEOJ 1983.
13 Chang 1986a: 16.
14 Chang 1986a: 17.
15 Chang 1986a: 18.
16 See Anonymous 1977.
17 Chang 1986a: 18.
18 Barnes 1990a.
19 See Barnes 1990a.

20 M. Tanaka, personal communication, May 1992; these figures are not absolute but depend on the method of calculation.
21 M. Tanaka, personal communication, May 1992.
22 Chang 1981a: 148.
23 Barnes 1990b.
24 See, for example, Shanghai Institute of Ceramics 1986.
25 Including conservation and restoration, material and technology, production places, environment, subsistence, prospecting and arti-fact analysis, dating etc.
26 See, for example, Editorial Committee of Kobunkazai 1984.

Chapter 3: The Earliest Inhabitants

1 Stanley 1979: 146; also Stanley 1981.
2 See Jia 1980, figure facing p. 2.
3 Munthe et al. 1983.
4 Jurmain et al. 1990: 287.
5 Wu & Wang 1985: 36–37.
6 Jia 1975: 43; Jurmain et al. 1990: 412–13.
7 See Shapiro 1974.
8 Binford & Ho 1985; Binford & Stone 1986; Jia 1989.
9 Jia 1980.
10 Wu & Wang 1985: 39–40.
11 Movius 1949.
12 Pope 1989.
13 Ho & Li 1986.
14 Olsen 1987.
15 Sohn 1974.
16 Sohn 1973.
17 Serizawa 1978a.
18 See Reynolds 1985.
19 Oda & Keally 1986.
20 Bahn 1987.
21 Based on Birdsell 1972.
22 Based on Weidenreich 1943, 1969.
23 Cann 1988; Stringer 1989.
24 Based on Weidenreich's work and successors (Weidenreich 1943, 1969; Coon 1962; Aigner 1975; Wolpoff, Wu & Thorne 1984).
25 Anonymous 1992; Barinaga 1992.
26 Wolpoff & Thorne 1991; Templeton 1993.
27 IVPP 1980.
28 White 1983.
29 Suzuki & Hanihara 1982.

Chapter 4: Innovations of Modern Humans

1 Inada 1987.
2 Zhang 1990: 131.
3 You et al. 1986.
4 Olsen 1987; but such an interpretation is subject to the same criticisms levelled at the postulated use of similar tools in the Jomon for horticulture – see Chapter 5, 'Incipient Cultivation?'
5 Jia & Huang 1985a: 220.
6 Nakano 1987.
7 Serizawa 1982.
8 Yi & Clark 1985.

9 Aikens & Higuchi 1982: 78–83.
10 Asahi Shinbun newspaper, 14 Feb. 1991.
11 Kim, W.Y. 1973.
12 Inada 1987.
13 Nakano 1987.
14 Aikens & Higuchi 1982: 82.
15 Inada 1987.
16 Aikens & Higuchi 1982: 82.
17 Suzuki 1973; Suzuki et al. 1984.
18 Kamaki 1984.
19 Renfrew, C. 1975.
20 Jia & Huang 1985a: 218.
21 Bednarik & You 1991.
22 Sohn, P.K. 1974.
23 Sherratt 1980: 90.
24 Archaeometry 30.2: 301–2 (1988).
25 Oda & Keally 1973. The Narita #55 site in Japan has produced radiocarbon ages of 30,200±1000 and 29,600±960 (uncalib.). In Australia, the earliest edge-ground axe/adzes are 20,000 years old, and in Papua New Guinea fully ground axes date back to 10,000 years ago.
26 Yasuda 1978.
27 Tsukada 1986.
28 Matsuyama 1981.
29 Fagan 1987; Ikawa-Smith 1986.

Chapter 5: Littoral Foragers

1 Rowley-Conwy 1984.
2 Koyama & Thomas 1981.
3 E.g. Keally 1984.
4 Price 1981; Aikens et al. 1986.
5 In the strict sense, 'foraging' implies unplanned, opportunistic behaviour while 'hunting and gathering' implies scheduled seasonal rounds. 'Foraging' and 'foragers' are used here in the latter sense for brevity.
6 Sherratt 1980: 98.
7 Akazawa 1980.
8 Koike 1980.
9 Nakano 1987.
10 Howells 1986; Hanihara 1985, 1986.
11 Harunari 1986.
12 See Nelson 1975.
13 Nelson 1993.
14 Nelson 1993.
15 Kent & Nelson 1976.
16 Nelson 1975.
17 See Nelson 1993.
18 Nelson 1993.
19 Suzuki, M. 1973; Suzuki, M. et al. 1984.
20 Kamikawana 1968.
21 Nishida 1983.
22 Barnes 1985; Koike 1986; Aikens & Dumond 1986; Braun 1986.
23 Nelson 1993.
24 Crawford 1983, 1986; D'Andrea 1992.
25 Egoma and shiso in Japanese.
26 Ikawa-Smith 1980.
27 Gorman 1970.
28 J. Renfrew, personal communication.
29 Tsukada, cited in Chang 1981b: 184.
30 Tsukada 1986: 42.

Chapter 6: Agricultural Beginnings

1 See Chang 1981a; Rodwell 1984a.
2 Chang 1986a: 95.
3 See Chang 1981b; Liu 1985.
4 Compare Chang 1969 and 1986a.
5 See Kato 1987: 30; Nishida 1983.
6 Bailey 1981.
7 As at Torihama; see Aikens & Higuchi 1982: 127–30.
8 Namgyongni, a Chulmun settlement where rice was found together with foxtail millet (Nishitani 1986: 5).
9 Long- (*indica*) and short-grained (*japonica/sinica*) rice. The latter was first named *japonica* for its wide-spread occurrence in Japan, but the trend is to rename it *sinica* after China where it seems to have originated.
10 Liu 1985.
11 Li, H.L. 1983: 42.
12 Bray (1984: 492) states that this occurred in the Medieval period, but it is possible that dry rice was grown earlier. More research is needed to elucidate this point.
13 Chang 1981b: 179.
14 Bray 1984: 436.
15 See Ho, P.T. 1975a.
16 Olsen, Olsen & Qi 1980; Rodwell 1984a.
17 See Rodwell 1984b.
18 Chang 1986a: 103.
19 Nelson 1993; Nagamine 1986, cited in Nelson 1993.
20 Chang 1981a: 152.
21 Li, H.L. 1983.
22 Bray 1984.
23 Chang 1986a: 226.
24 Chang 1986a: 162.
25 Chang 1986a: 260.
26 The term 'East Coast' is adopted from Rawson 1980 and formalized here.
27 The term 'Longshan' is being phased out in favour of the term 'Dawenkou' (J. Rawson, personal communication, 1992); in this book 'Longshan' will be used to refer to the Late Neolithic cultures as before, but 'Dawenkou' will be employed for the Middle and Late Neolithic ceramic tradition originating in the East Coast cultures.
28 Huber 1981; Rawson 1980: chapter 1.
29 Huber 1983.
30 Zhang 1985.
31 Zhang 1985.
32 Cf. Pearson 1981.
33 First put forward in English in Chang 1959: 93; see also Chang 1977: 97–100.
34 Pearson 1974.
35 Li, H.L. 1983.

Chapter 7: The Emergence of Neolithic Elites

1 Andersson 1923.
2 See Chang 1986a: 181–89 for general description.
3 Chang 1986a: 186.
4 Pearson 1981, 1988; Pearson & Underhill 1987.
5 Chang 1986a: 169.
6 Chang 1986a: 254.
7 Chang 1986a: 255.
8 Huang 1992.
9 Chang 1986a: 250, 270, 275.
10 Chang 1986a: 190–91.
11 Li, C. 1956.
12 Chang 1986a: 273.
13 Fried 1967.

Chapter 8: The Mainland Bronze Age

1 Bishop 1941; Loehr 1949, cited in Chang 1986a: 234.
2 At the Non Nok Tha site in Thailand, the manufacture of bronze is known from between 2500–2000 BC (see Higham 1989: 99–104; Bayard 1979). New excavations in Thailand again raise the possibility of its early use in Southeast Asia (Charles Higham, personal communication, 1991–92).
3 Ma, C. 1980: 1.
4 Barnard 1980–81.
5 Rawson 1980: 13.
6 Chang 1986a: 389.
7 Ge & Linduff 1990; although radiocarbon dates corresponding to early Shang have been obtained for Sanxingdui, these are not acknowledged by many archaeologists, who believe the site to belong to a later period.
8 *Zhongguo Wenwu Bao* (15 Nov. 1990: 1). Thanks to Sarah Allan for drawing this site to my attention.
9 Zhang et al. 1983: 22.
10 Lin 1986: 249–50.
11 The site of Erlitou is sometimes partially ascribed to the Xia culture, corresponding to an ancient dynasty mentioned in early Chinese documents. This causes difficulties in archaeological periodization, however, requiring the insertion of a very brief 'Xia period' between the Late Neolithic and Shang periods. This is avoided here by considering Erlitou as potentially non-Shang in culture but definitely occurring in the Shang *period*, defined for the purposes of this book by the advent of the bronze industry.
12 In cases where Erlitou is considered to be Xia (see previous note), the Shang period is thought to begin with Erligang; therefore, Erligang is labelled as Early Shang. In any case, the styles of Erligang are not now thought to indicate chronological development but to represent the stylistic variety existing at Erligang and Anyang (see Thorp 1985).
13 The bronzes of Erligang and Anyang are quite different in style, and art historians generally believe there is an as yet undocumented phase of bronze development occurring between them. If this is ever identified, then it might be termed 'Middle Shang', especially in cases where Erligang is considered 'Early Shang' (see preceding note).
14 Bagley 1987: 111.
15 Renfrew & Cherry 1986.
16 Thorp 1985.
17 Sarah Allan, personal communication, June 1992.
18 Franklin 1983.
19 See Rawson 1980: 29.
20 Lewis 1990: 19.
21 Chang 1986b.
22 Period phases as defined for the purposes of this book.
23 Chang 1986a: 311.
24 Wheatley 1971.
25 See Chang 1980b: 237–38.
26 Hsu, M. 1986.
27 Hsu & Linduff 1988: 297.
28 Hsu & Linduff 1988: 300.
29 Except for Erlitou, which is ascribed by some to the Xia.

Chapter 9: Early Mainland States

1 Li, C. 1977.
2 The terms 'enemy' and 'friendly' are used here respectively as translations for *fang* and for *hou/bo* lords; see Chang 1980b: 216–17.

3 Chang 1980b: 219.
4 Mark Lewis, personal communication, June 1992.
5 See Chang 1980b: 211–19.
6 Chang 1980b: 70.
7 Chang 1980b: 77.
8 'Towns' and 'kinship groups' are translations for *yi* and *zu*, respectively. See Chang 1980b: chapter 3.
9 See Bagley 1977.
10 Chang 1980b: 210.
11 Chang 1978.
12 Chang 1980b: 58.
13 Chang 1980b: 210.
14 Hsu & Linduff 1988: 113.
15 Hsu & Linduff 1988: 158.
16 Hsu & Linduff 1988: 249–57.
17 Lewis 1990.
18 Falkenhausen 1990.
19 The measure of one Zhou *li* is said to be 'more than 1364.7 feet, English measure' (Creel 1970: 325, nn. 27); if 1 m = 3.28 ft, one *li* = 416 m.
20 Wheatley 1971: 411.
21 Chang 1980b: 161.
22 Tien 1978: 34.
23 Lewis 1990: 29.
24 Maspero 1978.
25 Lewis 1990: 17.
26 Piggott 1977; Pulleyblank 1966.
27 These data on the changing function of chariots are derived from Shaughnessy 1988.
28 See Shaughnessy 1988.
29 Lewis 1990: 17.
30 Lewis 1990: 54–61.
31 Lewis 1990: 60.
32 Luo 1980: 1.
33 Luo 1980: 6.
34 Barfield 1989.
35 Wang, Y.C. 1951: 176.
36 E.g. Gettens et al. 1971.
37 Wagner 1993: 80.
38 Wagner 1993: 73, 99.
39 Wagner 1993.
40 Wagner 1993.
41 Wagner 1993: 254.
42 Qi, Qin, Yan, Qiao, Wei, Han and Chu.
43 Li, X. 1985: 327.

Chapter 10: The Northern Frontier

1 See, for example, the seminal work by Jettmar 1967.
2 IVPP 1980: 123–26, 131–34.
3 Lattimore 1940; Huntington 1907.
4 Sherratt 1981.
5 Sherratt 1981.
6 Bray 1984.
7 These animals are identified together here for two reasons: it is very difficult to distinguish their bones from each other, and only one Chinese character is used to refer to them both.
8 Cui 1988: 69–74. My thanks to Nicola Di Cosmo for guiding me to this report.
9 Chang 1986a: 282.
10 Chang 1986a: 384.
11 Shaughnessy 1988.
12 Shaughnessy 1988: 227.
13 Barfield 1989.
14 Di Cosmo 1992.
15 Referred to as *yi* in Chinese.
16 Childe 1951.
17 Kim, J.H. 1978: 163. Here, *pinyin* romanization has been substituted for Wade-Giles spellings in the original.
18 Kim & Nishitani 1984: 84.
19 Townsend 1975; Nelson 1982: 541.
20 For this reason, Nelson 1993 avoids the term

'Bronze Age' altogether, preferring to call this period the 'Megalithic Age.'
21 Kim & Nishitani 1984: 84.
22 Kim & Nishitani 1984: 99.
23 Zvelebil 1986.
24 Kim, W.Y. cited in Choi, M.L. 1984: 59.
25 National Museum of Korea 1978–9, 1986.
26 See Kim, J.H. 1978: 130–34.
27 I,Konmu 1988.
28 Kim, W.Y. 1986a: 102, 107, 110.
29 Kim, B.M. 1982.
30 'Cist' and 'dolmen' are two terms adopted from European archaeology. A cist is most strictly defined as a burial facility constructed of flat stones stood on edge to form a box in which the corpse was laid; flagstones could be used to pave the bottom of the box and provide a cover. A dolmen is a much larger construction consisting of a large capstone with various understructures (see fig. 79). A cist is embedded in the ground, while dolmens characteristically stand above ground, although some might have been mounded with earth. In Japanese archaeological literature, the term dolmen was inaccurately applied to stone chambers found in tumuli as they were first described by Westerners late last century.
31 Kim & Nishitani 1984: 106.
32 Kim & Nishitani 1984: 108.
33 Choi, M.L. 1984: 67.
34 Choi, M.L. 1984.
35 Choi, M.L. 1984: 69–70.
36 Kang, B.W. 1991.

Chapter 11: The Spread of Rice Agriculture

1 Choe, C.P. 1982.
2 Nelson 1982.
3 Sahara 1987.
4 Hanihara 1985.
5 Hanihara 1987.
6 See fig.30. Also see Howells 1986; Brace & Nagai 1982.
7 As mentioned in the Preface, either of these events may be used as the beginning of the Yayoi period, depending on one's preference. I subscribe to the latter – the use of ceramic criteria. Here, then, Yamanotera is considered to be a Jomon pottery type.
8 Barnes 1993.
9 Akazawa 1982.
10 Akazawa 1981.
11 Oikawa & Koyama 1981.
12 Akazawa 1981.
13 M. Sahara, personal communication, 1989.
14 Nihon Kokogaku Kyokai & Shizuoka Kokogakkai 1988.
15 Tsude 1988.
16 See Hawkes 1974; Barnes 1982.
17 Fujiwara 1979.
18 Crawford 1992.
19 Hamada 1981: 153.

Chapter 12: The Making and Breaking of Empire

1 Creel 1964: 170.
2 Luo 1980: 2.
3 E.g. Cottrell 1981.
4 This discussion of armour is based on Dien 1981/2.
5 Li, X. 1985: 240–46.
6 Wang, Z. 1982.
7 See Dewall 1967 and Pirazzoli-t'Serstevens 1982: 81–88.

8 See Watt 1970; Meacham 1980.
9 This discussion is based on Loewe 1967.
10 See the popular account by Hopkirk 1980.
11 Loewe 1967.1: 84; Luo 1980: 6.
12 Yu 1967: 38.
13 Bulling 1960.
14 Loewe 1979.
15 In early historic Northeast Asia, shamans employed the mirror as a sun symbol; this symbolism has been projected back into the protohistoric Pen/Insular cultures by some researchers.
16 The autopsy was actually shown in a BBC television programme in the *Chronicle* series (1982) entitled 'China: Treasures of the Cultural Revolution.'
17 Wang, Z. 1982: 209.
18 Pirazzoli-t'Serstevens 1982: 41.
19 The commonly stated date is 119 BC, but the actual establishment of the monopoly was not accomplished until 117.
20 Dien 1981/82.
21 Liu, X. 1988: 13.
22 Nara Prefectural Museum of Art 1988a: 12.
23 Liu, X. 1988: 141.
24 Nara Prefectural Museum of Art 1988b.
25 Barfield 1989: 92.
26 Barfield 1989: 102.
27 Dunhuang 1981.
28 Juliano 1980.

Chapter 13: The Yellow Sea Interaction Sphere

1 Barnes 1986b.
2 Gardiner 1969: 9.
3 Kim, J.B. 1978.
4 Watson, B. 1961: 258–63.
5 Harada & Komai 1936.
6 Umehara 1954, 1956.
7 Koizumi 1935.
8 Kim, J.H. 1978: 145.
9 Pai, H.I. 1992.
10 Ikeuchi 1930.
11 Chronicles of the Wei Dynasty.
12 Not to be confused with Han China.
13 Sohn et al. 1970: 28.
14 Hatada 1969.
15 Choi, C.G. 1982.
16 *Korea Newsreview*, Jan. 1982.
17 I, K. 1988.
18 Kim & Nishitani 1984: 141.
19 Taylor 1990: 41.
20 Taylor 1990.
21 MacCord 1960; the site was named 'Able' by the troops.
22 Taylor 1990: 214.
23 Hamada & Umehara 1923.
24 Tsunoda & Goodrich 1951.
25 Tsunoda & Goodrich 1951: 2.
26 Young 1958.
27 Takemoto 1983.
28 Tsunoda & Goodrich 1951: 14.
29 Tsunoda & Goodrich 1951: 16.
30 Hudson & Barnes 1991.
31 Sahara et al. 1989: 33.
32 Sahara 1975.

Chapter 14: The Mounded Tomb Cultures

1 Aston 1972; Kim, P.S. 1983.
2 See Li, X. 1985: 93–105.
3 Pusan 1985.
4 See Barnes 1990d for a review of Peninsular state-foundation myths.

5 Ji'an 1979.
6 See Barnes 1988b.
7 Kim, W.Y. 1986b defines these three Koguryo mural types.
8 Kim, W.Y. 1992.
9 Kim, W.Y. 1983: 53ff.
10 Nelson 1993.
11 See Miki 1974.
12 See Kidder 1964.
13 See Barnes 1990d: 141.
14 Price 1978.
15 Barnes 1986b.
16 See Lee, K.B. 1984; Aston 1972.
17 Kim, C.S. 1971; Miller 1974.
18 Kiley 1973.
19 Nelson 1991.
20 Nelson 1993: 265.
21 Lee, K.B. 1984: 38.
22 Barnes 1987.
23 Anazawa & Manome 1986.
24 Best 1980.
25 Hook 1982: 186.
26 See 'Kogoishi' entry in KEOJ 1983.
27 See Adams 1975.
28 Hirano 1977.
29 See Hudson 1989.
30 See 'Horserider Theory' entry in KEOJ 1983.
31 See Barnes 1990d: 138–41; Grayson 1977.
32 Kidder 1985; Edwards 1983.
33 See Barnes 1990d: 138–40.

Chapter 15: East Asian Civilization

1 See 'Taika Reform' entry in KEOJ 1983.
2 Hook 1982: 186.
3 Inoue 1977.
4 Lee, K.B. 1984: 76.
5 Barnes 1988a.
6 See Barnes 1988b: chapter 6 for details.
7 Lee, K.B. 1984: 63.
8 The actual unit of measurement was one *cho* (2.45 acres or 0.992 hectares).
9 See Kidder 1972: chapter 7 for details.
10 Lee, K.B. 1984: 76.
11 The roads (-*do*) formed part of the district names, e.g. Hokurikudo, Hokkaido; some of the roads and the district names are still in use today.
12 Lee, K.B. 1984: 77.
13 Piggott 1977.
14 Lee, K.B. 1984: 77.
15 Crawford & Takamiya 1990; D'Andrea 1992; Crawford 1992.
16 See Kim, W.Y. 1983.
17 Hook 1982: 191.
18 Yamamura 1974.
19 Hayashi 1975.

Chapter 16: Epilogue

1 Ball 1989.
2 Addis 1984.
3 Liu & Bai 1983.
4 Liu & Bai 1983.
5 Mao 1984.
6 Yin 1984.
7 Kim, W.Y. 1983: 73.
8 Keith 1979: 232.
9 Kim, Y.H. n.d.
10 Institute of Archaeology 1984.
11 Barnes 1986–88.
12 Kyoto-shi Maibun 1980: 49.
13 *yashiki*.
14 Maekawa 1991: 8.

Further Reading and Bibliography

Further Reading

Book titles are given in upper case letters; shorter works are in lower case.

PREFACE

The UNESCO series, RECENT ARCHAEOLOGICAL DISCOVERIES, is a selective introduction to the succession of periods and the variety of archaeological remains in each of the East Asian countries; each volume is brief and well illustrated: China (Institute of Archaeology 1984); Korea (Kim, W.Y. 1983); and Japan (Tsuboi 1987).

CHAPTER 1: ORIENTATION

Detailed national archaeologies are available in standard textbooks for each country: THE ARCHAEOLOGY OF ANCIENT CHINA (Chang 1986a); ANCIENT CHINA: ART AND ARCHAEOLOGY (Rawson 1980); PREHISTORY OF JAPAN (Aikens & Higuchi 1982); ANCIENT JAPAN (Pearson 1992); and THE ARCHAEOLOGY OF KOREA (Nelson 1993). For general archaeological method and theory, read ARCHAEOLOGY: THEORIES, METHODS AND PRACTICE (Renfrew & Bahn 1991).

CHAPTER 2: ARCHAEOLOGY EMERGENT

Japan: Almost archaeology: early archaeological interest in Japan (Bleed 1986); The 'idea of prehistory' in Japan (Barnes 1990a); An objective view of Japanese archaeological works in Korea (Arimitsu 1966); The origins of bureaucratic archaeology in Japan (Barnes 1990b). *China*: CHILDREN OF THE YELLOW EARTH: STUDIES IN PREHISTORIC CHINA (Andersson 1934); Archaeology and Chinese historiography (Chang 1981c).

CHAPTER 3: THE EARLIEST INHABITANTS

PALAEOANTHROPOLOGY AND PALAEOLITHIC ARCHAEOLOGY IN THE PEOPLE'S REPUBLIC OF CHINA (Wu & Olsen 1985); ATLAS OF PRIMITIVE MAN IN CHINA (IVPP 1980); PEKING MAN: THE DISCOVERY, DISAPPEARANCE AND MYSTERY OF A PRICELESS SCIENTIFIC TREASURE (Shapiro 1974); On problems of the Beijing-Man site: a critique of new interpretations (Jia 1989); History of Early Palaeolithic research in Japan (Ikawa-Smith 1978).

CHAPTER 4: INNOVATIONS OF MODERN HUMANS

Modern *Homo sapiens* origins (Wolpoff, Wu & Thorne 1984); The microlithic in China (Chen 1984); Recent developments in the late Pleistocene prehistory of China (Olsen 1987); Palaeolithic art from China (Bednarik & You 1991); Japan and Korea at 18,000 BP (Reynolds & Kaner 1990).

CHAPTER 5: LITTORAL FORAGERS

Vegetation in prehistoric Japan: the last 20,000 years (Tsukada 1986); Postglacial foraging and early farming economies in Japan and Korea (Rowley-Conwy 1984); Maritime adaptation of prehistoric hunter-gatherers and their transition to agriculture in Japan (Akazawa 1981); The Western-language Jomon (Kaner 1990); AFFLUENT FORAGERS (Koyama & Thomas 1981).

CHAPTER 6: AGRICULTURAL BEGINNINGS

The domestication of plants in China: ecogeographical considerations (Li, H.L. 1983); The relationship of the painted pottery and Lung-shan cultures (Huber 1983); The Chinese Neolithic: recent trends in research (Pearson & Underhill 1987).

CHAPTER 7: THE EMERGENCE OF NEOLITHIC SOCIAL DEVELOPMENT

Chinese Neolithic burial patterns: problems and methods of interpretation (Pearson 1988); Liangzhu: a late Neolithic jade-yielding culture in southeastern coastal China (Huang 1992); The Neolithic of northeastern China and Korea (Nelson 1990).

CHAPTER 8: THE MAINLAND BRONZE AGE

CHINESE BRONZES: ART AND RITUAL (Rawson 1987); THE GREAT BRONZE AGE OF CHINA (Wen 1980); Sanxingdui: a new Bronze Age site in southwest China (Ge & Linduff 1990); ANCIENT CHINESE AND ORDOS BRONZES (Rawson & Bunker 1990); On bronze and other metals in early China (Franklin 1983).

CHAPTER 9: EARLY MAINLAND STATES

SHANG CIVILIZATION (Chang 1980b); SOURCES OF SHANG HISTORY (Keightley 1978); WESTERN ZHOU CIVILIZATION (Hsu & Linduff 1988); EASTERN ZHOU AND QIN CIVILIZATION (Li, X. 1985); SANCTIONED VIOLENCE IN EARLY CHINA (Lewis 1990); IRON AND STEEL IN ANCIENT CHINA (Wagner 1993).

CHAPTER 10: THE NORTHERN FRONTIER

Historical perspectives on the introduction of the chariot into China (Shaughnessy 1988); THE PERILOUS FRONTIER: NOMADIC EMPIRES AND CHINA (Barfield 1989); Chapter xx in THE PREHISTORY OF KOREA (Kim, J.H. 1978).

CHAPTER 11: THE SPREAD OF RICE AGRICULTURE

From Toro to Yoshinogari: changing perspectives on Yayoi archaeology (Hudson 1990); The transitions to agriculture in Japan (Crawford 1992); Paddy field soils (Barnes 1990e).

CHAPTER 12: THE MAKING AND BREAKING OF EMPIRE

THE FIRST EMPEROR OF CHINA (Cottrell 1981); THE HAN CIVILIZATION OF CHINA (Pirazzoli-t'Serstevens 1982); HAN CIVILIZATION (Wang, Z. 1982); ART AND POLITICAL EXPRESSION IN EARLY CHINA (Powers 1991).

CHAPTER 13: THE YELLOW SEA INTERACTION SPHERE

Culture contact and culture change: the Korean peninsula and its relations with the Han dynasty commandery of Lelang (Pai, H.I. 1992); Chiefly exchange between Kyushu and Okinawa, Japan, in the Yayoi period (Pearson 1990); Yoshinogari: a Yayoi settlement in northern Kyushu (Hudson & Barnes 1991).

CHAPTER 14: THE MOUNDED TOMB CULTURES

Early Korean States (Barnes 1990d); **The Kolp'um system: basis for Sillan social stratification** (Kim, C.S. 1971); **EARLY JAPANESE ART: THE GREAT TOMBS AND TREASURES** (Kidder 1964); **PROTOHISTORIC YAMATO: ARCHAEOLOGY OF THE FIRST JAPANESE STATE** (Barnes 1988b); **Chiefly lineages in Kofun-period Japan: political relations between centre and region** (Tsude 1990).

CHAPTER 15: EAST ASIAN CIVILIZATION

CAMBRIDGE HISTORY OF CHINA: SUI AND T'ANG CHINA (Twitchett & Fairbank 1979); **EARLY BUDDHIST JAPAN** (Kidder 1972); **THE HISTORIC CITY OF NARA: AN ARCHAEOLOGICAL APPROACH** (Tsuboi & Tanaka 1992); **The Silk Road and the Shosoin** (Hayashi 1975); **The *ritsuryo* system in Japan** (Inoue 1977); **Decline of the ritsuryo system: hypotheses on economic and institutional change** (Yamamura 1974).

COLLECTIONS OF PAPERS

THE ORIGINS OF CHINESE CIVILIZATION (Keightley 1983); **STUDIES OF SHANG ARCHAEOLOGY** (Chang 1986b); **NEW PERSPECTIVES ON CHU CULTURE DURING THE EASTERN ZHOU PERIOD** (Lawton 1991); **WINDOWS ON THE JAPANESE PAST** (Pearson et al. 1986); **PACIFIC NORTHEAST ASIA IN PREHISTORY** (Aikens & Rhee 1992); **BIBLIOGRAPHIC REVIEWS OF FAR EASTERN ARCHAEOLOGY 1990** (Barnes 1990c).

Bibliography

Adams, E.B. (1975) 'Silla Buddhist reliefs of a Mirok grotto.' *Korea Journal* 15.7: 59–64.

Addis, J.M. (1984) 'The evolution of techniques at Jingdezhen with particular reference to the Yuan Dynasty.' In *Jingdezhen Wares: The Yuan evolution*, pp. 11–19. Hong Kong: Oriental Ceramic Society of Hong Kong.

Aigner, Jean S. (1975) 'The Palaeolithic of China.' *Proceedings, 13th Pacific Science Congress.* Vancouver.

Aigner, Jean S. (1981) *Archaeological Remains in Pleistocene China.* Munich: C.H. Beck.

Aikens, C.M. and Dumond, D.E. (1986) 'Convergence and common heritage: some parallels in the archaeology of Japan and western North America.' In Pearson et al. 1986: 163–80.

Aikens, C.M. and Higuchi, T. (1982) *Prehistory of Japan.* New York: Academic Press.

Aikens, C.M. and Rhee, S.N. (1992) *Pacific Northeast Asia in Prehistory.* Washington State Univ. Press.

Aikens, C.M., Ames, K.M. and Sanger, D. (1986) 'Affluent collectors at the edges of Eurasia and North America: some comparisons and observations on the evolution of society among north-temperate coastal hunter-gatherers.' *University Museum, University of Tokyo Bulletin* 27: 3–26.

Akazawa, Takeru (1980) 'Fishing adaptation of prehistoric hunter-gatherers at the Nittano site, Japan.' *Journal of Archaeological Science* 7: 325–44.

Akazawa, Takeru (1981) 'Maritime adaptation of prehistoric hunter-gatherers and their transition to agriculture in Japan.' *Senri Ethnological Studies* 9: 213–58. Osaka: National Museum of Ethnology.

Akazawa, Takeru (1982) 'Cultural change in prehistoric Japan: the receptivity process of rice agriculture in the Japanese archipelago.' *Advances in World Archaeology* 1: 151–211.

Akazawa, Takeru et al. (1980) *The Japanese Palaeolithic: a techno-typological study.* Tokyo: Rippu Shobo.

Anazawa, Wakou and Manome, Jun'ichi (1986) 'Two inscribed swords from Japanese tumuli.' In Pearson et al. 1986: 375–95.

Andersson, J.G. (1923) *The Cave Deposit at Sha Kuo T'un in Feng Tien.* Palaeontologia Sinica D-1.1. 43 pp.

Andersson, J.G. (1934). *Children of the Yellow Earth: studies in prehistoric China.* London: Kegan Paul, Trench, Trubner.

Anonymous (1977) *The Outline of Korean History (until August 1945).* P'yongyang: Foreign Languages Publishing House.

Anonymous (1992) 'African Eve theory takes a step back.' *New Scientist*, 15 Feb.

Archaeology Quarterly (Kikan Kokogaku) (1986) 'Yamataikoku o Kokogaku Suru.' Special issue.

Arimitsu, K. (1966) 'An objective view of Japanese archaeological works in Korea.' *Transactions of the Korean Branch, Royal Asiatic Society* 42: 75–79.

Asahi (1980) *Yamatai-koku no Michi e* [On the road to Yamatai]. Tokyo: Asahi Shimbun. (in Japanese)

Asahi-cho (1982) *The Historic Site of Fudodo: an outline and summary of its facilities.* Toyama Pref.: Asahi Township. (in Japanese)

Aston, W.G., trans. (1972) *Nihongi: chronicles of Japan from the earliest times to AD 697.* Tokyo: Tuttle.

Auboyer, J. et al. (1979) *Oriental Art, a handbook of styles and forms.* London: Faber & Faber.

Bagley, R.W. (1977) 'Pan-lung-ch'eng: a Shang city in Hupei.' *Artibus Asiae* 24: 165–219.

Bagley, R.W. (1987) 'The Zhengzhou Phase (The Erligang Period),' and 'The appearance and growth of regional bronze-using cultures.' In *The Great Bronze Age of China*, ed. Wen Fong. London/New York: Thames & Hudson/The Metropolitan Museum of Art.

Bahn, Paul G. (1987) 'Excavation of a palaeolithic plank from Japan.' *Nature* 329: 110.

Bailey, G. (1981) 'Concepts of resource exploitation: continuity and discontinuity in palaeoeconomy.' *World Archaeology* 13.1: 5–8.

Ball, David (1989) Translation of *The Discovery of Ru Kiln.* Manuscript, Centre for Asian Studies, Univ. of Adelaide.

Barber, E.J.W. (1991) *Prehistoric Textiles.* Princeton Univ. Press.

Barfield, Thomas J. (1989) *The Perilous Frontier: nomadic empires and China.* Cambridge, MA: Basil Blackwell.

Barinaga, M. (1992) '"African Eve" backers beat a retreat.' *Science* 255: 686–87.

Barnard, Noel (1980/81) 'Wrought metal-working prior to Middle Shang (?): a problem in archaeological and art-historical research approaches.' *Early China* 6: 4–20.

Barnes, G.L. (1982) 'Toro.' In *Atlas of Archaeology*, ed. K. Branigan, pp. 198–201. London: Book Club Associates/MacDonald.

Barnes, G.L. (1985) 'The Asian textured-pottery horizon: whitewash or Mesolithic mosaic?' Paper delivered at the Prehistoric Society Spring Conference, Norwich.

Barnes, G.L. (1986a) 'Paddy field archaeology in Nara, Japan.' *Journal of Field Archaeology* 13: 371–79.

Barnes, G.L. (1986b) 'Jiehao, Tonghao: peer relations in East Asia.' In *Peer Polity Interaction and Socio-Political Change*, ed. C. Renfrew and J. Cherry, pp. 79–92. Cambridge Univ. Press.

Barnes, G.L. (1986–88) 'The origins of bureaucratic archaeology in Japan.' *Journal of the Hong Kong Archaeological Society* 12: 183–94.

Barnes, G.L. (1987) 'The role of the *be* in state formation.' In *Specialization, Exchange and Complex Societies*, ed. E. Brumfiel and T. Earle, pp. 86–101. Cambridge Univ. Press.

Barnes, G.L. (1988a) 'Walled sites in Three Kingdoms settlement patterns.' In *Papers of the 5th International Conference on Korean Studies I*, pp. 436–64. Songnam: Academy of Korean Studies.

Barnes, G.L. (1988b) *Protohistoric Yamato: archaeology of the first Japanese state.* Ann Arbor: Museum of Anthropology and Center for Japanese Studies, Univ. of Michigan.

Barnes, G.L. (1990a) 'The "idea of prehistory" in Japan.' *Antiquity* 64.245: 929–40.

Barnes, G.L. (1990b) 'The origins of bureaucratic archaeology in Japan.' *Journal of the Hong Kong Archaeological Society* 12: 183–96.

Barnes, G.L., ed. (1990c) *Bibliographic Reviews of Far Eastern Archaeology: Hoabinhian, Jomon, Yayoi and early Korean states.* Oxford: Oxbow Books.

Barnes, G.L. (1990d) 'Early Korean States: a review of historical interpretation.' In Barnes 1990c: 113–62.

Barnes, G.L. (1990e) 'Paddy field soils.' *World Archaeology* 22.1: 1–17.

Barnes, G.L. (1992) 'The development of stoneware technology in southern Korea.' In *Pacific Northeast Asia in Prehistory*, ed. C.M. Aikens and S.N. Rhee, pp. 197–208. Washington State Univ. Press.

Barnes, G.L. (1993) 'Miwa occupation in wider perspective.' In *The Miwa Project Report*, ed. G.L. Barnes and M. Okita, pp. 181–92. British Archaeological Reports S582. Oxford: Tempvs Reparatvm.

Bayard, Donn (1979) 'The chronology of prehistoric metallurgy in northeast Thailand: Silabhumi or Samrddhabdhumi?' In *Early South East Asia*, ed. R.B. Smith and W. Watson, pp. 15–32. Oxford Univ. Press.

BBC2 Television (1982) *China: treasures of the Cultural Revolution* [archaeological excavations]. 'Chronicle' series.

Bednarik, R.G. and You, Y. (1991) 'Palaeolithic art from China.' *Rock Art Research* 8.2: 119–23.

Best, Jonathan W. (1980) 'The Sosan triad: an early Korean Buddhist relief sculpture from Paekche.' *Archives of Asian Art* 33: 89–108.

Binford, L. and Ho, C.K. (1985) 'Taphonomy at a distance: Zhoukoudian, "The Cave Home of Beijing Man"?' *Current Anthropology* 26: 413–42.

Binford, L. and Stone, N.M. (1986) 'Zhoukoudian: a closer look.' *Current Anthropology* 27.5: 453–75.

Birdsell, J. (1972) *Human Evolution.* Chicago: Rand-McNally.

Bishop, C. (1941) *Origin of the Far Eastern Civilization.* Smithsonian War Background Series. Washington, DC: Smithsonian Institution.

Bishop, M.C. (1989) 'The articulated cuirass in Qin dynasty China.' *Antiquity* 63: 697–705.

Bleed, P. (1986) 'Almost archaeology: early archaeological interest in Japan.' In Pearson et al. 1986: 57–67.

Bowen, G. (1979) 'Report on stone tools from Chongok-ni.' *Chindan Hakbo* 46/47: 48–55.

Brace, C.L. and Nagai, M. (1982) 'Japanese tooth size: past and present.' *American Journal of Physical Anthropology* 59: 399–411.

Braun, D.P. (1986) 'Midwestern Hopewellian exchange and supralocal interaction.' In *Peer Polity Interaction and Socio-Political Change*, ed. C. Renfrew and J. Cherry, pp. 117–26. Cambridge Univ. Press.

Bray, F. (1984) *Science and Civilisation in China 6.2: Agriculture.* Cambridge Univ. Press.

Bryan, A.L. (1978) 'An overview of Paleo-American prehistory from a circum- Pacific perspective.' In *Early Man in America.*, ed. A.L. Bryan. Occasional Papers no. 1, Dept. of Anthropology, Univ. of Alberta.

Bryan, A.L. (1986) *New Evidence for the Pleistocene Peopling of the Americas.* Orono, Maine: Center for the Study of Early Man.

Bryan, A.L. (1991) 'The current status of research on Pleistocene Americans.' Paper presented at the 13th INQUA Conference, Beijing.

Bulling, A. (1960) *The Decoration of Mirrors of the Han Period: a chronology.* Geneva: Ascona.

Cann, Rebecca L. (1988) 'DNA and human origins.' *Annual Review of Anthropology* 17: 127–43.

Chang, K.C. (1959) 'A working hypothesis for the early cultural history of south China.' *Bulletin of the Institute of Ethnology, Academia Sinica* 7: 43–103.

Chang, K.C. (1968) *The Archaeology of Ancient China.* Revised/2nd edn. Yale Univ. Press.

Chang, K.C. (1969) *Fengpit'ou, Tap'enk'eng and the Prehistory of Taiwan.* Yale Univ. Publications in Anthropology, vol. 73. Yale Univ. Press.

Chang, K.C. (1977) *The Archaeology of Ancient China.* 3rd edn. Yale Univ. Press.

Chang, K.C. (1978) *'T'ien Kan:* a key to the history of the Shang.' In *Ancient China*, ed. D.T. Roy and T. Tsien. Hong Kong: Chinese Univ. Press.

Chang, K.C. (1980a) 'The Chinese Bronze Age: a modern synthesis.' In *The Great Bronze Age of China*, ed. F. Wen, pp. 35–50. London/New York: Thames & Hudson/The Metropolitan Museum of Art.

Chang, K.C. (1980b) *Shang Civilization.* Yale Univ. Press.

Chang, K.C. (1981a) 'In search of China's beginnings: new light on an old civilization.' *American Scientist* 69: 148–60.

Chang, K.C. (1981b) 'The affluent foragers in the coastal areas of China: extrapolation from evidence on transition to agriculture.' *Senri Ethnological Studies* 9: 177–86. Osaka: National Museum of Ethnology.

Chang, K.C. (1981c) 'Archaeology and Chinese historiography.' *World Archaeology* 13: 156–69.

Chang, K.C. (1983) 'Sandai archaeology and the formation of states in ancient China.' In *The Origins of Chinese Civilization*, ed. D. Keightley, pp. 495–522. Univ. of California Press.

Chang, K.C. (1986a) *The Archaeology of Ancient China.* 4th edn. Yale Univ. Press.

Chang, K.C., ed. (1986b) *Studies of Shang Archaeology.* Yale Univ. Press.

Chen, Chun (1984) 'The microlithic in China.' *Journal of Anthropological Archaeology* 3:79–115.

Cheng, Dong and Zhong, Shao-yi (1990) *Ancient Chinese Weapons: a collection of pictures.* Beijing: Chinese People's Liberation Army Publishing House. (in Chinese with English summary)

Childe, V.G. (1951) *Social Evolution.* New York: Schuman.

Chinese Culture Foundation (1987). *Stories from China's Past: Han Dynasty pictorial tomb reliefs and archaeological objects from Sichuan Province, People's Republic of China.* San Francisco.

Choe, C.P. (1982) 'The diffusion route and chronology of Korean plant domestication.' *Journal of Asian Studies* 41.3: 519–29.

Choi, Byong-hyon (1987) 'Investigating the formation of Late-type Shilla pottery.' In *Sambul Kim Won-Yong Kyosu Chongnyon T'oe-im Kinyon Nonch'ong*, pp. 563–96. Seoul: Ilchisa. (in Korean)

Choi, Chong-gyu (1982) 'Aperçu sur les fouilles faites à Choyang-dong et leur signification.' *Revue de Corée* 14.2: 40–62.

Choi, Chong-gyu (1983) 'Examination of Wajil pottery and its significance.' *Kodai o Kangaeru* 34: 1–19. (in Japanese)

Choi, Mong-lyong (1984) *A Study of the Yongsan River Valley Culture.* Seoul: Dong Song Sa.

Choi, Mong-lyong and Shim, Chong-bo (1991) *Understanding Paekche History.* Seoul: Hag'yon Munhwa. (in Korean)

Chong, Chaehun and Cho, Yujon, eds. (1989) *Pukhan oe Munhwa Yusan II.* Seoul: Koryowon. (in Korean)

Chow, B. (1981) 'The animal remains discovered at Lishan Village, Wu'an, Hebei Province.' *Kaogu Xuebao* 1981.3: 303–47. (in Chinese)

Coon, C.S. (1962) *The Origin of Races.* New York: Knopf.

Cottrell, Arthur (1981) *The First Emperor of China.* London: Macmillan.

Crawford, Gary W. (1983) *Paleoethnobotany of the Kameda Peninsula Jomon.* Anthropological Papers 73, Museum of Anthropology, Univ. of Michigan, Ann Arbor.

Crawford, Gary W. (1986) 'Sakushu-Kotoni River plant remains.' In *The Sakushi-Kotoni River Site*, ed. M. Yoshizaki. Sapporo: Hokkaido Univ.

Crawford, Gary W. (1992) 'The transitions to agriculture in Japan.' In *Transitions to Agriculture in Prehistory*, ed. T.D. Price and A.B. Gebauer, pp. 117–32. Madison: Prehistory Press.

Crawford, Gary W. and Takamiya, Hiroto (1990) 'The origins and implications of late prehistoric plant husbandry in northern Japan.' *Antiquity* 64: 889–911.

Creel, H.G. (1964) 'The beginning of bureaucracy in China: the origin of the *hsien.' Journal of Asian Studies* 23.3: 155–84.

Creel, H.G. (1970) *The Origins of Statecraft in China, Vol. 1: the Western Chou empire.* Univ. of Chicago Press.

Cui, Xuan. (1988) 'Report on pre-Qin faunal remains in Inner Mongolia.' *Nei Meng-ku She-hui K'e-hsueh* 1988.1: 69–74. (in Chinese)

D'Andrea, A.C. (1992) *Palaeoethnobotany of Later Jomon and Yayoi Cultures of Northeastern Japan*. Ph. D. thesis, Dept. of Anthropology, Univ. of Toronto.

Daniel, Glyn and Renfrew, Colin (1988) *The Idea of Prehistory*. Revised & enlarged edn. Edinburgh Univ. Press. (Orig. 1962, London: C.A. Watts.)

Davis, Simon J.M. (1987) *The Archaeology of Animals*. London: Batsford.

Dewall, Magdalene von (1967) 'The Tien culture of southwest China.' *Antiquity* 40: 8–21.

Di Cosmo, N. (1992) 'Protohistoric agriculture in the Mongolian Basin.' Paper delivered at the East Asian Archaeology Network Meeting, Washington, DC.

Dien, A.E. (1981/82) 'A study of early Chinese armour.' *Artibus Asiae* 43.1/2: 5–66.

Dillehay, Thomas D. (1988) 'How new is the New World?' *Antiquity* 62: 94–97.

Dunhuang Institute for Cultural Relics (1981). *The Art Treasures of Dunhuang*. Hong Kong/New York: Joint Publishing Co./Lee Publishers Group.

Editorial Committee of Kobunkazai (1984) *Scientific Approaches to the Study of Cultural Property*. Kyoto: Domyosha. (in Japanese)

Edwards, W. (1983) 'Event and process in the founding of Japan: the horserider theory in archaeological perspective.' *Journal of Japanese Studies* 9.2: 265–96.

Esaka, T., ed. (1973) *Kodaishi Hakkutsu 2: Jomon pottery and shellmounds*. Tokyo: Kodansha. (in Japanese)

Esaka, T. and Noguchi, Y. (1979) *Kodaishi Hakkutsu 3: Figurine technology and beliefs*. Tokyo: Kodansha. (in Japanese)

Fairbank, J.K. and Reischauer, E.O. (1960) *East Asia, The Great Tradition*. Boston: Houghton Mifflin.

Fagan, Brian M. (1987) *The Great Journey: the peopling of ancient America*. London/New York: Thames & Hudson.

Falkenhausen, Lothar von (1990) 'The state of Yan and its northeastern connections.' Paper delivered at Society for American Archaeology Meetings, Las Vegas.

Falkenhausen, Lothar von (1991) 'Chu ritual music.' In *New Perspectives on Chu Culture during the Eastern Zhou Period*, ed. T. Lawton, pp. 47–106. Washington, DC: Smithsonian Institution.

Franklin, U.M. (1983) 'On bronze and other metals in early China.' In *The Origins of Chinese Civilization*, ed. D.N. Keightley, pp. 279–96. Univ. of California Press.

Fried, M. (1967) *The Evolution of Political Society*. New York: Random House.

Fried, M. (1975) *The Notion of Tribe*. Menlo Park: Cummings.

Fuji, N. (1966) 'Climatic changes of postglacial age in Japan.' *The Quaternary Research* 5.3/4: 149–56. (in Japanese with English summary)

Fujita, F. (1987) 'A few perspectives about slit earrings of Jomon period.' *Japan Society for Southeast Asian Archaeology Bulletin* 7: 7–9. (in Japanese)

Fujiwara, Hiroshi (1979) 'Fundamental studies of plant opal analysis 3: estimation of the yield of rice in ancient paddy fields through quantitative analysis of plant opal.' *Kokogaku to Shizen Kagaku* 12: 29–42. (in Japanese with English title and summary)

Gai, Pei (1991) 'Microblade tradition around northern Pacific rim: in view of China.' Paper presented at the 13th INQUA Conference, Beijing.

Gardiner, K. (1969) *The Early History of Korea*. Univ. of Hawaii Press.

Ge, Yan and Linduff, K. M. (1990) 'Sanxingdui: a new Bronze Age site in southwest China.' *Antiquity* 64: 505–13.

Geng, Xiushan (1982) 'Transgressions and regressions in the eastern China [sea] since the late Pleistocene epoch.' In *Acta Oceanologica Sinica* 1.2: 234–46.

Gettens, R.J., Clarke, R.S. Jr. and Chase, W.T. (1971) 'Two early Chinese bronze weapons with meteoritic iron blades.' *Freer Gallery Occasional Papers* 4: 1–77.

Golany, G.S. (1992) *Chinese Earth-Sheltered Dwellings*. Univ. Press of Hawaii.

Gorman, Chester (1970) 'The Hoabinhian and after: subsistence patterns in Southeast Asia during the late Pleistocene and early Recent periods.' *World Archaeology* 2.3: 300–20.

Grayson, J. (1977) 'Mimana: a problem in Korean historiography.' *Korea Journal* 17.8: 65–69.

Guidon, N. and Arnaud, B. (1991) 'The chronology of the New World: two faces of one reality.' *World Archaeology* 23.2: 167–78.

Hamada, K. and Umehara, S. (1923) *The excavation of Kimhae Shellmound*. Chosen Sotokufu, Taisho 9–nendo Koseki Chosa Hokoku, vol. 1. Government General of Chosen. (in Japanese)

Hamada, Tatsuji (1981) 'Where were the artifacts made: centring on their chemical components.' In *Kokogaku no tame no kagaku 10 sho*, ed. H. Mabuchi and T. Tominaga, pp. 135–56. (in Japanese)

Han, Defen and Xu, Chunhua (1985) 'Pleistocene mammalian faunas of China.' In *Palaeoanthropology and Palaeolithic Archaeology in the People's Republic of China*, ed. Wu, R. and Olsen, J.W., pp. 267–86. Orlando: Academic Press.

Han, Yong-hui (1982) 'The artifacts from the Majangni house remains.' *Report of the Research of Antiquities of the National Museum of Korea* 14, appendix.

Han'guk Kogohak Yon'guhoe (1984) *Han'guk Kogohak Chido* [Korean Archaeological Maps]. Han'guk Kogohakpo Special Issue 1. Seoul

Hanihara, Kazuro (1985) 'Origins and affinities of Japanese as viewed from cranial measurements.' In *Out of Asia: peopling the Americas and the Pacific*, ed. R. Kirk and E. Szathmary, pp. 105–112. Canberra: The Journal of Pacific History.

Hanihara, Kazuro (1986) 'The origin of the Japanese in relation to other ethnic groups in East Asia.' In Pearson et al. 1986: 75–84.

Hanihara, Kazuro (1987) 'Estimation of the number of early migrants to Japan: a simulative study.' *Journal of the Anthropological Society of Nippon* 95.3: 391–403.

Harada, Y. and Komai, K. (1936) 'Showa 9–nen oyobi do 10–nendo dojoshi no chosa' [Investigation of the walled site, 1934–35]. *Koseki Chosa Gaiho: Roran doseki Showa 10*, pp. 33–47. (in Japanese)

Harunari, Hideji (1983) 'The history of personal ornaments: the foraging period.' *Kikan Kokogaku* 5: 18–22. (in Japanese)

Harunari, Hideji (1986) 'Rules of residence in the Jomon period: based on the analysis of tooth extraction.' In Pearson et al. 1986: 293–312.

Hatada, T. (1969) *A History of Korea*. Santa Barbara, CA: American Bibliographical Center, Clio Press.

Hawkes, Jacquetta (1974) 'Toro, Japan.' *Atlas of Ancient Archaeology*. London: Heinemann.

Hayashi, Ryoichi (1975) *The Silk Road and the Shoso-in*. New York/Tokyo: Weatherhill/Heibonsha.

Hearn, Maxwell K. (1980) 'The terracotta army of the First Emperor of Qin (221–206 BC).' In *The Great Bronze Age of China*, ed. Wen Fong, pp. 351–68. London/New York: Thames & Hudson/The Metropolitan Museum of Art.

Herrmann, A. (1966) *An Historical Atlas of China*. Chicago: Aldine.

Higham, C. (1989) *The Archaeology of Mainland Southeast Asia*. Cambridge Univ. Press.

Higuchi, T., ed. (1979) *Nihon Bunka no Rekishi 1: Pre- and Proto-History*. Tokyo: Shogakkan. (in Japanese)

Hirano, Kunio (1977) 'The Yamato state and Korea in the fourth and fifth centuries.' *Acta Asiatica* 31: 51–82.

Ho, C.K. and Li, Z.W. (1987) 'Paleolithic subsistence strategies in North China.' *Current Research in the Pleistocene* 4: 7–9.

Ho, Ping-ti (1975a) 'The indigenous origins of Chinese agriculture.' In *The Origins of Agriculture*, ed. C. Reed, pp. 413–84. The Hague: Mouton.

Höllmann, T.O. (compiler) (1983) *Neolithische Gräber der Dawenkou-Kultur in Ostchina*. Materialien zur Allgemeinen und Vergleichenden Archäologie, vol. 2. Munich: C.H. Beck.

Hook, B., ed. (1982) *Cambridge Encyclopedia of China*. Cambridge Univ. Press.

Hopkirk, P. (1980) *Foreign Devils on the Silk Road*. Oxford Univ. Press.

Hotta, Mitsuru (1975) *Noyama no Ki II* [Trees of field and mountain, II]. Tokyo: Hoikusha. (in Japanese)

Howells, W.W. (1986) 'Physical anthropology of the prehistorical Japanese.' In Pearson et al. 1986: 85–100.

Hsu, C.Y. and Linduff, K.M. (1988) *Western Chou Civilization*. Yale Univ. Press.

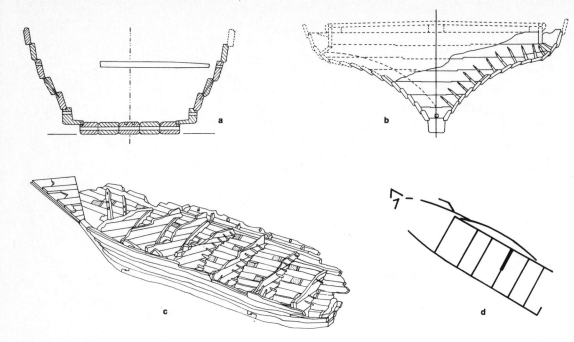

129 *Hull constructions of two medieval ships wrecked in Korean waters. The 11th-century Wando ship (a), made in Korea, had a flat bottom, while the Chinese Shinan ship (b, c, d), which sank in the early 14th century, was keeled and compartmented.*

The wreckage of the ship itself was later raised, restored and reassembled at a new purpose-built governmental research institute established at the nearby Korean port of Mokp'o.

Based on documentary evidence and bolstered by sculptures such as the *haniwa* ship from 5th-century Kyushu, researchers have long thought that prior to the 16th century

> shipwrights ... built vessels with squared-off ends, flat, keelless bottoms, and bulkheads that divided the interior into compartments. [By constrast,] Western ships had pointed ends, rounded hulls with keels, no bulkheads, and also different sails and rigging.[8]

The recovery of the Shinan and Wando ships off the southern Peninsular coast revealed greater variety in early ship-building techniques than anticipated by this statement. The 11th-century Wando ship, made in Peninsular Koryo and representing a 'traditional Korean boat style',[9] did have a flat bottom, but cross-timbers only functioned to hold the sides together rather than to form compartments. The Shinan ship, built in Yuan-period China, was not flat-bottomed but had a V-shaped cross-section and a large bar keel, though it otherwise conformed to expectations. The Wando ship was carrying a cargo of locally produced ceramics to Peninsular markets, whereas the Shinan ship was probably *en route* from southern China to Japan. Thus, the difference in construction might reflect the distance to be travelled and the requirements of coastal versus open-sea sailing. The different purposes were also reflected in

130 *Chinese coins salvaged from the Shinan wreck. All date to AD 1310; the largest is 4.28 cm in diameter and weighs 18.1 g.*

Hsu, Minfu (1986) *The Origins of Chinese Traditional Architecture.* Ph.D. Thesis, Dept. of Architecture, Univ. of Edinburgh.

Huang, Tsui-mei (1992) 'Liangzhu: a late Neolithic jade-yielding culture in southeastern coastal China.' *Antiquity* 66: 75–83.

Huber, L.G.F. (1981) 'The traditions of Chinese Neolithic pottery.' *Bulletin of the Museum of Far Eastern Antiquities* 53: 1–256.

Huber, L.G.F. (1983) 'The relationship of the Painted Pottery and Lung-shan cultures.' In *The Origins of Chinese Civilization*, ed. D.N. Keightley, pp. 177– 216. Univ. of California Press.

Hudson, Mark (1989) 'Ethnicity in East Asia: approaches to the Wa.' *Archaeological Review from Cambridge* 8.1: 51–63.

Hudson, Mark (1990) 'From Toro to Yoshinogari: changing perspectives on Yayoi archaeology.' In *Bibliographic Reviews of Far Eastern Archaeology 1990*, ed. G.L. Barnes, pp. 63–112. Oxford: Oxbow Books.

Hudson, Mark and Barnes, Gina L. (1991) 'Yoshinogari: a Yayoi settlement in northern Kyushu.' *Monumenta Nipponica* 46.2: 211–35.

Hughes, David W. (1988) 'Music archaeology of Japan: data and interpretation.' In *The Archaeology of Early Music Cultures*, ed. E. Hickmann and D.W. Hughes. Bonn: Verlag für systematische Musikwissenschaft.

Huntington, Ellsworth (1907) *The Pulse of Asia.* London.

I, Konmu (1988) 'Preliminary report of the excavation at Tahori, Uichang.' *Pangmulgwan Shinmun* June: 4. (in Korean)

Ikawa-Smith, F. (1978) 'Introduction: the Early Paleolithic tradition of East Asia.' In *Early Paleolithic in South and East Asia*, ed. F. Ikawa-Smith, pp. 1–10. The Hague: Mouton.

Ikawa-Smith, F. (1980) 'Current issues in Japanese archaeology.' *American Scientist* 68: 134–45.

Ikawa-Smith, F. (1986) 'Late Pleistocene and Early Holocene technologies.' In Pearson et al. 1986: 199–216.

Ikeuchi, H. (1930) 'A study of Lo-lang and Tai-fang, ancient Chinese prefectures in Korean Peninsula.' *Memoirs of the Research Department of the Toyo Bunko* 5: 79–95.

Im, H.J. and Kwon, H.S. (1984) *Osanni Site: a neolithic village site on the east coast.* Archaeological and Anthropological Papers of Seoul National Univ., vol. 9. (in Korean with English abstract)

Im, Mu-byong (1969) *Kumgangsa: a temple site of the Paekche dynasty.* Kungnip Pangmulgwan Kosok Chosa Pogo 7. Seoul: National Museum of Korea. (in Korean)

Inada, T. (1987) 'The Palaeolithic Age.' In *Recent Archaeological Discoveries in Japan*, ed. K. Tsuboi, pp. 5–23. Paris/Tokyo: UNESCO/Centre for East Asian Cultural Studies.

Inoue, Mitsusada (1977) 'The *ritsuryo* system in Japan.' Acta Asiatica 31: 83–112.

Institute of Archaeology (1984) *Recent Archaeological Discoveries in the People's Republic of China.* Paris/Tokyo: UNESCO/Centre for East Asian Cultural Studies.

Ito, Akio (1971) *Zur Chronologie der frühsillazeitlichen Gräber in Südkorea.* Munich: Verlag der Bayerischen Akademie der Wissenschaften.

IVPP (1980) *Atlas of Primitive Man in China.* Beijing: Science Press.

Jeon, Young-rae (1990) *Kankoku Seidoki Jidai Bunka Kenkyu* [Research on the Korean Bronze Age] Seoul: Shina. (in Japanese)

Jettmar, Karl (1952) 'Zum Problem der tungusischen "Urheimat".' *Wiener Beiträge zur Kulturgeschichte und Linguistik* 9: 484–511.

Jettmar, Karl (1967) *Art of the Steppes: the Eurasian animal style.* London: Methuen.

Ji, G.J. and Han, B.S. (1982) *Chungdo.* Kungnip Pangmulgwan Kojok Chosa Pogo 14. Seoul: National Central Museum. (in Korean)

Jia, Lanpo (1975) *The Cave Home of Peking Man.* Beijing: Foreign Language Press.

Jia, Lanpo (1980) *Early Man in China.* Beijing: Foreign Language Press.

Jia, Lanpo (1989) 'On problems of the Beijing-Man site: a critique of new interpretations.' *Current Anthropology* 30.2: 201–5.

Jia, Lanpo and Huang, Weiwen (1985a) 'The Late Palaeolithic in China.' In *Palaeoanthropology and Palaeolithic Archaeology in the People's Republic of China*, ed. Wu, R. and Olsen, J.W., pp. 211–23. Orlando: Academic Press.

Jia, Lanpo and Huang, Weiwen (1985b) 'On the recognition of China's Palaeolithic cultural traditions.' In *Palaeoanthropology and Palaeolithic Archaeology in the People's Republic of China*, ed. Wu, R. and Olsen, J.W., pp. 259–65. Orlando: Academic Press.

Ji'an County Relics Preservation Centre (1979) 'The preservation of two Koguryo stone mound tombs at Ji'an.' *Kaogu* 1979.1: 27–32, 50. [in Chinese]

Juliano, Annette L. (1980). 'Buddhism in China.' *Archaeology* 33.3: 23–30.

Jurmain, R., Nelson, H. and Turnbaugh, W.A. (1990) *Understanding Physical Anthropology and Archeology.* St. Paul: West Publishing.

Kamaki, Y. et al. (1984) 'Study on the palaeo-cultural communication through sourcing of obsidian and sanukite implements.' In *Kobunkazai no Shizen Kagaku-teki Kenkyu*, ed. the Kobunkazai Editorial Committee, pp. 333–59. Tokyo: Dohosha. (in Japanese)

Kamei, S. (1965) 'Nature in the Japanese Pleistocene: fauna.' In *Nihon no Kokogaku 1: Sendoki jidai*, ed. S. Sugihara, pp. 59–70. Tokyo: Kawade Shobo. (in Japanese)

Kamikawana, A. (1968) 'Sites in middle Yamanashi-ken and Middle Jomon agriculture.' *Asian Perspectives* 11: 53–68.

Kanaseki, H. and Sahara, M. (1985/1986) *Yayoi Bunka no Kenkyu* vols. 5/6. Tokyo: Yuzankaku. (in Japanese)

Kaner, Simon (1990) 'The Western-language Jomon.' In *Bibliographic Reviews of Far Eastern Archaeology*, ed. G.L. Barnes. Oxford: Oxbow Books.

Kang, Bong-won (1991) 'A megalithic tomb society in Korea.' *Journal of Korean Ancient Historical Society* 7: 135–222.

Kaogu 1974.6: 130.

Kaogu Xuebao 1978.1: 8.

Kato, S. (1987) 'The Jomon culture.' In *Recent Archaeological Discoveries in Japan*, ed. K. Tsuboi, pp. 24–36. Paris/Tokyo: UNESCO/Centre for East Asian Cultural Studies.

Keally, C.T. (1984) 'Unequal privilege in Jomon society: a pilot study.' *Sophia International Review* 6: 34–42.

Keally, C.T. (1990) 'Environment and the distribution of sites in the Japanese Palaeolithic environmental zones and cultural areas.' Paper presented at the Indo-Pacific Prehistory Association Congress, Yogyakarta, Indonesia.

Keightley, D. (1978) *Sources of Shang History: the oracle-bone inscriptions of Bronze Age China.* Univ. of California Press.

Keith, D.H. and Kim, H.E. (1979) 'Yellow Sea yields shipwreck trove: a 14th-century cargo makes port at last.' *National Geographic*, August: 230–43.

Kent, K.P. and Nelson, S.M. (1976) 'Net sinkers or weft weights?' *Current Anthropology* 17.1: 152.

[KEOJ] (1983) *Kodansha Encyclopedia of Japan.* Tokyo: Kodansha.

Kidder, J.E. Jr. (1957) *The Jomon Pottery of Japan.* Artibus Asiae, Supplementum 17. Switzerland: Ascona.

Kidder, J.E. Jr. (1959) *Japan Before Buddhism.* London/New York: Thames & Hudson/Praeger. (Rev. edn. 1966)

Kidder, J.E. Jr. (1964) *Early Japanese Art: the great tombs and treasures.* London/Princeton: Thames & Hudson/Von Nostrand.

Kidder, J.E. Jr. (1965) *The Birth of Japanese Art.* London: Allen & Unwin.

Kidder, J.E. Jr. (1968) *Prehistoric Japanese Arts: Jomon pottery.* Tokyo: Kodansha.

Kidder, J.E. Jr. (1972) *Early Buddhist Japan.* New York: Praeger.

Kidder, J.E. Jr. (1985) 'The archaeology of the early horse-riders in Japan.' *Transactions of the Asiatic Society of Japan*, 3rd series 20: 89–123.

Kiley, Cornelius J. (1973) 'State and dynasty in archaic Yamato.' *Journal of Asian Studies* 23.1: 25–49.

Kim, Byung-mo (1978) *Aspects of Brick and Stone Tomb Construction in China and South Korea – Ch'in to Shilla Period.* Ph.D. thesis, Univ. of Oxford.

Kim, Byung-mo, ed. (1982) *Megalithic cultures in Asia.* Hanyang University Monographs, no. 2, Seoul.

Kim, Byung-mo and Ch'im, Kwang-ju (1987) *Isong Sansong: a preliminary excavation report.* Hanyang University Museum Series no. 5. (in Korean).

Kim, C.S. (1971) 'The *Kolp'um* system: basis for Sillan social stratification.' *Journal of Korean Studies* 1.1: 41–72.

Kim, Dal-su et al. (1986) *From Kaya to Yamato.* Tokyo: Take

Shobo. (in Japanese).

Kim, Jeong-hak (1978) *The Prehistory of Korea*. Univ. Press of Hawaii.

Kim, Jung-bae (1978) 'The question of horse-riding people in Korea.' *Korea Journal* 18.9: 39–50; 18.11: 41–52.

Kim, Pu-sik (1983) *Samguk Sagi*. Modern Korean translation by Yi, P.D. Seoul: Eul-Yoo.

Kim, Won-yong (1960) *Studies on Silla Pottery*. Seoul: Eul-Yoo.

Kim, Won-yong, ed. (1973) *Archaeology in Korea 1*. Seoul National University.

Kim, Won-yong (1981) 'Korean archaeology today.' *Korea Journal* 21.9: 22–44.

Kim, Won-yong (1983) *Recent Archaeological Discoveries in the Republic of Korea*. Paris/Tokyo: UNESCO/Centre for East Asian Cultural Studies.

Kim, Won-yong (1986a) *Art and Archaeology of Ancient Korea*. Seoul: Taekwang.

Kim Won-yong (1986b) 'Wall paintings of Koguryo tombs.' In Kim 1986a: 389–400.

Kim, Won-yong, ed. (1989) *Kankoku no Kokogaku* [Korean Archaeology]. Tokyo: Kodansha. (in Japanese)

Kim, Won-yong (1992) 'The characteristics of Koguryo mural tombs.' In *Meikai o irodoru*, p. 8. Fukuoka: Fukuoka Kyoiku Iinkai. (in Japanese)

Kim, Won-yong and Nishitani, Tadashi (1984) *Kankoku Kokogaku Gaisetsu* [Outline of Korean Archaeology]. Tokyo: Rokko. (in Japanese)

Kim, Won-yong et al. (1985) *Osanni Site II*. Archaeological and Anthropological Papers of Seoul National University, vol. 10. (in Korean with English summary)

Kim, Won-yong et al. (1987) *Mongch'on T'osong Northeastern Sector Excavation Report*. Seoul: Seoul National University Museum. (in Korean)

Kim, Yong-han (n.d.) 'Two shipwrecks from Korean water.' Xerox. Mokpo Conservation Institute for Maritime Archaeological Finds.

Kitano, K. (1976) *Kawachi Nonaka Kofun no Kenkyu* [Investigations of the Nonaka Tomb in Kawachi]. Kyoto: Rinsen Shoten. (in Japanese)

Kobayashi, T., ed. (1988) *Kodaishi Hakkutsu 3: Jomon people and their tools*. Tokyo: Kodansha. (in Japanese)

Koike, H. (1980) *Seasonal dating by growth-line counting of the clam, Meretrix lusoria: toward a reconstruction of prehistoric shell-collecting activities in Japan*. Univ. of Tokyo Press.

Koike, H. (1986) 'Jomon shell mounds and growth-line analysis of molluscan shells.' In Pearson et al. 1986: 267–78.

Koike, H. and Chisholm, B. (1991) 'Paleodiet of hunter-gatherers in Japan estimated by ^{13}C-^{15}N and lipid analyses.' *The Quaternary Research* 30.3: 231–38.

Koizumi, Akio (1935) *Tomb of the Painted Basket*. Koseki Chosa Hokoku 2. Korea: Chosen Koseki Kenkyukai. (in Japanese)

Koizumi, Akio (1986) *Chosen Kodai Iseki no Henreki* [Travels to Ancient Korean Sites]. Tokyo: Rokko. (in Japanese)

Kondo, Y. and Takashi, Y. (1974) *Yayoi Jidai no Shakai* [Society in the Yayoi Period]. Tokyo: Toseido. (in Japanese)

Koyama, S. and Thomas, D.H. (1981) 'Affluent Foragers: Pacific coasts east and west.' *Senri Ethnological Studies, vol. 9*. Osaka: National Museum of Ethnology.

Kuhn, Dieter (1988) *Textile Technology: spinning and reeling*. Science and Civilisation in China 5.IX. Cambridge Univ. Press.

Kuraku, Yoshiyuki (1989) *Kodaishi Fukugen 5: Yayoijin no Zokei*. [Reconstructing Ancient History, 5: Portraits of Yayoi people]. Tokyo: Kodansha. (in Japanese)

Kyoto-shi Maibun [Kyoto Institute of Archaeological Research] (1980) *Heian Kyoseki Hakkutsu Shiryosen*. Kyoto.

Lao, F., Ye, H. and Cheng, Z. (1986) 'Ancient long kiln and kiln furniture in Zhejiang Province.' In *Scientific and Technological Insights on Ancient Chinese Pottery and Porcelain*, ed. Shanghai Institute of Ceramics, pp. 314–20. Beijing: Science Press. (in English)

Lattimore, Owen (1940) *Inner Asian Frontiers of China*. New York.

Laufer, B. (1912) *Jade, study in Chinese archaeology and religion*. Field Museum of Natural History, publication 154; Anthropological Series 10.

Lee, Dianfu and Sun, Yuliang (1990) *Koguryo Kansa*. Seoul: Samseong. (in Korean).

Lee, Ki Baek (1984) *A New History of Korea*. Harvard Univ. Press.

Lewis, Mark (1990) *Sanctioned Violence in Early China*. Albany: State Univ. of New York Press.

Li, Chi (1956) *Ch'eng-tzu-yai: the black-pottery culture site at Lung-shan-chen in Li-ch'eng-hsien, Shan-tung province*. Yale Univ. Publications in Anthropology, vol. 52. Yale Univ. Press.

Li, Chi (1977) *Anyang*. Univ. of Washington Press.

Li, H.L. (1983) 'The domestication of plants in China: ecogeographical considerations.' In *The Origins of Chinese Civilization*, ed. D.N. Keightley, pp. 21–64. Univ. of California Press.

Li, Jiazhi (1985) 'The evolution of Chinese pottery and porcelain technology.' In *Ceramics and Civilization 1: ancient technology to modern society*, ed. W.D. Kingery, pp. 135–62. Columbus, OH: American Ceramic Society.

Li, Xueqin (1985) *Eastern Zhou and Qin Civilizations*. Yale Univ. Press.

Lin, Yun (1986) 'A reexamination of the relationship between bronzes of the Shang culture and of the Northern Zone.' In *Studies of Shang Archaeology*, ed. K.C. Chang, pp. 237–74. Yale Univ. Press.

Littauer, Mary Aiken (1977) 'Rock carvings of chariots in Transcaucasia, Central Asia and Outer Mongolia.' *Proceedings of the Prehistoric Society* 43: 243–62.

Liu, Jun (1985) 'Some observations on the archaeological site of Hemudu, Zhejiang Province, China.' *Bulletin of the Indo-Pacific Prehistory Association* 6: 40–45.

Liu, Xinru (1988) *Ancient India and Ancient China: trade and religious exchanges AD 1–600*. Delhi: Oxford Univ. Press.

Liu, Xinyuan and Bai, Kun (1983) 'Reconnaissance of ancient kiln sites.' In *Ching-te-chen: views of a porcelain city*, ed. R. Tichane, pp. 395–416. New York: New York State Institute for Glaze Research.

Loehr, Max (1949) 'Weapons and tools from Anyang, and Siberian analogies.' *American Journal of Archaeology* 53: 126–44.

Loewe, Michael (1967) *Records of Han Administration*. 2 vols. Cambridge Univ. Press.

Loewe, Michael (1979) *Ways to Paradise: the Chinese quest for immortality*. London: Allen & Unwin.

Loewe, Michael (1989) 'Some early Chinese maps.' *Needham Research Institute Newsletter* no. 6.

Lubbock, Sir John (1865) *Pre-Historic Times, as illustrated by ancient remains and customs of modern savages*. London: Williams & Norgate.

Luo, Zewen (1980) 'The Great Wall.' In *The Great Wall*, compiled by Yu Jin, pp. 1–7. Beijing: Wenwu. (in Chinese and English)

Ma, Chengyuan (1980) 'The splendor of ancient Chinese bronzes.' In *The Great Bronze Age of China*, ed. Wen Fong, pp. 1–19. London/New York: Thames & Hudson/The Metropolitan Museum of Art.

MacCord, Howard A. (1960) 'The Able site, Kapyong, Korea.' *Asian Perspectives* 2.1: 128–38.

Maekawa, Kaname (1991) *Studies of Urban Archaeology*. Tokyo: Kashiwa Shobo. (in Japanese with English summary)

Maejima, M. (1985) *Japan's Ancient Archaeological Sites, 20: Shimane*. Osaka: Hoikusha.

Mainichi Shimbun (1992) 21 May.

Mao, Philip W.C. (1984) 'Qingbai wares.' In *Jingdezhen Wares: The Yuan evolution*, pp. 32–38. Hong Kong: Oriental Ceramic Society of Hong Kong.

Maspero, Henri (1978) *China in Antiquity*. Univ. of Massachusetts Press.

Matsuyama, Toshio (1981) 'Nut gathering and processing methods in traditional Japanese villages.' *Senri Ethnological Studies* 9: 117–40. Osaka: National Museum of Ethnology.

Meacham, William (1980) *Archaeology in Hong Kong*. Hong Kong: Heinemann Asia.

Medley, Margaret (1976) *The Chinese Potter: a practical history of Chinese ceramics*. Oxford: Phaidon.

Miki, Fumio (1974) *Haniwa*. Tokyo/New York: Shibundo/Weatherhill.

Miller, Richard J. (1974) *Ancient Japanese Nobility: the* kabane *ranking system.* Univ. of California Press.

[Minpaku] (1977) *National Museum of Ethnology: exhibition catalog.* Osaka: Kokuritsu Minzokugaku Hakubutsukan. (in Japanese)

Mizuno, S. and Kobayashi, Y. (1959) *Zukai Kokogaku Jiten.* Tokyo: Tokyo Sogensha. (in Japanese)

Morgan, L.H. (1877) *Ancient Society.* New York: World Publishing.

Morse, E.S. (1879) *The Shell-mounds of Omori.* Memoirs of the Science Department, vol. 1, pt. 1, University of Tokyo, Japan.

Movius, H.L. (1949) 'The Lower Paleolithic cultures of southern and eastern Asia.' *Transactions of the American Philosophical Society* n.s. 38, pt. 4.

Munthe, Jens et al. (1983) 'New fossil discoveries from the Miocene of Nepal include a hominoid.' *Nature* 303: 331–33.

Müller-Karpe, H. (compiler) (1982) *Neolithische Siedlungen der Yangshao-Kultur in Nordchina.* Materialien zur Allgemeinen und Vergleichenden Archäologie, vol. 1. Munich: C.H. Beck.

Nabunken (1991) *Annual Bulletin of the Nara National Cultural Properties Research Institute for 1990.* Nara: Nabunken. (in Japanese with English title and table of contents)

Nakano, Masuo (1987) 'Lipids analysis and archaeology.' In *The International Congress 'Development and Isolation in the Pacific'*, pp. 34–36. Osaka/Tokyo: Indo-Pacific Prehistory Association/ Japanese Society for Oceanic Studies/National Museum of Ethnology.

Nara Prefectural Museum of Art (1988a). *Silk Road: oasis and steppe routes.* Nara.

Nara Prefectural Museum of Art (1988b). *Silk Road: ocean route.* Nara.

National Museum of Korea (1978–9) 'Songguk-ri Site I.' *Kungnip Pangmulgwan Kojok Chosa Pogo* 11. (in Korean with English summary)

National Museum of Korea (1986) 'Songguk-ri Site II.' *Kungnip Pangmulgwan Kojok Chosa Pogo* 18.

Nelson, Sarah M. (1975) *Han River Chulmuntogi: a study of early Neolithic Korea.* Occasional Paper no. 9. Program in East Asian Studies, Western Washington State College.

Nelson, Sarah M. (1990) 'The Neolithic of northeastern China and Korea.' *Antiquity* 64: 234–48.

Nelson, Sarah M. (1993) *The Archaeology of Korea.* Cambridge Univ. Press.

Nelson, Sarah M. et al. (1982) 'The origins of rice agriculture in Korea: a symposium.' *Journal of Asian Studies* 41.3: 511–48.

Nihon DDK and Isarago Team (1981) *The Isarago Shellmound Site.* Tokyo: Nihon Denshin Denwa Kosha, Minato-ku Isarago Kaizuka Iseki Chosakai. (in Japanese)

Nihon Kokogaku Kyokai & Shizuoka Kokogakkai (1988) *Nihon ni okeru Inasaku Noko no Kigen to Hatten* [The Origins and Development of Rice Agriculture in Japan]. Shizuoka. (in Japanese)

Nishida, Masaki (1983) 'The emergence of food production in Neolithic Japan.' *Journal of Anthropological Archaeology* 2: 305–22.

Nishitani, T. (1986) 'An archaeological journey to Koguryo.' *Furusato no Shizen to Rekishi* 182: 1–7. (in Japanese)

Oda, S. and Keally, C.T. (1973) 'Edge-ground stone tools from the Japanese Preceramic culture.' *Busshitsu Bunka* 22: 1–26.

Oda, S. and Keally, C.T. (1986) 'A critical look at the Palaeolithic and "Lower Palaeolithic" research in Miyagi Prefecture, Japan.' *Journal of the Anthropological Society of Nippon* 94.3: 325–61.

Oikawa, A. and Koyama, S. (1981) 'A Jomon shellmound database.' *Senri Ethnological Studies* 9: 187–200. Osaka: National Museum of Ethnology.

Olsen, J.W. (1987) 'Recent developments in the late Pleistocene prehistory of China.' In *The Pleistocene Old World, Regional Perspectives*, ed. O. Soffer, pp. 135–46. New York: Plenum.

Olsen, S., Olsen, J.W. and Qi, G.Q. (1980) 'Domestic dogs from the Neolithic of China.' *Explorers Journal* Dec.: 165–67.

Ono, Y. (1992) 'The palaeoenvironment of Japan and East Asia at the period of maximum cold.' In *Senshi Mongoroido Shudan no Kakusan to Tekio Senraku*, ed. T. Akazawa. Univ. of Tokyo Museum. (in Japanese)

Otsuka, H. and Kobayashi, S. (1982) *Kofun Jiten.* Tokyo: Tokyodo. (in Japanese)

Pai, Hyung Il (1992) 'Culture contact and culture change: the Korean peninsula and its relations with the Han Dynasty commandery of Lelang.' *World Archaeology* 23.3: 306–19.

Pearson, R. (1974) 'Pollen counts in North China.' *Antiquity* 48: 226–28.

Pearson, R. (1981) 'Social complexity in Chinese coastal Neolithic sites.' *Science* 213: 1078–86.

Pearson, R. (1988) 'Chinese Neolithic burial patterns: problems and methods of interpretation.' *Early China* 13: 1–45.

Pearson, R. (1990) 'Chiefly exchange between Kyushu and Okinawa, Japan, in the Yayoi period.' *Antiquity* 64: 912–22.

Pearson, R. (1992) *Ancient Japan.* Washington, DC: Sackler Gallery, Smithsonian Institution.

Pearson, R., Barnes, G.L. and Hutterer, K., eds. (1986) *Windows on the Japanese Past: studies in archaeology.* Ann Arbor: Center for Japanese Studies, Univ. of Michigan.

Pearson, R. and Underhill, A. (1987) 'The Chinese Neolithic: recent trends in research.' *American Anthropologist* 89: 807–22.

Piggott, Stuart (1977) 'Chinese chariotry: an outsider's view.' *Colloquies on Art & Archaeology in Asia*, vol. 7. London: SOAS.

Pirazzoli-t'Serstevens, Michèle (1982) *The Han Civilization of China.* Oxford: Phaidon.

Pope, G.G. (1989) 'Bamboo and human evolution.' *Natural History* Oct.: 48–57.

Powers, M.J. (1991) *Art and Political Expression in Early China.* Yale Univ. Press.

Price, B.J. (1978) 'Secondary state formation: an explanatory model.' In *Origins of the State*, eds. R. Cohen and E. Service. Philadelphia, PA: Institute for the Study of Human Issues.

Price, T.D. (1981) 'Complexity in 'non-complex' societies.' In *Archaeological Approaches to the Study of Complexity*, ed. S.E. v.d. Leeuw, pp. 55–97. Amsterdam: Institute of Pre- and Proto-History, Univ. of Amsterdam.

Pulleyblank, E.G. (1966) 'Chinese and Indo-Europeans.' *Journal of the Royal Asiatic Society.* 1966: 9–39.

Pusan University Museum (1985) 'Kimhae Yeanni Tomb Cluster 1.' *Pusan Taehakkyo Pangmulgwan Yujok Chosa Pogo* 8. (in Korean)

Rawson, J. (1980) *Ancient China: art and archaeology.* London: British Museum Publications.

Rawson, J. (1987) *Chinese Bronzes: art and ritual.* London: British Museum Publications.

Rawson, J. and Bunker, E. (1990) *Ancient Chinese and Ordos Bronzes.* Hong Kong: Oriental Ceramic Society.

Reischauer, Robert Karl (1937) *Early Japanese History, Parts 1, 2.* Princeton Univ. Press.

[Rekihaku] (1987) *Report on the Excavation of the Nishiyagi Site, Akashi City.* Bulletin of the National Museum of Japanese History, vol. 13. (English summary)

Renfrew, Colin (1975) 'Trade as action at a distance.' Reprinted in C. Renfrew, *Approaches to Social Archaeology*, pp. 86–134. Edinburgh Univ. Press.

Renfrew, Colin and Bahn, Paul (1991) *Archaeology: theory, methods and practice.* London/New York: Thames & Hudson.

Renfrew, Colin and Cherry, John (1986) *Peer Polity Interaction and Socio-Political Change.* Cambridge Univ. Press.

Reynolds, T.E.G. (1985). 'The Early Palaeolithic of Japan.' *Antiquity* 59: 93–96.

Reynolds, T.E.G. and Barnes, G.L. (1984) 'The Japanese palaeolithic: a review.' *Proceedings of the Prehistoric Society* 50: 49–62.

Reynolds, T.E.G. and Kaner, S. C. (1990) 'Japan and Korea at 18000 BP.' In *The World at 18000 BP. Vol. 1: high latitudes*, ed. O. Soffer and C. Gamble, pp. 296–311. London: Unwin Hyman.

Rodwell, S. (1984a) 'China's earliest farmers: the evidence from Cishan.' *Bulletin of the Indo-Pacific Prehistory Association* 5: 55–63.

Rodwell, S. (1984b) 'The common fowl in early China.' *Journal of the Hong Kong Archaeological Society* 11: 124–27.

Rowley-Conwy, P. (1984) 'Postglacial foraging and early farming economies in Japan and Korea: a west European perspective.' *World Archaeology* 16.1: 28–42.

Rudolph, R.C. and Wen, Yu (1951). *Han Tomb Art of West China*. Univ. of California Press.

Sahara, Makoto (1975) 'Once there was a war: changes in stone projectile points.' *Kodaigaku Kenkyu* 78: 26–28. (in Japanese)

Sahara, Makoto (1979a) *Nihon no Genshi Bijutsu 2: Jomon Doki 2* [Jomon Pottery 2]. Tokyo: Kodansha. (in Japanese)

Sahara, Makoto (1979b) *Nihon no Genshi Bijitsu 7: Dotaku*. Tokyo: Kodansha. (in Japanese)

Sahara, Makoto (1987) 'The Yayoi Culture.' In *Recent Archaeological Discoveries in Japan*, ed. K. Tsuboi, pp. 37–54. Paris/Tokyo: UNESCO/Centre for East Asian Studies.

Sahara, M., Takashima, T., eds. (1989) *Yoshinogari: a Yayoi village in Saga Prefecture (3rd c. BC – AD 3rd c.)*, exhibition catalogue. Nara: Kashiwara Prefectural Museum. (in Japanese)

Sahoe Kwahagwon Kogohak Yon'guso, ed. (1977) *Choson Kogohak Kaeyo* [Outline of Korean archaeology]. Seoul: Saenal, reprinted 1988. (in Korean)

Sasaki, K. (1986) *Japanese Culture and the Japanese*. Tokyo: Shogakkan. (in Japanese)

Scarre, C. (1988) *Past Worlds: the Times Atlas of Archaeology*. London: Times Books.

Segalen, Victor (1978) *The Great Statuary of China*. Univ. of Chicago Press.

Seoul National Museum (1980) *Joong-do Site 1*. Report of the Research of Antiquities of The National Museum of Korea, vol. 12.

Serizawa, Chosuke (1978a) 'The Early Palaeolithic in Japan.' In *Early Paleolithic in South and East Asia*, ed. F. Ikawa-Smith, pp. 233–47. The Hague: Mouton.

Serizawa, Chosuke (1978b) *A Palaeolithic Stone Industry Excavated from the Iwato site, Oita Prefecture, Japan*. Records of Archaeological Material, no. 2. Sendai: Laboratory of Archaeology, Faculty of Arts and Letters, Tohoku Univ.

Serizawa, Chosuke (1982) *A Palaeolithic Stone Industry Excavated from the Mosanru Site, Hokkaido*. Records of Archaeological Material, no. 4. Sendai: Laboratory of Archaeology, Faculty of Arts and Letters, Tohoku Univ.

Service, E. (1975) *Origins of the State and Civilization: the process of cultural evolution*. New York: W.W. Norton.

Shanghai Institute of Ceramics, ed. (1986) *Scientific and Technological Insights on Ancient Chinese Pottery and Porcelain*. Beijing: Science Press. (in English)

Shapiro, H.L. (1974) *Peking Man: the discovery, disappearance and mystery of a priceless scientific treasure*. London: Allen & Unwin.

Shaughnessy, E.L. (1988) 'Historical perspectives on the introduction of the chariot into China.' *Harvard Journal of Asian Studies* 48.1: 189–237.

Sherratt, Andrew, ed. (1980) *Cambridge Encyclopedia of Archaeology*. Cambridge Univ. Press.

Sherratt, Andrew (1981) 'Plough and pastoralism: aspects of the secondary products revolution.' In *Pattern of the Past*, ed. I. Hodder. Cambridge Univ. Press.

Shi, Zhilian (1984) 'Images of women on brick carvings of the Northern Song Dynasty.' In *Recent Discoveries in Chinese Archaeology: 28 articles by Chinese archaeologists describing their excavations*, pp. 88–89. Beijing: Foreign Languages Press.

Shimonaka, K., ed. (1979) *Sekai Kokogaku Jiten* [World Archaeology Dictionary]. Tokyo: Heibonsha. (in Japanese)

Shimoshino, Nobuyuki, ed. (1989) *Kodaishi Fukugen 4: The advent of Yayoi agricultural villages*. Tokyo: Kodansha. (in Japanese)

[Shiojiri] (1984) *Idojiri Eastern Sector Prefectural Allotments Excavation Report for 1983*. Nagano-ken: Shiojiri City Board of Education. (in Japanese)

SNU (Seoul National University Museum and Dept. of Anthropology) (1976) *The Hunamri Site 3*. Archaeological and Anthropological Papers of Seoul National University, vol. 7.

Sohn, Pow-key (1973). 'The Upper Palaeolithic habitation Sokchang-ni, Korea: a summary report.' *Publication of Yonsei University Museum, English Series*, no. 1.

Sohn, Pow-key (1974) 'Palaeolithic culture of Korea.' *Korea Journal* 14.4: 4–11.

Sohn, P.K., Kim, C.O. and Hong, Y.S. (1970) *The History of Korea*. Seoul: Korean National Commission for UNESCO.

Stanley, Steven (1979) *Microevolution: pattern and process*. San Francisco: W.H. Freeman.

Stanley, Steven (1981) *The New Evolutionary Timetable*. London: Harper & Row.

Stringer, C.B. (1989) 'The origin of early modern humans: a comparison of the European and non-European evidence.' In *The Human Revolution: behavioural and biological perspectives on the origins of modern humans*, ed. P. Mellars & C. Stringer, pp. 232–44. Edinburgh Univ. Press.

Suzuki, H. and Hanihara, K., eds. (1982) *The Minatogawa Man: the Upper Pleistocene man from the island of Okinawa*. Univ. of Tokyo Press.

Suzuki, Masao (1973) 'Chronology of prehistoric human activity in Kanto, Japan, parts 1 & 2.' *Journal of the Faculty of Science, Univ. of Tokyo* sec. 5, vol. 4, pt. 3: 241–318; sec. 5, vol. 4, pt. 4: 395–469.

Suzuki, Masao et al. (1984) 'Obsidian analysis: 1974–1984.' *St. Paul's Review of Science* 4.5: 131–40.

Takemoto, Toru (1983) The Kyushu dynasty: Furuta's theory on ancient Japan. *Japan Quarterly* 30.4: 383–87.

Tanabe, Shozo and Tanaka, Migaku (1978) *Nihon Toji Zenshu 2: Yayoi, Hajiki*. Tokyo: Chuo Koronsha. (in Japanese)

Tanaka, Migaku (1984) 'Japan.' In *Approaches to the Archaeological Heritage*, ed. H. Cleere, pp. 82–88. Cambridge Univ. Press.

Taylor, Sarah J. (1990) *Ploughshares into Swords: the iron industry and social development in protohistoric Korea and Japan*, Ph.D. thesis, Univ. of Cambridge.

Templeton, Alan R. (1993) 'The "Eve" hypotheses: a genetic critique and reanalysis.' *American Anthropologist*.

Tenri Sankokan (1990) *10th Special Exhibition: Bronze Mirrors of Ancient China*. Tenri Univ. Press. (in Japanese)

Thomsen, C.J. (1848) *A Guide to Northern Antiquities*. Translated by J. Lubbock.

Thorp, R. (1985) 'The growth of Early Shang civilization: new data from ritual vessels.' *Harvard Journal of Asian Studies* 45.1: 5–76.

Thorp, R. (1987) 'The Qin and Han imperial tombs and the development of mortuary architecture.' In *The Quest for Eternity*, ed. S.L. Caroselli, pp. 17–38. London: Thames & Hudson.

Tien, Ko (1978) 'Tombs with sacrificial slaves, Early Western Chou dynasty.' *New Archaeological Finds in China* 2: 32–36. Beijing: Foreign Languages Press.

Till, B. and Stuart, P. (1988) *Images from the Tomb: Chinese burial figures*. Vancouver: Art Gallery of Greater Victoria.

Townsend, A.H. II (1975) *Cultural Evolution during the Neolithic Period in West Central Korea*. Ph.D. thesis, Univ. of Hawaii.

Tsien, Tsuen-Hsuin (1962) *Written on Bamboo and Silk*. Univ. of Chicago Press.

Tsuboi, Kiyotari (1987) *Recent Archaeological Discoveries in Japan*. Tokyo: Centre for East Asian Cultural Studies.

Tsuboi, Kiyotari and Tanaka, Migaku (1991) *The Historic City of Nara: an archaeological approach*. Paris/Tokyo: UNESCO/Centre for East Asian Cultural Studies.

Tsude, Hiroshi (1987) 'The Kofun period.' In *Recent Archaeological Discoveries in Japan*, ed. K. Tsuboi, pp. 55–71. Paris /Tokyo: UNESCO/Centre for East Asian Cultural Studies.

Tsude, Hiroshi (1988) 'Land exploitation and the stratification of society: a case study in ancient Japan.' *Studies in Japanese Language and Culture* 4: 107–30. Faculty of Letters, Osaka Univ. (in English)

Tsude, Hiroshi, ed. (1989) *Kodaishi Hakkutsu 6: King and Populace in the Kofun Period*. Tokyo: Kodansha. (in Japanese)

Tsude, Hiroshi (1990) 'Chiefly lineages in Kofun-period Japan: political relations between centre and region.' *Antiquity* 64: 923–28.

Tsukada, Matsuo (1986) 'Vegetation in prehistoric Japan: the last 20,000 years.' In Pearson et al. 1986: 11–56.

Tsunoda, Ryusaku and Goodrich, L. Carrington (1951) *Japan in the Chinese Dynastic Histories: Later Han through Ming Dynasties*. Perkins Asiatic Monographs 2. South Pasadena, CA: P.D. and Ione Perkins.

Twitchett, D. and Fairbank, J.K. (1979) *The Cambridge History of China: Vol. 3 Sui and T'ang China*, pt.1. Cambridge Univ. Press.

Umehara, S. (1954, 1956) 'Two remarkable Lo-lang tombs of

wooden construction excavated in Pyongyang, Korea.' *Archives of the Chinese Art Society of America* 8: 10–21; 10: 18–29.

Underhill, Anne P. (1990) *Changing Patterns of Pottery Production during the Longshan Period of Northern China, ca. 2500–2000 BC.* Ph.D. thesis, Univ. of British Columbia.

Wagner, Donald B. (1985) *Dabieshan: traditional Chinese iron-production techniques practised in southern Henan in the twentieth century.* Scandinavian Institute of Asian Studies Monograph Series, no. 52.

Wagner, Donald B. (1993) *Iron and Steel in Ancient China.* Leiden: Brill.

Wang, Laiyin (1984) 'Jade shrouds of the Han dynasty.' In *Recent Discoveries in Chinese Archaeology*, pp. 76–78. Beijing: Foreign Languages Press.

Wang, Yu-ch'uan (1951) *Early Chinese Coinage.* Numismatic Notes and Monographs, no. 122. New York: American Numismatic Society.

Wang, Zhongshu (1982) *Han Civilization.* Yale Univ. Press.

Watabe, T. (1990) 'Wet-rice technology as seen from Han-period materials.' In programme to the Fourth International Symposium: Higashi Ajia kara mita Nihon Inasaku no Kigen, Fukuoka, 17 March 1990. (in Japanese)

Watson, Burton (1961) *Records of the Grand Historian, Vol. 2.* New York: Columbia Univ. Press.

Watson, William (1961) *China before the Han Dynasty.* London/New York: Thames & Hudson/Praeger.

Watson, William (1971) *Cultural Frontiers in Ancient East Asia.* Edinburgh Univ. Press.

Watson, William (1974) *Style in the Arts of China.* New York: Universe Books.

Watt, J.C.Y. (1970) *A Han Tomb in Lei Cheng Uk.* Hong Kong: Urban Council.

Weidenreich, Franz (1943) *The Skull of Sinanthropus pekinensis: a comparative study on a primitive hominid skull.* Palaeontological Sinica n.s. D 10, n.s. 127.

Weidenreich, Franz (1969) 'Interpretations of the fossil material.' In *Early Man in the Far East*, ed. W.W. Howells, pp. 149–157. Oosterhout N.B., Netherlands: Anthropological Publications.

Wen, Fong (1980) *The Great Bronze Age of China.* London/New York: Thames & Hudson/The Metropolitan Museum of Art.

Wheatley, P. (1971) *The Pivot of the Four Quarters.* Edinburgh Univ. Press.

White, T. (1983) Review of Eldredge & Tattersall, *The Myths of Human Evolution. Nature* 303: 90.

Wolpoff, M.H., and Thorne, A.G. (1991) 'The case against Eve.' *New Scientist*, 22 June, pp. 37–41.

Wolpoff, M.H; Wu, Xinzhi and Thorne, A.G. (1984) 'Modern *Homo sapiens* origins: a general theory of hominid evolution involving the fossil evidence from east Asia.' In *The Origins of Modern Humans: a world survey of the fossil evidence*, ed. F.H. Smith and F. Spencer, pp. 411–83. New York: Liss.

Wu, G.D. (1938) *Prehistoric Pottery in China.* London: Kegan Paul, Trench, Trubner.

Wu, Rukang and Olsen, John W., eds. (1985) *Palaeoanthropology and Palaeolithic Archaeology in the People's Republic of China.* Orlando: Academic Press.

Wu, Xinzhi and Wang, Linghong (1985) 'Chronology in Chinese palaeoanthropology.' In *Palaeoanthropology and Palaeolithic Archaeology in the People's Republic of China*, ed. Wu, R. and Olsen, J.W., pp. 29–51. Orlando: Academic Press.

Xu, Pingfang (1992) 'Recent archaeological excavations.' Paper delivered at the Symposium on Chinese Archaeology, 11–13 November 1992, SOAS, Univ. of London.

Yamamura, Kozo (1974) 'The decline of the ritsuryo system: hypotheses on economic and institutional change.' *Journal of Japanese Studies* 1.3: 3–37.

Yasuda, Y. (1978) 'Prehistoric environment in Japan: palynological approach.' *Science reports of the Tohoku University* 7th series (Geography) 29.2: 117–281.

Yeung, Kin-Fong (1987) *Jade Carving in Chinese Archaeology, Vol. 1.* Hong Kong: Chinese University Press. (in Chinese and English)

Yi, Chang-gon (n.d.) *Research Related to the Analysis of the Composition of Copper Coins from Sinan.* Seoul: Cultural Properties Research Institute. (in Korean)

Yi, S. and Clark, G. (1985) 'The "Dyuktai culture" and New World origins.' *Current Anthropology* 26.1: 1–20.

Yin, Weizhang (1984) 'Archaeological studies of recent years.' In *Recent Discoveries in Chinese Archaeology: 28 articles by Chinese archaeologists describing their excavations*, pp. 98–102. Beijing: Foreign Languages Press.

You, Y.Z., Xu, Q.Q., Li, Y. and Ho, C.K. (1986) 'Seasonality and site structure of Late Paleolithic sites from Northeast China.' *Current Research in the Palaeolithic* 3: 97–102.

Young, John (1958) *The Location of Yamatai: a case study in Japanese historiography, 720–1945.* Johns Hopkins University Studies in Historical and Political Science 75.2.

Yu, Ying-shih (1967) *Trade and Expansion in Han China: a study in the structure of sino-barbarian economic relations.* Univ. of California Press.

Zhang, Senshui (1985) 'The Early Palaeolithic of China.' In *Palaeoanthropology and Palaeolithic Archaeology in the People's Republic of China*, ed. Wu, R. and Olsen, J.W., pp. 147–89. Orlando: Academic Press.

Zhang, Senshui (1990) 'Paleolithic research in China.' In *Anthropology in China: defining the discipline*, ed. G. E. Guldin. Armonk NY: M.E. Sharpe.

Zhang, Zhong-pei (1985) 'The social structure reflected in the Yuanjunmiao cemetery.' *Journal of Anthropological Archaeology* 4: 19–33.

Zhang, Z., Sun, T. and Wang, D. (1983) 'Introduction to the bronzes of Yunnan.' In *The Chinese Bronzes of Yunnan*, pp. 19–24. London: Sidgwick & Jackson.

[Zhejiang et al.] Zhejiang Cultural Properties Research Institute, Shanghai City Cultural Properties Committee, and Nanjing Museum (1989) *Jades of the Liangzhu Culture.* Beijing: Wenwu. (in Chinese)

Zhongguo Wenwu Bao 15 Nov 1990. (in Chinese)

Zhou, Shirong (1984) 'An ancient football game portrayed in bronze.' In *Recent Discoveries in Chinese Archaeology: 28 articles by Chinese archaeologists describing their excavations*, pp. 68–71. Beijing: Foreign Languages Press.

Zvelebil, Marek (1986) *Hunters in Transition.* Cambridge Univ. Press.

Sources of Illustrations

Line illustrations

CB = Crane Begg, principal artist.

Box 1: Not to scale. a. Chang 1986a: fig. 116, Machang Neolithic pottery, Liuwan; b. Chang 1980b: fig. 61, occupational emblems on Shang bronzes; c. Redrawn by author after Keightley 1978: fig. 5, inscribed turtle plastron, and fig. 2, prepared scapula; d. Li, X. 1985: fig. 85, inscribed bronze bell from tomb #1, Chengqiao, Liuhe; e. Li, X. 1985: fig. 21, inscribed oath of allegiance on jade from Qinyang, *ca.* 22 cm ht.; f. Li, X. 1985: fig. 194, inscribed bamboo slips from tomb #25 at Yangtian, Changsha.

Box 2: Compiled after Hook 1982, Blunden & Elvin 1983, and Fairbank & Reischauer 1960. '…loyalty, reciprocity…': McMorran, I. in Hook 1982: 317. 'new historical consciousness': McMorran, I. in Hook 1982: 319. 'wide learning…': Fairbank & Reischauer 1960: 379.

Box 3: Compiled after IVPP 1980, Aigner 1981 and Han & Xu 1985.

Box 4: Compiled after Bryan 1978, 1986, 1991, Gai 1991, Dillehay 1988; see also Guidon & Arnaud 1991. 'At least…': Dillehay 1988: 95. Figure after Fagan 1987: 91, 100.

Box 5: Not to scale. See Nelson 1993 on Yunkimun pottery. See Chang 1968: 88 on *Shengwen. Shengwen* is written with the same Chinese characters as *Jomon* and also means 'cord-marked.' a. Cord-marked rim sherd from the Omori site, after Morse 1879: pl. 9; b. Carved rouletting sticks and their patterns, after Kidder 1957: fig. 2; c. Yungkimun pottery from the Osanni site, after Kim, W.Y. et al. 1985: fig. 17; d. Jomon pottery after Sahara 1979a: 38, 50, 54; e. Chulmun pottery from the Chit'amni site, after Kim, J.H. 1978: fig. 12.4; f. Shengwen pottery from the Banpo site, after Müller-Karpe 1982: fig. 4; g. Dapenkeng pottery after Chang 1969: fig. 83.

Box 6: Not to scale. a, b. after Müller-Karpe 1982: 7–25, 6–1; c. after Huber 1981: fig. 161; d. after Chang 1977: fig. 61; e. after Wu 1938: fig. 43–31; f. Wu 1938: fig. 45–30; g. after Wu 1938: fig. 46–d; h. after Chow 1981: fig. 12.4; i. after Chang 1977: fig. 73, Huading culture; j. after Chang 1977: fig. 74, Beiyinyangying phase; k. after Chang 1977: fig. 68, Miaodigou II culture; l. after Wu 1938: fig. 53–f, Gaolizhai site; m. after Chang 1986a: fig. 167, Beiyinyangying site; n. after Chang 1977: fig. 74, Beiyinyangying phase; o–v. after Höllmann 1983: p. 178–18, Shanzhuang I site.; p. 176–18, Sanlihe I site; p. 193–21, Xixiahou site; p. 82–9, Dadunzi 1 site; p. 141–2, Ganshancun site; p. 148–17, Jingzhiz-

hen site; p. 82–12, Dadunzi 1 site; p. 92–11, Dafanzhuang site. The Dawenkou expansion has previously been discussed by K.C. Chang (1977: 144–84) as the 'Lungshanoid' expansion.

Box 7: Not to scale. a. after Fujita 1987: fig. 2; b. after Yeung 1987: pl. XX–15 upper, Songze site, pl. XXI–1 lower, Songze site; c. after ibid.: pl. XXIII–3, Xuejiagang site; d. after ibid.: pl. XXIV–17, Sidun site; e. after Chang 1986a: fig. 149, Hutougou site; f. after Huang 1992: fig. 1; g. Yeung 1987: pl. XXIV–3, Sidun site; h. after Huang 1992: fig. 8. i. after Rawson 1980: fig. 27. See Rawson 1980: 80ff. on Liangzhu jade technology.

Box 8: See Lao et al. 1986 on Zhou stoneware kiln development. a. Hongshan kiln at Silengshan, after Chang 1986a: fig. 147; b. Shang kiln at Zhengzhou, after Medley 1976: 27; c. Late Zhou kiln at Jianglin, after Li, J. 1985: fig. 7.

Box 9: Condensed from Wagner 1993. 'Several hundred tons…': Wagner 1993: 265. Figure: reconstruction of 1st-century blast furnace at Zhengzhou, after *Kaogu Xuebao* 1978.1: 8. Wagner (1985: 46) believes that both the height and bellows size of the furnace were actually greater than shown.

Box 10: On the language of the Rong, see Hsu & Linduff 1988: 209. On the Tungusic homeland, see Jettmar 1952.

Box 11: Not to scale. Text based mainly on Kuhn 1988, and Kanaseki & Sahara 1985. a. after Kanaseki & Sahara 1985: 174, Yayoi-period spindle rod, 22.5 cm long, Onitora site; b. after Kuhn 1988: figs. 33, 35, 37, 62, Chinese Neolithic spindle whorls, 4–6 cm diameter; c. after Kanaseki & Sahara 1985: 157, a Yayoi-period fish trap from Yamaga site, unscaled; d. bronze figurine of backstrap loom weaver, Yunnan, early Han Dynasty, after Barber 1991: fig. 3.1; e. after Kanaseki & Sahara 1985: 179, backstrap loom parts from several Yayoi sites; f. after Li, X. 1985: fig. 161, woven structures of silk brocade of the Middle Zhou period, recovered from Zuojiatang tomb no. 44; g. after Kuhn 1988: fig. 181, scene of gathering mulberry leaves cast on a Zhou-period bronze vessel, 5th century BC; h. after Kuhn 1988: fig. 189.

Box 12: See Wang, Z. 1982: chap. 8. 'Of all the historical dynasties…': K.C. Chang in the foreword to Wang, Z. 1982: xix. 'Profoundly foreign…': Segalen 1978. Not to scale. a. after

Tsude 1989: fig. 240, tomb of Liu; b. after Thorp 1987: fig. 6, at Luoyang; c. border bricks after Watt 1970, pl. 2, scale 1:5; brick plaque of gate towers after Till & Stuart 1988, fig. v; d. after Powers 1991: fig. 97, bas relief in tomb at Maocun, dated AD 175; e. after Powers 1991: fig. 136, drawing of painting in ink and colours, Houshiguo tomb no. 1, 2nd century AD; f. granary after Watt 1970: fig. 5–4, Lei Cheng Uk tomb, Hong Kong; paddy field after Watabe 1990, fig. 46, Late Han; ploughing model after Watabe 1990, fig. 50, W. Jin.

Box 13: See Barnes 1992 for full exposition of the problem. Not to scale. a, b. after Seoul National Museum 1980: fig. 10–1, 2; c. after Han, Y. 1982: fig. 6; d. after Choi, C.G. 1983: fig. 1; e. after *Kaogu* 1974.6: 130; f. after Meacham 1980: 165, Bronze Age vessel from Hong Kong.

Box 14: On riveted armour, see Bishop 1989. See Wang, L. 1984 on the Mancheng tombs. Not to scale. a. Qin armour redrawn by H.A. Shelley after Dien 1981/82: 46; b. Lee & Sun 1990: fig. 27, Donggou Tomb #12; c. Mongch'on 1985: fig. 61, bone armour plates from storage pit #4, Mongch'on T'osong; d. Kim, D.S. *et al.* 1986: p. 74, iron cuirass from Pokch'on-dong tomb #4; e. Otsuka & Kobayashi 1982: fig. 37, stone sculpture from Sekijinyama Tomb surface; f. author after Kidder 1965: fig. 82, from Kuai, Gunma Pref., 133 cm ht; g. Otsuka & Kobayashi 1982: 411; h. Kim, W.Y. 1960: pl. 29–2, from Gold Bell Tomb, 21.3 cm ht; i. Kim & Shim 1987: 127–13, iron horse figurine from Isong Sansong; j. Nabunken 1991: 60, reconstruction of horse sacrifice pit at Otsukuri Tomb.

Box 15: 'Bells to look at/listen to…': M. Tanaka. 'visual memory': Hughes 1988. a. Shang carved bone ocarina after Li, C. 1977: fig. 43; b. after Hughes 1988: fig. 11–3, Yayoi ocarina; c. decorative scene on Late Zhou bronze object; d. Yayoi bell 'for listening' on left, after Maejima 1965: fig. 15; bell 'for looking' on right, ht. c. 80 cm, after Shimonaka 1979: 769; e. after Hughes 1988: fig. 16, Kofun-period *haniwa* zither-player, drawn by K. Fujita; f. after Hughes 1988: figs. 4–5 Jomon spatulate zithers, left 54.1, right 43.7 cm; g. Till & Stuart 1988: fig. i, Tang tomb figurine, 3-colour ware.

Chapter 2: 7. From Barnes 1990b.

Chapter 3: 8. Compiled after Wu & Olsen 1985. 9. Wu & Wang 1985: fig. 21. 11. Zhang, S.

1985: fig. 9.6. **12.** Movius 1948: fig. 7. **13.** Base map after Jia & Huang 1985b: fig. 14.1; artifacts after Wu & Olsen 1985: figs. 8.3, 8.5, 9.3, 9.7, 10.3, 10.12, 10.14, 11.1–4. **14.** Rekihaku 1987: fig. 34. **15.** After Jurmain et al. 1990: figs. 14-4, 21 and Box 14–2: fig. 1.

Chapter 4: **17.** CB after Geng 1982: fig. 3; Chard 1974: map 1; Tsukada 1986: fig. 7; Yasuda 1978; Ono 1992: fig. 3; Kamei 1965: fig. 8; the scientific names of the animals shown are: *Canis lupus, Sinomegaceros yabei, Mammuthus primigenius, Palaeoloxodon naumanni, Panthera pardus, Ursus arctos, Bos primigenius, Equus equus, Sus scrofa,* and *Bison priscus* as described in Keally 1990. **18.** a–g. author based on Akazawa 1980: fig. 9; h. after Akazawa 1980: fig. 13. **19.** After Reynolds & Barnes 1984: fig. 2; author after Inada 1987; artifacts after Oda & Keally 1973: fig. 3. **20.** Based on Akazawa 1980: fig. 11. **21.** CB after Serizawa 1978b: pl. 5, Iwato site; and after Inada 1987: fig. 13, Sunagawa site. **22.** After Aigner 1981: fig. 46. **23.** Not to scale; a. pecked deer (undated) at Ulchi site, after Sohn 1974; b. stone rod (9.5 cm long) from Iwato site, cultural horizon 1 (13–21,000 BP), Serizawa 1978b: pl. 9; c. incised pebble from Kamikuroiwa site Initial Jomon layers (10,700–12,165 BP), after Aikens & Higuchi 1982: fig. 3.6. **24.** Trees, author after Hotta 1975; maps, CB after Minpaku 1977: 147 and Sasaki 1986: fig. 20.

Chapter 5: **25.** CB; climatic scales after Fuji 1966; southwestern Taiwan after Chang 1969: fig. 89; Kanto region after Akazawa 1982: fig. 4–9. **26.** After Oikawa & Koyama 1981: fig. 3. **27.** CB after Koike 1980: 90 (left); after Suzuki 1980: fig. 3 (below). **28.** CB after Esaka 1973: figs. 58–9. **29.** Adaptation of T. Kobayashi by G. Miller; with permission of the Univ. of British Columbia Laboratory of Archaeology. **30.** After Hanihara 1985: figs. 5. **31.** All same scale; compiled after Kim, J.H. 1978: fig. 9; Townsend 1975: fig. 47; Nelson 1979: fig. 26. **32.** Base map, CB; ceramics after Kidder 1968: 92–3; earrings after Harunari 1985: fig. 2; Fudodo house after Asahi-cho 1982: 42; shell and arrowheads after Nihon DDK & Isarago 1981: pls. 41, 51; quern after Shiojiri 1984: 101.

Chapter 6: **33.** After Chang 1986a: figs. 52, 54. **34.** After Bray 1984: fig. 4; Golany 1992: fig. 2.8; Shimojo 1989: fig. 26. **35.** Not to scale. a–b. after *Kaogu Xuebao* 1981.3; c–h. after Chang 1986a: figs. 178, 181, 183–4. **36.** Not to scale; after Chang 1986a: figs. 52, 64, 126, 214; and author after Kondo & Takashi 1974: 20. **37.** CB after Chang 1981a: 153; updated based on Chang 1986a and Xu 1992. **38** After Pearson 1981: fig. 2. **40.** Not to scale; a. after Chang 1986a: fig. 173; b, c. author after Kondo & Takashi 1974: 17; d. after Chang 1986a: fig. 174. **41.** a. after Golany 1992: fig. 1.3; b–d. after Chang 1978: fig. 41; e. after Chang 1986a: fig. 68. **42.** CB after Chang 1986a: fig. 77.

Chapter 7: **44.** Ceramics after Chang 1986a: figs. 143–4, 154–6; map, CB. **45.** CB after Chang 1986a: fig. 148. **46.** Dawenkou III, grave 10; after Höllman 1983: figs. 32–3. **48.** CB after Chang 1986a: fig. 226. **49.** CB after Barnard 1980–81: fig. 10.

Chapter 8: **50.** CB after Barnard 1980/81: fig. 5. **51.** Base map, CB based on Chang 1980b: fig. 84. Northern Complex objects after Lin 1986: figs. 49, 51; see his text for discussion of reciprocal

influences with Shang. Sanxingdui objects after Ge & Linduff 1990: figs. 11, 13, 14. Yangzi Basin objects after Sahara 1979b: 74; *see also* Falkenhausen 1991. **53.** a–c. after Rawson 1987: fig. 9; d. after Huang 1992: fig. 6; e. after Cheng & Zhong 1990: 39. **54.** Compiled after Watson, W. 1961: fig. 20, socketed axes; and after Cheng & Zhong 1990: 23, 25, 27. For western connections, *see* Watson, W. 1971. **55.** After Li, X. 1980: fig. 20. **56.** CB based on Chang 1977: figs. 106, 154 and Chang 1986a: figs. 226, 262, and measurements. **57.** CB after Chang 1980b. **58.** CB after Chang 1977: fig. 168.

Chapter 9: **60.** CB after Chang 1980b. **61.** CB based on Herrmann 1966: 5–6 and Luo 1980: fig. following p. 6. **62.** After Li, C. 1977: fig. 20. **63.** After Shimonaka 1979: 481–2. **64.** CB after Barnes 1988a: fig. 4. **65.** Author after Li, X. 1985: figs. 166–7, 171, 176. **66.** C. Gait-Utime after Scarre 1988: 193. **67.** After Li, X. 1985: figs. 143–5.

Chapter 10: **68.** After Littauer 1977: figs. 16, 20. **69.** After Davis 1987: fig. 6.3. **70.** After Li, X. 1985: figs. 53, 134. Upper: from Tomb no. 1, Nanshangen; lower: from Jincun, Luoyang. **72.** After Kim, J.H. 1978: fig. 84. **73.** Author after Chang 1986a: fig. 260. **74.** After SNU 1976: pls. 1, 3, 7. **75.** Not to scale; compiled from Jeon, Y.R. 1990: fig. 148; and after Kim, J.H. 1978: fig. 65. **76.** Not to scale; a. after Kim, J.H. 1978: fig. 65; b. CB after Kim, W.Y. 1983: fig. 17; and c–e. after Sahara 1979b: 74. **77.** a,c,d. after Jeon, Y.R. 1990: figs. 1, 8; b, e. after Kanaseki & Sahara 1986: 109, 115; b. CB. **78.** After Kim, J.H. 1978: 172. **79.** After Kim, B.M. 1985: figs. 36–8.

Chapter 11: **80.** After Barnes 1986a: fig. 1. **81.** After Akazawa 1982: fig. 4.3. **83.** After Tanabe & Tanaka 1978: 62–3. **84.** Not to scale; 'shaman', S. Machida, in Kobayashi 1988: fig. 240; Figurine burial after Esaka & Noguchi 1979: fig. 202; figurine after Kidder 1959: fig. 13–d; mask after Mizuno & Kobayashi 1959: 739; stone plaques after Esaka & Noguchi 1979: fig. 223; spouted pot after Sahara 1979a: 60. **85.** After Tsude 1988: fig. 7. **86.** After *ibid.*: fig. 1. **87.** CB after Higuchi, ed. 1979: fig. 232 and Tsude 1988: fig. 8. **89.** After Shimoshino 1989: fig. 183. **90.** Human figures redrawn by author after Kondo 1979: 34; a. weaponry: upper after Jeon, Y.R. 1990: fig. 9; lower after Kanaseki & Sahara 1986: 119–2; b. Peninsular bell 18 cm; after Kim, J.H. 1978: fig. 65.

Chapter 12: **91.** Author after Wang, Z. 1982: fig. 28. **92.** Map, author after Cotterell 1981: 19; plans and sections from Hearn 1980: figs. 121, 123. **93.** a. after Sahara 1979b: 74–21; b. after Watson, W. 1961: fig. 66; 1st c. BC bronze drum from Shizhaishan. **94.** After Segalen 1978: 29, 34. **95.** After Kim, J.H. 1978: 72. **96.** a–d. after Auboyer 1979: 424–5; e–k. after Tenri 1990: figs. 12–16, 21–22. **97.** Author after Loewe 1979: figs. 3, 4, and Pirazzoli-t'Serstevens 1982: fig. 23. **98.** CB after Watson, W. 1974: pl. 60. **99.** CB after Hayashi 1975: fig. 203.

Chapter 13: **101.** Author after Asahi 1980: 11. **102.** After Kim, B.M. 1978: figs. 33, 40–41. **103.** After Umehara 1954: figs. 1, 4, 6, 10, 13. **104.** Author after Koizumi 1986: fig. 118. **105.** After Ji & Han 1982: figs. 6–7. **106.** After Kanaseki & Sahara 1985: 133. **107.** After *Archaeology Quarterly* 1984.6: frontispiece. **108.** From the Kar-

ako-Kagi site; redrawn by H.A. Shelley after *Mainichi Shimbun* 1992.5.21. **109.** Plans after Hudson 1990: figs. 19–20; figures, S. Iwanaga in Kuraku 1989: fig. 282.

Chapter 14: **111.** a. after Kim & Nishitani 1984: fig. 88, Jian Ryangmin #73 tomb; b. *ibid.*: fig. 89, the General's Tomb; c. after *ibid.*: fig. 131, Chisan-dong #44 tomb; d. after Kim, W.Y. 1983: fig. 21, Tomb #155; e. after Otsuka & Kobayashi 1982: fig. 27, Goshikizuka Tomb. **112.** a. after Miki 1974: fig. 14; b. after *ibid.*: fig. 53; c. after Miki 1967: fig. 33. **113.** a. after Sahoe Kwahagwon 1977: fig. 128.2, Liaodong Fortress tomb; b. after *ibid.*: fig. 130.2, Ssanggidung Tomb; c. Ito 1971: fig 32.4, Chunghyo-ri A Tomb #8; d. after Otsuka & Kobayashi 1982: fig. 20, Kanayama Tomb. **114.** a. after Lee & Sun 1990: fig. 24, Anak Tomb of the Dancers; b. after Kim & Nishitani 1984: fig. 90, Anak Tomb #3; c. after *ibid.*: fig. 97, Jiangxi Damu Tomb; d. after Lee & Sun 1990: fig. 29, Jian tomb motifs; e. after Otsuka & Kobayashi 1982: fig. 126, Mezurashikizuka Tomb. **115.** After Ito 1971: figs. 35, 38. **116.** After Kitano 1976: figs. 74, 76. **117.** Left, after Anazawa & Manome 1986: fig. 5. **118.** Author after Kim, W.Y. 1986b: pls. 4–43, 44.

Chapter 15: **119.** Mongch'on after Kim, W.Y. et al. 1987: fig. 4; Panwolsong after Kim, W.Y. 1989: 238; distribution after Han'guk Kogohak Yon'guhoe 1984: 40–1. **120.** After Tsude 1987: fig. 46. **121.** After Choi & Shim 1991: frontispiece. **122.** Author. **123.** a. after Choi, B.H. 1987: figs. 4, 6, 10; b. after Kim, W.Y. 1986a: 360, 24 cm ht; c. after Im, M.B. 1969: 24–5. **124.** Thames & Hudson. **125.** Author based on Lee, K.B. 1984: 70. **126.** Map, author; Heijo capital and Nara palace after Tsuboi & Tanaka 1991: 59; northern forts based on Reischauer 1937. **127.** After Tsude 1988: fig. 6.

Chapter 16: **128.** a. after Shi 1984: 88; b, c. H.A. Shelley after Zhou 1984: 68, 70. **129.** a. CB after Keith 1979: 234; b, c, d. CB after Kim, Y.H. n.d. **130.** After Yi, C.G. n.d.: figs. 63–4. **131.** Courtesy of H. Matsumoto, Munakata Shrine Museum, Fukuoka, Japan. **132.** Author after Institute of Archaeology 1984: fig. 78.

Plates

21 Collection of Arthur M Sackler, USA
22 British Museum
23 Collection of Mrs Walter Sedgwick, London
24 The Art Institute of Chicago (Sonnenschein Collection)
25 Britain–China Friendship Association
26 China Publishing House
27 From *The Great Bronze Age of China*, 1980, fig. 8
28 Fogg Museum of Art, Harvard University
29 Metropolitan Museum of Art, New York
30 China Publishing House
31 China Publishing House
32 Victoria and Albert Museum; Crown copyright
33 Victoria and Albert Museum; Crown copyright
34 From William Watson, *China*, Thames and Hudson, 1961, pl. 74
35 Imperial Household Museum, Tokyo
36 Photo R.E. George. Collection of E. Spencer-Churchill, Northwick Park, Glos. England.
37 China Publishing House
38 British Museum; photo John R. Freeman

39 Shang Dynasty
40 British Museum
41 British Museum
42 Photo Seth Joel
43 Shaanxi Museum of Qin Dynasty
44 Photo Seth Joel
45 British Museum
46 China Publishing House
47 Nelson Gallery of Art, Kansas City, Missouri
48 Gina Barnes (reproduction)
49 Gina Barnes (reproduction)
50 People's Republic of China
51 People's Republic of China
52 Gina Barnes
53 Kyoto University
54 Kyoto University
55 National Museum, Tokyo
56 H. Ohashi Collection
57 National Museum, Tokyo
58 Gina Barnes
59 Gina Barnes
60 Hong Kong Museum of History (Gift of Father Maglioni)
61 National Museum, Tokyo

62 Seattle Art Museum
63 Gina Barnes
64 British Museum; photo Edwin Smith
65 Gina Barnes
66 Gina Barnes
67 National Museum, Tokyo
68 National Museum, Tokyo
69 Metropolitan Museum of Art, New York
70 National Museum, Tokyo
71 National Museum, Tokyo
72 National Museum, Tokyo
73 Asian Art Museum of San Francisco
74 Gina Barnes
75 Cave no. 428, Dunhuang, Gansu, China
76 Gina Barnes
77 Gina Barnes
78 Gina Barnes
79 Gina Barnes
80 Shosoin treasury of Todaiji temple, Japan
81 Gina Barnes
82 Gina Barnes
83 Shibayama Board of Education
84 Edward B. Adams
85 Nara National Institute of Cultural Properties

Index

ARCHAEOLOGY 7, 9, 13, 16, 22–3, 26, 28–9; associations 32–4, 38, 41; colonial 26, 30, 32, 35, 38, 209; ethno– 89; historic 16, 19, 71, 265, 267; *27*; and politics 36, 266–7; prehistoric 16, 19, 22, 27, 39, 269; protohistoric 16, 18, 19, 23, 26–7, 39, 130, 208, 216, 221, 241, 269; *27*; rescue 35–7, 268; **2**; scientific 41; theoretical 40–1, 95; underwater 263; urban 267.

ARCHITECTURE 28, 103, 108, 110, 113, 116–17, 126–7, 129, 146, 197, 200–1, 219–20, 224, 226, 248–9, 251, 255, 260, 266; *40, 48, 93, 108–9, 112–13, 120, 124*; *Box 12 (p. 201)*; **78, 80**. bricks 116, 130, 196–7, 200–1, 203, 209–10, 249, 251, 266; *98, 102, 128*; **77**. defensive walls 146–7, 192, 196–7; *61*; **45**. dwellings 39, 51, 60, 68, 75, 78, 80, 92–3, 104, 108, 127, 155–6, 161–2, 189, 200, 215; *28–9, 32, 74, 87, 105, 109, 112, 120*. granaries 104, 187, 200, 255; *109, 120*; **52, 56**. hearths 66, 78, 80, 108, 155–6, 215; *98, 105*. pagodas 249, 251, 260; *121*; *76, 77*. palaces 27–9, 33–4, 36, 109, 126–7, 130, 196, 206, 221, 223, 246, 248–9, 251, 253, 255, 257, 267; *57, 122, 126*; **80–2, 85**. storage facilities 92, 104, 108, 245. tamped earth 113, 117, 126, 129, 146, 223, 255, 257; *64*. temples 107, 109, 110, 127, 129, 130, 135 (see also BUDDHISM: temples). tiles 129–30, 209, 249; *123*; **79**. tombs 196, 200–1; *58, 97, 102, 111, 113*; *Box 12 (p. 201)*.

ARMOUR 152, 192, 203, 230–2, 245, 266; *53, 67, 92*; *Box 14 (pp. 230–1)*; **42, 67**.

ART 98, 124, 176, 200–2, 226, 266; *35, 96*; *Box 12 (p. 201)*. animal images 80, 98–9, 110, 114–15, 121, 153, 157, 200, 226, 230–1, 266; *23, 35, 51, 68, 70, 94, 96, 104, 123*; *Box 7 (p. 115)*; **16, 21–4; 25–6, 32–4, 51, 62**.